BILL HAYWOOD'S BOOK

drawn by
Lydia Gibson

WILLIAM D. HAYWOOD

(1869-1928)

BILL HAYWOOD'S BOOK

THE AUTOBIOGRAPHY OF
WILLIAM D. HAYWOOD

NEW YORK
INTERNATIONAL PUBLISHERS

Library of Congress Catalog Card Number 74-77419
ISBN 0-7178-0012-1; 0-7178-0011-3 (pbk)

Copyright, 1929, by
INTERNATIONAL PUBLISHERS CO., INC.

Printed in the U.S.A.

This printing, 1977

209

CONTENTS

CHAPTER		PAGE
I.	Boyhood Among the Mormons	7
II.	Miners, Cowboys and Indians	21
III.	Homestead and Hard Times	38
IV.	Silver City	56
V.	The Western Federation of Miners	71
VI.	Telluride	90
VII.	Tin Houses and Autocracy	108
VIII.	Cripple Creek	122
IX.	In the Crucibles of Colorado	139
X.	"Deportation or Death"	155
XI.	Industrial Workers of the World	174
XII.	"Undesirable Citizens"	190
XIII.	The Boise Trial	207
XIV.	The World Widens	223
XV.	The Lawrence Strike	239
XVI.	"Article 2, Section 6"	254
XVII.	The Pageant	261
XVIII.	The U. S. Industrial Relations Commission	278
XIX.	Raids! Raids! Raids!	290
XX.	The I.W.W. Trials	310
XXI.	The Prison	327
XXII.	With Drops of Blood	339
XXIII.	The Centralia Tragedy	352
XXIV.	Farewell, Capitalist America!	359
XXV.	Haywood's Life in the Soviet Union	363
	Appendices	366

BILL HAYWOOD'S BOOK

CHAPTER I

BOYHOOD AMONG THE MORMONS

My father was of an old American family, so American that if traced back it would probably run to the Puritan bigots or the cavalier pirates. Neither case would give me reason for pride. He was born near Columbus, Ohio, and with his parents migrated to Iowa, where they lived at Fairfield. His brother and cousins were soldiers in the Civil War; all of them were killed or wounded. My father, when a boy, made his way across the prairies to the West. He was a pony express rider. There was no railroad across the country then and letters were carried by the Pony Express, which ran in relays, the riders going at full speed from camp to camp across the prairies, desert and mountains from St. Jo, Missouri, to San Francisco on the Pacific coast.

My mother, of Scotch-Irish parentage, was born in South Africa. She embarked with her family at Cape of Good Hope for the shores of America. They had disposed of everything, pulled up by the roots, and left her birthplace to make their way to California. The gold excitement had reached the furthest corners of the earth. People without the slightest knowledge of what they would have to contend with were leaving for the West. There were no palatial steamships in those days; it meant months of dreary, dangerous voyage in a sailing vessel. The danger was not past when they landed in port; there was still the train ride of eighteen hundred miles, and then the long trip across the plains and mountains in covered wagons drawn by oxen. There was the constant dread of accident, of sickness, and of the hostile Indians, red men who had been forced in self-protection to resent the encroachment of the whites.

On the way across the prairies, my uncle, then a small boy, was lost. The family did not know what had become of him. They searched the long wagon-train in vain. He was in none of the prairie schooners, he was not among the stock drivers who drove the extra oxen, cows and mules. The train could not stop and one family could not drop behind alone to search the boundless prairies. They gave him up for lost and went on with the wagon train, grieving for him. When they pulled down Emigrant Canyon, they saw the beautiful Salt Lake Valley. The dead sea, Great Salt Lake, spread out in front of them. To the right lay the new city of Zion, which had been founded by the Mormons in 1847. Here the family abandoned the wagon-train because of sickness and had to wait for the train following, with the hope that my uncle had been picked up and brought along. It was but a few days after their arrival that my grandmother, walking along the street, saw her son with a basket of apples on his arm. She gathered him up, apples and all, and took him home to his sisters. He had gone with the train ahead and had reached the city a week or two earlier.

My grandmother started a boarding house in Salt Lake City. My father boarded there and met my mother. He was then a very young man; when they married, he was about twenty-two and my mother was a girl of fifteen. I was born on the fourth of February, 1869, before a railroad spanned the continent.

I have but one remembrance of my father. It was on my third birthday. He took me from the house and set me up on a high board fence, which he climbed over, lifting me down on the other side. We went through an alley-way to Main Street, then to a store where he bought me a new velvet suit, my first pants. We called on many of his friends on the way home, and I was loaded with money, oranges and candy. My father died shortly afterward at a place called Camp Floyd, now known as Mercur. When my mother learned of his illness she started for Camp Floyd, taking me with her, but before her arrival he had died of pneumonia and was buried. When we visited his grave, I remember digging down as far as my arm could reach.

Salt Lake City is built in a bend of the Wasatch range. To the east the mountains rise high and stark, to the north is Ensign Peak, near the top of which is a tiny cave that has been explored by all the adventurous youngsters of the town. To the southwest, in the Oquirrh Mountains, lies much of the wealth of Utah. Here are the mining camps of Stockton, Ophir, Mercur, and Bingham Canyon, where is the great Utah copper mine. To the immediate west is the Great Salt Lake, whose waters are so dense with salt that no animal life can survive.

On the islands in the Salt Lake are nests of thousands of sea-gulls, which are sacred in Utah because of the fact that during a plague of grasshoppers the gulls fed upon the pests, eating millions. They would swallow as many grasshoppers as they could hold, then spew them up and swallow more, and in this way the sea-gulls helped to save a part of the farmers' crop, the total loss of which would have meant starvation for the Mormons.

Salt Lake valley is threaded by the Jordan River, and to the north are warm and hot springs. The grandeur of the scenery and the beauty of the city itself were counteracted by the bad feeling generated by the Mormon Church. Especially was this true during my boyhood days, when the atmosphere was still charged with the Mountain Meadow Massacre, the destruction of the Aiken party, and the threats of the Mormons against the Apostates. These threats were thundered from the lips of Brigham Young, Hyde, Pratt, and other church officials. Of course, they did not make the impression on me that they did on older people, though I remember distinctly some of the features of the trial of John D. Lee, who was a leader of the Mormons and Indians who killed nearly a hundred and fifty men, women and children at Mountain Meadow. The massacre occurred after Lee had got the emigrants to surrender their arms. Lee himself and other Mormons had a bitter hatred against these particular emigrants, who were from Arkansas and Missouri, where the so-called Mormon prophet, Joseph Smith, and his brother Hyrum had been murdered in the jail at Carthage, Missouri. I remember seeing a picture of John D. Lee sitting upon his coffin before he was executed at Mountain Meadow. The laws of Utah Territory provided that when a man was sentenced he could take his choice of the means of execution, either shooting or hanging. John D. Lee chose shooting, and was taken from the county seat where he was tried, to Mountain Meadow, the scene of his crime, which undoubtedly had been instigated by others higher in authority. But twenty years passed by between the massacre and the execution in 1877.

It was at about this time that I first saw Brigham Young, the president of the Mormon Church, on the street, although I had seen

him before in the Tabernacle, and had heard him deliver his vigorous sermons against apostacy. A short time later he died, supposedly
from eating green corn; but rumors were current that he had poisoned himself. If these rumors were true, it was probably because
of John D. Lee's conviction and the demand on the part of the
Gentiles, as all non-Mormons were called, for the arrest and trial
of Brigham Young in connection with the massacre, at the time of
which he had been governor of the Territory and United States
Indian Agent. The Mormons had sensibly cultivated friendly relations with the Indians, and they undoubtedly prevented the massacre
of another party of emigrants who came through at about the same
time.

The house where I was born was built of adobe, on First South
Street, between West Temple and First West. It was divided into
four apartments, two on the ground floor and two above. The interesting feature of this house was the family who lived above us,
a woman who had been a widow with two grown daughters. At
the time of which I write they were all married to the same man,
so that the daughters were wives of their own stepfather. Polygamy
has always been a religious tenet of the Mormon Church.

Some four years after the death of my father, my mother re-
married, and we went to a mining camp called Ophir, to live. Ophir
Canyon was steep. On the right the mountains were precipitous,
broken with gulches. On the left were lower hills. The canyon
widened where the town was built, giving room enough for two or
three streets. Lion hill was at the head of the canyon. Over the
mountain back of our house was Dry Canyon, where the Hidden
Treasure mine was located. At this and other mines of the camp
my stepfather worked. The ridge near the Hidden Treasure was
strewn with great bowlders of copper pyrites. The Miners' Delight
mine was a tunnel with some open works which were the playground
of the boys of the camp. There we found many beautiful crystals
which we loved to collect.

Mrs. Whitehead was my first teacher. The schoolhouse at Ophir
was built at the upper end of the town and was little more than a
lumber shack. From the windows in the late winter we could see
the snow slides coming down the mountain side from which all the
timber had been cut. The first winter a slide filled the canyon below
the town, through which a tunnel had to be cut for the stage to come

through, and to let the water out. At the noon recess Mrs. Whitehead would appoint a monitor who would report to her how we behaved in her absence. One day Johnnie O'Neill and I were reported for fighting, and when school was called to order, he was called up and given a whipping with the ruler. I ran pell-mell for the door and home, where I told my mother that I was not going to school any more because the teacher was going to whip me for fighting, and there hadn't been any fight. That night my mother took me to Mrs. Whitehead's house and I told them I guessed I knew when I was fighting and when we were wrestling. The matter was patched up and I went back to school the next day. However, Johnnie O'Neill and I had many a fight, both before and after this wrestling match.

One morning I was going to school, which was only a short distance from our house, when I saw Mannie Mills across the street pull his gun from his pocket and shoot at Slippery Dick, who was walking just ahead of me. Dick also began shooting and they exchanged several shots when Mills fell on his face, dead. Several people ran up to him. Slippery Dick blew into the barrel of his six-shooter, put it in his pocket and walked away. I followed him until he went into a nearby saloon. That was the first time I saw a shooting scrape. It was not the only one that occurred in Ophir, which was regarded as one of the wildest mining camps in the West. Another day I went to the scene of a shooting scrape and saw two members of the Turpin family and another man lying dead on the ground.

There was an explosion one night under a corner of Duke's hotel. The next morning I was in front of Lawrence's store when a woman, called "Old Mother" Bennet, came walking down the street muttering something about "burning down the town." A man who was sitting on the edge of the sidewalk jumped to his feet and struck her in the face. It was Johnny Duke, the owner of the hotel. This woman and her man had bragged about planting the powder, and after the incident on the sidewalk both were arrested and the Vigilance Committee drove them down the canyon that very afternoon.

Another day two schoolmates of mine were playing in the livery barn. They were in the room where the hostler slept and found a pistol under the pillow. Accidentally, Pete Bethel pulled the trigger and killed Willie Duke. When I heard the shot I ran to the stable and found Willie dead. I saw the blood running out of his head. Little Pete Bethel was scared speechless.

These scenes of blood and violence happened when I was seven years old. After the talk of massacres and killings at Salt Lake City, I accepted it all as a natural part of life.

It was an event when the Dutch shoemaker's family arrived in the camp. A day or two after their arrival I was playing down by the creek near the shoemaker's house when I saw a little girl in the shadow of a clump of willows. Going over to her, I found that she was very pretty, with cheeks like big red apples. When I spoke to her she only smiled. I took her hand, then I kissed her and she seemed to like that. Some one called, her mother, I guessed. Breaking away from me she ran to the house, smiling back at me over her shoulder. The next day I went back and there she was, dipping up a bucket of water from the creek. I went up quietly and put my arms around her, when she turned and scratched my face, spat at me and lifted the bucket as though to throw the water over me. I ran away, not knowing what had come over her. Later I found that it was not she at all; it was her twin sister.

Most of the boys in the camp had slingshots. I was going to make one for myself. I was back of the house trying to cut a handle from a scrub-oak, when the knife slipped and penetrated my eye. They sent me to Salt Lake immediately for medical attention, and for months I was kept in a dark room. But the sight was gone.

When I returned to Ophir, school was closed and I did my first work in a mine. I was then a little past nine years of age. It was with my stepfather, who was doing the assessment work at the Russian mine.

School opened again, and I went another term. This time Professor Foster was the teacher, a stern-looking old Mormon from Tooele, but an excellent teacher. He taught me to understand history, to dig under and back of what was written. He was a lantern-jawed, gray-mustached old man with gray eyes, and I never saw him whip a child.

Hardly a week passed without a fight with some boy or other, who would call me "Squint-eye" or "Dick Dead-eye," because of my blind eye. I used to like to fight.

After this term of school the family returned to Salt Lake City. Zion, as the Mormons called the city, was intended originally as the

capital of an empire of the Mormon Church. When gold was discovered in California, the emigrants swarmed through Utah on
their way to the gold fields of the West. Some dropped off at Salt
Lake City and stayed, but curiously enough, in spite of the stam-
pede for gold, no Mormons joined in the rush or left their territory.

The Temple Block, where the Tabernacle, the Assembly Hall,
the Endowment Houses and the Temple were enclosed within high
walls, was the heart of the city; around it everything centered. In
the Tabernacle, where eight thousand people could gather, I heard
Adelina Patti sing one night when I was a young boy. I have never
forgotten it.

The city was built with wide streets that were numbered from
the Temple Block. Along the gutters ran streams of mountain water
which was used to water the gardens with which every house was
surrounded.

The population was divided. Mormons were the dominant factor. The others, even the Jews, were known as Gentiles. The Mormons controlled most of the business and all of the farms. Many
of the larger enterprises, factories and farms, were owned by the
church, which maintained tithing offices, a newspaper and an his-
torian's office. The Gentiles of the Territory were miners, business
men, saloon keepers, lawyers and politicians. The *Deseret News* was
the official paper of the Mormons, while the *Salt Lake Tribune* spoke
for the Gentiles. Against the Gentiles there was a bitter antipathy,
as the older Mormons could not forget the outrages they had suffered, their property that had been destroyed, the killing of their
leaders, their final abandonment of the states where they had lived,
and their search for a new home where they could be safe from
persecution, and which was now being invaded by their old-time enemies. That spirit of bitterness has somewhat died down with the
newer generation, but when I was a boy it was at its height.

We lived for years near the house that was my birthplace, in different rented houses, always surrounded by polygamous families;
the Taylors, the Evanses, the Cannons. John Taylor, one time president of the Church of Latter Day Saints, as the Mormons call their
church, lived across the street from us. He had eight wives in one
half block. Next door to our house was one of several families
of William Taylor, a brother of the president, and the first house
from theirs was the home of Porter Rockwell. He had the repu-

tation of being a Danite, or one of the Destroying Angels, an associate of the notorious Bill Hickman. Concerning these Destroying Angels, it was said that their function was to avenge the church by doing away with such offenders as apostates. Rockwell was a mysterious being to the boys of the neighborhood, most of whom were Mormons. All had heard of the terrible things that he and Hickman were accused of, through rumors and whispers in their families. There was nothing definite, but enough to arouse the curiosity of the youngsters so that when we saw Porter Rockwell on the street, with his long gray beard, gray shawl, gray slouch hat, and iron gray hair falling over his shoulders, we would run along in front of him, staring back at his not unkindly face. After Porter Rockwell died, some boys in the neighborhood thought it would be a good joke to haunt the big house where he had lived alone. One who worked in a drug store got some phosphorus, which we put on a sheet. We tied the sheet to a rope, and pulled it from the house to the barn. Breaking into the house, we rattled pieces of iron and crockery in an old keg, shook the windows and did other things to make a noise, so that one passing could not fail to notice the disturbance. The ghostly sheet and the continuous racket on dark nights gave the house the reputation of being haunted. All the boys who belonged to the gang were initiated with different hair-raising stunts.

The Sisters' Academy of the Sacred Heart was in the next block. They had a little building adjoining the girls' school where some small boys from the adjacent mining camps were boarded and given their first education. There were some day-scholars. Though not a Catholic, I was admitted to the school, where a nun called Sister Sylva was our teacher.

During vacation time my uncle Richard came to visit us from one of the near-by mining camps. Reading an advertisement one day in the paper that a boy was wanted on a farm, he talked it over with my mother, with the result that I was bound out to John Holden. For a period of six months at one dollar a month and board I was to be boy-of-all-work on the farm. There I milked two cows, fed the calves, cleaned out the stable, but my main job was driving a yoke of oxen.

One day I was in the field harrowing while Holden was plowing. A tooth of the harrow turned up a nest of field mice. They were curious little things. I had never seen the like before, and got down on my knees to examine them more closely. They were red, with no hair on their bodies. Their eyes were closed. The nest was a neat little home all lined with what seemed to be wool. It seemed only a few minutes that I looked at them, when all of a sudden I felt a smarting whip-lash across my body. Holden had crossed the field, picked up the bull-whip I had dropped, and struck me without saying a word. I jumped up and ran straight to the house, gathered up my few belongings, tied them into a bundle and started for home. As I crossed the fields some distance from Holden I sang out: "Good-by, John!" I walked to the city some ten miles distant. This was my first strike.

When I got home and told my mother that I had quit, because Holden had struck me with the whip, she was angry at the abuse, but was afraid of what he might do on account of the paper that she had signed, which was an indenture binding me to work for him. Holden came to our house the next day, my mother scolded him for daring to strike me with a whip. He admitted to having a bad temper and promised never to do it again, so I went back with him and served my time. Holden was a cruel man, cruel to his horses, cruel to his oxen, cruel to his wife, who often used to say that "it would be better to be an old man's darling than a young man's slave."

My next job was working for Mrs. Paxton, who had a small store. I ran errands and chopped kindling wood which she sold in packages. Her son, Clem Horseley, was chief usher in the Salt Lake Theater, and he added a little to the small wage of a dollar and a half a week that I was getting from his mother by giving me a job as an usher at fifty cents a night when there were shows at the theater. Besides showing people to their seats, we also acted as claquers, starting or increasing the applause at the end of each act. This job gave me an opportunity to see many plays that I should otherwise have missed. I became interested in the plays and trage-dies of Shakespeare, as Booth and Barrett appeared in Salt Lake City while I was working in the theater. I later became an ardent reader of Shakespeare. All sorts of shows were given at this theater; I saw everything from home talent to the stars that stopped over on their way to the coast. There were opera companies, oriental jugglers, and boxing exhibitions given here, although the theater was the property of the Mormon Church.

Then I got a job with old John C. Cutler. He was a good man to work for. His store was a fruit commission house. He was a fine, red-cheeked old man with a white beard, good-tempered and genial, who had many old cronies who visited him in the store. I once heard them discussing their different marital relations. Old man Cutler had two wives. The older one, the mother of four prominent Mormons of Utah, lived in Salt Lake City, the younger one in South Cottonwood. He remarked that he had yet another wife, a buxom lass who had a fine baby, but he added: "I don't know where she is now." Why he laughed when he said this, I never did understand. This old man would occasionally get stuck with consignments of grapes, bananas or other perishable fruit. He would turn these in to the tithing office of the church, where I would deliver them. Once in a while he would say to me, "William, do you think you can sell that fruit?" Once he sold me ten or twelve bunches of bananas at twenty-five cents a bunch, which I quickly disposed of at a dollar and a half a bunch; another time it was tomatoes at twenty-five cents a bushel; of these my mother and other women in the neighborhood made ketchup.

I used to go swimming with Joe and Heber Cutler in the Jordan River. I was caught with a cramp once and would have drowned if Joe had not come to my aid. I tried to repay this one night, when a warehouse back of John Cutler's store caught fire. I knew the boys were sleeping in the store, and a rumor was going through the crowd that there was powder in the warehouse. I ran up the street to rout them out, when I heard the explosion. The broken glass dropped out of the windows of the stores like a waterfall, but I got through uninjured. The Cutler boys had been awakened and had already escaped from the store, and the fire was soon extinguished.

When I was about twelve I ran a fruit stand on Elephant Corner for old man Reese. Around dinner time one day I heard some shooting down the street and saw a crowd gathering in front of Griggs' restaurant. I ran down to see what the trouble was. Two policemen were bringing a Negro out of the restaurant. From what the crowd said I understood that he had killed one policeman and the watermaster, and had wounded another policeman.

The policemen, with the crowd following, started toward Second South Street. I wondered why they did not go the shortest way to the jail; the route they took was nearly a block longer. As they went along Second South Street, a grocer left his store and joined the crowd, folding up his apron and tucking it into his belt as he walked along. This man, whose name I did not know, shouted: "Get a rope!" I thought to myself, "What do they want with a rope? The police have got him fast."

The crowd was increasing and getting more excited at every step. The added distance increased the number of the mob. As the jail was reached, I could see the prisoner and the policemen on the steps that led up to the door. It seemed to me that the policemen, instead of pushing the Negro into the prison, pushed him into the hands of the mob. I did not see him again until I had crowded in under the arms of the mob, which was then standing hushed as though stricken with awe. Then I saw the Negro hanging by the neck in the wagon shed. His face was ghastly, and although he was light colored, it was turning blue, with the eyes and tongue sticking out horribly. I looked at the swinging figure and thought over and over, "What have they done—what have they done—" It was as though a weight of cold lead settled in my stomach.

The leaders of the mob were not satisfied with the death of the man. Some one cried out: "Drag him out and quarter him! Hang him to a telegraph pole!" They dragged the limp body by the neck to the corner of the street, where Mayor Wells drove up and read the riot act, ordering them to return the body at once to the jail. This was my first realization of what the insane cruelty of a mob could mean. I learned then, too, that the mob was not composed only of those who would be willing themselves to do the dreadful deed that was done, but many were there out of curiosity to see what was going to be done. Each one there lent the strength of his presence to the leaders. I don't think more than three or four men there really wanted to kill that man.

A messenger boy has the opportunity to see things and know people intimately, and working as a messenger boy I had this chance. It put me in touch with all the leading citizens of Salt Lake City. People were not guarded in what they said before a young boy, and I heard their business plans, their scandals and their political schemes. In this way I came to know of the plans that were being matured against the Mormons, which finally resulted in the passage of the Edmunds Act, which forbade polygamy. In opposition to this plan, a scheme was framed up by the Mormons, who employed a woman and brought her to the city, established her in a house which was supplied with convenient peep-holes, and invitations were sent out to prominent Gentiles to visit the lady, who had with her some interesting young friends. Through a mistake, some invitations were also sent to Mormons, and the affair created a scandal in the city, on both sides, many would-be dignified and prominent men being involved.

I went one term to St. Mark's School. As I look back at it, it seems to me I must have been a queer pupil. In some of my studies I received excellent marks, in others I could make no headway. For history and geography I went up to the highest class in the school. My liking for these studies and my ability in them came, I am sure, from the earlier teaching I had received from old Professor Foster. In mathematics I went to the class below; in other studies I held with the regular class.

The term at St. Mark's was the last of my school days. About this time I made up my mind to change my name from William Richard Haywood, Richard being the name of the uncle who had bound me out to the farmer and whom I therefore did not like, to my father's name, William Dudley Haywood. My mother concluded that this could be done if I was confirmed in church. She was an Episcopalian. This was the last time that I attended a church service.

I heard Ben Tillman, Senator from South Carolina, lecture in Salt Lake City, and it was from him that I got my first outlook on the rights of the Negroes. In the course of the lecture he showed his bitter antipathy toward the Negro as a man and as a race. A Negro sitting beside me asked him a question; his reply was a ferocious and insulting attack, with reflections on the colored man's mother. He referred to his questioner as a "saddle-colored son of Satan," and went on to tell him what his mother must have been for the Negro to have been the color he was; this because the Negro obviously was of mixed blood. I looked at the Negro, and his pained expression caused me forever after to feel that he and his kind were the same as myself and other people. I saw him suffering the same resentment and anger that I should have suffered in his place; I saw him helpless to express this resentment and anger. I feel that Ben Tillman's lectures must have made many other people feel as I did. It seemed to me that I could look right into the breast of old Tillman and see his heart that was rotten with hate.

I met other public characters when I was a bellboy in the Continental Hotel and the Walker House. One evening a tall, dignified man, sitting with his feet against a railing in front of the hotel, asked me as I passed: "My boy, do you know who I am?" "No, who are you?" said I. He answered: "I am the world-renowned Beerbohm Tree, the great English actor!" I looked at him; I didn't know what he was driving at.

I met more interesting people, whom I could better understand. There was a Lightning Calculator, who stopped at the hotel; my lack of ability in arithmetic caused me to think he was one of the world's wonders. Then there was John L. Sullivan, who came through with a boxing combination; with him was Slade, a big Maori who came over to fight him, but Sullivan could lick a corral full like him. Sullivan I liked better than any of the rest. His show was at the Walker Opera House, in which I had a good seat. I saw him box with Herbert Slade, and knock out a man who tried to win the thousand dollars that he was giving to any one who would stand up against him during four rounds.

Dr. Zuckertort, the great chess player, stopped at the Walker House, and while there played simultaneously seventeen games blindfolded, which I thought a most remarkable feat. It so inspired me that I started then and there to learn chess.

While I was working at the Continental I was suddenly taken sick with typhoid pneumonia. I did not go back to my job at the Continental, and after my recovery my mother and I decided that I should learn a trade. In the house next to us was a family named Pierpoint. The man was a boiler maker, whose father owned a foundry and boiler shop. My mother spoke to the old man about me becoming an apprentice; but when they talked about drawing up the necessary papers I rebelled. I did not want to be bound out again as I had been to John Holden, where I could not quit until a certain term was served. My stepfather was then superintendent of the Ohio Mine and Milling Company in Humboldt County, Nevada. He decided that he could use me there. I bought an outfit in Salt Lake City, consisting of overalls, jumper, blue shirt, mining boots, two pairs of blankets, a set of chessmen, and a pair of boxing gloves. My mother fixed up a big lunch, mostly of plum pudding. She said: "You will be back in a few weeks." Bidding my little sweetheart and my family good-by, I left for Nevada. I was then fifteen years old.

CHAPTER II

MINERS, COWBOYS AND INDIANS

THIS was my first long journey. We passed through Ogden, going around Great Salt Lake, as the Luzon cut-off had not then been built. I was on the lookout for Corinne and Promontory, as I knew that these places had at one time been the stamping ground of my father and uncle. Promontory was the station where the golden spike was driven when the Central Pacific and the Union Pacific Railroads met from the east and the west. The iron horse, as the Indians called the railroad, had overtaken the covered wagons and ox teams.

For many miles after we left the lake, the lowland was covered with a crust of salt. Then we came to the sage-brush flats of Nevada, which seemed endless. As far as the eye could reach there was nothing but the long stretches of the gray-green shrub. The stations were few and the towns were small. We passed Elko, Battle Mountain and then the Humboldt River came into view on the right. On the morning of the second day I arrived at Winnemucca, went to the hotel, and immediately after dinner took the four-horse stage for Rebel Creek. The stage line extended in those days to Fort McDermitt, an army post. The stage was loaded with freight; I was the only passenger. Inside was a big buffalo coat and a buffalo robe; I thought there would be no chance to get cold. From Winnemucca past the Toll-house was a road through sand hills, which was built of sage-brush laid the width of the wagon track. When tramped down it was for a short time serviceable, but the sands were ever shifting, so that new roads were continually in the process of being built.

We arrived at Kane Springs for supper. It was already dark and getting very cold. When we went to the station, the driver got a drink of whisky. I felt warmer after a cup of hot coffee. After the horses had been changed for a new team, the driver said: "We are ready; let's go!" I piled into the coach. The buffalo robe and the coat were gone; they belonged to the driver. It was a cold, clear night. In front of us and a little to the right we could see the majestic outline of Granite Peak, in the shelter of which the winter snows were stored, furnishing some water to the flats below. This was my first view of the Santa Rosa range.

When we reached Rebel Creek it was late at night. I had been thinking about unrolling my blankets for a bed. I climbed down from the stage, cold and shivering, and found that supper had been prepared and a clean white bed was awaiting me.

A spring wagon was provided, into which I threw my roll of blankets and my valise, and we drove to Eagle Canyon, two miles up which the Ohio mine was located. There was not a tree in sight; nothing but the scrubby willows that grew along the little stream that flowed down the canyon. There was but one house. It was built of lumber and was about twenty-eight feet long, fourteen feet wide, divided in two by a partition. In the front room bunks were ranged; double length and three high. In this room there were no chairs, no tables, no furniture of any kind other than a desk and the stuff belonging to the men, consisting almost entirely of blankets and clothing, and a few suitcases and bags thrown under the lower bunks.

The second room had a big cook-stove in the corner, a kitchen table and a cupboard along one wall. Along the other wall, where there was a window, was a long table covered with brown flower-patterned oil-cloth, with benches running the full length on either side. Overhead on the beams were piled the groceries and other supplies and the bunk of the Chinese cook, which was reached by a ladder. Charley Sing was a good cook, and kept his part of the house scrupulously clean. The other room was also clean, as far as being free from vermin was concerned, but the lumber was without paint and had never seen a plane. There was a little porch in front, a bench over which hung a looking-glass, washpans, a water-bucket alongside the bench, and towels hung against the side of the house. The well was near the creek, in the bottom of the gully. Below the house stood an old stone cabin, half dug-out, with logs, brush, and dirt for a roof. One corner of this was fixed up for use as an assay office. The rest was used for storing cases of canned foods, vegetables, and other supplies.

My stepfather came down from the mine a few minutes ahead

of the other men who were working there. He was glad to see me. After meeting the men and having dinner, I unrolled my blankets and spread them on some hay in the bunk over the desk. I put on my overalls and jumper and digging boots that same afternoon and went to work in the mine. My first job was wheeling rock from a shaft that was being sunk at the end of an open cut. I soon found that a wheelbarrow loaded with rock was more than I could handle, so I made the loads lighter and took more trips. I was glad enough when quitting time came.

When we got down to the house it was already dark. The usual mining camp meal was ready, and every one pitched in with a hearty appetite. It was but a few minutes afterward, when the dishes were cleared away, that the men gathered around the table again, reading, playing cards or chess as best they could by flickering candle-light. Others were stretched out in their bunks, or sitting on the edges of them, and so the winter evenings were passed. There was no place to go. The closest town was Winnemucca, sixty miles away. There was one saloon at Willow Creek, the post office, four miles away, but this was seldom patronized, though occasionally some of the men who went to the station brought back a couple of bottles of whisky.

Though miners situated as we were could not keep in close touch with current events, we were all great readers. I remember the second Christmas I was there, one of my relatives sent me a book on baseball. This would have been interesting enough some years before but I was now in a place where one side of a baseball team could not be scratched up in a long day's ride.

I did not have many books of my own, but the miners all had some. One had a volume of Darwin; others had Voltaire, Shakespeare, Byron, Burns and Milton. These poets were great favorites of my stepfather. We all exchanged books, and quite a valuable library could have been collected among these few men. Some received magazines, and there were four or five daily papers that came to the camp. That they were a week old made little difference to us.

I had a friend about whom I have not yet spoken. This was Tim. He was much more than the ordinary dog one usually meets. A shepherd type, as large as a good-sized collie, his coat was black with brown points and a white patch at his throat. He was quick and strong and had limpid brown eyes. He did not speak my language, but I could understand his tail-wagging, his joyful bark, fierce growl, pathetic whine, and low, peculiar croon. There was something about Tim that always made me think of him as a real person. It was as though the personality of some lovable human had found a place in his being. Instinct was not the only attribute that actuated Tim, although perhaps for scientific reasons I should not venture to assert that Tim could think. Anyway, you know him now well enough to understand the kind of companion such a dog could be to a boy at a mine sixty miles from a railroad, with the nearest neighbor four miles away. The one boy in that section of the country I saw only occasionally, but Tim was with me all the time. He and I had heaps of fun. I helped him out in many a desperate fight we had with lynx, wild-cat and badger.

John Kane was the assayer and ore-sorter at the mine. He took a great liking to me and taught me assaying. He was a big, heavy-set, good-natured Irishman with a heavy black mustache and pleasant eyes. When I went to work with him I helped him prepare the samples that were to be assayed. No work I ever did in my life was as fascinating as assaying. These first small ventures into the realm of chemistry led me to feel that I would like to become a mining engineer. I made up my mind to learn this profession and wrote to the Houghton School of Mines and the Columbia School of Mines to learn their requirements for entrance. I secured some books on assaying and surveying and devoted much time to study. But I never entered either of these colleges. I found myself with other responsibilities and my further education was secured in the school of experience.

I took a shotgun one day and started up the canyon looking for grouse or sage-hen, when I ran across a Basque sheep-herder who suggested, "Maybe you want deer?" I told him that would be fine. We went together to his camp on the ridge that divided Eagle Creek from Rebel Creek, where he got his rifle and we started around the summit toward a clump of scraggly poplar trees. There was a thick undergrowth of manzanita. Pointing to a big flat rock on one side of the wood, he handed me his rifle and said, "You go there. I stay here few minutes. Then I go through, maybe deer come out." I walked over and climbed up to the flat rock, from which I had a clear view of all that side of the woods. Presently I heard the crash of undergrowth, and out burst a beautiful big stag with splendid antlers. I stared at him amazed, when he turned and bounded down toward the bed of the creek, heading into the brush again. In a short time the Basque came plodding through the manzanita over to where I was sitting and asked me: "Did you see deer?" I told him that I had and started to explain what a big buck it was. He interrupted me by asking, "Why you no shoot?" Only then the thought struck me what a splendid shot I could have had at that buck! I tried to tell the Basque that I had forgotten to shoot, but he took his rifle and marched off without a word. I must have had an attack of the "buck-ague." If I had scared up the deer and left the Basque to do the shooting we would have had venison for supper.

One morning as I came out of the dry gulch on my way to the station I saw a bunch of saddle horses and a crowd of men in front of Andy Kinniger's place at the mouth of Willow Creek. I hurried on, and heard that Kinniger had been shot and the surgeon from Fort McDermitt was then trying to find the bullet. It was somewhere in the dead man's skull. I marveled at the skill with which the surgeon had removed the top of the skull to probe down the spinal column where the bullet had lodged. Kinniger had been shot some time the previous evening while he was seated in a chair leaning back against a clump of willows. Later it was proved that Kinniger was killed by One Arm Jim, a Piute Indian, who was arrested, tried, and sentenced to hang. No one could find any motive for the Indian's action, and every one believed that he was an accessory. A petition was circulated and the sentence of One Arm Jim was commuted to life imprisonment in the Carson Penitentiary. I saw him there many years afterward, when I visited the pen to see Preston and Smith, who were serving life sentences. These were two miners from Goldfield whose story I will tell later. I recall an interesting feature about the penitentiary yard, which had been made by excavating into the mountain side. A rough half circle was dug out, leaving sheer walls, in places sixty to eighty feet high. On the floor of the yard were the imprints of what must have been an elephant or mastodon of prehistoric times, also the footprints of a man which were half again as large as an ordinary man's footprints. These impressions were made in mud apparently, but had hardened to solid rock. Involuntarily one followed the footprints as they led to the wall. There one-half of the animal's track was left exposed, the other half was covered by eighty feet of solid rock and alluvial soil.   One realized that it was just a little too late; the animal had passed by, perhaps two hundred thousand years before.   The wall of time had arisen to prevent our following.

People were sociable in the frontier country.   A dance was quite an event.   It would be planned some weeks ahead, and people would gather from thirty to forty miles around.   It was not unusual for some of the ranchers with their families to drive forty miles to a dance, dance all night and all next day, then drive home.   As for dancing partners, there were girls and old women from the ranches, and sometimes Indian squaws would take part.   At an impromptu dance at Kinniger's place Mrs. Snapp from the station at Rebel Creek played the dance music on a three-stringed fiddle, accompanied by Tom Melody, who had contrived a tambourine by putting beans in an empty cigar box.

But more interesting were the Indian dances, where, in a circle cleared on the sage-brush flat, the Indians would gather for their pow-wow and dance sometimes the snake-dance, the ghost-dance, the sun-dance, or some other just as mysterious.   Their only music was the drums and the lilt of the squaws.   The tunes were plaintive and fantastic, and sounded much alike to me.   In the night when the fires were lighted, the hypnotic rhythm of the drums and the springy furtive dance steps of the Indians, accompanied by the low crooning song, were thrillingly weird.

The story of the massacre of the Piute Indians at Thacker Pass was told to me first by Jim Sackett, one of the volunteers who took part in the killing.   I also heard the story from Ox Sam, a Piute who had made his escape, one of the only three survivors.

I first heard this hair-raising narrative when old Sackett happened to be a chance visitor at the Ohio mine.   It began with an explanation of the many depredations on the part of the Indians throughout southern Oregon and northern Nevada, which caused the white men to organize a volunteer company which, he said, was for mutual protection.   This company had been famous as the crack Indian fighters of that section.   Their quarters were at Fort McDermitt; from this base they scoured the country looking for Indians.   McDermitt was on the western slope of the Santa Rosa range, in the mouth of a branch of the Quin River.

Sackett was an old pensioner who roamed about the country doing little, as he was then too old to work much. There were only a few of his type left. He was at home in the mountains at the cabins of the prospectors or at the ranches along the river in the valley. He wore his hair and his beard long, both grizzled gray. His eyes were weak and looked as though they were sore from alkali dust. As he talked he would squirt tobacco juice at an object he had located as a target, and hit it with remarkable precision. His story started:

"That day we had camped at the mouth of Willow Creek, just above where Andy Kinniger's house stands now. We were settling down for a good night's sleep when the call came for boots and saddles. Now what's up? The outfit was ready to move in a very short time, mules packed and horses saddled. The captain coming up pointed across the valley in the direction of what is now called Thacker Pass, saying, 'If you look close you can see a fire there. Before dusk I thought I could see smoke but now I see the fire. It is an Indian camp. We've got to get there by daylight. We'll start when it gets a little darker.' It was a long ride across the sagebrush flat and through the meadows as we got close to the river, which we had to swim. More meadows and then the sage-brush again. One of the horses stepped into a badger hole and broke his leg. We couldn't kill him until next day. They might have heard the shot and we did not want to alarm them. Here the company divided; part were sent ahead to ride down the pass to the camp, a small detachment was left with the pack animals and extra saddle horses, the rest of us rode up the pass.

"Daylight was just breaking when we came in sight of the Indian camp. All were asleep. We unslung our carbines, loosened our six-shooters, and started into that camp of savages at a gallop, shooting through their wickiups as we came. In a second, sleepy-eyed squaws and bucks and little children were darting about, dazed with the sudden onslaught, but they were shot down before they came to their waking senses. The other detachment came rushing in but did no shooting until they were close up. From one wickiup to another we went, pouring in our bullets. Then we dismounted to make a closer examination. In one wickiup we found two little papooses still alive. One soldier said, 'Make a clean-up. Nits make lice.' When Charley Thacker spoke up, saying, 'I'd like to keep those two if there ain't no serious objection.' Before it was decided, some one sang out, 'There's one gettin' away!' He was already a mile off on a big gray horse going like the wind. Some of us began to shoot, several got on their horses and started after him. But it was too late, he escaped. They soon returned. Those of the Indians who were only wounded we put out of their misery, and then mounted and rode away, Charley Thacker carrying his two papooses behind him."

These young ones grew to manhood and were known as Jimmy and Charley Thacker. When I knew them they had gone back to the nomadic life of the Indians. Both were fine, stalwart men; as men, I imagine, much better than those who had helped kill their fathers and mothers, relatives and friends.

Old Sackett's tale seemed to pull a lot of the fringe off the buckskin clothes of the alluring Indian fighters I had read about in dime novels. There was nothing I had ever read about, with heart palpitating, of killing women and little children while they were asleep. The old volunteer's exploits were at a discount with me after that, and declined even more when Ox Sam, some months later, told me in his pidgin English what had happened at Thacker Pass. He made no additions to the story, but it was the feeling in the things he said that Sackett did not possess. The old Indian buck was one day sitting on a sack of charcoal at the door of the half dug-out cabin which we used as an assay office. I went out and sat down beside him, asking him how his squaw Maggie and his papooses were. "Pretty good," he answered. I said, "Sam, tell me about Thacker Pass." He glanced up with a distant look in his eyes, murmuring, "Long time ago. No much talk about now." But I said, "Sam, I would like to know why the white men kill Indians. Do you know?" Sam's eyes narrowed. "Yes, I sabe. You no sabe?" I told him that I did not. Sam began:

"Long time ago same time I born, maybe before, no white man stay in Nevada. That time Piute live pretty good. In spring, catch em plenty fish, dry em, smoke em. Lots duck, lotsa goose, smoke em, too. In the fall, kill em deer, jerk em meat. First time frost come, catch em plenty pine-nut. All time lotsa rabbit, lotsa sage-hen. Piute no sabe big ranch, no make em farm, all same live pretty good. Some time Bannock, some time Shoshone man steal em Piute squaw. We make em fight. Some time Piute steal Shoshone, Bannock squaw; make em pretty good fight. Some time make em big gamble; some time big dance; some time big pow-wow. Hot, cold, all same. Piute live. When him die, make up big pile rock, him stay inside. Got bow and arrow, good knife, kill em good pony, Piute go happy hunting ground. Everything good. "White man, he come. He make em little farm, some time marry Piute squaw. That's pretty good. Mix em blood all same like Bannock, Shoshone. Pretty soon come more white man. Him prospector; him pretty good. I no sabe, all time dig hole, make em big pile rock, dig em more hole. He no stay long one place. Soldier man come. No sabe soldier. He no got em farm, he no dig em hole, he no do nothing; say all time 'Uncle Sam.' He all live one house, no woman. I no sabe. All time talk em 'squaw, squaw.' He got fire-water, give em Piute, make em crazy all same white man. All Indians have big pow-wow. Big Chief say, what matter now? Too much trouble all time. Indian like em fire-water, fire-water he no good. Soldier give Indian fire-water. No like fire-water. Indian sell em mink-skin, badger-skin, all kind of skin to soldier. Sell em squaw, too, for fire-water. By and by Indian he crazy. No more fire-water, all same crazy. Chief say soldier not much good. Indian say all white men not much good. Pretty soon white man kill em Piute. Indian no much sabe, he kill em white man. That's pretty bade time. Soldier hunt Piute all same coyote. That's time Thacker Pass. Lots of Indians going Quin River sink to get ducks, goose. That morning soldier come quick, shoot, shoot. I cut wickiup skin behind, go quick and get on big white horse, ride fast; soldier no catch em, no shoot em. I ride Disaster Peak. Long time hide. My father, my mother, my sisters, my brothers, I no see no more. Long time ago. Not much talk about now."

Old Sam ended with a tremor in his voice and moisture in his eyes. "Yes, I sabe, I sabe." Grasping his hand, I said, "You stay a little while, Sam. We'll have dinner pretty soon."

There was a wide historical meaning in the brief story that Ox Sam, the Piute Indian, told me. It began when the earliest settlers stole Manhattan Island. It continued across the continent. The ruling class with glass beads, bad whisky, Bibles and rifles continued the massacre from Astor Place to Astoria.

Half-way between the camp and the mouth of the canyon there was a big ledge of quartz, the outcropping of which stood high, cleaving the mountain from base to summit. Charley Day, who was then working in the Ohio mine, had located this cropping, but said that he never intended to do the assessment work on it. One night he said, "I'll give you the Caledonia mine if you want it." With the thought of being a mine owner, I accepted from him the quit-claim deed, to make which binding I gave him the legally required sum of one dollar. I used to pass this claim with the idea of working it some time, but having come into possession of it so cheaply, I ignored its possible value. Some years later I worked in it as a miner, after Doctor Hanson of Winnemucca had relocated it, organized a company and erected a quartz mill. I had neglected the assessment work and my right had long before expired. It came into the possession of the Caledonia Mining and Milling Company. When the first lot of ore was run through the mill every one was excited as to what the returns were going to be. We had heard different reports as to how the assays were running and that some nuggets had been caught in the battery or ore-crusher. But we never knew the returns, as a nephew of the doctor ran away with the entire output, and as far as I knew was never caught. After this episode there was an air of discouragement and pessimism about the mine. The men did not know whether they were going to get their pay or not, and shortly afterward I quit.

Coming down the trail from the mine one day, John Kane and I were skylarking and I jumped on his back. He fell and broke his leg. The other men helped carry him down to the bunk-house; I started off to Rebel Creek to get a team and spring wagon to take John to the hospital at Fort McDermitt. We put a mattress in the wagon, got John in and started on the thirty-mile drive to the surgeon. It must have been a painful trip for him, but the surgeon did a good job and six weeks later John was back at work. That is, he was working in the assay office hobbling about on a crutch.

Men situated as we were sometimes form close friendships. This was true of Pat Reynolds and myself. Pat was the oldest man on the job, tall, raw-boned, with a red chin-whisker, bushy eyebrows and a strawberry mark on the outer corner of his left eye. It was this old Irishman who gave me my first lessons in unionism. Pat was a member of the Knights of Labor, and some of the things he told me about this organization I could not well understand at the time. I had never heard of the need of workingmen organizing for mutual protection. In that part of the country there did not seem to be a wide division between the boss and the men. The old man who was the boss slept in the same room and ate at the same table and appeared the same as the rest of the men. But Pat explained that he was not the real boss; that none of us knew the owner of the mine. Mentioning the large ranches in the vicinity, he said, "The owners live in California, while the men who do all the work and make the ranches and mines of value are here in Nevada." He told me about the unions he had belonged to, the miners' union in Bodie, California, and the Virginia City Miners' Union in Nevada, organized in 1867, the first miners' union in America. These two unions were among the first that formed the Western Federation of Miners. It was some time before I got the full significance of a remark that he made, that if the working class was to be emancipated, the workers themselves must accomplish it. Early in May, 1886, this thought was driven more deeply into my mind by reading in the newspapers the details of the Haymarket Riot, and later the speeches that were made by the men who were put to trial. The facts and details I talked over every day with Pat Reynolds. I was trying to fathom in my own mind the reason for the explosion. Were the strikers responsible for it? Was it the men who were their spokesmen? Why were the policemen in Haymarket Square? Who threw the bomb? It was not Albert Parsons or any one that he knew; if it had been, why did Albert Parsons walk into court and surrender himself? Who were those who were so anxious to hang these men they called anarchists? Were they of the same capitalist class that Pat Reynolds was always talking to me about? The last words of August Spies kept running through my mind: "There will come a time when our silence will be more powerful than the voices you are strangling to-day." It was a turning point in my life.

I told Pat that I would like to join the Knights of Labor. From this time, although there was never an opportunity to join, I was a member in the making.

Soon after this I made my first visit home since I had begun to work in the mine. After a few weeks I returned to Nevada. The next year was a year of financial crisis, and panics of this kind affect the miner as well as the workers in other industries. The Ohio mine was closed down, and I was left in charge. I lived alone at the camp with my dogs for company, and did my own cooking.

Some time later I returned to Utah and went to work in the Brooklyn mine. My first job there was firing the boilers and running the top car, taking away the waste and ore that were sent to the surface. The Brooklyn was an inclined shaft fourteen hundred feet deep, in which there was a skip that was hauled up by the engine for which I was firing the boilers. For a while I worked in what was called the Mormon stope; it had been given this name because several of the men employed there were from the San Pete valley, a strictly Mormon section. I worked in several different places in this mine, which was producing lead. There were men going to and coming from the hospital all the time, suffering from lead poisoning. This is one of the serious vocational diseases with which the workers have to contend, but there was no provision made for them. In that part of the country the miners were sent to hospitals in Salt Lake City which they themselves maintained. Every miner had one dollar a month taken out of his wages by the company for hospital services. Their transportation to and from the hospital the workers had to pay themselves. A crowd of lead miners presents a ghastly appearance, as their faces are ashen pale.

There are many dangers to which a miner is exposed besides rheumatism, consumption, lead poisoning, and other diseases. One of these is the constant danger of falling rock when a mine is not kept closely timbered. I was working but a short distance from Louis Fontaine when he was killed by a slab of rock from the roof that crushed his head on the drill that he was holding. We got the body out of the stope on a timber truck, ran it to the station, and put all that was left of Louis in the skip. We rang three bells for the surface. Some of us laid off to go to the funeral.

The men rode on the skip coming up to dinner at quitting time. Four could sit in the skip on either side, two on the crossbar, and one on the angle to which the steel cable was fastened. One day I got on the cable behind the man on the angle and rode all the way to the top. It was one of the most hair-raising experiences of my life. The cable was whipping the timbers at the top and the rollers on which the skip ran up the steep incline. I was afraid every second that my hands would be caught as I held on to the cable behind my head, and I gripped the man in front of me with both legs to keep from turning on the rope.

While at the Brooklyn mine, I sent to Nevada for my sweetheart,

Nevada Jane Minor. We were married and went to live in Salt Lake City, where our first child was born, a boy who died at birth. Shortly afterward we returned to Nevada, where I spent some time doing assessment work for Thad Hoppin, and prospecting. I later went to work on the Hoppin ranch.

A cowboy's life is not the joyous, adventurous existence shown in the moving pictures, read about in cheap novels, or to be seen in World's Exhibitions. The cowboy's work begins at daybreak. If he is on the ranch he rolls out of bed, slips on his pants, boots and hat and goes to the barn to feed his saddle horses. It is his greatest pride that he does not work on foot. Coming back, he washes his face and hands at the pump, and takes his place at the long table; the Chinese cook brings in piles of beefsteaks, potatoes, hot cakes, and "long butter," as the flour-gravy is called, because on a big cattle ranch where there are thousands of cows, ofttimes there will be not one milk cow, and no butter but what is hauled many miles from town to the ranch.

There are various kinds of work for the cowboy to do during the different seasons on a cow ranch. The cattle are not pastured or herded, but run wild on the mountains and sage-brush flats. They are rounded up in the Spring and Fall, the round-up being called the "rodeo." This and other words commonly used in the southwest come down to us from the days when this part of the country was a Spanish colony, and Spanish was the usual language. The foreman, who was called major-domo, of the biggest ranch in the neighborhood issued the call for the rodeo. Cowboys from all the ranches in a radius of a hundred miles or more came with their saddle horses, each bringing three or four. The bedding consisted of a couple of blankets and a bed-canvas. When traveling with the rodeo, the men rolled up their bedding and put it in the chuck wagon which also carried the cooking utensils and the grub. Starting from the home ranch the outfit would camp on the banks of a stream or near a spring or sometimes would be compelled to make a dry camp, in which case they hauled along barrels of water for the emergency. After supper we stretched our beds on the ground, gambled and otherwise amused ourselves, telling stories of past experience and singing lilting and rollicking songs. A horse-wrangler or two guarded the paratha, the herd of saddle horses. We all went to sleep as soon as night fell. At the first break of day, the cook was up getting breakfast. The wranglers brought the horses. The cowboys went to the corral. Each roped his horse out of the band, saddled and bridled it and then went to the chuck wagon for breakfast.

After eating we rolled cigarettes, mounted our horses and started for the mountains, some going up one canyon, some up another. We rode to the highest summits. Turning, we drove before us all the cattle on that part of the range. The round-up took place in the valley below, where the cattle were brought together. The cowboys formed a circle around them, fifty or a hundred cowboys spaced out around several hundred head of cattle. Two or four cowboys from the biggest ranch rode among the herd and drove out the cows and young calves; they were able to recognize their own by the brands and earmarks on the cows. The task was then for the cowboys from each ranch to brand and earmark the calves that belonged to the ranch they were working for. The parting out continued until all the cows and young calves were separated from the herd. The other cattle were started back to the mountains. Two or three small fires were lit in the corral and the first bunch of cows was driven in; the other bunches were held to await their turn. We roped the calves by the hind legs and dragged them near the fire by taking a turn with the rope around the horns of our saddles. We cut the ears of the calves with our own peculiar marks, crop, under-bit, swallow-fork or other designs. The brand of the ranch was burnt into hip or shoulder. This proceeded until all the calves were branded and earmarked, the males gelded, leaving one out of every twenty-five or fifty for breeding purposes, selecting those which in the opinion of the cowboys would make big, strong animals. Outside of the bawling and bellowing of the calves and cows, there was silence; we had little to say while at work, as we were nearly choked with dust.

Meanwhile the chuck wagon had moved on to the next camping ground. If the horses had not had a hard day's work we would start for our supper at a long, swinging lope, singing ribald songs at the top of our voices. Unsaddling the horses where we were going to make our beds for the night, we washed up and were ready with ravenous appetites for grub. The day's work was done. The round-up took several weeks; we went up one side of the valley and down the other side.

Another round-up took place every fall, when beef steers were gathered for the market. It was carried on in much the same way though we used to take more care not to drive the animals fast because of the weight that would be lost from marketable steers.

When beef was needed for the camp, a young heifer or steer was killed. The cowboys as a rule used to barbecue the head and other parts of the animal. This was done by heating rocks which were put into a hole that had been prepared, the head and pieces of meat being wrapped in pieces of wet canvas, put on top of the hot rocks and covered with dirt. In the morning we would dig it out, remove the canvas and the hide, and with a little pepper and salt the main part of our breakfast was ready.

Wild horses are more fleet-footed than cattle and more difficult to handle. After the round-up of horses, those that were wanted for harness and saddle were kept in field or corral until the slack season of fall and winter, when they were broken to work or ride. This was the most exhilarating part of a cowboy's life. There was much excitement in riding wild horses as well as in handling them, not only for the rider but for the onlookers. Some horses were extremely vicious, biting, striking and kicking fiercely, to say nothing of their bucking propensities.

"I'm going to ride that roan colt to-day," said Tom Minor, my brother-in-law, as we were rolling out of bed in the bunk-house of Hoppin's ranch.

"I bet he'll pitch some," remarked John White.

"Oh, I don't know," said Tom, "I think he'll be as easy as a rockin' chair."

After breakfast six or eight cowboys went out to the corral. It was a bright, sparkling morning, the air was clean with a light frost. John White had a lasso on his arm and moved toward the horses, saying, "They're full of ginger this morning, Tom," as he threw his rope around the neck of a rangy roan colt, and sat back on the rope. Two of the boys ran up to help him, and Minor started toward the horse, his hands slipping along the taut lasso.

"Whoa, Rockin'-chair," he purred, reaching out his hand to the colt, which was used neither to its new name nor to the smell of human beings. The horse reared and struck out with both fore feet. After repeated efforts and much stroking, a halter was finally slipped over its head, and a leather blindfold was pulled down over its eyes. The lasso was taken off and the colt stood quivering in every nerve. Tom kept murmuring, "Whoa, Rockin'-chair." With sidewise and forward motions, they got the horse near the fence and tied him to a post. Tom tossed a blanket on him, but he kicked, snorted and bucked until he got it off. This was repeated until the colt came to the conclusion that he was not being hurt. He was led out to the open field, where, with much careful persuasion, he was hackamored and saddled. Minor, fastening on his big roweled spurs, with a quirt on his right wrist and reins in the left hand, which was on the horn of the saddle, placed his left foot in the stirrup and was on. He reached over and pulled up the blindfold, hit the colt on the shoulder with his quirt, and Rockin'-chair began to buck, all four feet bunched, his head down between his forelegs. His back bulged up like a camel's hump, while Minor was gouging him with his spurs and whipping him with his quirt. White sang out, "Lovely Jesus! but can't he buck? Some Rockin'-chair!"

The horse twisted, corkscrewed, cavorted and did everything a horse could do except roll. When he was completely exhausted Tom rode him back to the corral and got down. Then one of the boys took Rockin'-chair and unsaddled him. Minor said to the group who had come to shake hands with him, "He's a tough gazabo. We'll save him for the Pendleton round-up."

The cowboys and miners of the West led dreary and lonesome lives. They had drifted westward from points of civilization, losing contact with social life. Young and vigorous, they were bursting with enthusiasm which occasionally broke out in wild drinking sprees and shooting scrapes. They were deprived of the friendship of women, as the country was not yet settled, and when they visited the small towns on the railroad they gave vent to their exuberant feelings.

We saw dust coming up the valley road one day and wondered who it might be. Looking again a little later, we could see a sorrel team and a light buggy, but we did not recognize the occupant even when he pulled into the yard. We went out and asked him to unhitch and have supper. He told us that his name was Henry Miller. We had never seen him before, but knew him as one of the biggest ranch owners of the West. Putting his team in the barn after watering the horses and giving them a feed of hay, we took Miller to the house and seated him in the kitchen while we set about preparing supper. One of us—there were only two men on the ranch at that time—reached up and took down a package of coffee from the shelf, when Miller broke in: "Now I see why Hoppin goes broke. He feeds de ranch-hands Arpuckle's coffee! No vunder he goes broke; I vould go broke, too, if I gif my men Arpuckle's coffee!" We did not comment on this outburst, as the coffee seemed cheap enough to us. In the course of the evening Henry Miller told us how he had made his tremendous fortune. He said: "I starts out mit a basket of meat on my arm; I peddles it from house to house. I make me not vun fortune, but tree fortunes; I make vun fortune for Lux, vun for de goddam lawyers and tieves, and vun for mineself. If it vas not for de goddam lawyers and tieves, I own now de whole dam state of California. Anyhow, I got it some land; I can travel from mine wheat ranch in Modesto to de Whitehorse ranch in Oregon mit a team and stop on mine own land every night." Lux was his business partner; Miller and Lux was a powerful firm of meat-raisers and wheat-growers in California, which exploited the state in the early days.

We were always busy on the Hoppin ranch. According to the season, sheep-shearing, breaking horses, handling the cattle, or haying kept us on the go. There were three hay ranches, one alone of which was three thousand acres.

At this time Fort McDermitt was abandoned by the army. There was no industrial center anywhere near, and the Indians were practically all exterminated. My father-in-law was appointed custodian of the government property. My wife and I went to live alone at the old deserted army post until the family could arrange to move there from Willow Creek.

CHAPTER III

HOMESTEAD AND HARD TIMES

THE old fort was typical of many of its kind to be found throughout the West at that time. It was built in a hollow square around a parade ground of well-kept lawn. When entering the big gate in the barbed wire fence, the barns and stables were on the right, while on the left was a big granary, which was set up off the ground on piles. On top of each pile, before the sills were laid, a tin pan had been placed upside down to prevent rats or mice from getting in. The soldiers' barracks were on one side of the parade ground, the officers' houses on the other. These were small but neat, well-built dwellings of lumber. The officers used to see that they were kept warm in winter, as they had great ricks of mahogany wood which cost from forty to sixty dollars a cord and which had to be brought on mule-back for long distances on mountain trails. We took up our abode in what had been the captain's house. Our furniture was scanty; there were neither blinds nor curtains at the windows, nor a carpet on the floor. A big bed, chairs, and a table, besides our cooking outfit, was the extent of our household goods.

My wife spent her time making baby clothes. She startled me one morning sooner than we had expected by saying that she was suffering from labor pains. We were alone. We had planned to get Mrs. Vance, who was acting as a midwife for her neighbors and who lived ten miles away. My wife said that she did not think the baby would come during the time it would take me to drive over and get the old woman, so I hitched up and started at breakneck speed for help. When I got to the Vance farm the old lady put on her hat and coat and got into the wagon; I was not two hours in making the twenty miles.

Just ahead of us my wife's father and mother pulled in from Willow Creek. Mrs. Vance hurried into the house while I drove the team back to the barn and left them for the old man to unhitch. I went to the house on a run, where I found that my wife's mother had fainted when she heard her daughter's groans and realized what was about to happen. There she lay on the floor, and as Mrs. Vance came into the room she, too, fell down in a faint. I went and got a dipper of water and threw it hastily in their faces, and left them where they fell.

I have confronted many desperate situations but nothing so serious as this, and none that required the same nerve and coolness on my part. I did not know what had to be done, and I thought my wife was going to die, she seemed to be in such terrible pain. I said some words of encouragement to her as she lay moaning with the increasing pangs, and I grabbed the doctor book and hurriedly read all that I could find on childbirth.

A baby girl was born. I had tied and cut the navel cord when Mrs. Vance came to her senses. I was too busy to notice her until, just as I was cleaning up the afterbirth, my mother-in-law also came out of her faint. At last they were calm enough to go and heat some water and wash my wife and the baby, who was as bright and healthy as though she had had expert attention at her birth in, stead of only the unskilled help of her father.

My wife came through safely. All through the confusion caused by the old ladies' unaccountable behavior, she had kept cooler than any of us. While she was still in bed, Old Jim Horsehead, a Piute Indian, would come every morning and flatten his nose against the window pane and ask:

"How you wife and baby?"

He showed the greatest interest in the progress of the baby. The accusation of cruelty is only due to prejudice against the Indians; I have known many Indians and have found them more friendly and more loyal to their friends than many other people.

In the Spring I joined a government surveying corps to plot that part of the country around Black Rock and Quin River Sink. Moran, the surveyor, had taken the precaution to get his men in good shape for the work. The first month we were busy preparing stakes, cutting them the right length, sharpening them, and running preliminary lines. In the month of April we did nine hundred miles of measured work, an average of thirty miles a day, Sundays included.

After we were through surveying I went to Paradise Valley, where I worked during the haying for the Reese brothers. Aaron Reese was a russet-faced, heavy set Welshman with a red beard.

There was a fine bunch of men on his ranch who had a great store of good stories to enliven spare moments.

The way they broke horses to harness on this ranch gave me all the thrill of a Ben Hur chariot race. We would hitch a gentle, well-broken horse on the off side of a mowing-machine, having lifted the sickle bar and tied it securely. While the wild horse was being hitched beside the other, the driver would seat and brace himself. The men holding the wild horse would let go. With a desperate plunge to free himself from the contraptions that were all new in his life, the broncho would jump and rear at the rattle and clatter of the machine behind him. There was nothing to do but let the horses run. The gentle horse would crowd when the rein was pulled, and make the wild one circle in wide rings. After a short time they were driven back and unhitched. After two or three exercises of this kind we would put the colt to regular work cutting grass.

I was with a threshing outfit that season after the haying was done. There were a lot of small farmers who had grain to thresh. We had a good crew of men with our machine and put through more grain than had ever been threshed in that valley before. The boss of the outfit wanted to pay twenty-five cents a day less than the previous season. Every man on the job quit, leaving the threshing machine standing alone in the field.

Up to this time I had never drunk much, and had gambled but little. The day we quit the threshing machine everybody went to town. A dice game was running in Gillinan's saloon. I began to play and before the night was over I had won everything but the key of the front door. Gillinan borrowed money and won back from me most of his property but the money I had won I sent home.

From Paradise Valley I went back to Eagle Creek and was working in the Caledonia mine when my brother-in-law got word to me that the McDermitt reservation had been thrown open to entry, that is, people could settle upon it, taking as much as one hundred and sixty acres of land. The law required that the settler should build a house and till the land for five years, after which it would belong to him. This was what was called "homesteading." It was late at night when I got this word, but I got out of bed and started to Fort McDermitt on horseback. There were not more than five or six hundred acres of the fort land, and this was where we located our homesteads. There were two of us, my father-in-law and myself, so there would not be room for any more settlers except on the government hay reservation in the bottom-land, where my brother-in-law Jim took up his homestead. We knew there was but little chance of the word getting out about the land being open to entry, but we lost no time in getting there first as these farms were worth striving for. I can remember the thoughts about having a home of my own that ran through my head as we loped along. We got to McDermitt early in the morning, and after breakfast at once started to run our lines; that is, to mark our boundaries.

My farm was just below the old army post, where the valley was widest. We built foundations on the three places, and I went to Winnemucca for lumber, out of which I built a one room house with a lean-to kitchen. This room I lined with burlap and whitewashed it. It made a fine wall and ceiling as tight as a drum. I moved my wife and baby down into the new house.

Life began to take on a new aspect; every tap of work I did, building fences, digging ditches, was all for ourselves. Now it was a question of where to build the barn, where the chicken coop should be, where the corral, and what kind of trees to set out. It was very fine land, the loam was deep and would grow anything.

There were so many things we needed that money was an immediate necessity. I left home for Tuscarora, a mining camp some hundred and twenty-five miles distant. The first night I stopped at Thompson's Mill at Willow Creek. There were four other men gathered there that night. The place had been abandoned, but the stove and cooking utensils were still there. All of us had some grub with us, and we got supper ready, consisting of bacon, flapjacks and coffee. While we sat at the table eating, some one remarked that we were a strange group. We looked at him inquiringly, and he said:

"Every man here has lost one eye."

Sure enough, this was true. We were the only one-eyed men in the county and we were all together that night.

The next morning we started out, some going down the canyon. I went across the summit to Paradise Valley. Here I met Billy Townsend, a farmer who was going to Tuscarora with a load of produce. He agreed to take me with him and I stopped that night on his farm. Next morning we started out with a six-horse team and two wagons. We went through Squaw Valley and across Soldier Summit, where we spread our blankets on the ground. The next morning we were covered with a blanket of snow and the entire country as far as we could see was white.

When we got to Tuscarora, Townsend said:

"I've got to get out of here as soon as I can sell out. I haven't a minute to lose or I'll be snowed in. I think I can dispose of the grain and other stuff quick, but I don't want to be bothered with those chickens. I'll be glad to get fifty cents apiece for them; think you could sell 'em?"

He had two crates full of chickens. I said I'd try, and did sell them, with some gain to myself which came in handy before I got to work.

The next morning I started rustling at the mine for a job and finally took a lease on a stope in the Navajo mine which was on the slope of Mount Blitzen. In cleaning up the lease we had to lower the ore by means of rope to the tunnel that ran to the main shaft, there to be hoisted to the surface. This meant handling the sacks several times. When we got it on top we carried it to a jig to wash the screenings. The bulk of the ore we sent directly to the sampler and it was paid for by the mining company. The rest of the ore we sent after we had worked it through the jig which was a contrivance worked by hand in which the values settled in the bottom, while the waste was washed off at the top. Around the shaft house were mountain-high piles of sage-brush, as at this mine they fired the boilers with these Lilliputian oaks. The brush was wet down before it was pitched into the fire box.

Later I worked at the Commonwealth mine. In the stope where I was working, among other men was one Joy Pollard, whose name I mention because of the fact that many years afterward I met him again in Cripple Creek, Colorado, and he was one of the delegates to the initial convention of the Industrial Workers of the World in Chicago.

Tuscarora was an interesting old camp. There were mines right in the center of the town and there were no company boarding houses or company stores. The miners either lived at home, boarded in restaurants, or lived with private families. The saloons were typical of a mining camp and were well patronized. Usually a long bar ran the length of one side, with two or three tables in the front, and a card room in the rear. Faro and poker were the favorite games. I was standing at the bar in Louis Engel's saloon one night when the barkeeper said:

"Bill, take a look at that group at the faro table."

They were eight men and one woman. Every one of them had killed from one to six men. The woman, Molly Forshay, had killed her paramour, had been tried and sentenced to life imprisonment in the state penitentiary. After about two years in prison she revealed the fact that she was to become a mother. To quiet the scandal involving the warden, the governor pardoned her.

A teamster who was hauling freight on the road from Tuscarora to Elko could be seen knocking around the saloons, gambling and smoking but never indulging in drink; got married, but the wife soon got a divorce. Later the teamster put on dresses, got married again, this time to a man, and raised a large family. They called her the "Tuscarora what-is-it." She had donned men's clothing so that she could make more money than was paid for women's work.

Drinking, gambling, and dancing were not our only amusements. We had a Lyceum club, study and debating classes which gave the young people the opportunity to learn something of history, literature, and so forth.

Tom Minor was working on the "P-bench" ranch near Tuscarora. He came to town one day and we decided to go home on a visit. Tom of course had his own outfit. I got a horse and saddle, and the morning we started out he rode an outlaw broncho which he called "Cherokee Bill." We rode down Independence Creek to the Owyhee River and stopped at a ranch for the night. Next morning early we started out with a few slices of bread and bacon. The first thing to do was to swim the river; it was high and wide and the water was cold. The horse I was riding swam low, there were only his eyes, ears and nose in sight. I got soaking wet to the waist. Tom's horse was a high swimmer and he got wet only about to the knees. The Owyhee River into which Jack Creek emptied was a tributary to the Snake River, which wriggled its way through Idaho and Oregon to the Columbia River. Up these various streams thousands of miles to the very foot of Mount Blitzen came the salmon from the Pacific Ocean to spawn. As we climbed out of the Owyhee River we could see the top of Buckskin Mountain which was at the head of McDermitt Creek. Tom pointed to it, saying:

"It's a long ride and maybe a dry camp."

For the want of canteens we had filled two bottles full of water. As the sun got higher and the day warmer we rolled the bottles up in our coats and tied them to our saddles. There was no road. The distant mountain ahead was our only means of direction. We were now in the Diamond-A desert. Such names as "P-bench" and "Diamond-A" come from the branding marks used by the ranches in this part of the country; the ranches themselves are called after their brands.

There was no growth on the desert except a low scattered browse, which sheep fed upon in winter when there was snow to slake their thirst. As the miles passed, the size of old Mount Buckskin increased in our vision. It was a clear day and the mountain appeared to be nearer than it really was.

Our horses began to fag along in the late afternoon. We had made no stop since the early morning. Our clothes had dried on us. Neither we nor the horses had had a bite to eat. Our water was all gone except a little in the bottom of the bottles. We got down and stretched ourselves, and the horses nibbled at the browse. We ate a slice of bread and bacon, and drank what water we had, then mounted and set out again. The sun had gone down. We were making slow progress when we heard the sharp chatter of a magpie.

"There's water!" we both cried at once, but there was nothing in sight except barren desert. We turned a little to the right and made for the place the sound had come from. The horses became restless and broke into a lope. In less than a hundred yards we came to a deep canyon with sheer precipitous walls. Far below us lay the green fresh grass, the crystal stream and the willows that fringed it. As far as we could see there seemed to be no break in the cliffs. We rode along the edge. The horses, we knew, were hungry and thirsty; there under their very noses were fresh water, green grass, and no way to reach it. What must a horse think under those circumstances?

We came at last to a narrow gully running down into the canyon, very steep and filled with sliderock. We rode down with no other mishap than a bad scratch on my horse's left hind leg. We unsaddled, picketed Cherokee Bill, and turned Preacher loose, had a long drink, ate a bite and stretched out with our saddles for pillows, pulling our saddle blankets up over us when the night got cool. At break of day we were on our way, riding up the canyon until we came to an easy place to get up to the flat above. To our right across the flat we saw the Haystack Mountains, a group of low hills rising sharply from the plain, so much alike that cowboys invariably got lost among them during the round-ups.

We got home early in the afternoon. The family was glad to see us and I was delighted to be back with my wife and baby. But the happiness was marred by the condition of my wife, who was suffering from a renewed attack of what doctors had called rheumatism. When a girl she had been thrown from a horse and her spine was injured. It affected her joints, which were badly swollen and gave her much pain, from which she suffered all her life.

I decided as a last resort to take her to Kyle Springs, a distance of about a hundred and forty miles. Loading our bedding, food, and camping outfit on a spring wagon, and leaving the baby with her grandmother, we started out with a splendid pair of palamina horses, cream colored with white manes and tails. We made the Hill the first day, the second day drove to Winnemucca and the next to Kyle Springs. The curative properties of these waters were known far and wide, but the place was now deserted, as the mines in that part of the country had been worked out. There was a house of four or five rooms on a barren, bleak spot near Cinnabar Mountain. Unionville and other old mining camps were in the mountains across the valley, eight or ten miles away. There were small farms and ranches here and there.

We were alone for three weeks or a month, except during a few days when some Indians camped at the springs. My wife was practically helpless, unable at that time to walk so that I had to carry her everywhere, and she could not even dress herself. In the morning I would get up and dress, feed the horses, clean up the stable, ride one horse and lead the other to water—the only fresh water was up the canyon about a mile. Coming back I would wash, cook and carry a little breakfast to my wife, and clean up the dishes. Then I would roll her in a blanket and carry her up to the springs. There I dug a hole in the mud and put her in, covering her up to the neck with the oozy warm mud. Having done up her long hair in a towel, I fastened another towel on two stakes stuck in the mud for a pillow. I stripped before beginning the mud-bath, steaming and other processes that we went through every day. From the mud-hole, which was outside in the open air, I carried

Nevada into the plunge, rinsed the mud off, and wrapped her in the blankets to carry her back to the house. In the afternoon I would again carry her to the springs, this time to dip her in the alum baths, which were in a hole, so small that I had to be careful not to scratch her on the rock. After this came another turn in the steam bath, and a plunge.

After we had been at the springs nearly a month, and had visited the different ranches nearby, I stood my wife on the scales one day when we were in Unionville, and found that she weighed only eighty-eight pounds. This was a loss of twenty-five pounds or more from her usual weight. We concluded that the treatment I was giving her at the springs was too severe, and we decided to go home, where we tried snake-oil, sage-baths, and other Indian remedies.

At the fall rodeo of the cattle ranches of nothern Nevada there were some bad men among the cowpunchers, quick on the trigger and ready to shoot at the drop of a hat, some of the best broncho-busters of the West and some who were experts with their riatas. The outfit was camped for two nights on the left bank of the Humboldt River, a few miles from the lively little town of Winnemucca, where the cowboys did much drinking, wild riding and reckless shooting, which was nothing out of the ordinary. This was the scene of a tragic fight between two cowboys, one armed with a double action six-shooter, the other with a riata. I'll give you the story as Walter Rice, one of the participants, told it to me when he came to Mc-Dermitt. I was crossing the parade ground one day when I saw a vaquero coming down the road, easily discernible from the way he rode, and from his outfit. He wore chapereros, the leg guards of the cowboys, made of goatskin with the long hair outside, a sombrero was set on the back of his head, and long tapaderos flapped in unison with the nodding head of his big fine-looking cream-colored horse. Before I recognized him he called out:

"Hello, Bill!"

Touching his horse with the spurs he rode up on a jump, pulling his mount back on its haunches just as he reached me. He put out his hand with a western "How?"

"Good," I said, "get down and look at your saddle. Put up your horse and have a bite."

We started back toward the barn.

"I don't know whether I'm going to stay long. I've got a story to tell you." Pulling out the makings, he rolled a cigarette.

"All right," I said, "but wait till after dinner. I guess you're hungry."

"Hungry is no name for it. I crossed the Diamond-A desert yesterday without a stop, and rode from the other side of Buckskin Mountain this morning."

Knowing the distance, I looked at him and remarked,

"You must have been in a big hurry."

"Yes. Yet I don't know but what I'm going the wrong way. You haven't heard anything?"

"Not a thing. But let's eat. Then you can tell your beads."

After dinner we went out and sat on the grass. Rice said:

"I think I killed a man before I left camp."

Surprised, I asked how.

"Give me a match. I'll tell you just how it happened," he said, after wetting with his tongue the cigarette he had been rolling. "I was riding for the P-bench ranch with the rodeo. We camped just north of Stauffer's field on the Humboldt, and had the saddle horses in the field. The first night some of the boys come back from town pretty drunk. I had rolled my bed down next to Mex Ricardo. I didn't pay much attention to him, took off my gun and slipped it between the blankets under my coat that I had rolled up for a pillow. Next morning when I got up, I straightened the blankets a little, rolled them up in the canvas, washed and went to breakfast. After breakfast I went back for my gun. It was gone. None of the boys had seen any one around my bed. I didn't think of Ricardo at the time. But I sure was mad. That gun was a beauty, pearl-handled, blue-barreled, thirty-eight on a forty-five frame. A kind of a keepsake that I hated to lose. Where I got it is another story.

"Nearly every one was saddled up before I caught a wall-eyed pinto that I rode that day. We were moping along through the low hills between the river and the Toll-house when Tom Baudoin, riding just behind me, sung out, 'Rice, I thought you said you'd never sell your gun?' 'What for would I want to sell it?' I said; 'I couldn't buy a better one.' 'Oh!' he says, 'I thought you sold it to Ricardo. You just let him take it, huh?' 'No, I'm damned if I did,' I told him, 'I'd like to see that Mexican right now.'

"We got through early that afternoon. When we had parted out the beef steers and had done what little branding there was to do, the sun was still high. Everybody worked lively; guess they wanted to get to town, for it 'ud be their last chance to clean up for quite a while. I met Ricardo at the chuck wagon and said to him, 'What did you do with my gun?' He answered kind of sheepish-like, 'I throwed it in the river.' I told him he'd have to be a damned good diver because I was going to make him get it. He was kind of playing me for a jug-belly, I guess. He said, 'Don't get sore; I'll give it back to you in the morning,' and walked off with his plate and knife and fork. Pretty soon I saw him cinching his saddle. I knew he was going to town.

"He didn't show off much that night before the senoritas. I hadn't unsaddled Pinto yet. I went over and climbed on. My rope was coiled loosely over the horn. I started after Mex, caught up with him, told him I wanted my gun and wanted it damn quick. I wasn't expecting him to shoot. He had my gun inside the belt of his chaps. He pulled and plugged me through the arm here."

Pulling up his coat-sleeve, Rice showed me his left fore-arm, bandaged with a bloody handkerchief, and continued:

"When he shot, his horse started to pitch, but Ricardo fired again, just grazing my leg. That didn't hurt much, but my arm did. I knew that I'd have to do something and do it quick. When his horse stopped bucking he'd get me sure. So I grabbed my riata, held the coils on this arm but it couldn't do much, swung my loop and tossed the string on him just as the bay colt he was riding quit jumping. I took my turns and started for camp. He struck the ground with a thump. I could feel that we were pulling up sage-brush, but I didn't stop until we got to the wagon.

"There was some excitement. One of the boys took my rope off. I coiled it up and asked the fellers who were looking at Mex if he was dead. They couldn't tell. I said, guess I'll go for a doctor and get this fixed up while I'm in town. My arm was bleeding a stream. 'Let me tie that up before you start,' said one of the boys, taking his bandanna off his neck. He tied it tightly around my arm above the wound. It didn't take a minute. Guy Kendrick made the ride with me.

"We went after old Doc Hansen, told him there was a man hurt in camp who had got caught in a rope and dragged. He sent for a saddle horse and asked what was the matter with me; I guess I looked kind of pale. I showed him my arm and without asking what happened he said, 'I'll dress that for you while we're waiting for the horse. Be sure to come back in the morning; got to be careful of infection.' We went out to our horses. I said, 'You go on. I'm going to get a bottle of whisky.' But I didn't. I waited till they crossed the bridge and followed them. When we got close to camp I rode out into the sage-brush and dropped the reins. I knew Pinto would stand. Dodging through the sage-brush I got close enough to see what was going on. I could tell from the way Doc and the fellers were acting that Mex was dead. I went back to where I left Pinto and thought things over for a few minutes.

"Should I go into town and give myself up? Next day the outfit would leave and I'd be alone and in jail. No telling how long I would be there. Would need a lot of money for a lawyer. So I piled on to old Pinto and waved my hat to the camp, although it was dark, and hit the trail for the P-bench ranch. I didn't make it till the next night. Woke Tom Minor and told him what had happened. I washed and fixed my arm a little, had something to eat, a few hours' sleep, and early the next morning Tom woke me; he had breakfast ready, a lunch fixed and two horses saddled. He said, 'I'm going to the forks of the road with you.' There he bid me good-by. 'If you don't go back, the flag-tailed nag is yours. He's good for a long ride if you have to make it.' I waited a few minutes, turned and rode down Jack Creek, swam the Owyhee at Bacon's ranch. You know the rest. Now I want to take care of my arm for a day or two and stay under cover."

That day we rode across the valley to Washburn canyon and fixed him up in a little deserted cabin there. Two days later I went back. Rice was gone. A note written on the margin of a newspaper was on the table under a cup. It read: "Get my gun. I'll do as much for you. It was a present from my sweetheart. Send it to her. I'll get it when I go back to Idaho."

I got his gun from Billy Higginson, one of the cowboys, who had picked it up where Ricardo had dropped it when he was jerked from his horse. I sent it as requested to the address that he had given.

It was a long time before Rice ventured to visit his old stamping ground. His sweetheart had received the gun, but no word from

Rice. She thought that he had changed his mind and had sent back the present she had given him. After weary months of waiting she gave the gun to another fellow. One day Rice rode into his home town. He had her picture in the conchas of his bridle. Tying his horse in front of a saloon, he walked in to look for old acquaintances. He was about to take a drink when a young fellow came in and walking up to him said:

"Stranger, you'll have to take them pictures off your bridle."

"What?" said Rice. Then it occurred to him what had happened. "You—"

Both began to shoot at the same time. Rice was killed with the present from his sweetheart.

After we returned from Kyle Springs I worked on my farm, putting in head-gates, cutting fence-posts and digging ditches. When the old mining fever would come back I would go to the mountains and do some prospecting. I relocated the Wild Deer mine on Flat Creek, and two other claims over the ridge on Granite Creek. Here very rich gold ore was later discovered, and it became the site of National City, a one time flourishing mining camp.

This was the period of an extreme financial crisis that really amounted to a panic. It was hard to find a job at any kind of work. My brother-in-law, Jim Minor, and I went to Delamar. The first day we rode to Jack Baudoin's place. He was an old settler, very proud of his reckless son, Tom. He had a pair of wild horses in the corral, necked together with a strong rope, and asked us if we would drive them to the Owyhee River, saying that it would be no bother, they would go along the road without trouble. When he turned them out of the corral the next morning they started direct for Grassy Mountain. Jim started after them and after a ride of ten miles or more turned them toward the ford, but they broke again and swam the river. We followed, turned them and they swam back. Even tied together by the necks as they were, they kept us on the run. It was late afternoon when we got them into the corral at the station.

When we got to Delamar we found a crowd of unemployed men, but asked for a job only to learn that there would be no chance of work in the near future. So we started for home. The first night we stopped at Billy Beers', who lived on a big ranch with a big family and a big lot of cattle. Everything was big about Billy

Beers, he was a big hearty fellow himself, and he liked big meals. When we sat down at table, the steak platter was not as heavily loaded as he thought it ought to be and he said with gentle good-nature:

"Mamma, can't we have some steak? God damn it, can't we have some steak? Here we've got a thousand head of god-damned steers and a god-damned Chinaman to cut them up any time you want it, and we can't get a god-damned steak? God damn it, mamma, now can't we have some steak?"

During these days of stress and privation my father-in-law received official notice from the government that the land upon which we had homesteaded was to be reserved for the Indians. This did not affect my brother-in-law, Jim, who had taken up his homestead on the hay reservation, but it was a fearful blow to the old man and to me. It seemed as if a black curtain had been pulled down on the future; there was no ray of hope. I broke out in a spirit of desperation and said that we should not starve as long as I had the old Springfield rifle and there were cattle on the range. Shortly afterward I moved my wife and baby to Winnemucca. There was nothing left; no compensation for the work I had put into the homestead, for the house I had built, the fences I had run, the trees I had set out.

My money was all used up. There was no chance of getting a job around that part of Nevada, so I started for Angels' Camp in California, beat my way to Auburn only to learn that there had been a fire in the camp and a lot of men were out of work there too. I met a contingent of Coxey's Army heading east, caught up with them at Reno, Nevada. With another fellow I made the trip through the Truckee snow-sheds in a box-car; it was so cold that the frost hung in festoons inside the car from the top and sides. We had to keep walking up and down the car to keep from freezing to death.

From Reno I went with a crowd of the army to Wadsworth. Some of them told me that they were going to Washington, D. C., to demand work, that there were other armies of jobless men going from the South and East for the same purpose. One said that "General" Coxey was going to ask Congress to pass a law to build roads, another said something about "non-interest-bearing bonds," but it seemed to me that they were all going to Washington as a living petition to demand work or that work should be started by the government for the unemployed. It was one of the greatest unemployed demonstrations that ever took place in the United States, although but few in numbers finally reached Washington. The various armies crossed the country in freight trains, sometimes forcing the railroad companies to furnish transportation, and the mayors of the towns where they appeared in numbers were compelled to provide them with the necessary food, in order to get rid of them and send them on their way.

At Wadsworth I met a railroad man whom I had known before. He invited me to his house for dinner and that afternoon we went down the river on a fishing trip. He caught a trout, one of such trout as are to be found only in the Truckee River. We had it for supper.

That night I hustled around and found that there was a train-load of cattle to be shipped to Chicago, and I got a job going with them. There were four or five other men. It was our job when the train stopped to get out with prod-poles and jab the prod into any steer that happened to be lying down. This was to keep them from being trampled to death or smothered by the other steers.

I dropped off at Winnemucca and went home more depressed than I had ever been in my life. I could not understand the problem of unemployment, nor could I find the reason for thousands of men crossing the continent to go to Washington. My thoughts went back more and more to the talks I had had with Pat Reynolds. These panics in which the workers were the chief sufferers were the outgrowths of the capitalist system. But the cure or preventive did not then occur to me. I struggled along in mental darkness.

Suddenly came a great rift of light. This was the strike of railroad men in 1894. Freight trains loaded with perishable fruit for the eastern markets were side-tracked, also train-loads of coal and other products going west. The strike of the American Railway Union was spreading. The governors of several states had called out the militia. At Sacramento, California, in response to an order to fire, the militiamen jabbed their bayonets into the ground and refused to shoot.

The militia of Winnemucca refused to answer the call to mobilize. Most of them were railroad men, to whom the militia was a social affair. They did not feel inclined to shoulder arms to protect the railroad company's property. The town was flooded with oranges and other produce from the side-tracked cars, but it was better to eat them than to let them rot. Coal would be needed for the winter and the boys were not going to kill each other for laying in a supply for cold weather. The members of the A.R.U. were aroused against the railroad interests. The federal soldiers had been sent to Chicago by President Cleveland against the workers who were striking at the Pullman Car Shops. Eugene V. Debs had been arrested with others, charged with conspiracy to murder, and when this charge was dropped, they were sent to prison for contempt of court. The membership of the organization was indignant at the flagrant injustice. I listened to and took part in the many hot discussions. Here, I felt, was a great power. It was not the fact that produce had been removed from the cars and the strikers were that much ahead. The big thing was that they could stop the trains. It was a lesson of the Knights of Labor, an echo of the voice of the Chicago martyrs.

My little girl was taken sick with typhoid pneumonia and I sat at her bed side for days and nights at a stretch. When the crisis of her illness came and she began to recover I did not think that I was going to be able to sleep. I walked the house through, I walked the town, I went home and darkened the room and drank whisky. When I finally went to sleep I slept twenty-four hours without waking.

My wife, then able to be up and around, went out one afternoon and returned to find that the house had been robbed. Several of our little keepsakes had been stolen. This outraged our feelings more than the loss injured us, because in the mining camps and on the ranches it had never been necessary to turn the key in the lock. We would leave home, even for days, and hang the key on the door-post. If a stranger came by, he might go in and feed himself or sleep in the house, clean up afterward, and go on his way after hanging the key up in its place. No one ever stole. Contrary to the slanders against them, the Indians never stole even from the deserted mining camps where ownerless pots and pans and tables were left behind. I once left the house at the Ohio mine for months; when I returned the door was open, but the guns and blankets, so valuable to the Indians, had not been touched.

Gold was found at a place called Kennedy, and a mining excitement broke out. I went there and fixed up a cabin with Al Richardson, got a job with the Imperial Mining Company. I remember going to bed one night and waking the next morning to find that four houses had been put up along the road overnight. Later we took a contract to run a tunnel a hundred feet. We were to sharpen our own tools, wheel our own dirt and furnish our own powder. When we examined the face of the old tunnel which we were to continue, we found that some novice had worked there and the face of the tunnel was scooped out in the center like the bottom of a pot. It was porphyry and would break big if we put our holes in right, so we agreed that at eight dollars a foot we could make good wages, put this sum in as our bid, and got the contract.

Jerry-the-bum adopted me in Kennedy. Jerry was a rough-haired Skye terrier. When he came to live in my cabin I made him as comfortable as I could and he followed close at my heels wherever I went. The men about the town said:

"You think you've got a dog, don't you? He won't stay with you. That's Jerry-the-bum."

But Jerry seemed to like me as well as I liked him. I missed him one day when I was downtown at the post office. On my way home I saw him sitting up on the seat of a freight-wagon. I said:

"Hello, Jerry, what are you doing up there?"

He didn't seem to hear me. Coming up closer, I said:

"Come on, let's go home."

Jerry turned his head away.

"Well," said I, "if that's the way you feel about it, so long!"

Jerry was gone a couple of weeks when I heard a scratching on the door. I opened it and he came in wagging his stub of a tail just as though nothing had happened. I gave him something to eat and he appropriated his old corner. He never left me again as long as I stayed in Kennedy. Jerry had the wanderlust; he would ride around with freighters wherever they might happen to go, when the fit came over him, to Winnemucca, Seven Troughs, Sulphur Mines and lots of other places.

Downtown one night in Tom Powell's saloon, Tom said to me:

"I think you could make some money if we'd start a poker game."

Without hesitating I opened the game and ran it every night, working during the daytime. I laid up about eight hundred dollars that month.

The camp shut down and was deserted even more rapidly than it had sprung up. I went back to Winnemucca and lost most of the money that I had with me at faro. Fortunately I had sent my wife a good part of my winnings from Kennedy before this.

In Winnemucca I worked for a short time driving a team. Leaving my family there, I went to Washburn, to run the boundary lines on a farm that my father-in-law had homesteaded there. We hauled my little house from the place of which I had been dispossessed and set it up as an addition to the house that he had built on his new homestead.

Some men came along who were going to Silver City, Idaho, for a race meet. I asked them to carry along my blankets, as I had also decided to go to Silver City. I expected to get there ahead of them, as they had to go slowly to keep their horses in trim.

Looking down the valley, over the enchanting sagebrush flats and the mountains where I had spent so much of my life, and where I had expected to live, I left Nevada. I did not return until many years later.

CHAPTER IV

SILVER CITY

THE road to Silver City was through a country that was rugged, bleak, and gray. No habitations except the occasional stations, most of them deserted, and a farm here and there. Not a tree to be seen in the entire distance, nothing but crooked, gnarled sagebrush, greasewood and stretches of browse. At least this was true until one came to the river; there the country was broken up into foot-hills with high mountains behind them.

Approaching the first summit, my thoughts went back to a story told me by Bill Coulter years before, about being chased down this road by Indians when he was driving a stage. I could imagine the flying stage-coach and Bill throwing the buckskin into his team, with a band of Indians behind whooping and yelling but never getting close enough to the galloping horses to shoot an arrow at the driver.

Before I got to Jack Baudoin's I was hungry and thirsty. I had a few dollars in my pocket, but I thought, Hell, what good is money, anyway? Here at least was one place where a car-load of twenty-dollar gold pieces would not buy a square meal. Why should money buy a meal, I wondered; money did not seem to me an equivalent of value, an equivalent of labor, or an equivalent of anything else. This was something that I would have to look into.

At Jordan Valley I turned my horse in to pasture, hung my saddle and bridle up in the livery stable, and took stage for Silver City.

When we got there, I went into a Chinese restaurant, and afterward knocked around the town for an hour or so. I was looking for a place to sleep that night. A man said to me:

"I've got a bed in the old Potosi shaft house. You can roll in with me until your blankets come, but you'd better come up and look at the place so if you happen to come in late you won't stumble and fall down the shaft in the dark."

I went up to the shaft house with him. There were several rolls of blankets scattered about a deep open shaft into the old mine, without any cover or railing around it. I used this place as a lodging house for some days after my blankets arrived. I did not go to the races, but asked the men to get my saddle and horse in Jordan Valley on their way home, and take them back to the ranch.

The first morning I was up early and went to the Blaine mine, rustling a job. I did this for several mornings and sometimes at the noon hour as well, but without success. Hutchinson was the name of the manager; he had been in Nevada years before. I spent all the money I had and went to old Hutch again and told him that I'd have to have some kind of a job.

"What can you do?" he asked me. I told him I could do most anything around a mine.

"Can you run car?"

"I'm a miner, but I can run car."

"All right. Come on in the morning."

That day I met Dave O'Neill downtown; I had known him in Tuscarora. He handed me a five-dollar gold piece, saying:

"Bill, you might need this."

I said to him, "I am broke, Dave, but I'm going to work in the morning."

"Well," he said, "Keep it anyway. You can hand it to me payday."

Loans of this kind were a general custom among the miners, and it was seldom or never that they were not repaid. Within the last three years Herman Andrigg, with whom I worked in Silver City, where he was champion driller, repaid a loan I made to him more than a quarter of a century ago.

I went to the old shaft house, rolled up my blankets and carried them to the Blaine mine bunk-house. The bunk next to the door was vacant. This just suited me. The bunk-house was a long rambling place with bunks built two high along the walls, accommodating, I suppose, about sixty men. The air was none too good at best, as the opening and shutting of the door was almost the only ventilation.

In the bunk-house, while we sat around the stove or lolled in the bunks, all the old tales of the different mining camps would be related by men who had been on the scene of action, or who had heard the stories at first hand. Bill Pooley, a "Cousin Jack," as we called the Cornishmen, of whom there were many in Silver City, was a good story teller. He once told us about a friend of his who had had smallpox. Bill said:

"When he got well, 'e was so deep pitted that 'e 'ad to shave 'isself with a brace and bit."

Nothing pleased the Cousin Jacks better than to get a lease where they could make wages or a little more. They called this "tributing." A number of them had "tributed" on the Poor Man mine. Simon Harris, the superintendent of the mine, decided to stop this kind of work and to work all the men on wages. Eight or ten of the Cousin Jacks were sitting about a big round table in the Brewery Saloon. They were complaining and lamenting about the loss of their tributes, when one of the group said to another:

"See 'ere, Tussy, can't thee pray? Can't thee pray for we tributes?"

Tussy answered; "It's been a long time since I made a prayer, but I'll try." He began:

"Dear Lord, dost thee know Simmon 'Arris, superintendent of the Poor Man mine? If thee know en, we wish for thee to take en and put en in 'Ell, and there let the bugger frizzle and fry, until 'e give us back we just tributes. And when 'e do, dear Lord, we ask thee to take en out of 'Ell again, an' grease en up a bit and turn of en loose. Amen."

All were pleased with the prayer, and bought another gallon of beer in Tussy's honor. Like all prayers, however, it was ineffective. Leasing was abolished and the Cousin Jacks lost their tributes.

There were six or seven car-men in the Blaine mine. We started work ahead of the miners. Our work was to push the cars in the tunnel back to the chutes where the men were working in the stopes above. When we lifted the gates in the chutes the cars would fill without any trouble. It was only from the face of the tunnel, before connections were made with the adjoining Black Jack mine, that we had any shoveling to do. When the cars were loaded, we would push them out, and going down a place called the short cut we would step on the foot-board behind and the cars would gain such speed that we could ride all the way to the dump. The ore we dumped in a bin and from there it was run to the mill which stood in the canyon a few hundred yards below the tunnel.

After a few days I was put to work in the short cut stopes. In my stope, on the opposite shift, worked a man by the name of Matt McLain. When he became shift boss I was working for him. He came into the stope one day where I had a platform rigged up. Leaning his arms on the staging he began talking about old times in Pennsylvania. He said:

"You've heard of the Molly Maguires?"

I said that I had; every one had heard of the Molly Maguires.

"But," he went on, "you never heard how they were trapped. There was a certain Franklin B. Gowen who was manager of one or more of the mines in Shamokin Valley. He decided to wipe out the Molly Maguires, which was a kind of a labor organization that would not stand for a reduction of wages. Gowen employed the Pinkerton Detective Agency, and they sent one of their stool-pigeons whose real name was McParland.

"He came into Pottsville as James McKenna. He had a little bundle tied on the end of a stick over his shoulder when he walked into town and inquired for a place to stop. He found a boarding house that suited him. One evening he went as though by chance into Barney Hogle's saloon and invited everybody in the place to have a drink. When he paid for the drinks, he displayed a roll of bills and incidentally remarked that he had just quit his ship at Philadelphia; that he had got tired of the sea and was going to get a job on land for awhile if he could. He asked Hogle if he could get work in that neighborhood.

"Hogle was one of the bond-masters of the Molly Maguires, that is, he was one of the leaders of this organization that had been transplanted from Ireland and now in Pennsylvania was made up principally of coal miners. Hogle was also a saloon-keeper, and he had seen young McKenna's wad of money. The young Irishman was a good spender and Hogle wanted to cultivate him as a customer. But not wanting to seem anxious in this regard, he answered McKenna by saying that it took a pretty good man to hold a job there.

"McKenna flared up. 'I'm a pretty good man,' he said, buying another drink, 'I'll sing a song, dance a jig, or fight with any man in the house for the whisky for everybody.' He sang an Irish song, he danced an Irish jig. Looking about he saw a likely lad sizing him up. Sidling up to the young miner, he said, 'Is it yez that'll be wanting to try me out?' 'I will that,' was the reply.

"Every one adjourned to the handball court in the rear. McKenna played handball a few minutes, then they stripped for the fight, which was to be a 'fair go.' The audience was all Irish, and nothing tickled their fancy more than a good fight. They selected a referee and squared off. The miner cut McKenna on the cheek, but Mac countered to the jaw with his left, and jabbed his right to the ribs. 'That's the b'y,' shouted a voice. Then with a straight left to the chin the miner drove Mac against the end wall. Mac recovered quickly and with both hands punched the miner about the body, forcing him to a clinch.

"The next round the miner feinted with his left and landed a slam on Mac's nose. The blood spurted as Mac swung and got the young fellow at the point of the jaw, keeling him over. The fight was finished. Every one had been highly pleased. McKenna washed his bloody nose; his right eye was nearly closed. Shaking hands with the young miner, he said, 'Yez were a better man than I thought ye wuz.' Back in the bar-room there were more drinking and dancing. It was declared by all to have been a fine night.

"McKenna patronized this place frequently and got work through the influence of Hogle. All his associates were Molly Maguires. This was just what he wanted. Some time later he was asked to become a Molly Maguire. Of course he readily assented, but said that to be a good Molly Maguire perhaps one ought to have had more experience than had fallen to his lot. It was but a short time after he had joined that he was employed in some kind of official capacity in the organization.

"This gave him the opportunity for which he was looking. Through the skulduggery of this detective, a number of young miners were involved in a murder; at least they were mixed up in it to such an extent that they were charged with murder. A warrant was issued for Tom Hurley. McKenna, who by this time was suspected by the miners, saw Hurley on a train, and started after him. Hurley went to the rear of the train. McKenna and the other dicks who were with him were intercepted here and there in following him, and Hurley had time to drop off the train.

"When the young miners appeared for trial, McKenna testified against them and gave his name as James McParland, a Pinkerton detective. The price the Molly Maguires paid for trusting their affairs to a saloon-keeper was the lives of ten of their members who were executed, and fourteen who were sentenced to from two to seven years in the penitentiary. McParland would probably have been unable to wriggle his slimy way into the organization without Hogle's help."

This was the first time I had ever heard of an agent provocateur. I later learned that it was the first time that such a method had been used against the working-class in America. McLain's story made a deep impression on me.

On June 19, 1896, I was working with two others, cutting out for a station in the Blaine tunnel where they were going to sink a shaft. I was up on a staging, and got down to ask one of the car-men if I could ride his car out. With his assent I started. A big rock on the front end of the car struck the first chute I came to, tipping it up so that my right hand got caught between the car and the bottom of the chute, getting badly mangled. My candle had been put out by the jolt, and I was left in total darkness. I groped my way back to where Big Barney Quigley was working in a cross-cut. I called to him and he came out and walked with me to the doctor's office. We were about three thousand feet in the tunnel then. There was no "first aid," nor bandages, it was just a question of getting there some-how and keeping the bleeding hand from knocking against the wall as we went out. I remember that even at this late season of the year we walked through open cuts where the snow was more than six feet deep.

When we got to the doctor, he said that part of my hand would have to be amputated. I told him that I did not want to go through life doubly crippled. I was already handicapped by the loss of an eye. If there was any chance of saving the hand I wanted him to try to do it. He said:

"We'll try," and dressed the hand. I refused to take an anæsthetic, in spite of the pain, because I was afraid that he would take off the fingers while I was unconscious. After some days the hand showed that it was beginning to mend. It had to be dressed every day and I carried it in a sling a long time.

My wife and little girl had then just come to Silver City. While I was looking for a house to live in we were stopping at the Idaho Hotel. As I was unable to work because of my broken hand, the miners took up a collection and presented me with a purse of money that tided us over this emergency very well. I bought a two-room house from a miner named Schilling who was leaving camp, paying part down and the rest in installments. We moved into our new home.

In the early part of the following August, Edward Boyce, president of the Western Federation of Miners, came to Silver City for the purpose of organizing the miners. Two meetings were held in the county court house, one on the eighth and one on the tenth of August. I attended both, though I did not know then that I would ever be able to go back to work in the mines, as I was still carrying my arm in the sling. But I was greatly interested in what Boyce had to say. Here was a man who had been through the Cœur d'Alenes strike of 1892. He was tall, slender, had a fine head with thin hair. His features were good, but his teeth were prominent. This was due to salivation, contracted while working with quicksilver in a quartz mill. This is a vocational disease met with quite often among mill men.

With more than a thousand other miners he had been arrested by the Federal soldiers when they were sent to the Cœur d'Alenes at the request of Governor Shoup. A bull-pen was built in which the prisoners were confined for more than six months. This was a rough lumber structure two stories high. There was no sanitation provided, and the excrement of the men above dripped through the cracks in the plank floor on the men below. They became vermin-infested and diseased, and some of them died.

The Helena-Frisco mill had been blown up. A story afterward appeared in *Collier's Weekly*, implicating George A. Pettibone. Pettibone was the head of the assembly of the Knights of Labor at Gem. He was already well known among the miners. The story related in a graphic manner how some boxes of powder had been put into the water flume some hundreds of feet up the mountainside. The boxes slid down the flume at a tremendous velocity and exploded when they struck the mill; it was a long gun. The unreliability of the story was shown in the attempt to implicate Pettibone by asserting that he had been so badly injured that he lost one of his arms. I knew Pettibone in after years; neither one of his arms or hands had ever been hurt, though his feelings were badly embittered by the conditions of the mining camps of the Cœur d'Alenes before the strike of '92. He could never forget the maggots in the meat, nor the swarthy weasel-faced stool-pigeon called Serengo, in the employ of the Mine Owners' Association organized by John Hays Hammond.

Boyce related how the Western Federation of Miners had been conceived while he and thirteen others were in the Ada county prison at Boise, Idaho. Jim Hawley, their attorney, who had been a miner, suggested to them that all of the miners of the West should come together in one organization. This thought met the approval of the prisoners, as the miners' unions then in existence were scattered assemblies of the Knights of Labor. Boyce explained how, when they were released, a convention was called on May 13, 1893, in Butte, Montana, and the Western Federation of Miners was organized.

He described the first big strike that occurred after the formation of the W.F.M. This was in Cripple Creek, Colorado, in 1894. Every man in the district had gone on strike to prevent a reduction of wages and to establish the eight-hour day. Some of the mine owners of this district, then reputed to be millionaires, had formed themselves into an organization called the Mine Owners' Association. They knew that they could not depend upon Governor Waite, who had been a miner and was elected on the Populist ticket, but they knew that they could rely on the county commissioners and the sheriff of what was then El Paso county. These officers, at the instigation of the Mine Owners' Association, hired and equipped a small army of deputies, thirteen hundred or more men, who were provided with two hundred saddle horses, gatling guns, and other up-to-date instruments of war.

Previous to this the governor had sent the militia to the district, but upon investigation found that there was no occasion for the presence of the soldiers, and withdrew them. The sheriff mobilized his deputies and started to Cripple Creek. Two hundred of them got as far as Wilbur. The miners learned of their presence and sent a detachment of men against them. There was some shooting and one or two were killed on each side.

Governor Waite now made a personal investigation. He addressed the miners in their hall at Altman. He called out the militia at once and sent them to Cripple Creek with instructions to place themselves between the miners and the hired thugs. The miners were barricaded upon the crest of Bull Hill, where they had a strong fort and proposed to fight to the finish in protection of their wives and families and their rights as workingmen.

The commanding officer, General Brooks, notified the assembled deputies that if they did not disperse he would fire upon them. They left the camp the next day for Colorado Springs. They were so incensed at their failure at Cripple Creek that they tarred and feathered Tarney, the adjutant general of the state, who was in charge of the soldiers at Cripple Creek.

Governor Waite had been elected by the workers of the state. The mine owners knew that they couldn't fool with him, because upon his taking office he had ordered out the militia and had trained their cannon on the city hall in Denver, when the previous office-holders representing the mine owners and their business interests had refused to give up office.

Boyce reminded us that Governor Waite had the distinction of being the only governor in the United States who had ever called out the soldiers to protect the workers.

He told us about the conviction of Ed Lyons and Mike Tully, who had been charged with blowing up the Strong mine. Later they were released from the penitentiary and the stockholders of the mine sued Sam Strong, one of the owners, for the damages resulting from the explosion.

At these meetings Boyce initiated several hundred charter members of the Silver City Miners' Union Number 66 of the Western Federation of Miners.

"That is a good strong pledge," said I to Tom Fry, who was standing at my shoulder. The court room where the meetings were held was crowded. There were miners and mill workers from the Black Jack mine, the Florida mill, the Trade Dollar, the Blaine, the Poor Man, and the smaller mines of the camp. Every seat and every bit of standing room was filled. The charter was held open for some time to allow as many as possible to become charter members.

I was elected a member of the finance committee, and at various times filled the different offices of the union. While I was in Silver City I never missed a meeting of the Miners' Union except when I was working on the night shift, and I always took an active part in the work of the organization.

Two others and myself went as a committee to visit the Black Jack mine and invite one John Taylor who was working there either to become a member of the union, or leave the camp. Taylor became indignant and said that the superintendent told him that he did not need to join the union. We told him that the superintendent was not running the union; "the union is being run by the men of this camp." We had no further discussion with him, but when the shift came out of the mine at noon all of the men around the bunkhouse, including the night shift, resolved themselves into a committee of the whole, and told Taylor to roll his blankets and hit the trail. He did this without any loss of time. I met Taylor years later, under strange circumstances.

Stewart, the master mechanic at the Trade Dollar mill, was another man to whom we had to extend a special invitation to join the union. We explained to him that we could make no distinctions as to men in the camp; that we wanted to make it a thoroughly organized camp; that he would get as much benefit as any other member, sick and death benefits as well as hospital service—for the union very soon owned its own hospital. Stewart joined under protest and in after years attempted to repay me with interest. But that is another story.

There were nearly a thousand men employed in Silver City. There was a continual coming and going, but these two were the only men with whom we had any trouble. The membership included all those working in the mines, skilled and unskilled alike, and also those in and around the mills. There was only a slight difference in pay between the skilled and the unskilled men. As the Western Federation of Miners developed, all of its struggles were for the men underneath, for the lower paid men, as we came to learn that when the unskilled worker got a wage upon which he could live decently there was no danger of the skilled men falling below this level.

All the men in and around the mines worked every day of the week, including Sundays, and the mills were never closed down even for holidays.

In 1896, in his annual report to the Western Federation of Miners, Ed Boyce said that he hoped that, before the time of the next convention, the martial tread of twenty-five thousand armed miners would be heard throughout the West; that the time had come when the miners would have to protect themselves from thugs such as were used in the Cœur d'Alenes, in Cripple Creek and in Leadville; that he trusted every miner would get a modern rifle and a supply of ammunition.

At one time I was on a committee appointed to see Joseph Hutchinson, the manager of the Trade Dollar Mining Company, about the pay of the men who were sinking. There was at that time a winze being sunk on the Trade Dollar Mine for which the men were being paid only three dollars and a half a day, which was fifty cents less than the union wage for sinking. Hutchinson said:

"Well, that complies with your constitution," taking a copy of the constitution of the union from his desk; "there is no provision here for sinking a winze."

Taking a copy of the constitution from my pocket, I said:

"If you will read this you will see that we have corrected that error. Most men would rather work in a shaft than in a winze. At least, there is no reason why the wages should not be the same."

"I agree to that," he told us, "but I wish that when you change your constitution you would be good enough to keep us supplied with the latest issue."

It was not always because of skill or ability that men became superintendents or managers. One night there was a fire in the Chinese laundry in the back street. Some one suggested that the place ought to be blown up to keep the fire from spreading. Joe Hutchinson remarked that a box of powder would do the work. I told him:

"You don't want to put fifty pounds of powder under that shack! You'd break every window in town. Four or five pounds will lift it out by the roots."

They got the fire under control without the use of powder. The superintendent had probably never used a pound of powder in his life; he was superintendent through the success of his father.

I haven't described Silver City, which was built in a canyon between two towering peaks, War Eagle and Florida mountains. The bottom of the gulch was full of bowlders and rocks which had been turned up by the early gold diggers. The town was but two streets wide, the rear street occupied by prostitutes, black, white and Chinese. There were seventeen saloons in the town, besides other business houses. In the Winter the snow was often packed as deep as the first story windows. The little houses and cabins of the miners would be covered, nothing but the stovepipes sticking up through the snow. I had marked the trail to my house by sticking willows down on either side, and pulling them up as the snow increased in depth.

One night I dropped into the corner saloon. There is a corner saloon in every mining camp, and this one differed little from any of them. There was a billiard and pool table, a stud-poker and a faro game were running. I went over to the faro game, put down a dollar, and won on the turn.

"Give me silver," I said to the dealer, and asking the boys who were standing around to have a drink, we went over to the bar. I noticed a man sitting in a corner with his hat pulled down over his face. I asked Ben Hastings, the bartender:

"Who is that man?"

Ben answered, "That's old McCann; he don't drink much, but he'd sell his soul for a dose of morphine."

I called to McCann, "Come on, pardner, have a drink." As he came up, he pushed his hat back a little, and said:

"Hullo, Bill, you don't remember me. I used to know you in Tuscarora."

Staring at his emaciated face, at last I recognized his features, haggard and aged by the use of the drug to which he was addicted.

As I went out later, I noticed McCann speaking to one of the boys who worked in the Trade Dollar mine.

The next morning, on my way to work, I saw a light in McCann's cabin, and that evening I heard that he had gone to the stage office early in the morning, having dragged down a box on a hand sled, to be shipped out. The sheriff was at the stage office when McCann arrived there. He took McCann and the box to his office. When the box was opened there it was found to contain a lot of rich ore. McCann was charged with robbery and put in jail.

After several hours in the cell, his cravings began. He called the sheriff and said to him:

"A.B., you know that on account of my nerves I have been taking morphine, and I've got so I can't get along without it. You'll get me some at the post office drug store? If you tell them there it's for me they'll know how much I want."

"Why, sure, Mac, I'll do that," said the sheriff. He went away, and Mac began pacing up and down the cell. Already his temples were throbbing, his body wet with cold sweat. Up and down, up and down he went, more restless and goaded every minute. The hours dragged along, but the sheriff did not come back. In the night he thought he was going to die. His tortured nerves seemed to crack and ravel inside him. Before morning came he longed for death. He called to the guard, his voice shaking:

"I've got to get some morphine. You can get it!"

The guard answered:

"I can't leave here any more than you can. You'll have to wait till the sheriff comes in the morning."

It was late when Crocheron, the sheriff, came back. Mac was standing at the door of the cell. He reached a scrawny arm scarred with many jabs of the hypodermic needle through the bars of the cell, and said desperately:

"Give it to me, sheriff, for God's sake give it to me! I'm dying."

The sheriff pulled the little blue bottle out of his pocket.

"I'll give it to you, Mac. But I must have the names of the men who gave you that ore to ship out."

Mac staggered, tripped on the food pan, and collapsed on the floor. Dragging himself back to the bars, he looked the sheriff in the eyes and said:

"I can't tell you."

The sheriff walked off and left Mac in his agony.

A short time later the court was in session, and Mac, more dead than alive, was brought in for trial. The prosecuting attorney told him:

"McCann, the mining company has no desire to prosecute you. But they do want to know the names of the men who gave you that ore."

McCann, lifting his worn and exhausted face, said:

"I cannot tell you."

He was convicted and sentenced to seven years in the Boise penitentiary and he died there while serving his term.

Ben had said he would sell his soul for a dose of morphine. But he suffered untold agonies rather than sell his friends.

On the twenty-eighth of June, 1897, my youngest daughter was born. My wife did not recover her health for months. She was bedfast, and the domestic cares of the family fell entirely upon my shoulders, as there was not a woman or girl in the camp that we could get to work outside her own home. They came up in the evenings after their own work was done, and helped us in neighborly ways, but until the wife of the colored barber came to town I had to do the work myself. The baby from its birth slept with me. Afraid of smothering her if I laid her at my side, every night I put her on my breast. If she had been in a cradle I should not have heard her cry when she was hungry, so soundly did I sleep.

Though I was, not working, the butcher and store-keeper and others with whom I dealt said to me:

"Don't worry, Bill, things will be all right soon. Remember, you can always have anything you want from us."

At that time I gambled some and drank a little, but I quit both. While I had sometimes made winnings, in the long run I had been much the loser.

Sometimes I took my wife to visit the neighbors, the baby in one arm and her in the other. I remember one evening being down to see Mrs. Morris at the foot of the hill. When we started home there had been a drift of snow, and I had my wife on one arm, the baby on the other, and the little girl on my back. I carried them all three up the hill.

The Blaine mine was worked through a tunnel in the side of a mountain, and the mining was done above as well as below the level of the tunnel. Coming out we walked Indian file on a plank laid between the tracks. One day Theodore Buckle, a florid, big, fine-looking young Hollander, was just behind me, and we scuffled and joked as we went along. He went to dinner in a boarding house, I ate my lunch in the blacksmith shop. Going back to the mine after dinner, he was a few minutes ahead of me. Some of the men had to climb a hundred and ten feet to the first level above, and from there to the stopes which were still above this. There were some ahead of Buckle, some behind him. He was just climbing up into his stope when a slab of rock fell and crushed the life out of him. We managed to raise the rock high enough to get his body from under it and carried it down to the hundred-and-ten-foot level. There, for want of a better stretcher, we tied the corpse to a short ladder which we lowered down the man-way to the main tunnel. We sent a committee to town with the body.

On another occasion we heard a shot, back near the station on the same hundred-and-ten-foot level. Then some one called to us and we hurried out to find that MacDonald, who had only been at work a short time, had his entire face blown off. He was still alive and we contrived to lower him down the man-way. One of the boys had run out ahead and sent for a wagon. We got him to the hospital as quickly as we could, where he soon died. MacDonald had evidently been biting a fulminating cap to fasten it on a fuse that he was getting ready to fire his holes. Many of the miners did this instead of using their knives to clinch the cap, or pincers that were made for the purpose.

The question of the eight-hour law was beginning to stir the miners of Idaho, and at the coming session of the legislature they were going to try to have a bill enacted to provide for an eight-hour day for men employed in mines, mills and smelters. Joseph Hutchinson was sent as a lobbyist, supplied with funds by the Trade Dollar Company to work against the bill. This action could be expected from the mine owners, but James R. Sovereign, one-time Master Workman of the Knights of Labor, then editor of the paper owned by the miners' unions of the Cœur d'Alenes, the *Idaho State Tribune,* did a treacherous piece of work in publishing an editorial against the eight-hour law. He proved a faker and sell-out, no better than his predecessor, Powderly. The bill was defeated by the legislature, but later established by the miners. It was the Western Federation of Miners, through its attorney, John H. Murphy, that carried the first eight-hour law passed in the United States, the Utah law, to the United States Supreme Court, where it was declared constitutional. But the miners and the mill men of Utah had to fight to compel its enforcement.

I was elected as a delegate from the Silver City Miners' Union to the convention of the Western Federation of Miners which was held in 1898 in Salt Lake City.

CHAPTER V

THE WESTERN FEDERATION OF MINERS

THERE were delegates from most of the mining camps of the West: copper miners from Butte, Montana; lead miners from the Cœur d'Alenes, Idaho; gold miners from the Black Hills of South Dakota and from Cripple Creek, Colorado; silver miners from Virginia City, Nevada, which was called the mother of mines. The miners' unions of most of these places had been old assemblies of the Knights of Labor. Here they were all meeting together. Miners' delegates came from many other places besides; British Columbia had her representatives as well as Arizona. There were mill men and smelter men and one or two coal miners. We were the men who, with the United Mine Workers, a body of coal miners, produced the mineral wealth of America. Each union that we represented was an integral part of the Western Federation of Miners. We were one of the three industrial unions that existed at that time, and the only one that had a vision of the day when with other unions in other industries, we could live by the slogan "All for One, One for All."

Here were men who had fought in the tragic strikes of Cœur d'Alenes, Cripple Creek, and Leadville. We were talking of plans which would strengthen our position and back up the rifles that many of us already possessed. We wanted the other workers in and around the mining camps organized with us.

Edward Boyce in his presidential report recommended the formation of an organization that would be a support to the miners and a benefit to the organized men and women. He also called attention to the importance of a Miners' Home for crippled, sick and aged miners, who as a rule under the present conditions died as charity patients, when a mere pittance from each of us would mean a guarantee of care and shelter.

One of the delegates, in speaking of the Spanish War, then going on in Cuba and the Philippines, predicted that the result would be an increase in the standing army, which then consisted of twenty-five thousand men; that these soldiers would be maintained in idleness to be used on such occasions as the Cœur d'Alenes strike, the American Railway Union strike and as they already had been used in many other strikes.

The American Federation of Labor had chartered an organization known as the Northern Mineral Mine Workers. Although they were not represented at this convention, later all the unions comprising this body became parts of the Western Federation of Miners.

I should mention here that the Western Federation of Miners had at one time applied to the A. F. of L. for a charter and had sent two delegates to the convention of that organization. These delegates, Boyce and Clifford, reported that in their opinion the Western Federation of Miners would gain little or nothing by affiliating with the A. F. of L. They said that the sessions which they had attended had developed nothing that would be of advantage to the working class. The chief interest seemed to be the reëlection of Samuel Gompers and other officers, and the transfer of the headquarters of the A. F. of L. from the industrial city of Indianapolis to the political swamp at Washington.

The initial convention of the Western Labor Union, which was held at Salt Lake City at the same time as the convention of the W.F.M., was made up of delegates representing various trades around the mining camps and other western towns. One delegate I remember, MacArthur of San Francisco, from the International Seamen's Union, opposed the launching of the Western Labor Union on the ground that it would be in opposition to the American Federation of Labor, but expressed his earnest support of the Western Federation of Miners. He had forgotten, if he ever knew, that the A. F. of L. itself was organized in opposition to the Knights of Labor.

Daniel McDonald of Butte was elected president of the new organization. I was elected to the executive board. The Western Federation of Miners became a chartered body of the Western Labor Union.

While these conventions were in session, Sam Gompers with Henry White, who was afterward involved in a scandal about selling the labels of his union, the United Garment Workers, and others of Gompers' lieutenants, arrived in the city. He came, he said, to see Ed Boyce, to urge the reaffiliation of the W.F.M. with the A. F. of L.

What he really wanted was to address the convention, but it would have been useless. When Gompers came to the building where the convention was being held, it was amusing to see the big broad-shouldered men of the West taking the measure of this undersized individual that called itself the leader of labor. This squat specimen of humanity certainly did not personify the membership of the American Federation of Labor. Sam was very short and chunky with a big head that was bald in patches, resembling a child suffering with ringworm. He had small snapping eyes, a hard cruel mouth, wide with thin drooping lips, heavy jaws and jowls. A personality vain, conceited, petulant and vindictive. Looking at him, I could realize the passion of cruelty with which this person would wield power if he had it. It was easy to understand how Gompers could plead for men who were facing the noose of the executioners—with his tongue in his cheek and his heart reeking with hypocrisy. One could realize that he might even refer jokingly to the defeat of a great labor struggle, if it were being conducted by an organization that was not strictly in accordance with his views. To look at him was to know that he could protest against giving relief to women and children.

When Gompers had appeared before Governor Oglesby in 1887 ostensibly in behalf of the Chicago martyrs, having been urged by labor men in Chicago to go to Springfield, his opening words were:

"I have differed all my life with the principles and methods of the condemned."

Before Gompers says anything more, let us see who the men were, from whose principles and methods he had all his life differed. They, eight of them, were the spokesmen of the working class. Some of them had been members of the International Workingmen's Association.* Some were members of the Knights of Labor. These men were working day and night in the interests of the strikers at the McCormick Harvester Company. Some of them had, on May first, 1886, addressed the members of the Lumber Shovers' Union. The police attacked this meeting; some of the strikers were killed and many of them were injured. It was decided to hold a protest meeting in Haymarket Square on May fourth. A great gathering assembled,

---

* Better known as the First International, it was founded by Karl Marx and others in London, on September 28, 1864. Shortly before the International was dissolved in 1874, its General Council was moved to America.

which was addressed by Spies, Parsons and Fielden. Carter Harrison, mayor of Chicago, attended the meeting. Leaving early, he notified the police that everything was being conducted in an orderly way and that the police need not go to the meeting. In spite of the mayor's order, Captain Bonfield sent one hundred and seventy-six policemen to disperse the meeting. It was Fielden who was speaking when Captain Ward gave the order for the workers to disperse, and not Spies, as Gompers said. A bomb was thrown that killed seven policemen and many of the workers. Who threw the deadly missile was never known, but eight men were arrested: August Spies, Albert Parsons, Louis Lingg, Adolph Fisher, George Engel, Oscar Neebe, Samuel Fielden and Michael Schwab. They were charged with being accessories to murder. They were put on trial and convicted before a prejudiced judge, by a picked jury that was rewarded by the Chamber of Commerce. Before sentence was passed upon them, these men gave to the working class their principles. August Spies said:

In addressing this court, I speak as the representative of one class to the representatives of another. . . . I have been indicted on the charge of murder as an accomplice or accessory. Upon this indictment I have been convicted. There was no evidence produced by the state to show or even to indicate that I had any knowledge of the man who threw the bomb, or that I myself had anything to do with the throwing of the missile. . . . If there was no evidence to show that I was legally responsible for the deed, then my conviction and the execution of the sentence, is nothing less than a wilful, malicious and deliberate murder, as foul a murder as may be found in the annals of religious, political or any other persecution. . . .

Spies spoke for eight hours. He arraigned the social system and he proved that violence was constantly and extensively used to overawe the industrial class, and that legal and political remedy had been denied them. He said:

I believe that the state of caste and classes, the state where one class dominates over and lives upon the labor of another class, and calls this order; yes, I believe that this barbaric form of social organization, with its legalized plunder and murder, is doomed to die and make room for a free society, voluntary association for universal brotherhood. You may pronounce sentence upon me, honorable judge, but let the world know that in A.D. 1886, in the State of Illinois, eight men were sentenced to death because they believed in a better future, because they had not lost faith in the ultimate victory of liberty and justice. . . . These are my ideas; they constitute a part of myself. I cannot divest myself of them nor would I if I could. And if you think that you can crush out these ideas that are gaining ground more and more every day, if you think you can crush them out by sending us to the gallows, if you would once more have people suffer the penalty of death because they have dared to tell the truth, and I defy you to show where we have told a lie, I say if death is the penalty for proclaiming the truth, then I will proudly and defiantly pay the costly price. Call your hangman. Truth, crucified in Socrates, in Christ, in Giordano Bruno, in Huss, in Galileo, still lives. They, and others whose number is legion, have preceded us on this path; we are ready to follow.

Michael Schwab said:

It is not much that I have to say, and I would say nothing at all, if keeping silent did not look like a cowardly approval of what has been done here. To term the proceedings during the trial 'justice' would be a sneer. Justice has not been done. More than this, could not be done. If one class is arrayed against the other, it is idle and hypocritical to think about justice. . . . I have not the slightest idea who threw the bomb on the Haymarket, and I have no knowledge of any conspiracy to use violence on that or any other night.

Oscar Neebe told of his work among the bakers and brewers of Chicago, and the improvements secured in wages and hours of labor by direct action. He had worked for the education of laboring men. When he was sentenced to life imprisonment he said: "I am sorry I am not to be hung with the rest of the men."

Adolph Fisher said:

You ask me why sentence of death should not be passed upon me. I will only say that I protest against being sentenced to death because I have committed no crime. I was tried in this room for murder, and convicted of anarchy. I protest against being sentenced to death because I have not been found guilty of murder. But however, if I am to die on account of being an Anarchist, on account of my love for Liberty, Equality and Fraternity, I will not remonstrate. If death is the penalty for our love of the freedom of the human race, then I say openly that I have forfeited my life. This verdict is a death-blow against free speech, free press and free thought in this country.

Said Louis Lingg:

I despise you. I despise your order, your law, your force-propped authority. Hang me for it.

George Engel told the court:

All I have to say in regard to my conviction is that I was not at all
surprised. For it has ever been that men who have endeavored to en-
lighten their fellow-men have been thrown into prison or put to death.

Samuel Fielden said:

The nineteenth century commits the crime of killing its best friends.
It will live to repent it. But as I have said before, if it will do any good
I freely give myself up.

In a speech lasting many hours, Albert Parsons said:

I am a socialist. I am one of those, although myself a wage-slave, who
hold that it is wrong, wrong to myself, wrong to my neighbor, and unjust
to my fellow-man, for me, wage slave that I am, to make my escape
from wage-slavery by becoming a master and an owner of slaves myself.
. . . This is my crime before high heaven. This and this alone is my
crime. . . . The only sacred right of property is the natural right of
the working man to the product which is the creation of his labor.

These were the principles from which Samuel Gompers had
"differed all his life."

The Knights of Labor was at that time a strong, growing organization with nearly eight hundred thousand members. Its rapid growth
at this period made it evident to Gompers that the organization of
craft unions that he had started, the A. F. of L., could not meet
with success if the revolutionary demands of the workers were encouraged. Gompers in his plea to Governor Oglesby for clemency,
had said:

If these men are executed, it would simply be an impetus to this so-
called revolutionary movement which no other thing on earth can give.
These men would, apart from any consideration of mercy or humanity,
be looked upon as martyrs. Thousands and thousands of labor men all
over the world would consider that these men had been executed because
they were standing up for free speech and free press.

We ask you, sir, to interpose your great power to prevent so dire a
calamity.*

---

* Samuel Gompers: "Seventy Years of Life and Labor." Vol. II, pp. 180-
181.

Gompers' warning to the governor had expressed his life-ambition, which was to prevent the growth of the revolutionary working class movement.

I remember speaking coolly and calmly, and pleaded as strongly as I could for the exercise of the governor's clemency, at least to grant a reprieve to the men for a considerable time, so that an opportunity might be had to establish their innocence, if they were innocent.

The qualifying word, "if," measures Sam Gompers' loyalty to the revolutionary working class movement of America. This was written thirty years after Governor John P. Altgeld in reviewing the case, had said:

None of the defendants could be at all connected with the case. The jury was picked. Wholesale bribery and intimidation of witnesses was resorted to. The defendants were not proven guilty of the crime charged under the indictment.

The reason and manner of Gompers' plea on behalf of the men about to die had made the delegates at Salt Lake City realize the wide difference between the pure and simple trade union, and the Western Federation of Miners, which had inscribed on its charter: "Labor produces all Wealth, Wealth belongs to the producers thereof."

The revelation of what could be termed nothing less than treasonable action on the part of Gompers increased the growing hatred against the man, and this hatred extended to the council of the A. F. of L. when we learned the facts about what they had done during the American Railway Union strike in 1894. It was generally known that when Gompers got on the train at Indianapolis to go to Chicago he had said:

"I am going to the funeral of the A.R.U."

A funeral without a corpse would be a strange thing. What Gompers meant was that they were going to kill the American Railway Union and thereby provide the necessary corpse for the funeral. And this was what they proceeded to do. A conference of the Executive Council of the A. F. of L. was called, and met at the Briggs House in Chicago. In addition to the council there were fourteen delegates from the affiliated unions, the First Grand Master of the Brotherhood of Railway Trainmen, and the Grand Secretary and

Treasurer of the Locomotive Firemen. Eugene V. Debs appeared before this conference and asked that they present to the Railroad Managers' Association the proposition that the strikers return to work at once as a body, upon the condition that they be restored to their former positions, or, in the event of failure, to call a general strike. Five members of this conference, Gompers being one, were appointed to draft resolutions. Here are extracts from their proposals:

> The great industrial upheaval now agitating the country has been carefully, calmly and fully considered, and a conference of the Executive Council of the American Federation of Labor and the executive officers and representatives of the national and international unions and Brotherhoods of Railway Men, called to meet in the city of Chicago, on the twelfth day of July, 1894. In the light of all the evidence obtainable and in view of the peculiar complications now developing in the situation, we are forced to the conclusion that the best interests of the unions affiliated with the American Federation of Labor demand that they refrain from participating in any general or local strike which may be proposed in connection with the present railroad troubles. . . .
>
> We further recommend that all connected with the American Federation of Labor now out on sympathetic strike should return to work, and those who contemplate going out on sympathetic strike are advised to remain at their usual vocations.*

This was the blade of treachery, with a handle made of a double cross, that was plunged into the breasts of the strikers of the Pullman car shops. It caused the death of the American Railway Union. It sent Eugene V. Debs and his co-workers to prison. Gompers, writing about the event in after years, said:

> The course pursued by the Federation was the biggest service that could have been performed to maintain the integrity of the Railroad Brotherhoods. Large numbers of their members had left their organization and had joined the American Railway Union. It meant, if not disruption, weakening to a very serious extent.**

The A. F. of L. had also refused to live up to the pledge given during the Leadville strike of 1896. This and other information becoming general among the delegates, the Western Federation of Miners was firmly determined to have no further connection with the

---

* *Ibid.*, pp. 411-412.
** *Ibid.*, p. 414.

A. F. of L. The A. F. of L. had made a record of treason, treachery and avarice that must not be forgotten.

Representatives of the Utah Federation of Labor paid their respects to the convention of the Western Federation of Miners, and did not forget to remind the delegates that the W.F.M. was the only organization that had assisted the Utah workers in carrying the eight-hour law to the United States Supreme Court.

These conventions had been a significant point in my life. I keenly realized the importance of the revolutionary labor movement, and now had a deeper understanding of the struggles that had been made and the sacrifices demanded of the workers in their efforts to emancipate themselves from wage-slavery. I knew the struggle must go on and I was determined to take an active part in it.

While I was in Salt Lake City I had many pleasant visits with my relatives. I had not seen my mother and sisters for some years, or my cousin Mae Gudgell, with whom I had carried on a correspondence since I had left home. I went to see my uncle Dick, who during the course of the afternoon referred to his "baby boy." Charley was then a big, fine strapping boy of about sixteen. I thought of myself at eleven years old, when my uncle Dick had bound me out to John Holden, saying that I was old enough to earn my own living.

When I returned to Silver City I at once went to work in the Blaine mine. I was then president of the union and made my report of the convention at the next meeting. The Western Federation of Miners began the publication of a monthly called the *Miners' Magazine*. I wrote some articles for it, and at one time sent in a bunch of ninety subscriptions. The union had then what was practically the same as the shop-steward system. These were neither business agents nor walking delegates, but members appointed by the union on both shifts at every mine, and the same at the mills. It was the duty of these "vigilants," as we called them, to report the conditions of work about the mine or mill on their shift, and also to see that every man was a member of the union in good standing.

Ed Boyce made a visit to Silver City and commended the union on the progress that had been made. Silver City was then not only organized, but completely unionized. Every man working in the camp was a member of the union. With two or three other miners, I went with Boyce to Delamar, where he met with the members and officers of the union there. On the trip we discussed many things. He went rather deeply into the history of the Knights of Labor, and toid us something of the International Workingmen's Association. We talked about the educational work so necessary among the miners. The headquarters of the W.F.M. was then in Butte, Montana. The general situation of the organization was improving. There were no serious controversies anywhere, but trouble was fomenting, especially in the lead district of the Cœur d'Alenes.

My work in the union kept me busy during my extra time when I was off shift. I was again elected delegate to the convention, which was to be held once more in Salt Lake City. Just before leaving for the convention, we got the rumble of the explosion in the Cœur d'Alenes, the newspapers and a wire from W.F.M. headquarters bringing the story. The men of Silver City were not excited, but every one was thinking about what might happen further, and they were mad clear through.

The Bunker Hill and Sullivan Company, and the Last Chance were paying fifty cents a day less than all the other mines of the Cœur d'Alenes. The mines paying three and a half a day had posted notices that they would reduce wages. The miners determined that this should not happen, and they directed their energies to bringing the lower paid mines up to the higher paid standard. This was stubbornly resisted by the companies that were trying to rob the miners of one-seventh of their pay.

When the power drills were introduced the work of the miners was changed. The men did not object to the installation of the machines, but many skillful miners were not physically capable of handling one of the big sluggers. No consideration was shown to them; they were put to running cars, shoveling ore, or as roustabouts at fifty cents a day less than the miners had been receiving. This would make a corresponding reduction in their standard of living. Fifteen dollars a month less for all miners, thirty dollars a month less for miners who could not handle the big drills. It could be summed up as less food, less clothes, less house-room, less schooling for the children, less amusements, less everything that made life worth living. The situation was discussed in all its different phases at all the meetings of the union. There was no means of escape from the gigantic force that was relentlessly crushing all of them beneath its cruel heel. The people of these dreadful mining camps were in a fever of revolt. There was no method of appeal; strike was their only weapon.

On April 29, 1899, a big demonstration was held at Wardner. All the members of all the unions in the district were there. The last warning had been sounded. The fuses were lit. Three thousand pounds of dynamite exploded. The Bunker Hill and Sullivan mill was blown up, ripped and smashed, a mass of twisted steel, iron and splintered timbers. The miners had released their pent-up resentment. There may have been some who regretted the destruction of that which workers had built, but the constraint of the entire population was for the time-being relieved.

The managers and superintendents, who had found no words of encouragement for the despairing miners, now became voluble in their demands for state assistance. They could wreck a whole population, but now they raised a maudlin cry because a mill had been destroyed. Governor Frank Steunenberg, a sheep rancher, appealed to President McKinley for Federal soldiers, which were dispatched immediately to the Cœur d'Alenes mining district. Armed force was imposed upon a peaceful people without inquiry or investigation on the part of either the governor of the state or the president of the United States, at the first request of the mining companies. When the soldiers arrived martial law was declared. More than twelve hundred men were arrested without warrant and held for months in prison without any charge being preferred against them. There was no insurrection in the Cœur d'Alenes, there was no interference in the function of the courts, yet hundreds of men were punished with months of imprisonment in the bull-pen, a structure unfit to house cattle, enclosed in a high barbed-wire fence. The miners of the West became embittered at the vicious treatment imposed upon their brothers in the lead mines of Idaho. Money was raised in every mining camp, in every smelter town and in many other places, and sent to the suffering women and children. It was shown that the mining company was responsible for the damage. Indignant resolutions condemning the outrages flooded Congress.

At Salt Lake City I found the shadow of the Cœur d'Alenes pervading the convention. The delegates could think or talk of little else. Twelve hundred members were in prison, nine of them indicted for murder, women and children were living under the dark menace of martial law. The legislature, the courts and the army were against us. Every man brought the question home to himself. If this dreadful thing happened in Leadville in the Cœur d'Alenes, how long before it happens in Butte, in the Black Hills, in Nevada? What is to stop it happening in the camp where I live? Must wages and hours and the conditions under which we live and work always be subject to the will and whim of the boss?

The only answer I could find in my own mind was to organize, to multiply our strength. As long as we were scattered and disjointed we could be victimized.

At this convention I had a suggestion to offer about changing the design of the lapel button that we wore. The emblem upon it was then a machine-drill on a tripod. This was unsuitable because it did not include all the workers in the industry, and because these dangerous machine drills had come to be known as "widow makers." The design was changed, and later changed again, to the symbol of three stars, signifying education, organization, and independence, with a pen, a hammer, and a drill between the stars. This remained the emblem of the W.F.M. I was elected to the executive board of the W.F.M. at this convention. In the fall a meeting of the board was held at headquarters in Butte, Montana.

In approaching Butte I marveled at the desolation of the country. There was no verdure of any kind; it had all been killed by the fumes and smoke of the piles of burning ore. The noxious gases came from the sulphur that was allowed to burn out of the ore before it was sent to the smelter. It was so poisonous that it not only killed trees, shrubs, grass and flowers, but cats and dogs could not live in the city of Butte, and the housewives complained that the fumes settling on the clothes rotted the fiber.

The city with the copper soul was built around the mines of Butte. The people of this mining camp breathed copper, ate copper, wore copper, and were thoroughly saturated with copper. The smoke, fumes and dust penetrated everywhere and settled on everything. Many of the miners were suffering from rankling copper sores, caused by the poisonous water. The old iron and tin cans were gathered up and dumped into a pool where the water from the mines percolated and precipitated copper on the scrap iron, eating out the iron and converting the cans into copper.

The toll of death in Butte was abnormal. The sick benefits paid to the members of Butte Miners' Union aggregated hundreds of thousands of dollars. The funeral benefits were frightfully large. The city of the dead, mostly young miners, was almost as large as the living population, even in this very young city. Human life was the cheapest by-product of this great copper camp.

The mines had been discovered by prospectors who had drifted up from Utah. Marcus Daly and W. A. Clark were both miners who had been in Tintic and Ophir Canyon. They were pioneers in Butte. Clark had a brother, Buckskin Clark, who lived at Ophir while I was there.

The main building of Butte was called the Big Ship; it had a copper keel, it was founded on copper. It was a company store, with offices on the sixth floor where schemes of copper were hatched. Dublin Gulch was the home of the "Paddy-come-latelies," the Irish "big-wheelers" direct from the old sod.

Butte Miners' Union Number 1 of the W.F.M. was at that time the largest union in America, with a membership often as high as five thousand. It was the greatest single social force of the working class in the western part of America. The tremendous power of this big union was not always used to the best advantage; it nearly always allowed itself to be divided on questions of strategy, tactics, and political issues. Otherwise it could have been the directing energy of the entire state of Montana.

The Miners' Hall was commodious but not nearly large enough to accommodate the membership. Boyce, Williams and I attended a meeting of the union. When I spoke, it was to compliment the union highly on the splendid work that it had done.

In Butte were the Engineers' Union and the Smeltermen's Union, both parts of the Western Federation. The men organized in the Engineers' Union were not machinists but the engineers who ran the hoisting engines and other engines about the works. Some of the engines were "first motion." The men who ran these got six dollars a day and were at that time the highest paid men in the organization. It required a clear mind and a steady arm to operate these engines, with which they pulled the men thirty to thirty-five hundred feet out of the mines. More responsibility rested upon the engineers than upon any other men around the mine. It will be recognized that speed was essential in hoisting the men and the ore. In some mines there were double and even triple decked cages. Most of the mines of Butte are very hot, but the fellow who named the Never-Sweat mine did not know that it would be the hottest of all.

The work in the Butte mines was all underground. The veins are worked through deep shafts, with tunnels or levels running from the shafts usually one hundred feet apart. The ore is worked or stoped out between the levels, dropped down chutes to the level below, and run to the shaft in small cars and hoisted to the surface. At present the ore is not burnt in the open but taken direct to the smelter.

It was decided by the meeting of the executive board that John C. Williams, board member from Grass Valley, California, and I should go to the Cœur d'Alenes to convey the greetings of the W.F.M. to the strikers and to report conditions as we found them in the strikebound district, which was then under martial law.

We left Butte and caught the Great Northern at Missoula. Burke was to be our first stop. That part of the Rocky Mountains where the Cœur d'Alenes mining district is situated, is scarred and gashed with gulches and deep canyons. The mountain sides are rugged, with cliffs and outcroppings of rock. There are old and rotten stumps of the trees that have been cut for mining timber, railroad ties and firewood. Everywhere bushes and shrubs, wild strawberries and other wild fruits grow in abundance. Where the forests have not been depleted either with the ax or with devastating fires, there are bear, deer, and other game. In the cold, clear streams are mountain trout. The Cœur d'Alenes lake is like a transparent gem in the rough setting of the mountains. It is a delightful place for a summer outing, but a frightful place to live during the long winters, with the continual fear of snowslides, the digging out of the snow-bound houses, the floundering to and from work through snow waist-deep. The railroad runs around the mountains, through tunnels, across deep chasms on skeletons of steel, up and down narrow canyons where there is just room enough for the roadbed. Before the coming of the iron horse, the burro was the only means of transportation, the hunter, the prospector and the Indian were the only inhabitants.

Dutch Jake, with a partner, was rambling around these mountains, maybe forty years ago. One day they picketed their burro and went gouging around the rocks and crevices, looking for "paydirt" or a vein of ore. When they got back, they found that their burro had got the rope he was tied with tangled in some shrubs and could only move a foot or two. They went to untangle the rope, and found that the donkey, stamping and trampling the ground, had uncovered a ledge of rich lead ore. Here they located the Bunker Hill and Sullivan mine, which became one of the richest producers in the Cœur d'Alenes district. Dutch Jake made some money, and in later years he bought a building in Spokane in which he ran a saloon. There he had a fine painting of the burro that had found the mine for him and his partner.

At Burke we saw Mrs. Paul Corcoran, and gave her the greetings of the W.F.M. We assured her that we would do everything in our power to secure Paul's release from the penitentiary. Mrs. Corcoran was a young, black-haired Irishwoman with two beautiful children. While martial law prevailed in the Cœur d'Alenes, Paul Corcoran, secretary of Burke Miners' Union Number 10 of the W.F.M., had been tried on a charge of murder for causing the death of one Bartlett Sinclair on the day of the big explosion. Paul Corcoran was in no way responsible. His arrest and the charge of murder against him were because he was secretary of the strongest union in the lead district. The companies that manipulated the state legislature and defeated the eight-hour law, the companies that intended to cut wages, the companies that could at their mere request have federal soldiers and martial law in the district, were the companies that employed a special prosecutor to conduct the trial of Paul Corcoran. He had been convicted and sentenced to seventeen years in the penitentiary at Boise, Idaho. The special prosecutor was William A. Borah, now United States senator for the state of Idaho. He is still a responsible mouthpiece of the exploiting class.

We stopped at Mrs. Fox's boarding house at Burke, which was well known to most of the miners of the West. I have heard many stories of her warm-heartedness. A miner coming to Burke was always welcome to a meal at her place. She caused much amusement among her boarders. One time when new cabbage was just in, the old lady had cooked up a lot. It was just what the miners were longing for and they kept asking for more. Bringing up the last plate full, she said:

"Take that, ye sons of batches, and I'll bring yez a bale of hay in the marnin'."

Burke's one street was so narrow that there was just room enough for the railroad track. When the train was in, a wagon could not pass on either side. The canyon was so deep that the sun had to be nearly at zenith to shine down into the town.

At Mullen we met Paddy Burke and a few other members of the union. Our activities were of necessity under cover, because of the district being under martial law. We avoided the hang-out of the soldiers. Our purpose was to get a word of encouragement to the men in the bull-pen. We wanted them to know that we had come to the Cœur d'Alenes to bring to them the sympathy and the united support of the organization, in the interests of which they were enduring the degradation of imprisonment in the vermin-infested hole. The miners in the bull-pen had gotten some scantlings and long planks, and had lifted the end of the roof and hung out a sign that they had painted on sheets. It read, "The American Bastille." This got under the hide of General Merriam, who seemed to think that his up-to-date bull-pen was not appreciated.

We met one of the eight men under indictment for murder who had escaped from the bull-pen. He said that most of the other boys who had come out with him had left the camp but that he was going to stay, as he had a good prospect of striking a ledge in his mine and he didn't want to lose it. I wanted him to tell me how he and the others had got out of the bull-pen.

"Why," he said, "there was nothing to it. Whatever was done, was done by the boys on the outside. Sergeant Crawford came to the guard-house where we were being held, one night. He said, get your clothes, you fellers are going to the hospital. We were soon ready and we started with a small detachment of soldiers, only two or three. When we got to the gate of the barbed-wire enclosure, Crawford advanced when challenged, 'Who goes there?' and answered, 'Sergeant Crawford with a detail to the hospital.' When we were outside, he told us to scatter. All except two of us have left the district."

Sergeant Crawford was sent to Alcatraz Island, California, for the part he played in the escape. In addition to the sentence of nine years he was dishonorably discharged from the army.

Paddy Burke also told us of an attempt to dig out of the bull-pen. The miners had sunk under one of the bunks, deep enough to get a roof for a tunnel that would not cave in if a wagon passed over it. As the tunnel increased in length the dirt was pulled out in a wooden box. They had to hide the dirt in the bunks or under them, and carried out some with the ashes. They were making good progress. In a short time hundreds of men would have been crawling through this little tunnel to the freedom of the mountains. But one day the man at work felt the air becoming dense and poisonous. He took the fire poker with which he was digging for want of a pick, and began jabbing at the roof to make a hole to the surface to let the bad air out of the tunnel. He rammed the poker into the posterior of a lazy soldier who was stretched out on the ground above. Yellowleg jumped up and yelled that he had been bitten by a snake. Other soldiers came running up to him but they could find no snake. They did find a little hole in the ground, and upon further investigation they found the tunnel. When the miners learned how their tunnel had been discovered they cursed their luck and they damned the soldier, but the joke was on them.

A company of the soldiers were colored men from Brownsville, Texas. We always believed that the government officials thought it would further incite the miners if armed black men were placed as guards over white prisoners. It did raise a storm of indignation, not so much against the colored soldiers as against those responsible for bringing any soldiers into the mining region. One of the officers, a dirty white scoundrel, sent letters to the wives and sisters of the men in the bull-pen, asking them to entertain the soldiers, saying that they would "receive due consideration." The hell-hound was not concerned about the men under him, his action was intended to add insult to the other injuries already inflicted upon the helpless prisoners. It was an insult in any case to ask the miners' families to have anything to do with soldiers, and it was a deliberate attempt to add race prejudice to the situation. Race prejudice had been unknown among the miners; there was no distinction in work or organization as to race, color or creed.

We saw that vile bull-pen from the train windows as we passed. A low, rambling one story building. There was a prison! Hundreds of men, many of whom I had worked with, were confined in it in squalor. They were men of my own kind. They were fighting my fight. If their wages had been cut, my wages would have been cut. They were the men who had made these mining camps. They had dug every pound of ore that ever came out of a mine. They and men like them had made the West. Their very lives, the living of their wives and children, were in jeopardy. Their appeals to the corporations went unheard. A mill had been blown up. If it was for this that they were in the bull-pen I should be there with them. I had not been in person at the demonstration at Wardner; but I was there in desire, in support. So was every miner of the West. We were united with the lead miners of the Cœur d'Alenes in their struggle against oppression.

During the long months that the miners were imprisoned, the companies were busy with schemes to strangle the unions. They brought thugs and ruffians, all of them gunmen, into the district, but the card that they most relied on was the General Employment Office which they established at Wallace. An ex-detective was put in charge of the office, which was conducted as a black-listing agency. To get a job in any mine in the district a man could not rustle as formerly at the mine, but had to go first to the employment office at Wallace and there pass a critical examination as to membership in the union, and previous places of employment. A physical description of all applicants was taken. A man passing muster was given a "rustling card" and told to go to the place that wanted men. Hundreds of non-union men and scabs were shipped into the district from Sudbury, a copper camp in Canada, from Joplin, Missouri, and other places. It was very evident that the unions were going to have hard sledding. But we were confident that whatever the future developments might be, the spirit of solidarity could never be crushed out of the members who understood the aims and ambitions of the W.F.M.

Before returning to Silver City I went to Rocky Bar and organized the miners and others eligible to membership in the union of the W.F.M. It was necessary for me to give them the latest information of the strike, and to tell them the purpose of the Miners' Union. From there I went to Blackbird, but there I did not organize, because I could not get the twenty-five members required for a charter.

Things in Silver City were about the same as they had been. I was working in the Florida tunnel when, thinking matters over one day, I took an empty box and on one side of it wrote a resolution condemning Governor Steunenberg for the imprisonment of the miners in the bull-pen and the presence of the soldiers and martial law in the Cœur d'Alenes. That night at home I wrote it on paper, and at the first meeting introduced it at the union. It was adopted and ordered published in the *Miners' Magazine*.

When they put machine drills in the Blaine mine I worked with Big Harry Palmer in a long cross-cut, running from the Blaine tunnel towards the Banner mine.

It was in this cross-cut, four thousand feet from the surface, that I turned off the air on the machine drill for the last time. It was three o'clock in the morning. I left for the convention that was to be held in Denver, Colorado, on the stage that same morning at six o'clock. Wallace Johnson and Billy Williams had been elected as delegates from the union. I was then a board member but not a delegate, and left a week ahead of them.

CHAPTER VI

TELLURIDE

THE convention was held at Oddfellows Hall on Champa street. Rumors were current that Butte Miners' Union Number 1 had made some complaint about the finances of the organization. Boyce, much to the amusement of all the other delegates, put all seven members of the delegation of Number 1 on the auditing committee, which had to audit the books of the year's work. It was a hard job at any time, but that year it was exceptionally so because of the receipts and disbursements in connection with the Cœur d'Alenes strike. The committee was expected to attend all the sessions of the convention, and to do the work on the books in between times. They brought in a satisfactory report, but none of them had any time to junket around the city.

Representatives of the American Federation of Labor were received at this convention. The warden announced their presence, Boyce appointed an escort, and when the silk-hat brigade entered he gave three sharp raps of the gavel. We all stood up until they reached the platform and sat down. Three raps, and we sat down. The orators were introduced one after the other. One told of the good work that was being done by the Western Federation of Miners for the striking teamsters in San Francisco, not only with financial help, but also in that the western mining camps had successfully boycotted goods from San Francisco. We were glad to help the teamsters in their strike, but many of us, I know, were thinking about what the American Federation of Labor executive board had not done for us in like circumstances.

When the speaking was finished, three raps of the gavel and we stood as the trade unionists filed out. They had received an attentive hearing. Not a word had been spoken except from the platform, not a murmur of applause, no vote of thanks. When the door closed, smiles spread over the faces of the delegates, and many of them burst out laughing. Then we quieted down to the business of the day.

At this convention Boyce asked me if I would be candidate for the office of secretary-treasurer. James Maher was going to quit, as he had been elected treasurer of Silver Bow county, Montana. I told him that I appreciated his suggestion but I was afraid that I would not be capable of filling the job. He said:

"I've been watching your work, and I would not have asked you if I didn't know that you were able."

"Well," I said, "if I'm elected, I'll do the best I can."

I told Johnson and Williams, the delegates from Silver City, that I was going to run for the office of secretary-treasurer. They encouraged me by saying they felt sure I would be equal to it, although it was a big job. I was elected.

The convention decided to move the headquarters of the W.F.M. from Butte, Montana, to Denver, Colorado, which was considered a more central location for the mining industry. There were at that time thousands of unorganized men in the iron and copper regions of Minnesota and Michigan. Then there were the smelters of Kansas and the lead mines of Missouri, which we were going to try to organize.

After the convention adjourned, Ed Boyce, Dave Coates and I were sitting in a restaurant, discussing the situation in Idaho while we ate. Boyce remarked that the board of pardons was going to meet there very soon, and if I were there I might be able to do something to help secure a pardon for Paul Corcoran. He added, "You'll want to move your family here right away; why not do both things on one trip? Could you leave to-night?" I replied, "I have only to pack my grip."

He asked Coates what time the trains left. Dave went to call up and inquire. Boyce said to me:

"Now Bill, take the check book with you and draw for any amount, if there is any chance for money to do any good. From Boise go to Silver City and get your family, and you can be back in a couple of weeks."

Coates returned from the telephone and told us the time a train left that night, and that he had engaged a sleeper for me.

"That's fine," I said, "I'm off."

Shaking hands, they both wished me the best of good luck. I went to the hotel, packed and got to the depot in time to catch the train for Idaho.

When I got to Boise, I met Tom Heney and John Kelly. Kelly had been elected member of the executive board in my place. They were both working in behalf of Paul Corcoran. Heney had petitions signed by nine of the jurymen who had convicted Corcoran. The other three jurors had left the state.

"But there's a more serious situation confronting us," he said; "Frank Martin, the state attorney, is balking. He's afraid of the Lewiston *Tribune*. If we could put five hundred dollars in the hands of the editor for advertising or subscriptions, he thinks it would stop any criticism that they might feel inclined to make."

The following day, the fourth of July, I went to the penitentiary, a mile or so from Boise. The forbidding looking buildings were surrounded by a high wall with a tower on each corner. Over the gate was a sign, "admission twenty-five cents." I told the warden who I was and that I wanted to see Paul Corcoran. He said, "This isn't a regular visiting day, but it's all right, anyway," and sent for Paul.

When Corcoran came in and I introduced myself, he was delighted. He was a fine looking man with a high forehead, a dark mustache, and clear, gray eyes. The year in confinement had already given him the prison pallor. He was working in the shoe shop. We sat down alongside each other at the table in the warden's office. The warden went out and there was no surveillance of any kind.

I spent most of the day with him. He knew that John Williams and I had been to see his wife and babies. He was deeply interested in what had occurred at the convention, and in every thing about the organization. I told him that I had come to meet with the board of pardons and that I already had arranged to see Governor Hunt the next day. "Don't stake too much on it but we are going to do our damnedest!" I said. Then I bid Paul good-by. When I left and looked back at those somber buildings with their bars and shadows, I had no premonition of the circumstances that were to make me better acquainted with their gloomy interior.

The next day I met Governor Hunt in his private office. He greeted me cordially and in the course of our long talk he said that "penitentiaries were not built for men like Paul Corcoran."

"You haven't seen Jules Bassett?" he asked. The board of pardons consisted of Bassett, Frank Martin, and the Governor. When I told him that I had not, he said, "You won't have to see him.

Bassett is all right. But I can't understand Frank Martin." I suggested that he might be afraid of adverse criticism. The governor remarked that there were some things worse than adverse criticism.

When I saw Heney and Kelly I repeated what the governor had said about Corcoran and the remark he had made about Jules Bassett and Martin. I told them that I felt that Corcoran would be pardoned if nothing unforeseen occurred, if not at this meeting of the board, then at the next.

As there was nothing more that could be done, I went directly to Silver City, which was only sixty miles away. The last half of the journey was by stage. I found my wife and babies had gotten along nicely while I was away. The next day I went up to the Blaine mine and was there when the shift came out at noon. The men congratulated me on my being elected secretary-treasurer, and wished me much success. After dinner when they were getting ready to go in, I saw Harry Palmer carrying an armload of drills out of the blacksmith shop. His partner had another load, and then they went back for more. I said to Harry, "It must have tightened up?"

"You never saw anything like it," he answered, "it's harder than the hubs of hell. Come on in and take a look."

"No," I said, "thank you. I'm not going underground again for a year. So long, boys!"

It took only a few days to get my affairs straightened out, and pack up all that we wanted to take with us. We left the house and furniture in charge of a friend, not knowing but what we would be returning after the next convention. With my wife, who was then able to walk, my little girl Vernie, and the baby Henrietta, we left Silver City to make our home for a time in Denver.

We rented a furnished house near the mint. It was within easy walking distance of the new office, which was in the Mining Exchange Building. There we had splendid quarters on the sixth floor. There were four rooms, one of them extra large, and two big vaults. In moving the office by freight from Butte, a lot of work had accumulated. There was mail for nearly three months that had not been opened. The accounts for this period had not been entered in the books. James Maher, my predecessor, had given me some good suggestions, but here was the work itself piled up in front of me. There were hundreds of letters to answer. We got two stenographers and in a short time we had cleaned up most of the correspondence. Shortly afterward Boyce and his wife left for Ireland. I caught their boat at Queenstown with a cable that read, "Paul pardoned." I thought it a good beginning.

The absence of Boyce increased the work. Night after night I stayed at the office until the small hours of the morning. I replied to all the letters that came addressed to Boyce as well as to all my own correspondence. I had to edit and write articles for the *Miners' Magazine*. I posted the books. All this when I was more familiar with the stormy end of a number two shovel than I was with a pen!

When the Boyces returned they lived at our house. He took up the work of the organization again in earnest. When there were matters of importance to discuss, we would sit down at his desk or mine and go over every angle of the situation carefully. When we had arrived at a mutual understanding he would say, as a rule, "Well, we are agreed," or "Let us agree on this." So the matter would stand. I never had to worry about a change of mind on his part. There would never be a reversal of plans or strategy, without mutual understanding.

Boyce asked me for a photograph of our baby, Henrietta, and ran it as a frontispiece in the *Miners' Magazine,* over the caption "our mascot."

Eleanor Boyce had been a school teacher in the Cœur d'Alenes, and was "grub-staking" her father and brothers who were working on a claim called the Hercules. One day she got a telegram saying that they had struck the ledge. It has proven to be one of the biggest mines of the West. She had become overnight worth more than a million dollars. Boyce said little or nothing then about his plans for the future. He had previously announced his intention to quit the presidency at the next election.

I said to Boyce one day at the office that, while Denver was a fine city for the headquarters, we could not stay there unless the thousands of unorganized smeltermen there and in surrounding towns were brought into the organization. It would be necessary to give that part of the organization work our immediate and most energetic attention. An eight-hour law had been passed in Colorado, similar in detail to the Utah law, but it was declared unconstitutional by the state supreme court. The efforts of the W.F.M. and other workers had been directed to securing an amendment to the Constitution, which was carried by the overwhelming vote of 46,714 majority. The American Smelting and Refining Company, the United Reduction Company, with other smelters and milling plants of the state, simply ignored the provision and continued to work men in eleven hours day shift and thirteen hours night shift. I devoted much of my time after office hours to organizing the men employed in the Globe, Argo, and Grant smelters. In this work I was ably assisted by Max Maelich, Joe Mehelic, E. J. Smith and other old-time smelter workers.

The 1901 convention was held in Denver. We had Eugene V. Debs and Thomas Hagerty present, and arranged for them to address a meeting in the Coliseum during the convention week. We got rooms for Debs and Hagerty in a little family hotel called the Imperial. I remember one evening when Debs had got into his pajamas. He was long and lanky and bald-headed, and sat in the middle of the bed with his feet crossed under him and a pipe in his mouth. He was spinning yarns about his past experiences. Hagerty was a Catholic priest, a big man physically, a good scholar, and a fairly good speaker. We expected him to make a strong appeal to the workers of his religious belief.

Debs was already well known to the delegates, as he had helped the W.F.M. as a speaker and organizer when the Cloud City Miners' Union had been on strike at Leadville in 1896. He was known to all of us as one of the finest orators in the labor movement. We all knew his weaknesses and some of us knew of his pathetic letter to John D. Rockefeller appealing for funds for his colonization scheme. In spite of these things we all liked him. He was a genial man and we admired the fight that he had led for the American Railway Union.

Debs was then a Socialist of some years' standing, and Boyce and I had joined the Socialist Party in Denver that year, after the Unity convention in Indianapolis. The principles of socialism were adopted and a vigorous campaign of education was advocated at this convention of the W.F.M. We were to form a bureau of education and our first move in the educational line was to arrange meetings for Debs and Hagerty, who was also a Socialist, through the mining regions. I had talked over with both of them our plans for continuing the eight-hour fight.

Charles H. Moyer was a smelter man from South Dakota. He was a member of the executive board, and this convention elected him president of the Western Federation of Miners. John C. Williams was elected vice-president, and I was reëlected secretary-treasurer. The convention was enlivened by the report of Vincent St. John, president of Telluride Miners' Union, in which he described the working conditions in the Smuggler-Union mine, where a strike had been declared on the first of May. We arranged to make a weekly of the *Miners' Magazine,* and also to employ an attorney as one of the regular staff of the organization. After the convention the executive board appointed John M. O'Neill, a miner from Cripple Creek, as editor of the weekly. O'Neill was a fluent and powerful writer and the magazine grew in popularity. We were fortunate also in securing the services of John H. Murphy, who was at that time attorney for the Brotherhood of Locomotive Firemen. He continued to hold that position as well as doing the legal work for the W.F.M.

In anticipation of the expense that would certainly be involved in a vigorous fight for the eight-hour day, I issued a circular letter describing the life of the smelter men, mill men and miners. I told of the work that we had done towards having an eight-hour law passed by the legislature in different states, and that in Colorado it had been defeated by a stroke of the pen. I told also how the constitutional amendment had been ignored when it was adopted later in Colorado. Now that we had to fight for the eight-hour day, it would involve one strike after another, some of which would become very bitter. We received from twenty to twenty-five thousand dollars in reply to this letter.

Telluride is an important silver and gold mining camp in the San Juan district of Colorado. The Smuggler-Union was one of the big mines there. Arthur Collins was the manager for this company, and introduced the piece system of mining. He would give miners a contract to break ore at so much per fathom. The miners boarded at the company boarding house. They were provided with tools and powder by the company. At the termination of the contract the expenses incidental to their work,—board, powder, candles, tool-sharpening, and so on,—were deducted from the amount owed them by the company. The price per fathom was continually reduced and the exactions of the company increased. In the beginning miners were required only to break the ore, but finally they were compelled to break it in a suitable size and shovel it down the mill-holes or chutes. Telluride Miners' Union of the W.F.M. declared a strike on the Smuggler-Union properties on May first, 1901, for the abolition of the contract system.

Though the union offered to guard the property without expense, guaranteeing protection to the company, the reply of Manager Collins was to employ scab deputies. An agreement was finally reached between Collins and the union, when the contract system was so changed that the miner received at least the union wage for the time that he was employed, and the miner could terminate the contract at any time. This settlement was not arrived at until a pitched battle had taken place between the union men and the deputies and other scabs. Charles Becker, the superintendent of the mine, was shot, two scabs were killed and several were wounded. The rest of the gang was escorted over the mountain. John Barthell, a union miner, was killed outright during the fight.

The *Telluride Journal* carried on a bitter campaign against the union until a close boycott was put on the sheet. Manager Collins succeeded in organizing a business-men's association to sustain the paper. This became later the Citizens' Alliance, the directing force of all the terrorism against the unions of the Western Federation of Miners. Some time later Arthur Collins was killed. Some one fired a load of buckshot into him as he stood near a window.

Governor Orman sent a commission to Telluride, composed of David Coates, then Lieutenant-Governor of the state, Senator Buckley, and John H. Murphy, attorney for the Western Federation of Miners. When this commission made its report it was to the effect that "everything was quiet in Telluride and the miners were in peaceful possession of the mines." This report created a commotion among the employing class in Colorado. The capitalist papers, especially the *Denver Republican,* carried editorials bitterly denouncing the miners.

One day I was at the First National Bank where the W.F.M. did business, when Fred Moffatt, vice-president of the bank, said to me:

"Is this report true that comes from Telluride, about the miners being in peaceful possession of the mines? If that is the case, what becomes of the men who have invested their money in these properties?"

I said: "If we follow your question to its logical conclusion, you'd have to tell me where the owners got money to invest in the mines. Who has a better right to be in peaceful possession than the miners?"

On the twentieth of November one of the tragedies in the history of the metalliferos mines occurred, at the Bullion tunnel of the Smuggler-Union mine. The tram house at the entrance of the tunnel caught fire A carload of baled hay had been unloaded at the mouth of the tunnel. The burning hay, lumber and timber caused a dense smoke, and the tunnel, with connections to the surface, formed a perfect chimney. Edgar Collins, a relative of the manager, and superintendent of the mine, directed spasmodic efforts to stop the flames. Then he gave his attention to removing Winchester rifles and ammunition from a nearby warehouse. Munitions of war were more important to him than the lives of the men inside the mine.

The fire had made great headway before any attempt was made to warn the men at work of their danger. When a messenger was sent in, he attempted to bring the men out by the same entrance he had gone in. All who followed his lead lost their lives, as did several others, though most of the miners escaped through other exits. The fire was still raging when a group of miners from the Tomboy mine, headed by the foreman, Billy Hutchinson, arrived at the scene. He at once gave orders to blow up the mouth of the tunnel. Had that been done as soon as it became evident that the fire could not be put out, all lives would have been saved. The first rescue party was driven back by gas and smoke, but they finally found twenty-five men who had been choked and smothered to death.

When the funeral took place, all mines of the camp were closed down, and delegations came from the surrounding mining camps. There were about three thousand men in line when their sixteen fellow-workers were buried at one time. Each miner carried a sprig of evergreen which he tossed into an open grave.

On the last day of the following February a terrible snowslide at Telluride carried away part of the Liberty Bell bunk-house, killing seventeen men. The terrific rush of snow had swept everything before it, rock, stumps, and brush, and had left a clean path behind. Avalanches happened frequently where the slopes were steep, and the forests had been cut down. They can be caused by a single drop of water from an icicle hanging on the branch of a tree far up the mountain side, or a flutter of a bird's wing might dislodge a particle of snow sufficient to start a mighty slide. A story appeared in a Denver paper in which Adjutant General Gardner was credited with the statement that the deadly snowslide was an evidence of the wrath of God against the unruly outlaw miners of San Miguel county. This foolish remark was intended as an insult to the miners, and it rankled deep in minds already sore from the sufferings of the strike, the fire, and the avalanche.

It is seldom that organizations find their monuments already built, but this unusual thing happened to the Western Federation of Miners. The monument had only to be named. One of the desperate struggles of the W.F.M. was with the gigantic Guggenheim Corporation and other smelting and milling interests in Denver, in connection with the working hours of smelter men. It had taken more than two years of persistent agitation to get sufficiently well organized to demand that the eight-hour law of the state be complied with. This was to be the first step. We had been hoping and working for the strength to strike to enforce this law.

A general meeting of smelter men who were working on the day-shift was held in Globeville town hall on the night of July third, 1903. This meeting was to be the deciding factor and to give the definite answer as to whether there was going to be a strike. Moyer was in Butte, Montana. I telegraphed him about the growing demands on the part of the smelter men for a strike, and of the meeting that was to be held. To my surprise, he wired to "postpone action till I return." Postponement seemed to me inadvisable, if not impossible. I said nothing about Moyer's telegram to the workers, and the program went ahead without a hitch. However, Moyer arrived in Denver just in time to take a desultory part in the meeting. The men were in earnest and enthusiastic, not to be tempered with any idea of delay. They were ready to strike, and wanted to do it at once. There was much rough and ready discourse about the indignities heaped upon them, the injustice of the long hours of work, the enormity of the "long change shift," in which a man worked twenty-four hours through when changing shift at the end of each two weeks.

Some of the workers assumed the high moral ground of compelling the smelter companies to comply with the law and constitution of the state, which made it mandatory that all men employed in certain designated hazardous or unhealthful occupations, including smelter men, should not labor more than eight hours. One contended that the long hours they were working gave married men no chance to get acquainted with their families. Their children were asleep when they left home for work in the morning, and were ready for bed when they returned at night. The general spirit of the meeting showed an awakening of minds long dormant through the inhuman hours of hard work, and of an active, interesting period for the smelting companies while the strike lasted.

It was decided that no one should leave the hall. At the hour of midnight a resolution declaring the strike was adopted unanimously. Outside, cannons boomed, anvils exploded, whistles blew. Fire-crackers were popping. It was the fourth of July. The noise and bedlam was the beginning of the celebration of the Declaration of Independence.

What a hollow mockery! What a miserable sham it seemed! In this stuffy little hall in the capital city of Colorado the spokesmen of thousands of wage-slaves were making their crude preparations for a bitter struggle, not for independence but for a shorter work-day. The fourth of July or any other holiday meant little to the smelter men, for their work must never cease. The fires that melted the ores, like the fires of hell, must never cool. There were no rest days, no Sundays, no holidays. These were the men with whom the real battle was to be fought. They wanted relief from a most vicious system of exploitation by a giant corporation, the head of which was Simon Guggenheim.

It was terrible to realize that most of these smelter workers now striking, fighting for the betterment of themselves and their families, gave little thought to the terrible injustices imposed upon the people of the United States by corporations, bankers, politicians, who have transformed what might have been a free republic into a bestial slave-shambles. Certain it was that these strikers would face priva-tion and imprisonment. They would have to contend with scabs, detectives, courts and perhaps soldiers, they would have insults and indignities heaped upon them, injunctions would be issued against them, and yet some of them would hurrah for the fourth of July!

The strike was to begin at once, as soon as the men on shift could be notified. The men knew that to be forewarned was to be fore-armed. The first knowledge that they proposed the company should have would be when the smelters closed down. The men left the hall in three divisions, the Argo smelter men first because that was farthest away, and then the Globe, the Grant smelter men last. It was intended that the calling of the strike should be simultaneous in the three big smelters. There were to be no parleys. "Quit work. Quit now. Strike!" That was the order. It was obeyed on the instant. The bosses were in a flurry. "Keep up the fires! The furnaces will freeze!" But their orders were not obeyed. The strikers shouted as they hurried about in flare and shadow, "Strike! Strike! The strike is on! Strike while the iron is hot!"

The smelters were in the suburbs of the city. It was some time before the patrol wagons with the Denver police arrived on the scene, and when they got there, there was little they could do. The men had quit work, the strike was on, the battle had begun.

At the Globe and Argo smelters, the bosses and office staff and as many officials as they could call up by telephone, managed to keep the fires going somehow, but at the Grant smelter the furnaces froze, the fires cooled, the metal and slag congealed. These furnaces never blew in again. The smokestack of the Grant smelter is one of the highest in America. Since the fourth of July, 1903, no smoke has curled from its top. It stands, let me dedicate it, a monument to the eight-hour day for which the Western Federation of Miners so valiantly fought.

At the meeting of the miners' committee in the Senate Chamber and the assembly hall, I described the conditions of the men who were working in the smelters, and the kind of homes they lived in, and compared a striker's home with the palace of ex-Governor Grant, who was one of the principal owners of the Grant smelter. There had been a description in the papers of the Grant home and some of the marvelous furniture it contained. I said that a single piece of Grant's furniture would buy a dozen such houses and furniture as the strikers had. I compared the rustling silk of the wives of the smelter owners with the clatter of babies' skulls; the infant mortality of the smelter district was higher than in any other part of the state. After I was through, ex-Governor Grant came to me with tears running down his cheeks and said that he himself was willing to have complied with the constitution of the state and would have tried to make the conditions of the men around the smelter better than they were, but that the company prevented him from taking any individual action.

I had just finished talking with Grant, when Manager Guiterman of the American Smelting and Refining Company, Guggenheim interests, came up and said to me:

"Mr. Haywood, we were taken by surprise when the strike was declared in our smelter, as Mr. Moyer had told me that there would be no strike without notification to the company."

I was astonished at this, as I did not think it possible that Moyer had intended to act as a traitor to the organization. He knew that he was not authorized by his position as president of the W.F.M. to make such a promise, either to Guiterman or to any one else. He further knew that the company would receive no notice if the workers could possibly avoid it, as they intended to make the strike effective. I did not take Guiterman's statement seriously; it seemed untenable and I let it pass as a slander.

The annual convention of the San Juan District Union of the W.F.M. met on August first and passed a resolution demanding the eight-hour day for mill and smelter men in its jurisdiction, to take effect not later than September first, 1903. A committee from the mill men of the Telluride Miners' Union was chosen, their demands formulated and presented to the Telluride Mining Association. The Association replied that some of the men included in the demand were under a contract that had more than a year to run, and that the scale submitted by the committee called for the same wage for an eight-hour day as was formerly paid for ten and twelve hours. A meeting of the union was called and the demands modified. All men under contract were to work as before. There was a general reduction of fifty cents a day wages, men working for four dollars would get three fifty, and three fifty men would get three dollars. Three dollars a day was to constitute the minimum wage of the camps. A committee of the union met a committee from the association composed of Bulkeley Wells, who had become manager of the Smuggler-Union mine after the death of Arthur Collins; Cooper Anderson of the Nellie mine, and A. C. Koch of the Alta. Wells, acting as spokesman, said he would submit the demands to the association. This committee seemed to think that a settlement could be reached on the terms submitted by the District Union. But no reply was ever received and a few days later the San Juan Mining Association, including all the mines of the district, was formed.

The mill men under the jurisdiction of Telluride Miners' Union decided to strike on September first. The miners were all laid off excepting a crew for the development work on the Tomboy mine and the Smuggler-Union property, which continued to operate the mill with the office force and a few scabs. Manager Wells himself put on overalls and took a place in the mills. A few days later the Federal Labor Union of the American Labor Union ordered out the cooks and waiters on the Smuggler-Union property. The miners were discharged and the shutdown was complete.

Discrimination continued in the Tomboy mine, so that a strike was declared against it on October twenty-first. Every man responded. Even the shift-bosses and foremen quit. Pickets to watch the mines were placed at Conn's store. Members of the Citizens' Alliance and deputy sheriffs tried to provoke a fight. They threw rocks at the store and fired a shot at one of the pickets. Next day the pickets were transferred to another store of Conn's near the Smuggler-Union mine. The members of the Citizens' Alliance got busy that night in Telluride and were standing on the principal street corners with shotguns and Winchesters. Bulkeley Wells came out of the *Journal* office with a sack of five rifles. A number of homes were invaded and union men were disarmed. Many men were arrested and held on charge of trespass, for going over a road that had been in constant use for twenty-five years. They were released on bond ranging as high as a thousand dollars.

The mine managers called the strike a violation of a contract that was entered into November twenty-eighth, 1901, and was not to expire until three years later. The union had already protested that the contract had been violated by the company; board had been raised from ninety cents to a dollar a day, black-listing and discrimination was the rule of the Tomboy company and the strike continued. Early in October interviews were held in Denver between the managers and the miners' representatives. Managers Chase, Wells, and Atchison came to the office of John H. Murphy, attorney of the W.F.M., where Miller, Murphy and myself went over the details of the strike with them. The mine managers seemed willing to grant all that the union demanded; we agreed that eight hours should constitute a day's work in the mills and mines, and that three dollars should be the minimum wage. Assistant Attorney General Melville, who was at this conference representing the governor, asked Bulkeley Wells if he was willing to pay the same money to a man on an eight-hour shift that he was paying to a man on a twelve hour shift. Wells replied, "Certainly. I know I can't get my old mill men back for less than three fifty a day."

When this conference was ended, we felt that the strike at Telluride had been definitely settled. But when the managers returned to Telluride there was a meeting of the Citizens' Alliance and things were again upset. Wells said after the meeting that if the matter had been left to himself, Chase and Melville for the owners and Miller, Murphy and Haywood for the miners, the whole thing could have been settled in an hour, but no such negotiations were attempted. The Citizens' Alliance sent a delegation of mine owners to the Governor with a request for troops. Governor Peabody, who had been elected the previous fall, immediately ordered the militia to Telluride. When we heard of this it was like a clap of thunder from a clear sky. I wrote to Oscar Carpenter, secretary of the Telluride Miners' Union, that the militia had been ordered there, and would arrive as quick as a special train could carry them. I told him that the "tin soldiers" were irresponsible and that great care would have to be taken to prevent an outbreak.

At once upon the arrival of the soldiers arrests began. Thirty-eight men were arrested at one swoop on charge of vagrancy; eighteen men at another time. Among them were Oscar M. Carpenter, and J. C. Barnes of the Federal Labor Union. Carpenter had my letter in his pocket when he was arrested. He tore it up and swallowed it to prevent its being read by the soldiers. I would rather they could have read the letter, as his destroying it made them think he had something to hide. These two were taken on a special train to Montrose and thrown in the jail there.

This much news we got by wire. Immediately there followed the proclamation of martial law, and the censorship of the press, telegraph and telephone cut Telluride off from the outside world. The press correspondents were notified that they must submit their stories to the Citizens' Alliance for approval. This order was naturally not popular with the reporters and stories got through to the Denver papers. We sent J. C. Williams, vice president, to Telluride to look after the finances of the strike in the San Juan district, and General Engley, of Cripple Creek, a veteran of the Civil War, to defend the arrested strikers.

One evening a literary entertainment was being held at the union hall, when a detachment of soldiers marched into the hall and read the martial law proclamation. That night, General Engley and J. C. Williams were deported with thirty-one men to the town of Ridgeway. Among them was Guy Miller, then president of Telluride Miners' Union. When they arrived in Ridgeway they were lined up on the sidewalk and told that they had been taken out of San Miguel county because they were not wanted there. A peculiar thing about many of the men who were deported was that they would not stay deported, but returned to Telluride to be run out again. When Williams came to headquarters in Denver, he told us how Joe Barnes had had himself shipped back to Telluride in a barrel.

Williams told us about the deportations. "At eight o'clock Captain Scholes came with a bunch of soldiers to get us. They took us to the court house, lined us up to march to the station. It was bitter cold, and a lot of the men were worried leaving their families like that without any one to look after them. I saw one of the wives coming along nearly at a run, carrying a little kid and crying as she came. She tried to fall in line with us beside her husband, but one of the dirty yellow-legs shoved her back on the sidewalk. We got down to the depot and they herded us onto the train, and just before we pulled out I saw the same woman on the platform, all in with hurrying, and her face twisted up with misery. She climbed on to the train. She couldn't afford to get left behind. She looked too sick to look after the baby, let alone work.

"They were mad clear through, being forced to leave their houses and families like that. They had lived there for years, and here they were being kicked out, 'not wanted,' by a bunch that thought it owned the town. A lot of them made up their minds to go back on the next train they could get."

Williams told us that the union had demanded of County Attorney Howe that the gambling joints should be closed during the strike. They knew that the miners would blow in a lot of their money, and they knew the union would be stronger if the money was in the men's pockets instead of in the pockets of the gamblers.

A. H. Floaten, manager of the coöperative store in Telluride, was with another batch of deportees. He came to Denver. When he appeared at the office, his clothes were torn and the front of his shirt was covered with blood. He told me that soldiers and gunmen had broken into his house one night when he was undressing for bed, that they dragged him out half dressed with his shoes in his hand. He had a gash an inch long on one side of his head, where he had been struck by a gun in the hands of Walter Kinley.

"Why don't you change your shirt?" I asked him.

"Well, I want people to see what happened to me."

"Every one will believe you just as well with a clean shirt on," I told him.

From the time of the deportations following the declaration of martial law, on January third, nothing of special interest occurred until the first of March, when thirty-four men were arrested on charge of vagrancy. Twenty-seven of them were fined $25.00 and costs and given until two o'clock the next day to pay their fines, leave the county, or go to work. Sixteen went to work on the sewers of the city. One of the men, Harry Maki, a Finn, refused to work. He was handcuffed to a telephone pole and left standing in the cold for many hours. Later he was kept in the county jail for thirty-six hours without food.

We had sent Attorney Edmund H. Richardson from Denver to Telluride after they had deported Engley, to help Murphy in the legal work. He didn't have as high an opinion of the law when he returned, although he had secured a reversal of the decision in the vagrancy cases. He said the miners had eleven hundred and forty-eight dollars in cash in their pockets between them when he brought them into court, and beside this they had the union back of them. The prisoners were discharged. Richardson's front teeth were loose. Walter Kinley, the gunman, had assaulted him when he was leaving the courtroom, in revenge for his severe cross-examination.

Our attorney, John Murphy, applied to District Judge Stephens for an injunction to protect the miners returning home from the members of the Citizens' Alliance. It was granted, but the military officials paid no attention to the order of the court. Murphy said it was a remarkable court order that was delivered by Judge Stephens the day he decided to adjourn the May term of court on account of the contempt of the Citizens' Alliance and the military who had invaded the district. The judge said: "It would simply be a farce to attempt to enforce the civil law in this county."

On August twenty-first a gang of mine-managers and gunmen led by John Herron, manager of the Tomboy mine, rode over the range to the Black Bear mine, a coöperative claim that was being worked by a group of Finns. The invaders rolled rocks against the shaft house until the men inside rushed out. They were lined up by Herron and his men and driven over the range. Some of these managers were the same men whom I had met in Attorney Murphy's office in Denver not much more than a year before. Then they had seemed amenable to reason. Now they were a mob of desperadoes, doing the dirty work of the Citizens' Alliance.

Shortly afterward the militia was recalled and the settlement of the strike followed. In the latter part of November the mines posted notices that the eight-hour day would be put into effect on the first of December, with a scale of wages identical with that demanded by the union fifteen months previously. The scale included the cooks, bakers, waitresses and dishwashers.

During the long period of this strike only seventeen members of the union had deserted, of the many hundreds of members in San Juan District. After the settlement of the strike, the Citizens' Alliance continued to keep in their employ gunmen such as Runnels, Meldrum and Kinley. These continued to threaten and intimidate the miners and they drove many men out of the district, telling them that any one who spoke against Governor Peabody could not remain in San Miguel county.

CHAPTER VII

TIN HOUSES AND AUTOCRACY

THE eight-hour fight in Colorado was looming up as one of the biggest things the organization had ever encountered. The unions of the Cripple Creek district sent some of their best men to the convention of May, 1902. Sherman Parker, Bill Easterly, Dan Griffis, Bill Davis, Charles Kennison, D. C. Copley and John Harper were there. St. John came from Telluride and Frank Smeltzer from Silverton. E. J. Smith represented the Denver smelter men. The convention was unanimous for pressing the eight-hour fight to a successful end. It endorsed what was being done by the mill and smelter men. All over the state, in Telluride, Durango, Florence, Canon City, Pueblo, Idaho Springs and Denver, the agitation for the eight-hour day was going on. This was soon to break in the Colorado industrial wars.

The convention again unequivocally endorsed the principles of Socialism. The policy and principles of the Western Federation of Miners were of much concern to the mine owners of the West, but some puerile-minded Socialists, such as Victor Berger, referred to the struggles that developed as "border feuds," intimating that they were not of much interest to the Socialist Party.

In my first articles in the *Miners' Magazine* I had proposed that the Western Federation should get control of mines by lease, bond, location or purchase. The idea seemed at the time a solution of some of the difficulties that we were constantly meeting. I introduced at this convention measures to this end, and was helped by Tom Hurley, who had been at one time a coal miner in Pennsylvania. I often wondered if he was the same Tom Hurley that McLain had told me about in his story of the Molly Maguires. He laid before the convention delegates definite plans of the coal beds of Routt county, which were then open to entry or location. Hurley reasoned that the W.F.M. could form a subsidiary company to get control of the land underlaid by coal, for the general organization.

There was no question about our ability to open, develop and operate the mines. That was the work we knew how to do, and we could do it better, more scientifically, with much greater regard for the health, lives and happiness of ourselves if we had the management. But large bodies move slowly. David Moffatt, president of the First National Bank of Denver, who had been a member of the board of arbitration in the first Cripple Creek strike in 1894, acquired the land in Routt county, taking it right off our plate, so to say. Other opportunities offered, but were simply neglected.

The effect of the acquisition of banks and mines upon a labor organization is now clearly shown, for example, in the Brotherhood of Locomotive Engineers. The scab mines of the Brotherhood in West Virginia are notorious examples. They are capitalistic ventures and are operated as scab concerns. Labor banks are not a coöperative effort of the workers, but a means of developing class collaboration. They strangle the principles of unionism and convert the members into part-time capitalists.

I realized the need of getting the women to help us in the Federation, and the convention adopted a resolution to form women's auxiliaries wherever it was possible, and urging us to strengthen the existing District Unions and organize others where it could be done.

The delegates were invited every year to visit the Underhill factory, where some two hundred girls were employed in making overalls and jumpers. The miners enjoyed the event, and so did the girls. Casual acquaintances were made, and often developed into real romances which resulted in the girls changing their vocation to that of a miner's wife in some outlying mining camp. After one of these visits, a resolution was offered by one of the delegates to introduce a uniform for a special rank in the organization. His idea was to deck us out like the Knights of Pythias or the Shriners. Susie Scheidler, one of the garment workers, had given me a miniature pair of overalls and a jumper to match, that she had made. I pulled them out of my pocket and held them up before the delegates. I supported the resolution, offering the overalls and jumper as a sample of the uniform we should adopt. Every one began to laugh. There was never any more nonsense about uniforms.

The mill and smelter men of Colorado City organized into a union of the Western Federation of Miners, early in 1902. The members of this little body were active, and the membership increased every meeting night. I went there on two occasions with President Moyer, and several times alone to help the new members in their work. We had D. C. Copley, Bill Davis and other members from the Cripple Creek district to help them at different times.

Colorado City was the site of some of the plants that reduced the ores from the Cripple Creek district. After the gold-bearing ore had gone through the reduction works there was little left but tailings and dross. None of the refined gold was left in Colorado City, nothing but waste and slum. This forlorn little industrial town of tents, tin houses, huts and hovels was bordered by some of the grandest scenery of nature. It was in the very shadow of Pike's Peak, only a short distance from the glorious Garden of the Gods. The wonderful medicinal waters of Manitou Springs were nearby, almost a suburb of the aristocratic residential city of Colorado Springs, with its beautiful homes where the owners and managers and other highly paid officials lived.

The officials of the reduction plant were arrogant and defiant. They adopted the old system that had been in vogue since the days of the Molly Maguires—that of employing Pinkerton detectives, spotters and stool-pigeons. From early in August until February, 1903, forty-one men had been discharged and had been told that it was because they had joined the union.

The Colorado City Mill and Smeltermen's Union Number 125 before declaring a strike sent a letter to the mill managers, calling attention to the discharge of many men because they had been members of the union, asking for their reinstatement and submitting a scale of wages. The union received no reply to this communication, but the companies continued their blacklisting until the fourteenth of February, when a strike was declared that closed down all the mills. The people of the town had discovered the Pinkerton detective who was leading the spies in their work at Colorado City. One day almost the entire population turned out and went to his rooming house, where they told him to pack up and get out of town, as they did not want him in their midst any longer. They escorted him to the edge of the town and he never returned.

The mill managers were supported by the Mine Owners' Association, and had the backing of the mongrel body called the Citizens'

Alliance. Secret meetings of these bodies were held, and plots were hatched that would bring the state militia to the scene.

Wherever it existed this Citizens' Alliance was a nest of venomous conspirators, with a banker at its head, a well-dressed, soft-palmed, white-collared parasite. The tough gambler, the lazy preacher, the nasty pimp, and others of the business element were found among its members. This body was fostered by the Mine Owners' Association, which likewise controlled and directed the State Militia, the county sheriffs, and through their office as many deputy sheriffs as it wanted. The constables and police of towns and mining camps as a rule were willing to do the bidding of the big mining companies. It would seem that these combined forces were strong enough for any legal purposes; but no, they must organize the Citizens' Alliance and employ ex-convicts, murderers and gunmen, such as Bob Meldrum, K. C. Sterling, Frank Varnick, D. C. Scott, Walter Kinley, Willard Runnels and many others of the same desperate character. With these plug-uglies the mine managers became close associates, and with their assistance villainous schemes were put into action. A. E. Carlton, banker, was the head of the Citizens' Alliance of Cripple Creek. A banker was the prime mover of the Alliance in the San Juan district. Another banker was the leader of the Citizens' Protective League at Idaho Springs, a small mining camp in Clear Creek county, a short distance from Denver.

Reporters from the Denver papers, and Alva Swain of the *Pueblo Chieftain*, came to the office of the W.F.M. They grouped themselves around my desk, two or three sat on the sill of the big half-circle window, and asked me various questions about the strike at Colorado City. I talked to them in detail, and they published the interview.

"The occasion of the strike was the refusal of the mill managers at Colorado City to treat with or recognize the union. Our men were discharged because they belonged to the union, and they were so informed by the managers. We asked the operators to reinstate these men and consider a wage scale. They would do neither. We claim a constitutional right to organize as do the operators, and we want wages that will enable our men to move into houses and not rear their families in tents. During the bitter cold weather the wives and children of many of the men were huddled together in tents because the wages paid would not suffice to pay house rent and provide other necessities. The scale we ask is lower than in any milling or mining camp in Colorado. The minimum scale paid is one dollar and eighty cents a day, out of which one per cent discount is deducted, and five cents taken off for compulsory insurance. We object to compulsory insurance. Checks are not drawn in favor of the men, but of the merchants with whom the men trade."

When the mill owners and representatives of the Mine Owners' Association realized that the strikers were masters of the situation, a picture was drawn by the corporations to present to the governor, that would justify the state militia being used to break the strike. The governor, in his message to the legislature, after having taken the oath of office, was emphatic in his assurance that he would uphold law and order. Such words coming from the chief executive of the state were wisely interpreted by the capitalist mill owners, who knew that the governor would never call out the state militia to prevent them from working men at starvation wages.

On the third of March, at the hour of noon, the governor who only a few months before had been living on usury, issued an order that gratified the mill managers. Moyer and I at once drafted the following address to the unions and the other workers of Colorado:

The chief executive of the State of Colorado has ordered the militia to Colorado City. The governor of this great commonwealth, after giving audience for several hours to Manager MacNeil and the representatives of the Mine Owners' Association, men who are pecuniarily interested in the degradation and subjection of labor, sends the armed power of the state to aid the merciless corporations in demanding their pound of flesh from the bone and muscle of men who have borne the tyranny of greed until patience has ceased to be a virtue.

Manager MacNeil acted as a deputy of the sheriffs and handed to the governor the following letter:

I hand you herewith a communication from the Portland Gold Mining Company, operating a reduction plant in Colorado City, and from the United States Reduction and Refining Company from which I have received requests for protection. I have received like requests from the Telluride Reduction Company.* It has been brought to my attention that men have been severely beaten and there is grave danger of destruction of property. I accordingly notify you of the existence of a mob and armed bodies of men patroling this territory, from whom there is danger of commission of felony."

It does not appear from the letter of the sheriff that he made a per-

---

* Not to be confused with Telluride, the mining camp previously mentioned.

TIN HOUSES AND AUTOCRACY 113

sonal investigation of the conditions existing in Colorado City. The communication from the corporations to the sheriff of El Paso county actuated the sheriff in placing in the hands of Manager MacNeil, a member of the corporations, an order to Governor Peabody, and upon the strength of this letter the armed force of the state is to be placed at the disposal of the corporations, to be used in intimidating labor to fall upon its knees in mute submission to the will of the oppressors. No word came from the citizens of Colorado City to the governor stating that there was a mob or insurrection. Depending absolutely on the unsupported representations of the corporations and a letter from the sheriff, an officer who from his own letter has failed to make a personal investigation, the governor of this great state has become a willing tool in the hands of corporate masters to place the armed machinery of Colorado in the hands of the corporations.

The governor listened attentively to the gory story of MacNeil, the representative of the corporations. Why did he not summon the representatives of labor and hear their evidence as to conditions in Colorado City? Is there only one side to a story when the interests of corporations are to be subserved and labor humiliated?

The Western Federation of Miners, through its executive officers, appeals to the laboring hosts of Colorado, to denounce this unpardonable infamy of the governor by pouring into the present legislature an avalanche of protests. The hour for action on the part of labor is at hand, and the voice of the producing class must be heard in thunder tones in the legislative chambers of the state, branding this shameless abuse of gubernatorial power with the malediction of their resentment.

CHARLES MOYER, President, W.F.M.
WM. D. HAYWOOD, Secretary-Treasurer.

Feeling ran high in Colorado City when the citizens learned that the State Militia had been called out by the governor and sent to their town. This was resented not only by the mill and smelter men, but in other and unexpected quarters. The mayor and members of the city council held a meeting and telegraphed a protest to the governor:

Governor Peabody, it is understood that the militia has been ordered to our town, for what purpose we do not know as there is no disturbance here of any kind. There has been no disturbance more than a few occasional brawls since the strike began, and we respectfully protest against an army being placed in our midst. A delegation of business men will call upon you to-morrow with a formal protest of the citizens of the city.

More than six hundred of the citizens of Colorado City signed a petition which was presented to the governor, requesting that the militia be recalled. The governor's answer was:

I will not recall the troops until the trouble is settled. There are no agitators running this administration. . . . If a man wants to work he has a perfect right to do so, and the troops are there to see that everybody's rights are protected.

On March tenth I expressed myself as follows, in the Denver papers:

The rights of personal freedom and liberty of speech are being violated. The strikers' pickets are being arrested on the public domain, when not attempting to encroach upon the company's property. They are not permitted to speak to the men in the mills, although their purpose is the peaceable one of persuading the men to quit work. So many of the non-union men have left the mills that the company is getting desperate.

Now, the situation is this: the miners of the state do not propose to submit to such oppression. They are advocates of law and order and they will not long permit it to be violated even by the state's chief executive. There is grave danger in pushing oppression too far, and it is certain that the miners are now in a mood to strike back. They will preserve their liberties and retain their rights if it is necessary to pass through the red sea of revolution in order to do so. Colonists had less occasion to rebel against the authority of King George than have the miners of Colorado to resist the oppression of Governor Peabody. '

During the progress of the strike the reporters came to the headquarters of the W.F.M. every day and sometimes several times a day. They asked me if I thought the mill workers of Colorado City would arbitrate their differences. I told them that I thought they would do anything within reason. On March sixth the *Denver Post* sent this telegram to the Colorado City mill managers:

Are you willing to submit to arbitration the troubles between your company and the mill workers employed by you, the arbitration board to be appointed by joint arrangements of the parties involved? Please answer at our expense. The Denver Post.

This is one of the replies they got:

There is no trouble between our company and mill workers employed by us. Our employees are and have been perfectly satisfied with wages and treatment. Wages paid by us more and hours of labor less than ore reducing plants with whom we compete. Our employees don't ask to arbitrate. Our plants are full handed and all our employees and plants require is protection from the violence of outsiders not employed by us. We would be pleased to have your representatives visit our plant and fully investigate.

C. E. MacNeil, vice-president United States Reduction and Refining Company.

In the same issue with these telegrams there was published a scathing editorial, which I quote at length here, because it sets forth the basis of the troubles that were developing and breaking out all over Colorado at this time.

C. E. MacNeil, stand up!
Was not this telegram of yours endorsed by the other mine managers? Is it true that it is a subterfuge?
Is it not a brazen falsehood from beginning to end?
Is it not a carefully worded telegram, prepared to hoodwink the people of Colorado?
Is it not intended to make the people believe the mill managers are more sinned against than sinning?
Are you not laughing at your own cunning and flattering yourself that you have made a master stroke and have fooled the people?
Your answer to each of these questions, if you are truthful, must be: "Yes."
Read your own telegram, Mr. MacNeil.
"There is no trouble between our company and mill workers employed by us."
Is it not a fact that your employees are on a strike?
You must answer "Yes."
"Our employees are now and have been perfectly satisfied with their wages and treatment."
Is it not a fact that your wages were so low that the men were hungry more than half the time?
Is it not true that your employees were forced to pay insurance and medical assessments and trade in your stores?
Is it not true that many employees were forced to live in tents because you would not pay them enough to pay for a house?
To each of these questions you must answer "Yes."
You say, "Wages paid by us are more and hours of labor less than ore reducing plants with whom we compete."
You know that is a barefaced lie, don't you?
Is it not a fact that the Woods Investment Company pays higher wages for less hours of work than you do?
Answer "Yes."
You say, "Our employees don't ask to arbitrate."
Is it not a fact that they have offered to arbitrate and you refused?
Is it not a fact that you say "There is nothing to arbitrate" to these men?
Is it not a fact that you are trying to break up the union?
Is it not a fact that you have refused and do refuse to recognize the rights of the men to organize?

Do you not know that this right is guaranteed by the Constitution of the United States that gives every man the right of liberty and pursuit of happiness?

Do you know that you are seeking to deprive these men of their liberty and deprive them of their happiness by grinding them down to the level of serfs?

You must answer "Yes" to these questions or tell a deliberate lie.

You say, "Our plants are full-handed and all our employees and plants require is protection from the violence of outsiders not employed by us."

Do you know that lies teem in every word of that sentence?

Craftily as you have couched that sentence, do you not know that it will not fool the people of Colorado?

Is it not a fact that your plants are not full-handed?

Is it not a fact that there has been no violence?

Is it not a fact that you had the troops called out to awe men who were asking only that you pay them money enough for their labor to allow them to live decently?

Is it not a fact that citizens of Colorado Springs and Colorado City to the number of hundreds have signed petitions to Governor Peabody declaring that there was no violence?

Do you know that these troops are costing the state of Colorado $2,000 a day and that there is absolutely no use for them in Colorado City?

Is it not a fact that you have those troops there just to excite violence?

You must answer "Yes."

Is it not true that your company has twelve million dollars of watered stock and pays dividends on starvation wages?

Answer "Yes."

Don't you know that you must answer "Yes" to these questions?

This is what the Western Federation of Miners stands for:

"To secure compensation fully commensurate with the dangers of our employment and the right to use our earnings free from the dictation of any person whomsoever."

Do you endorse that for yourself personally?

Answer "Yes."

Is there any reason why every man should not endorse that?

You must answer "No."

Here is another point the miners stand for:

"To establish as speedily as possible and so that it may be enduring, our right to receive pay for labor performed, in lawful money and to rid ourselves of the iniquitous and unfair system of spending our earnings where and how our employers or their agents or officers may designate."

Is that not right?

Will you consent to any one dictating to you how or where you will spend your salary?

Here is another point the miners stand for:

"To use all honorable means to obtain and promote friendly relations between ourselves and our employers, and endeavor by arbitration and conciliation or other pacific means to settle any difficulties which may arise between us, and thus strive to make contention and strikes unnecessary." Does this not show that your employees are ready to arbitrate? Is that not an honorable and fair stand for a man or men to take? You must answer "Yes." Mr. MacNeil, stand up. . . .

Such an editorial could not appear in America to-day. At that time the press was comparatively free and unhampered by either bankers or industrial capitalists, although the advertisers had the controlling influence on all papers. The papers of Colorado were largely dependent upon the miners for circulation. Twenty-five years ago the great interests, in their war upon labor, had not yet completed their united front, and an occasional voice of protest could be heard through a gap here and there in the iron ring. This has all been changed since Imperialism began to assert itself in America. Just preceding the World War, for example, one hundred and twenty-five of the most prominent papers all over the country were bought up for the preparedness campaign.

The governor could no longer maintain his pretense that there was nothing to arbitrate. Public sentiment became so strong that he was forced to use his office in bringing together both parties in the controversy. The governor called a meeting of the mill managers and the representatives of the W.F.M. at his office on March fourteenth. W.F.M. was represented by President Moyer and myself, with John Murphy. The atmosphere was heavy with antagonism. There was not a man there who was not bitterly opposed to the W.F.M. Mac-Neil was a dapper little man, the quintessence of the capitalist class, one who had never in his life spoken to a workingman except to give orders. He had the air of having been dragged in by the hair of the head to a meeting to which he was opposed before it started. Fullerton of the Telluride mill was of the same type, but younger and more pliable. Peck was a man of some experience who struck me as having at one time been a worker; with him we had little difficulty in coming to an agreement. The conference lasted from two o'clock Saturday afternoon until three Sunday morning, at which time we had come to terms with Peck and Fullerton. They agreed to the eight-hour day, no discrimination against union-men, reinstatement of the strikers, and that they would meet a committee of the union to discuss a scale of wages. MacNeil assumed a stubborn attitude, forcing himself out of the conference with the Portland and Telluride managers, but at the request of the governor he agreed to meet us the following day. We met MacNeil at the appointed time, but he refused to say that he would reinstate the strikers, or that he would meet a committee of the union on a question of wages, or that he would comply with the eight-hour law. Six men had come to an agreement. The governor had told us that he would withdraw the militia at once. One wretched little autocrat was able to strangle our efforts, and his stubbornness was responsible for the strike that followed. He could not have withstood the pressure alone. What powerful backing was pushing him on? The corporations? The church? The Citizens' Alliance? He must have come to that conference with definite instructions.

By March seventeenth the militia had not yet been withdrawn. We issued a statement of our efforts to arbitrate to the unions and the press.

Cripple Creek District Union Number 1 had been in closest connection with the strike at Colorado City, and knew all about the efforts that were being made in Denver with MacNeil and the settlements with the Telluride and Portland mills. Moyer had been in Cripple Creek at a conference of District Union Number 1, where it had been decided to call out the men working in mines furnishing ore to the Standard mill. This decision was not put into execution until four o'clock on the afternoon of March seventeenth, as a committee of business men asked to be given time to talk to MacNeil, to try to persuade him to accept the terms of settlement. The business men failed, and the ultimatum of District Union Number 1 went into effect. On the same day the governor withdrew the troops from Colorado City.

Governor Peabody sent a commission to Manager MacNeil at Colorado City, and to this commission MacNeil promised to comply with the eight-hour law and to adjust wages according to the terms of the other mills. While this was not the settlement we had demanded, District Number 1 determined to declare an armistice until May eighteenth, to give MacNeil opportunity to live up to the terms of his agreement with the governor's commission. When the news of this armistice reached the public of the Cripple Creek district there was a general jubilation and the mines began breaking ore to supply the plants of the United States Reduction and Refining Company. But MacNeil seemed to have forgotten that he had ever made any promises to the commission. The minimum wage for outside work was two dollars, and for inside work two sixty-five, at the Telluride and Portland mills, but MacNeil continued to pay only one seventy-five a day. District Union Number 1 took up the case again with MacNeil. They sent committees and had conferences, trying to induce him to pay the same wages as the other mills. MacNeil admitted that one dollar and seventy-five cents a day was not enough for any man to bring up a family on, but he positively refused to grant the request of the union.

The Mill and Smeltermen's Union of Colorado City was a part of Cripple Creek District Union Number 1. The miners of the District Union saw the necessity of helping the mill workers, whose fight was also theirs, and this call was issued:

All members of the Western Federation of Miners and all employees in and about the mines of the Cripple Creek district are hereby requested not to report for work Monday morning, August tenth, 1903, except on property shipping ore to the Economic mill, the Dorcas mill at Florence, and the Cyanide mills of the district.

By the twelfth, as rapidly as the committee could issue the order, the mines were closed down.

On the fourteenth, the Mine Owners' Association issued the following statement:

A general strike has been called on the mines of the Cripple Creek district by the executive heads of the Western Federation of Miners. At the time this strike was called, and, in fact, ever since the settlement of the labor difficulties in 1894, the most entire harmony and goodwill had prevailed between the employers and the employed in this district. Wages and hours of labor have been satisfactory and according to union standards, and general labor conditions have been all that could be wished.

Notwithstanding this, the heads of the Western Federation of Miners have seen fit to compel the cessation of all labor in the district, not because of any grievance of their own against the Cripple Creek operators, but for reasons entirely beyond our control. A no more arbitrary and unjustifiable action mars the annals of organized labor, and we denounce it as an outrage against both employers and the employed.

The fact that there are no grievances to adjust and no unsatisfactory conditions to remedy, leaves the mine operators but one alternative, and that alternative they propose to adopt fearlessly. As fast as men can be secured, our mining operations will be resumed, under former conditions, preference being given to former employees, and all men applying for work will be protected to the last degree.

In this effort to restore the happy conditions which have existed so long, we ask and confidently count on the coöperation and support of all our former employees who do not approve the methods adopted, as well as of the business men of the district who are equal sufferers with us.

In the resumption of operations, preference will be given to former employees, as before stated, and those desiring to resume their old positions are requested to furnish their names to their respective mines at an early date.

This article was signed by about thirty managers of mine properties, and also by C. C. Hamlin and A. E. Carlton, a banker who later became chairman of the Citizens' Alliance.

Five days after the strike was declared the miners of the district had a picnic at Pinnacle Park. John C. Sullivan, president of the Colorado State Federation of Labor, formerly a Cripple Creek miner, was one of the speakers. Moyer, Copley, Davis and others spoke. There was plenty of enthusiasm and determination among the miners and their families who had gathered in the park. When I was called on, I bantered a little with the Mine Owners' Association, the Citizens' Alliance, and the Pinkerton detectives, some of whom were present, and whom I charged with being responsible for the strike.

I told the miners:

The mine owners have said they would finish the El Paso tunnel themselves. I know there are many of you here who will lend them your cast-off overalls!

This raised a derisive laugh from men who knew what working underground was like. I went on:

I deny the statement signed by the mine owners, wherein they assert that the strike in this district was forced or compelled by the heads of the W.F.M. This strike is by members of the unions of this district. It is a strike of the W.F.M. against the inhuman conditions of life imposed upon the men working in the mills, reducing the ores that you produce. Our brothers, the mill men of Colorado City, have used every possible method to induce MacNeil to come to an agreement, or even to live up to his promises made to the commission that was sent to him by Governor Peabody. . . .

I challenge the mine owners when they say that affairs in this district have been all that has been asked for since 1894. This is contradicted by the continuous and bitter discrimination against members of the W.F.M. by the El Paso, Strong, Ajax, Gold-King and some other mines. Such action does not tend toward harmony and goodwill.

The laws of Colorado are good enough for a union man, but they are not good enough for the corporations of this state, or the corporations would not spend vast sums to corrupt every legislature that is elected. . . .

There are many mining camps throughout the West where every man working in or about the mines is a union man. Why cannot the same conditions prevail here?

The Western Federation of Miners was born of the oppression of the mine owners, but it has grown under that oppression. This organization is your life, your only security, and in this fight we must stand with it to the end.

After the picnic I had a chance to speak to the secretaries of the different unions. I urged them to send me photographs and descriptions of any "weak sisters" that broke ranks. I had an idea for a circular that I thought would stiffen them up for the fight.

We had passed through one convulsion of martial law, in the eight-hour struggle. Out of it had come a partial victory for the workers at Colorado City. The 1903 convention was in unanimous accord as to the progress made. The year's work was reviewed, the books were audited, plans were made to strengthen the organization, which had grown from 12,500 members, at the time I was elected secretary-treasurer, to more than double that number in 1903. We had accumulated some funds. The delegates seemed confident that the membership would respond to any assessments that might be required.

The struggle that we had tried so hard to avoid, but for which we had made some small provision, had begun.

CHAPTER VIII

CRIPPLE CREEK

In the latter part of July a compressor on the Sun-and-Moon mine at Idaho Springs had been blown up. The destruction had been charged at once to the Western Federation of Miners. A few nights later the homes of eighteen miners were invaded by the sheriff and his deputies. The men were taken to jail in spite of the tears and pleadings of their families. They were not formally arrested, as the sheriff had no warrants. He did not even make a charge against any of them, but the next morning he turned them over to a mob of the Citizens' Protective League, by whom they were roughly treated and escorted out of the town.

This was during the armistice before the second strike in Cripple Creek, and while the Denver smelter men's strike was absorbing some of our attention. A committee of the men from Idaho Springs came directly to headquarters at Denver, while the others followed the gang that had run them out, back to Idaho Springs. I talked over this affair at length with the committee and got John Murphy's advice over the telephone. We decided that the best thing to do would be to appeal to the governor. The committee started off to the capitol building and Murphy came over to the office to see me. He said when he came in that he didn't expect any favorable results from the visit to the governor, and that in his opinion we should immediately apply to Judge Owers of Clear Creek county, who had his offices in Denver, for an injunction against the members of the Citizens' Protective League in Idaho Springs.

It so happened that Governor Peabody told the committee that he could do nothing in the matter, that they should appeal to court. This we promptly proceeded to do. Judge Owers granted an injunction which he made permanent. When criminal complaints were filed by the miners against the members of the Protective League, Judge Owers cited bankers, gamblers, pimps, preachers and the rest of them to come into his court, and he read them a lesson they had never heard before.

Later Governor Peabody gave out an interview to the press in which he insulted Judge Owers. A few days after this—it was the same day that the Cripple Creek strike was declared, I remember—Judge Owers called me up on the telephone, saying:

"Haywood, at your convenience I'd like to talk to you on a matter of some importance."

I told him that I would come over to his office at once. When I got there, the judge was stretched out on a long wicker couch. He looked tired and worn, in bad health, but there was an inspiring flash in his eyes.

"Pull up a chair," he said. As I sat down, he went on: "I've been preparing to write a letter in answer to Governor Peabody, and I'd like to have you hear me dictate it. You may be able to offer some suggestions."

He called in his stenographer and, referring to some notes, he dictated the open letter that appeared in the *Rocky Mountain News.*

To his Excellency, Hon. James H. Peabody, Governor of Colorado; Dear Sir:—

In the *News* of Saturday, August fifteenth, 1903, you are reported as having, in an interview on the labor troubles at Cripple Creek, spoken as follows:

"I anticipate no trouble, however, either here or at Cripple Creek. The miners are beginning to understand that they cannot violate the law. They cannot assassinate men, neither can they destroy property. Not even if they do have the protection of District Judge Owers. For that reason I do not think we will have to order the militia out any place. But they must all understand that order must be preserved if they do not want the state to take a hand."

When I casually read the interview, I dismissed it from my mind as an error, on the theory that no man occupying the position of governor of this state could be so lacking in all sense of decency and justice as to make such a statement about a member of the judiciary. . . .

In the interview you directly charge the miners of the state as a body with violation of the law, assassination and destruction of property, and me, as a district judge, with protecting them in the commission of each and all of these crimes.

The law presumes all innocent until proven guilty. I am not aware and have not heard that any miner has as yet been tried, let alone convicted, of any crime connected with recent labor troubles in this state. I have not heard that any miners either as individuals or as a union or otherwise, have openly boasted of the commission of any crime or misdemeanor, or openly avowed responsibility for, or approval of the same in any manner, let alone by adopting and publishing resolutions approving thereof and offering to aid and abet the same. On the other hand, it is a matter of common knowledge that in Denver, Idaho Springs and elsewhere throughout the state, an organization has openly assumed the responsibility and boasted of its pride in the recent mob violence and outrage at Idaho Springs, and concerning which you have not so far raised your voice in condemnation or protest. . . .

When the expelled men from Idaho Springs appealed to you to be restored to their homes, you were prompt with a denial of help, based upon technical interpretation of your duty. You advised them with many platitudes to appeal to the courts for redress. They asked for bread and you gave them a stone, yet they followed your advice, and when the court, appealed to, restored them to their families, doing in two days what you dared not attempt in two weeks, you hasten with characteristic vacillation to serve your masters by expressing your chagrin and disapproval of the action of the court by publicly insulting the judge who presided, and who had the courage to perform the duty you recognized but shirked.

I fear, had fate been so kind to Colorado as to have made me a governor, I should be brutal enough to disregard the frantic appeals of hysterical sheriffs for militia, whenever the destruction of a chicken-house should be threatened, and I might even insist that the powers of a county should be used, before disgracing the state by ordering the militia at enormous expense to climb a hill and then climb down again. I might even, through lack of moral sense, were I governor, if appealed to by men claiming to have been expelled from their homes by a mob, feel it my duty, in defiance of precedent, to use the militia to restore them to their wives and children, and enforce the rights guaranteed my fellow-beings by the Constitution and the law. I might even, in such event, be impolitic enough to disregard the fact that the expelling mob was composed of "our best and most prominent citizens." . . .

In conclusion, may I venture to hope for a reply to this letter through the press as soon as you can get some one to write an answer for you, and will you kindly particularize your grounds of complaint against me?

Respectfully,

FRANK W. OWERS.

I told the judge that there was a difference between him and us. We used a dull ax on our opponents, he used a rapier. My only contribution to the letter was the last paragraph, where I suggested that the governor would have to get some one to write his answer for him. Evidently he could not find any one, as the letter remained unanswered.

After the letter had been disposed of, the Judge said:

"The Miners' Union at Leadville is having a hard time of it."

"Yes," I answered, "and it's getting worse. Since they've organized the Citizens' Alliance the bitter discrimination of the Mine Owners' Association makes it very hard for the union to get ahead. And it's hardest on our best members. You know, to lose their jobs is about the worst thing that can happen to them, and that usually happens first to the most active men."

"I know they've tried several times to hamper and handicap the miners' union," said the judge. He added, "Next week I'll be filling a temporary vacancy in the Leadville district. The judge there is taking a holiday. I want to suggest that if a carefully prepared application is presented, while I'm on the bench there, an injunction would be issued. John Murphy is a painstaking lawyer, talk things over with him. We want this injunction to be 'iron-bound and copper-cornered.'" After a little more talk, I left him, and went to see Murphy.

"This is rather unusual," said John, "but I'll make the application, and if the injunction is granted and enforced it will give the miners full protection."

Murphy went to Leadville while Judge Owers was on the bench. Here are some of the judge's remarks when the injunction was granted:

The appellants are members of the Cloud City Miners' Union Number 33, W.F.M. All of them are engaged in the mining industry, one of the chief industries of the State of Colorado, from whence a great part of the wealth of the people of the state is obtained. The appellants are the important factor in the production of all of this wealth. Without them production would at once cease, and in a short time the present populated mining region would become a howling wilderness, as the business element would soon leave if there were no mine workers to exploit. The appellants are most of them miners who every day shake dice with death. Not only is the labor of the men hazardous, but it is also unhealthful. The union which they have formed and of which they are members is their chief support; it is the medium through which their wages are maintained and their hours regulated. The union provides succor for them when injured or in sickness, and a funeral benefit for their families when they are called by the summons of death.

It is the opinion of eminent jurists that it is the law of state and nation that working men have the right of association and coöperation for their mutual benefit, which in this instance means that the men employed in and around the mines of Leadville have the right to belong to the Miners' Union.

The parties against whom this application for an injunction is directed are the owners of the mines in and about Leadville. Many are among the most prominent and substantial citizens of the community. Other owners are absentee stockholders. Such an injunction, if issued, would be against all owners. Some of the mining companies, it seems, have registered membership in the combination set forth (the Mine Owners' Association) in the names of their respective managers or superintendents. Cognizance will be taken of this fact.

None will at this time attempt to deny that the mines and property belong in fact and in accordance to the law to the present owners, though the charter under which the Miners' Union is working proclaims that "labor produces all wealth; wealth belongs to the producers thereof." This, or a similar maxim, was at one time expressed by Abraham Lincoln, but with this sentiment the laws and the courts of the land do not agree, and certainly the mine owners are not in sympathy with the notion. The mines belong to them and in this inalienable right they will have the protection of this and all other courts. The mine owners have the right to form themselves into a mine owners' union, not so named, but the equivalent. The mine owners' union can be used for the mutual lawful protection of their joint property. They have the right, after their lawful indebtedness is defrayed, and the meager wage of their employees deducted, to the accumulated residue or unearned increment. The mine owners' union or its members individually or collectively should not be, and are not, held in liability for the aged or injured who are in their employ. . . .

The citations of this petition are such as to lead one to imagine the remote possibility of the rights of the members of the miners' union having been infringed. The prayers of the appellants are, however, substantiated by a large number of affidavits. Therefore the opinion of this court is that the injunction be granted and at once issued. It is hereby made permanent. Violation of any clause is punishable by imprisonment for one year or fine of five hundred dollars or both.

This injunction granted to Cloud City Miners' Union enjoined the Mine Owners' Association from interfering in any way with the business of the Miners' Union, or discharging men because of membership in the organization. Although the regular judge of the district was not inclined to enforce the injunction, after Judge Owers' return to Denver, yet it did prevent the Mine Owners' Association of Leadville from joining forces against the miners with the associations of other districts.

A few days after my talk with Judge Owers, I went to see Senator Patterson at the Welton street office of the *Rocky Mountain News*. When I came in the senator was at his desk. He invited me to sit down and asked how things were going. I told him about the situation in Telluride, Idaho Springs, Colorado City, and about the smelter men's strike in Denver, and said that I wanted to speak to him about an article that he had printed charging the officials of the W.F.M. with having called the Cripple Creek strike. I explained to him that the members of the unions of Cripple Creek had called the strike through their district union.

"Oh," he said, "that's a small matter, Haywood."

"But, senator," I answered, "that's one of the charges that the Mine Owners' Association makes against us."

He said, "Well, we'll have to let it go this time. You can make the correction in some future statement that you publish."

This did not please me at all, but there was nothing to be done about it. Just as I was about to leave, the senator said:

"Haywood, where did this man Moyer ever make noise enough for you to find him?"

I told the senator who Moyer was, and that he had proven to be a very good organizer. He remarked emphatically:

"He has not the manly fiber or the stability required in a man to be the executive officer of such an organization as the Western Federation of Miners. I'm certain that you will find this to be true before you get through with him."

I remarked that the present situation would try the best of us, and thanked the senator for the generally friendly attitude of his papers.

Cripple Creek district was on the crest of a spur range of the Rocky Mountains. Here nature, the conjurer, had shaken up the porphyry dikes and into each split and seam had spurted up gold-bearing quartz or quartzite, which congealed. To the dismay of mining experts, the same old nature wizard split the mother granite and filled its cracks and crevices with gold. This untold wealth remained hidden through all the ages, until 1889, when a forlorn prospector, whose view of the scenery was obscured by the hind end of a jackass, dug with a dull pick into a streak of rich ore. That was the beginning of one of the world's greatest gold mining camps.

Men like that poor prospector have found the riches of the world. Wandering prospectors found the mines of Kalgoorlie, Witwatersrand, Klondike, Siberia, the diamond mines of Africa, the nugget of Ballarat, the iron mines of Sweden and America, the copper mines of Chile and Peru, the silver mines of Mexico. But the wealth they have found has always slipped into the coffers of the exploiters.

In 1903 the Cripple Creek district was producing twenty-four million dollars a year. Small cities and towns were built on these summits, some of them above timber line. Railroads climbed, twisting, tunneling, trellising mountains to the very shaft-mouths at the top.

Cripple Creek and Victor I found to be neat substantially built towns with streets and avenues, marked here and there with high smokestacks indicating mines in the center of town. The miners' unions in the different camps owned their own buildings, usually two stories with the lower floor rented to some merchant, and on the upper floor halls, club rooms and library. The halls were rented out to various fraternal societies. The Cripple Creek Miners' Union had a library of eight thousand volumes. The miners of this district as a body were as widely read men, and of as high a standard of intelligence, as could be found among workingmen anywhere. They lived in pleasant little cottages, with such flowers in the yards as would grow at ten thousand feet above sea-level. The town of Altman was the highest, over eleven thousand feet.

For years the miners and business men had associated with each other, belonged to the same fraternal societies. They were mostly American born. But the strike had been on only three days, when on August thirteenth, 1903, the merchants of Cripple Creek district, through the influence of the Citizens' Alliance, announced that from that day on, their business would be conducted on a cash basis. As usual, all the miners had paid their bills on the first of the month, and the merchants expected to catch the miners without enough money to carry them through the month.

George Hooten of the Anaconda Miners' Union came to Denver and talked over the situation with me. They needed potatoes badly in the district. I authorized him to look around the city and see what he could do with the jobbing merchants about getting two or three carloads of potatoes. He found three carloads of Greely potatoes, came back and told me what they would cost. I gave him a check for the amount, including the freight. When the potatoes arrived at Anaconda they were sold to the miners right out of the cars. Then we got some carloads of flour. As we bought in wholesale quantities and paid cash, we got lower prices and saved discounts and were able to sell these commodities to the strikers and their friends for less than they could be bought in any store in the district.

A little later Hooten, with Tom Parfet of Cripple Creek and John Harper of Victor, came to Denver to talk over the proposal I had made to the unions, to start stores as a means of distributing strike relief. It was the first time this had been tried in America. These three men had been appointed store managers by their unions, and it was the intention to put the stores in our own buildings as soon as we could have them vacated. With this agreement, the three managers went to the jobbers and wholesale merchants of Denver and selected their stocks of goods.

I got out a series of coupon books with the emblem of the organization on each coupon, each book containing coupons of different values. These were good at face value for anything in the store.

When our stores were vacated by the merchants who had occupied them previously, we moved in our stocks of clean, wholesome goods. There was a meat market, a grocery, and a green grocery in each store. The stores were a big success. We did a large cash business besides the strike relief. Not having to make big profits for the stockholders, nor large salaries for the managers, we were able to sell first class goods cheaper than they had ever before been sold in Cripple Creek district. We had the merchants so worried that they were in a state of insomnia. There was not a striker nor a working member of the union but was well pleased with the experiment. They realized an increase in real wages, through being able to buy necessities so much cheaper. We had good luck, too, in having such good men for managers, and in having our own stores from which we could not be evicted.

It seemed that the management of the El Paso mine was going to start a little circus of its own, as they built a high board fence all around that mine. For this and other work they paid the scabs in their employ a dollar an hour, which was large wages considering that the miners of the camp had not asked for more than three and a half a day. The members of the District Union were on the job and learned that an attempt was going to be made by the Mine Owners' Association to destroy the old shaft house at El Paso Number 2 in order to blame it on the strikers and have an excuse to bring in the soldiers. The miners prevented this by making the foul scheme public.

By this time the secretaries of the unions had sent me pictures of scabs and strike-breakers with detailed descriptions. I got out a circular, headed by a description of a scab in lurid terms. In the center of the poster was Bill Gleason, a notorious strike-breaker, one of the leaders among the scabs. Around his picture I put a circle of others, with their personal descriptions, and sent about two thousand of these to the Cripple Creek district to be posted up on telephone poles, billboards, and other public places. One miner pasted a copy on the plate glass window of a Victor store. Bill Gleason came along and recognized his picture. He became so angry that he pulled out his six-shooter and smashed the circular, plate glass window and all.

The strike had been on only two weeks when a conference was held with James Burns, the president of the Portland Mining Company, and a settlement was brought about which put seven hundred men to work. The Portland mine was one of the leading properties of the district. At that time it had produced seventeen million dollars in gold. The management was exceptional. During the strike of 1894 an agreement had been reached at once and the Portland never shut down during that strike, and would not have done so at this time if there had not been a misunderstanding between the manager and the committee from the district union. The district union reported to headquarters that when terms were reached with the Portland and the men went back to work, the city of Victor went wild with joy. We took it as an indication that the strikes on the other mines would not last long. It was about this time that we seemed to have reached an agreement with the mine managers of Telluride also, but the conspirators of the Citizens' Protective Association were at work.

A commission had been sent to Cripple Creek by the governor composed of John Chase, N. C. Miller and Tom E. McClellan. This commission, which came on what the people of the district described in their resolution of protest, as "a brief and stealthy visit," went through an alley into the rear entrance of the Victor Bank, and from there dodged around and reached Cripple Creek, where they called Sheriff Robertson into conference. The sheriff did not agree with them that the troops were necessary, but the mayors of Victor and Cripple Creek nevertheless submitted letters, identical in language from both of them, which said that the sheriff and other peace officers were utterly unable to preserve order and protect lives and property, and requested that the National Guard of Colorado be sent to the district immediately. The sheriff had told the commission that he had authority to employ all the deputies he needed, that he had the situation in hand, that there was no trouble in the district and had been none, no unusual assembly of men, saloons were closed at midnight. "The sending of troops here is a usurpation of authority on the part of the governor," he said.

The executive committee of District Union Number 1 stated that the commission had made no effort to see them, or to meet any representatives of the Western Federation, nor did they intimate any desire to hear the Federation's side of the difficulty. But the commission reported that they had made careful investigation among citizens and property owners, including the mayors of Cripple Creek and Victor, and said that they were "of the opinion that the lives of the citizens of the district are in imminent danger and personal rights are in jeopardy. Prompt action is necessary. . . . We find that a reign of terror exists in the district. We do not believe that the civil authorities are able to cope with the situation." This blood-curdling report was made in face of the fact that there had not been even a fist fight in Cripple Creek district, and the further fact that one of the leading mines—the Portland—was already at work.

A thousand soldiers got off the train at Cripple Creek, where everything was quiet. They established stations on every hill around the town, Cow Hill, Bull Hill, Pisgah, Nipple Hill, Squaw Hill, and St. Peter's Dome. Here they had telescopes, telegraph connections, heliograph signals, and search lights to rake the town. They took possession of the district. The citizens had to have passes from the military to go about their own town, or along their own roads.

These soldiers were under command of Adjutant General Sherman Bell, who was to receive from the mine owners thirty-two hundred dollars in addition to his regular salary. The mine owners had also agreed to pay five hundred thousand dollars for the maintenance of the troops while they were in the district. Here I should add that the mine operators of Telluride had also agreed to pay for the soldiers who went to the San Juan district.

After the militia arrived, a shipment of one thousand Krag-Jorgensen rifles was received from Wyoming, and sixty thousand rounds of ammunition. These war supplies could have come from no other source than the federal government.

At headquarters we got a telegram from Cripple Creek:

The civil power has been supplanted by military despotism. The laws of the state are overridden with impunity and the powers that be are using the glorious American flag to cover crimes against the Constitution of the illustrious State of Colorado and the bill of rights of the United States of America. The rights of property have supplanted the rights of the individual and a lawless mob (militia) are arresting citizens without authority and at their pleasure. Please arouse the citizens of the state and save us from this anarchism, militarism, un-American blatherskitism and Bellism.

It was signed, "Victims of Military Despotism."

The city council of Victor protested against the action of the mayor, saying that

he has wilfully misrepresented the conditions existing in this city, and we are informed as wilfully misrepresented the desires of the citizens. He left the council chamber when the council was in session to meet the advisory committee, without asking for an expression from any member of the council as to whether his contemplated action would meet with approval. His action was taken wholly upon his own motion and without knowledge or consent of any member of the council. We condemn it now and would have condemned it then, had we known his intention.

The conditions he represented do not exist and have at no time existed. The laws of the state and the ordinances of the city are and have been lived up to and respected by the citizens and property owners, and fully enforced by the officers of the law.

This protest was sent to the governor and to the press, and we got a copy at headquarters. Mass meetings were held in all the towns of the district, strong resolutions and petitions were drawn up. From Victor came a resolution that summed up the dreadful condition of things.

Even the Democratic Party and the Grand Army Post of veterans of the Civil War vigorously protested against the presence of the militia. The people of the district protested with a loud and unmistakable voice, but Governor Peabody's ears had been bought by the Mine Owners' Association.

The miners of the district took advantage of Labor Day, which fell upon September seventh that year, to make a splendid demonstration of their solidarity. Five thousand men were in line in Victor. The newsboys, forty of them, took part in the parade and made perhaps the best showing of any of the unions, as they were dressed in appropriate costumes and kept up a constant cheer and hurrah for the strike. Soldiers lined the sidewalks, and at some points were stationed in companies.

In Denver the officials of the Western Federation of Miners had been invited by the Trades Assembly to take part in the Labor Day parade. In accepting this invitation I paraphrased Spartacus' address to the gladiators: "Ye do well to invite the Western Federation of Miners, the fighting organization which has met on the industrial battlefield every shape of Citizens' Alliance, Chamber of Commerce, and Mine Owners' Association that the broad empire of the West can furnish. . . ." For the parade I had ten thousand scrolls printed with the constitutional amendments violated by the Peabody administration in a black border. Each of the paraders carried one of these scrolls as he marched through the streets of Denver.

While I was at the office, my wife, who was again bedridden, spent much of her time alone, although we had a woman working for us. Some one introduced a Christian Science reader to her. Having nothing to do, my wife began taking treatments from this woman, who professed to have the power of healing. Her imagination dwelt on the possibility of relief from her sufferings through the medium of Christian Science, as doctors had not been able to cure her. One charlatan woman and then another gave her treatments. Sometimes when she had a "claim," as they called an attack, she would have our oldest daughter, Vernie, telephone to one of these female ascetics, who would "hold" for her, or give her "absent treatments"—at so much per treatment. My wife became a devout reader of *Science and Health,* which was made up of the vagaries of a fanatical and ignorant old woman. To me it was all nonsense, based on that profane compilation of fables called the Bible. But it was useless for me to protest. If these so-called treatments gave her any comfort of mind, I could stand for it. But when it began to influence my children, it drove me nearly mad.

Liquor and I had been almost strangers. Now I found it to be a sympathetic mistress, that would lull me out of an ever-present, ever-growing misery. My work at the office was absorbing and steadily increasing. The strikes were not only growing in number but in intensity. We had a craven, underhand, murderous force to contend with, the Citizens' Alliance. After a day's work at the office, I would start home, stop in a saloon, maybe two, on the way, to get a drink of whisky to dull my mind against the thought of the superstition that was fastening my family in its meshes.

There were meetings in Denver at night, meetings out among the smelter men, meetings of the party, committee meetings, but never too much work. Never enough to keep my mind busy.

Mother Jones came to Denver about this time. I went to the Oxford Hotel to see her. She was a fine old woman with snow white hair and a baby complexion. She had a pleasant voice, but how it could rake and rasp when she was talking about her enemy, the capitalist class!

When she was a young woman, Mother Jones had struggled in the South against the yellow fever and had lost her husband and children, who had all died of the terrible disease. She came North, and in revolt against the helplessness of poverty, began to work at organizing the coal miners. Her work in West Virginia made a thrilling record. Wherever trouble broke out against the miners, Mother Jones went there. When a bridge was patrolled by soldiers, she waded the river in winter; when trains were being watched, the train crew smuggled her through. She always went where she wanted to go. When she came to Colorado, she had lost none of the courage and stubbornness that made this little old woman so hated and feared by the employers.

"Mother" went to Trinidad while the strike of the coal miners was on. One day I sent her a telegram saying that the troops were leaving for Trinidad in the morning. I later learned that this telegram was a great surprise to Governor Peabody, who said that at the time I had wired, he had not yet issued the order. He couldn't understand how I knew the troops were going, as he hadn't spoken about it to any one.

Shortly after the arrival of the soldiers in Trinidad, Mother Jones, with three other organizers, was deported. The old woman was hustled out without consideration, and had but a few moments to pack her things. She was shipped to Helper, and when she arrived there, they arrested her and put her in the pest-house, where they hoped she would catch smallpox or some other disease that would kill her. But she escaped the next day and came to Denver.

A notorious magazine, called *Polly Pry's Magazine,* printed a frightful tirade against Mother Jones. John Mitchell of the United Mine Workers seemed to think that there was some truth in the things that were written, and to his lasting disgrace he discharged Mother Jones as organizer, after all the brave work she had done for the miners of West Virginia, Pennsylvania, and elsewhere. I was glad to get her as an organizer for the W.F.M. She worked for us a short time during the Cripple Creek strike, but then took up her work among the coal miners again.

There were two jacks who came to Colorado during the coal-miners strike—one a jackass and the other the jack of spades; John Mitchell, president of the United Mine Workers of America, and John D. Rockefeller, Jr., among whose many interests was the Colorado Fuel and Iron Company.

The coal miners of the West had first been organized by the Western Federation, but as the United Mine Workers, made up only of coal miners, extended its jurisdiction, the coal miners dropped away from us and joined it. When John Mitchell came to Denver he stopped at the St. James Hotel, and passed the office of the W.F.M. on his way to pay his respects to the Citizens' Alliance! It was natural to suppose that he would have come to the Western Federation, if for no other purpose than to thank the organization for the support that it had given the United Mine Workers during the strike of 1902. The treasurer of the U.M.W.A. in compiling his report of the contributions, had mentioned the different unions and had given the sum total as coming from the international which they made up. But the unions of the W.F.M. were scattered all through the report. Sexton, the editor of the U.M.W.A. *Journal,* wrote an article in which he mentioned two or three contributions as being the total amount contributed by the Western Federation. I went through the report and found that the W.F.M. had been the largest contributor per capita of any organization in the United States. In addition to this financial support, we had offered to lay down tools in every coal mining camp where we were organized, if the U.M.W.A. would make the strike a general strike.

There were sixteen strikers of the U.M.W.A. from the northern field in jail in Denver for violating an injunction while Mitchell was there. He did not go to see them. He went to the Citizens' Alliance. The unions of the U.M.W.A. and the W.F.M. were fighting jointly for the eight-hour day. John Mitchell did not represent the workers who were on strike.

I have said that the coal miners of the West were first organized in the W.F.M., but this is not true as to all of them. Some, among them the miners of Hanna, Wyoming, were organized as independent bodies. A large majority of the Hanna Union were Chinese. There was a strike at Hanna in which the Chinese took the lead and when the white men were weakening after a long time on strike the Chinese went around to them and offered to double their relief, if they would but stand firm to win the strike.

A tragedy had occurred at Ely, Nevada. We felt it necessary to send John Murphy there to learn the details. When he returned it was to report that the union, deciding to make some demand of the company, had appointed a committee of three to see the superintendent. As the committee approached the office the superintendent, who had been notified of their coming, seemed to have become panic stricken. He started to shoot with a Winchester rifle, killing all three of the unarmed men. Murphy learned that the superintendent had at once made his escape from the town. Nothing was ever done to prosecute him for the three murders.

The smelter trust was successful in getting a unique crew of strike-breakers at Durango for a few days. They were Navajo Indians. But the native Americans did not take kindly to the work they were called on to do. One evening a pow-wow was held at which a young chief spoke:

"For a long time Navajo Indians live in this country. Long before white men come. We grow corn, we make blanket, we have lots of sheep. We get lots of deer, catch fish, live pretty good. White man come, he make smelter. Make everything hot like hell. Make fire-water; cold water hot. Make work night time. Night sleep time. Navajo no more work night time. Navajo no more work in smelter. To-morrow we go home."

The strike of the Denver smelter men was extending to the workers in other industries, and for a time it looked as though the city of Denver would be involved in a general strike, but the development was squelched by the typographical union, which, as a result of the disturbances, secured for themselves a seven-hour twenty-minute day. They callously left the smelter men alone to fight against eleven and twelve hours a day. In the course of my work I went to a meeting of the typographical union. When the president introduced me, he said that I would "entertain them for a few minutes." I told them, when I took the platform, that I had not come to entertain them. I had come to make an appeal on behalf of the Denver smelter men, who were workers the same as they, and to whom they owed a duty as union men, and that duty was to give the Denver smelter men their entire support. I left before the discussion, to speak at another meeting, and I never heard of any action being taken.

Governor Peabody said the soldiers were in Cripple Creek to assist the civil authorities. They showed this by arresting, among the first, County Commissioner Lynch and Justice of the Peace Reilly. They took Lynch from his dinner table, put him on a horse, and with troops and trumpets brought him into the presence of Generals Bell and Chase. They had served no warrant on him, and had made no charge, but the generals told him they did not want him to talk about the militia in the terms that he had used, and that he would have to quit bolstering up the strikers. After this catechising he was permitted to go home. The same treatment was given to Justice Reilly.

The bull-pen was established in connection with the military camp at Goldfield. Charles Kennison, president of the Cripple Creek Miners' Union Number 40, was the first man arrested and put in the bull-pen, although when he heard he was wanted he had given himself up to the sheriff. The sheriff turned him loose and then he was arrested by the military.

Sherman Parker, Bill Davis, Bill Easterly, Paddy Mullany, Lafferty and others were arrested without charge and thrown into the bull-pen. We got the firm of Richardson and Hawkins of Denver to take part in the defense of these cases, with Frank Hangs and old General Engley as well as John Murphy. These lawyers sued out writs of habeas corpus and had them served upon Chase and Bell.

There was much delay on the part of the generals in bringing the prisoners into court, and when they finally did so, it was under an armed force with a gatling gun trained on the courthouse and sharpshooters stationed on the roof of the National Hotel and adjoining buildings. While the court was in process of hearing the cases, twenty tin soldiers armed to the teeth stood with their backs to the judge, their rifles in their hands.

John Murphy, addressing the court, said:

"1 refuse to proceed with this case under the conditions which surround the court. This is not a civil process, this is an armed invasion." The prisoners were taken back to the bull-pen.

Next day they were brought back into court. This time the soldiers again filled the court, but they left their gatling gun behind them. Judge Seeds' argument for his decision to release the accused was long and very strong. In scathing language he discussed the usurpation of authority by the invading National Guard under Generals Chase and Bell. He ordered the prisoners discharged.

General Chase announced that he would not abide by the decision of the court, and to the dumfounded amazement of every one, he commanded the soldiers to take the prisoners, who were marched out of the court that had freed them. Later, in the evening, without any explanation, the men were released. The governor must have telegraphed Chase that he was going too far.

CHAPTER IX

IN THE CRUCIBLES OF COLORADO

THE Colorado militia was made up of clerks, business men and lawyers who in peace time were using the organization for dances, boxing matches and other amusements. Most of the clerks were members of Max Morris' union. Max was a member of the executive board of the American Federation of Labor, and the international union of which he was secretary was an artificial organization which existed for the purpose of allowing Max to hold his official position. He was a personal friend of Sam Gompers, who was frequently criticized for allowing a few hundred clerks to be represented on the executive board. Many of these so-called union men were at this time in Cripple Creek, Telluride and Trinidad doing the dirty work of the Citizens' Alliance.

The long campaign in Cripple Creek compelled the militia to offer bounty for substitutes, as they were being kept away from their businesses too long. The militia was then filled up with thugs from the slums of Denver, Chicago and other cities.

General Sherman Bell had three leaders of our women's auxiliaries arrested, Margaret Hooten of Anaconda, Estelle Nicholls of Cripple Creek, and Mrs. Morrison of Victor. They were brought before the generals and told that they would have to "behave themselves" or they would be put in the bull-pen. The women wanted to know just what was meant by "behaving themselves," but they got no answer to this question, and were turned loose.

Then Bell issued orders that all guns in the district must be registered. This order was not complied with to any extent, as most of the miners had no intention of turning over their arms, or even registering them with the military authorities. General Engley, the Civil War veteran and attorney for the Federation, deliberately strolled through the streets with his shotgun over his arm. John Glover, another lawyer, wrote a letter which he published, saying that he had two unregistered guns and if the militia wanted them they would have to come to his office for them. A detachment of soldiers did go to his office. He held them at bay, until, seeing that they were trying to fasten him in, he began to shoot. The soldiers returned a volley of twenty-five or more shots, one of which struck Glover in the arm. Then he surrendered and was put in jail. Before he was released they compelled him to say that he would not give an interview to the press about the incident.

General Bell, trying to earn his extra salary, sent a detachment of soldiers to the office of the Victor *Record* one night. The *Record* was publishing the official statements of the Western Federation. They arrested the entire staff, taking them off at once to the bull-pen. Emma Langdon, the wife of one of the linotype operators, herself a printer, got out the paper that night, with a flaring head-line, "Slightly Disfigured But Still in the Ring."

General Sherman Bell, anticipating the Kaiser's "me and God" by several years, announced to the people of Cripple Creek and the world at large: "No one knows but me and God and Governor Peabody what is going to be done." He wanted it known that he was "going to take no further orders from the civil authorities unless specifically instructed to do so by Governor Peabody."

General Tom McClellan said, "To Hell with the Constitution. We are not going by the Constitution, we are following the orders of Governor Peabody." The phrase, "To Hell with the Constitution," is famous to this day. This was such a glaringly unpatriotic statement, coming from a general of the militia, that I used it as the headline of a poster, printing below it some parts of the Constitution that had been violated by the soldiers and authorities of Colorado. The boys pasted these up at night on bill-boards and telegraph poles and other places. Next day soldiers under the orders of General Bell were busy scratching them off.

About this time the Citizens' Alliance managed to have us turned out of our offices in the Mining Exchange Building. This would have happened sooner, perhaps, but it had been our custom to pay a year's rent in advance. We moved into the Pioneer Building only a block away.

One night I had paper laid out on the dining room table at home. When my wife called out from the next room and asked what I was doing, I replied:

"I'm making more trouble for Peabody." I was at work on what became the notorious "desecrated flag" poster. I drew a rough picture of the United States flag, with a caption at the top, "Is Colorado in America?" On each stripe of the flag was an inscription:

Martial Law Declared in Colorado.
Habeas Corpus Suspended in Colorado.
Free Press Throttled in Colorado.
Bull-pens for Union Men in Colorado.
Free Speech Denied in Colorado.
Soldiers Defy the Courts in Colorado.
Wholesale Arrests Without Warrants in Colorado.
Union Men Exiled from Homes and Families in Colorado.
Constitutional Right to Bear Arms Questioned in Colorado.
Corporations Corrupt and Control Administration in Colorado.
Right of Fair, Impartial and Speedy Trial Abolished in Colorado.
Citizens' Alliance Resorts to Mob Law and Violence in Colorado.
Militia Hired by Corporations to Break the Strikes in Colorado.

I had a picture of Henry Maki chained to the flagstaff. The photograph had been taken in Telluride, where he was chained to a telegraph pole during the strike. Under this was the title "Under the Folds of the American Flag in Colorado," and under the flag, "If Old Glory is desecrated, it has been done by the Governor of Colorado. The strikers are struggling to enforce the laws of the state and to break not only the chains that bind Henry Maki, but the chains that bind all the workers." Following this was an appeal for funds for the Colorado strikers, with the signatures of Moyer and myself.

Victor Poole, a young miner, was in and out of the bull-pen and jail many times. Finally Governor Peabody declared the writ of habeas corpus suspended in his case, and said that he must remain in prison. We followed this decision by applying to the federal court. While the case was pending the military authorities, fearing that the writ would be granted, contrived to have charges preferred against Victor Poole for a minor criminal offense which had been forgotten if it had ever been committed. They turned him over to the sheriff of the county and in this way slipped from under a writ that would in all probability have been granted. Poole was not an official of the union. His continued persecutions caused much comment.

The Vindicator mine was under guard of the militia, but an explosion on the six-hundred-foot level that killed the foreman and superintendent was charged to the Western Federation of Miners. From the examination they made of the mine and the evidence introduced, the coroner's jury was unable to determine the cause of the explosion. Sherman Parker, Charles Kennedy, Bill Davis and Tom Foster were charged with this crime and placed under arrest, but the district attorney quashed the indictments for lack of evidence. The persecution of these men had become a byword in the district. They had been arrested and re-arrested, charged with nearly everything to be found in the annals of crime, but never once was any of them convicted of the slightest offense.

Parker, Davis and Foster were out at this time under large accumulated bail, though they had not been charged with any offense and no crime had been committed. None of the previous accusations having been fastened on these men, a serious charge was being framed up against them.

A certain lodging house in Cripple Creek was the rendezvous of the gunmen and detectives of the Citizens' Alliance. There the thugs planned their vicious conspiracies. It was there no doubt that Sterling and Scott arranged with Beckman, the Thiel detective, and McKinney, a rounder and pimp, the details of a proposed train wreck, the responsibility for which was to be placed upon Parker, Foster and Davis.

Scott had already inquired of a railroad engineer named Rush, where the worst place would be for a train wreck. Rush told him that if a rail were loosened at the high bridge, it would throw the train down an embankment, three or four hundred feet and kill or injure all the passengers. Scott told Rush that he must be on the lookout at a certain hour that night when he was driving his train.

At the identical spot near the high bridge, Rush stopped his train and took the fireman and others ahead, where they discovered that spikes had been pulled and a rail had been loosened. A wreck certainly would have occurred if he had attempted to run his train over the spot, carrying to death or injury between two and three hundred people. Kennison, the president of the Victor Miners' Union, and many other union men were on the train.

Sherman Parker, Bill Davis and Tom Foster were arrested as the principals of this terrible crime. When they were brought to trial McKinney was the star witness for the prosecution. He testified that he had done the job with the accused, but after a severe cross-examination admitted that he had testified at the instigation of Sterling and Scott, who had promised him a thousand dollars in cash and a ticket to anywhere he wanted to go. If he should be arrested and convicted, they had guaranteed him a pardon from Governor Peabody.

Beckman admitted that he would be willing to kill two hundred or more people for five hundred dollars. The attorneys for the Western Federation demanded his immediate arrest, and called upon the district attorney and his assistant to do their duty. But the detective was never arrested. Sterling and Scott also testified, but the slimy wretches fastened all the blame on their tools, Beckman and McKinney.

The final witness for the prosecution was Rush, the engineer, who testified that Scott had asked him where the worst place for a wreck would be, and that he had tipped him off that an attempt would be made at the place designated near the high bridge.

Without calling a single witness for the defense, without a word being said by the defendants in their own behalf or by the attorneys of the Western Federation in behalf of them, the judge ordered the jury to bring in a verdict of "not guilty."

A few days after this victory, Moyer and I went to Cripple Creek district to see the stores and visit the district union. Before we left I said to him:

"I don't propose to spend any time in the bull-pen."

"Well," he said, "what are you going to do if they arrest us?"

"Let's shoot it out with them," I said.

We took a couple of extra revolvers in a handbag. I told him:

"If we don't need these we can leave them with the boys."

Everything was perfectly quiet in Cripple Creek. We went to the hotel and left our grips, as we did not expect any attempt at arrest in the daytime. We visited the union stores at Goldfield, Victor and Cripple Creek, but for lack of time we did not go to Anaconda. The members of the district union reported that things were going along as well as could be expected. Some of them told amusing stories about the "desecrated flag" poster, and the sensation it had made when it was posted upon the billboards and telegraph poles. Some of the boys had pasted copies of the poster high up on the poles and said that the soldiers who were trying to scratch them off had to hang on like monkeys.

On our return trip we stopped at Colorado City to visit the mill and smelter men. There was a good spirit among them. They all felt certain that the strike against McNeil would be won. We returned to Denver very well satisfied with the outlook in the district.

The military authorities and the Citizens' Alliance did not like the turn affairs had taken, and had another convulsion of martial law. At this juncture there was a strange twist in the mentalities of Peabody and Bell, who had but a short time previously appealed to President Roosevelt for Federal soldiers. Now they sent a joint telegram offering to provide two thousand soldiers to help steal the republic of Panama for Roosevelt. Roosevelt, however, pulled off the job without help from Colorado.

The law-and-order element, which always means the silk-stocking people, were extremely busy in the Denver municipal elections. The ladies of Capitol Hill changed their costumes frequently, and each voted several times during the day. They were vying with the activities of Cooney-the-Fox, who was supposed to control the Democratic repeaters under the direction of Billy Green, the boss of Green county, which comprised the barrel-houses and houses of prostitution on Market Street. Even this section of the city had been invaded by the aristocracy of Capitol Hill. Little Billy was handicapped. He couldn't tell the well dressed, painted and powdered dames of Capitol Hill from the regular girls of the red-light district.

Reports from different wards came trickling into the office of the Western Federation, where we were quietly at work on election day. Dan MacDonald, president of the American Labor Union, had just arrived from Butte. He and Moyer were talking about the election, when one of them suggested that we should visit some of the voting booths of the nearby precincts, just to see what was going on. As we started I slipped my 38-caliber Colt into my hip pocket.

From the office we walked along Fifteenth Street to Larrimore, down to Eighteenth, then to Market. We saw some interesting groups, but no unusual activity. Then we made our way back to Eighteenth and Champa Streets, where we went into a saloon through the rear door; all saloons were supposed to be closed on election day. Mac and Moyer had a drink, I took a cigar.

As we were going out, we met a gang of deputy sheriffs, headed by a young man who was a nephew of Felix O'Neill, captain of the

Denver police. They all wore badges. Moyer sarcastically remarked:

"Pretty badges!"

O'Neill said sharply: "Don't you like 'em?"

Moyer replied, "Indeed I do: I'd like to have one for my dog."

He no sooner said it than one of them struck him squarely between the eyes. The man must have had on brass knuckles. As Moyer fell, his head struck the stone threshold and he lay quivering. The captain's nephew whipped out a big six-shooter, swung at Mac-Donald and struck him across the forehead, lifting his scalp about three inches. As Mac fell he broke his arm. I knocked the young fellow back and then had the whole bunch to deal with. I had not time to think how desperate was the situation: it was a fight for life. One of them struck me on the head with a gun. I dropped on my knees off the curb of the sidewalk, and drew my revolver. The captain's nephew was rushing up to give me another blow; I shot him three times in quick succession. He staggered back and started to run. I got to my feet and the other deputies ran away pell-mell, O'Neill following them with his gun pointing straight up in the air, and yelling like a Comanche Indian. I could not fire again as the opposite sidewalk was crowded with people. A policeman hurried up; he knew me, as they all did, and said:

"I'll have to take you to the station, Bill."

"Certainly," I replied, and stepped into the patrol wagon when it arrived. Meanwhile the ambulance came and took MacDonald and Moyer to the hospital.

At the station I was booked with assault to commit murder, and put in jail, only to be taken out a few minutes later to have my head dressed by the doctor. Young Jim, the captain's nephew, had just been brought in. I was told he had been badly hurt. I asked the doctor to fix him up first, as there was nothing serious the matter with me. My three bullets had hit him in the left arm, permanently crippling it. Two bullets had lodged in the bone, or I probably would have killed him, as his arm seemed to be across his body when I shot him. The surgeon remarked, as he was stitching the scalp wound in my head, that I was fortunate it was no worse. I said:

"I'm sorry I hurt him so badly, but from now on I'll carry a stronger shooting gun."

It was but a few minutes later that Coates and Pettibone came to the jail and I was released. I went home to report to the family these details of a quiet election day. Officially I never heard of the incident afterward.

Early in January, 1904, a vagrancy order was issued by General Sherman Bell. It was to include all the idle men in the district. This meant, of course, the striking miners. We at once issued the following notice from headquarters:

NOTICE

TO ALL MEMBERS OF THE WESTERN FEDERATION OF MINERS of the CRIPPLE CREEK DISTRICT: It has been decided in many courts that members of organized labor are not vagrants. Keep your union cards and refuse to be driven from home. If compelled to leave by force of arms, union men are advised to return immediately to the Cripple Creek district. The Western Federation of Miners will provide for all striking miners' families.

CHARLES H. MOYER, president, W.F.M.
WM. D. HAYWOOD, secretary-treasurer, W.F.M.

The Citizens' Alliance tried to fasten still another outrage on the Federation. A horrible accident had happened in the Independence mine. It was caused by the carelessness of Frank Gillese, a scab engineer from the Cœur d'Alenes. He was pulling the shift out of the mine at two-thirty in the morning, and for some unaccountable reason hoisted the cage above the shaft house floor, up into the sheave wheel, pulling the cable loose. The cage started back down the shaft. One man was thrown out on the floor of the shaft house, but fifteen were carried to a terrible death. In the eleven-hundred-foot drop the pressure of air pushed the men off the cage, and they were torn to ribbons on the walls of the shaft. It was twenty-four hours before they had gathered up all the remnants of the bodies.

This, like every other catastrophe that happened in the district, was charged to the Federation, although the Independence mine, like the Vindicator, was surrounded by soldiers, and the engineer was a scab.

The coroner's jury found that the company had neglected the usual precautions—there was no man at the landing to watch against accidents, there were no safety devices, the hoisting engine brakes were out of order and useless. This verdict made it impossible to connect the members of the W.F.M. with this terrible disaster.

There was, however, no investigation of the management, which, if the verdict of the jury was true, was guilty of nothing less than murder.

A newspaper writer came to Colorado to write about the industrial war, made several visits to the W.F.M. office, and seemed to be friendly to the organization. He gave me the proof sheets of the "Red Book," a pamphlet that was being issued by the Mine Owners' Association, containing the so-called "Criminal Record of the Western Federation of Miners." I at once started to prepare a counter document, the "Category of Crime of the Mine Owners' Association," which we called the "Green Book." We hurried this up so that it was ready for distribution before the Red Book was off the press.

In his concluding articles this writer said that the Federation was "unclean," and that we dared not permit a committee from the American Federation of Labor to audit our books. When this appeared in the Chicago paper, Ed Nockels, secretary of the Chicago Federation of Labor, telegraphed me asking if we would allow a committee of the A. F. of L. to audit the accounts of the Western Federation of Miners. To this I replied by wire that we would be glad to have this done, and that we would pay all expenses that might be entailed. The newspaperman's challenge was such a boomerang that he lost his job and has never been heard of as a correspondent since.

One of the owners of the Strong mine at Cripple Creek was Senator Scott of West Virginia. It was to him that the mine owners appealed to have a statement introduced in the United States Senate, viciously condemning the Western Federation of Miners. I quote a part of this statement of the mine owners, signed by C. C. Hamlin, and introduced by the senator:

During all these years an alleged labor organization known as the Western Federation of Miners has been endeavoring, with considerable success, to obtain a hold on this particular industry through the unionization of these mines, and the history of this campaign, with its record of murder, arson, dynamiting and riot, to say nothing of the more petty crimes, such as assaults, intimidation, threats and personal abuse, all committed for the purpose of intimidating and coercing men engaged in earning a livelihood, is enough to shock humanity. . . .

When an executive has been found big enough and brave enough and patriotic enough to rise above political expediency and take a firm stand in favor of law and order and the preservation of those rights guaranteed by the Constitution, as did Governor Steunenberg in Idaho in 1899, and as Governor Peabody is doing in Colorado to-day, protests such as that embodied in the resolution under consideration have gone up from certain quarters, either inspired by sympathy with the acts and purposes of this organization or with the hope of obtaining some political advantages through them, or, as we trust is the case with the present resolution, by ignorance of the facts which have engendered the condition. . . .

In 1901 the Smuggler-Union mine, at Telluride, Colorado, became involved in trouble with the Western Federation. The mine was using what is known as the contract system, i.e., the miners were paid according to the ground broken instead of by the day. It was admitted that a man who was willing to do a fair day's work could earn the union scale, which means a minimum of three dollars a day for eight hours' work, but nevertheless the Federation demanded that system discontinued. The management refused to abandon the contract system and the strike followed. Some non-union men were put to work, and on July third an armed body of union men attacked the mine, killed and wounded several persons, dislodged the non-union men, and took possession of the property. The non-union men were driven into the hills, and with their wounded companions were compelled to find their way on foot to places of safety. . . .

So that it will be seen that in all these strikes the Western Federation of Miners has not only indulged in coercion, picketing, threats and intimidation, but has resorted to riot, arson, bloodshed and general disorder as well, and in all of these localities, in times of outward quiet assaults, intimidation and even murder have been committed for the purpose of forcing men into the union. There can be no individual freedom where this organization gains a foothold. . . .

During the past few months the Cripple Creek district has been the center of the disorders generated by the Western Federation, both because it employs more labor than any other mining camp in the state, and because the Federation looked upon it as one of its strongholds and the best place to strike a decisive blow. . . .

This speech at the second session of the fifty-eighth Congress got the publicity that the mine owners were looking for, and they probably did not expect a reply.

As soon as I saw Senator Scott's statement, I telegraphed to Senator Patterson of Colorado and asked him if he would introduce a reply in the Senate. I got an immediate request to send on our reply at once. We wrote an answer of twenty-seven thousand words, which we sent to Senator Patterson. When he received it, he telegraphed me asking if he might change one word. I told him to make any change necessary. The senator explained to me later that the change he made was where we had called John Campion, a mine manager of Leadville, a liar. He said that Campion was a friend of his and he had no desire to apply that epithet to him. With this single change in the document he introduced it in the Senate and then telegraphed me to have the entire statement published in the following Sunday issue of his paper, the *Rocky Mountain News*.

I took the telegram and the statement at once to the editor, McKenna. When he looked at the bulky document, he said to me: "Haywood, this is a physical impossibility! It can't be set up on time."

"Well," I said, "we may be able to help you out on that. We have it set up in type now to run in the next issue of the *Miners' Magazine,* and we'll be glad to lend you the type, though it's a little larger than what you use."

"Just wait a minute. I'll go down and see the foreman."

When he returned he told me:

"Yes, we can use your type. We can set this up and tear it down next week." This referred to the union rule that everything used in the paper must be actually set up, torn down and distributed in the shop that printed it. I expressed an opinion about this "dummy work" that may not have been entirely complimentary to the typographical union.

The article ran to more than seven newspaper pages. The mine owners were so mad that they could have bitten the back of their necks when they read this statement of ours, introduced by Senator Patterson, in which we called upon the United States government for an investigation of the Colorado strikes, and offered to furnish all the assistance within our power.

Some time after this, Walter B. Palmer did make an investigation of the "Colorado Labor Disturbances," which was published over the name of Carrol D. Wright, U. S. Commissioner of Labor, but there was never any action on the part of the government.

From Senator Patterson's Senate Document, which was our reply to the Mine Owners' Association, we compiled our "Green Book" in answer to the "Red Book" already mentioned. Here are some of the mine owners' accusations against us, and our answers in part from the Senate Document, as they appeared in the "Green Book."

The Mine Owners said: That a large number of criminals and lawless men have been welcomed, supported and sheltered by the Western Federation of Miners. . . .

The Western Federation replied: That a large number of ex-convicts, gamblers, desperadoes and other criminals have been and now are knowingly employed and paid by the Colorado Mine Owners' Association and the Citizens' Alliance in Cripple Creek, Telluride and elsewhere in the state, as deputy sheriffs, guards, detectives, etc. . . .

The Mine Owners said: That the officers of that organization and a large number of the members, while perhaps not committing crimes themselves for which they can be prosecuted, do directly and indirectly advise or encourage the lawless among them to commit crimes. . . .

The Western Federation replied: That the officers of these organizations and a large number of the members have not only committed crimes themselves, for which they could and should be prosecuted and punished, but the organizations as such have directly and openly aided and abetted the same, and their members have boasted and approved of such crimes. . . .

The Mine Owners said: That these officers and this element preach disrespect for law and contempt for lawful authorities and openly and publicly, as individuals, approve of and gloat over the slugging, dynamiting and murdering of non-union men by their criminal associates. . . .

The Western Federation replied: That the association and alliance, while shouting hypocritically for "law and order," have openly defied the courts, destroyed liberty of the press, invaded the sanctity of the home, caused arrests without warrant, imprisoned men without charges of crime, driven men from the county after robbing them, and while declaring such men to be criminals of the deepest dye, have without compunction, dumped them on neighboring communities. They have tortured men and intimidated women and children to obtain confessions, and openly and publicly boasted and approved such crimes, as organizations, by adopting and publishing resolutions commendatory of them. . . .

The Mine Owners said: That where this organization has had its members in local public offices, or where it has had the power to influence peace officers and courts in this state, it has paralyzed the hand of justice and made it next to impossible to convict members of the Federation caught in the act of committing crimes. . . .

The Western Federation replied: That wherever the association or alliance have not had their members in public office, they have, wherever deemed necessary, compelled by violence and intimidation, the resignation of duly elected public officials and the appointment of their own creatures in the so-called vacancies. Wherever their members or tools are in office, or where they have had the power to influence peace officers and courts in this state, the law, as established since Magna Charta, has been subverted by decisions which have made the state a subject of derision to the entire country, the hand of justice has been paralyzed, and it has been futile to attempt conviction of their members, although caught in the act of committing crime and openly confessing and boasting of it.

This charge is supported and proven by the decisions themselves and by the following facts: The informations for riots and conspiracy which a court compelled an unwilling district attorney to file at Idaho Springs against some eighty members of these organizations, charging them as participants in a mob which had driven miners from their homes, were at the earliest possible moment dismissed by the same district attorney, and the criminals allowed to escape trial and punishment, though the whole community could have testified to their identity. At the same time, the same district attorney, aided by the attorneys of those organizations and backed by all the money needed, made two attempts by two separate trials to convict miners of the crimes of arson and conspiracy for which the same mob had pretended to expel them. They were each and all triumphantly acquitted without introducing evidence in their defense.

Not one of the mob of "best citizens" who exiled miners from Telluride has been prosecuted. When Judge Stevens issued his injunction to aid the exiles in returning home, the mob appealed to the governor of the state for force to defy the courts and he ordered out the militia, placed the leader of the mob in command, and the court stands defied and helpless to this day.

At Cripple Creek, a mob in brass and blue under orders from a puppet governor controlled by the association and the alliance, filled the courtroom with armed men, and defied the court in open session. While this mob of soldiers was in the district, it aided and abetted the members of the alliance and association, in compelling, by force and threats, the resignation of the duly elected sheriff and coroner and other civil officers of Teller county, and the appointment of their own creatures to the so-called vacancies.

Ever since this lawless governor recalled his mob of soldiers from Cripple Creek the reign of terror continues. Stores belonging to a foreign corporation have been looted in broad daylight by mobs led by A. E. Carlton, president First National Bank; Nelson Franklin, former mayor, and Cliff Newcomb, cashier First National Bank, and other 'law-abiding' citizens. Not one of these criminals fears arrest or punishment, and daily outrages are committed with impunity by mobs composed of members of the alliance and association, or acting under orders from them, and acting with the approval of the peace officers of the county, whom they forcibly installed in office. These crimes are committed with the consent and approval of the governor, who refuses to enforce the law and restore order on the pitiful pretense that he has 'not been officially notified. . . .

The Mine Owners said: That this organization, having formally and officially espoused the cause of the so-called Socialist Party, is opposed to our present form of government and is aiming at its overthrow, together with the abrogation of the present Constitution. . . .

The Western Federation replied: That these organizations have formally and officially espoused the cause of the so-called Republican Party, which they pretend to be still the party of Lincoln. That each of them is opposed to our present form of government and aiming at its overthrow. To this end they have destroyed and confiscated property, destroyed the freedom of the press, defied the courts, nullified the writ of habeas corpus, exercised the right of search without warrant, denied the right of trial by jury, exercised the power of banishment, denied the right of citizens to keep and bear arms, and trampled upon every other guarantee of personal liberty made by the constitution of the state and of the United States. Besides these and other violations of the constitutional rights of citizens, they are seeking to abrogate the Constitution and install a plutocracy, and to that end have adopted as their rallying cry a phrase, classic in its terseness and aptly descriptive of the men and their purpose, to wit: "To Hell with the Constitution."

The Mine Owners said: That this organization teaches its members to regard the wealth they produce from the property of others as their own, thus encouraging theft (of ore, for instance) and also inflaming the minds of its members against their employers, against the law, against organized society, against the peace and safety of the public. . . .

The Western Federation replied: That the organizations mentioned teach their members that the sole aim and end of existence is to acquire wealth without producing it, and that therefore the methods of trusts, stock watering, stealing ore from neighbors under the guise of trespass, buying the interests of widows and orphans in adjoining property without informing them of its value, and other similar methods used by predatory wealth, are respectable when compared to the economic theory that wealth should belong to him who produces it, or to Lincoln's assertions in his message to congress in 1864, that "to secure to each laborer the whole product of his labor is a worthy object of any government" and that "labor is superior to capital and deserves much the higher consideration." . . .

The facts which support and prove these charges made by the Federation are within the knowledge of every citizen of Colorado.

The appearance of the "Green Book" was a bad jolt to the Citizens' Alliance and the Mine Owners' Association. They were completely in the dark as to how we had gotten the material, and do not know until this day that the proof sheets were given to me by a newspaper writer. We distributed the "Green Book" free throughout the mining camps, and it was scattered broadcast throughout the West. The miners were delighted that it had appeared before the "Red Book"; the members realized that we were on the job at headquarters.

From the correspondence that was pouring into the office I could visualize the situation in the mining camps and smelting towns of the West. The strike at Colorado City had thrown out sparks that had kindled the fires of the eight-hour struggle in many places.

The big smelters of Pueblo were now on strike; the entire state of Colorado was in conflagration, nor did it stop at the state borders. The coal miners who had joined forces with us had extended their fight to Wyoming, to Arizona and New Mexico, covering all of district fifteen.

From various parts of this territory came reports of the terrorizing that was being carried on by the Reno Detective Agency, and other thugs and murderers employed by the Colorado Fuel and Iron Company and other coal companies, including those of southern Utah. These reports made gruesome pictures; the homes of miners being destroyed by dynamite, striking miners being shot to death; families being evicted from miserable shacks, their only homes, that were the property of the Rockefeller interests; miners being deported from homes, wives and children; the cruel beating of organizers Warjeon, Mooney and others.

As fearful as any other picture were those of the spies and detectives who had joined the organization to ferret out the plans of the union and report the work and whereabouts of the organizers.

Besides the newspaper reports and those brought in by messengers, there were letters, phone calls, telegrams from all sections. A telegram came saying that thirty-five miners had been killed in the Daly-West mine in Utah by an explosion of powder which had been stored unlawfully and criminally in the mine. We got word that three hundred and thirty-eight men had been blasted to death in Wyoming by a mine explosion. What with Fernie, the Independence disaster, and many others, this made a total of more than 1,087 deaths in preventable mine disasters that were charged against the mine owners and backed by juries' verdicts. Many were charged against the Western Federation, but these charges were not once upheld by the coroners' juries. I got letters about a strike in Keswick, California, and the deportation of miners from Dutch Flat. Then came news of scabs being shipped from the Cœur d'Alenes.

In addition to the regular correspondence with the secretaries of the unions, I sent them frequent bulletins of the strikes and asked for information about all the unions. They sent me pictures of the strikers, the union halls, demonstrations and so on, and I ran these in the magazine to create a wider mutual interest among the members of the Western Federation. I was trying to make Arizona acquainted with Alaska, Montana with Colorado; a sort of long-distance handshaking. I wanted to create a spirit of fraternity, and I did. There never was an organization like the Western Federation of Miners in that respect.

When I had been elected secretary-treasurer I was a novice in the labor movement. But the three years since I had shut off the air on the drill in the Blaine mine had been a severe course of training in the class struggle. I was never satisfied that the problems of labor could be solved by trade unionism, and parliamentary socialism was not a remedy.

I had seen time after time the weakness of craft unionism. The miners of Cripple Creek were scabs, many of them; the mill men of Colorado City were scabs, many of them. The railroads that connected them were manned by union men who were hauling scab ore to scab mills. That's craft unionism.

When I had wired John Mitchell that the miners of the West would lay down tools with the coal miners in a general strike, that was industrial unionism. It hadn't taken me three years to learn this. I have not had to change my mind about it.

Laws and legislative enactments were but will-o'-the-wisps unless we had the economic power—the strength of our union—to enforce them. Habeas corpus, the much boasted guarantee, was ineffective against martial law. Injunctions were useful only to the class that controlled the government.

While all these strikes were a severe test of the organization, I was doing everything I could to spread and intensify them. I hoped to see a situation like that of 1877, when strikes had spread over seventeen states, and cities and industries had been for a time under the control of the workers.

The membership was now being tested in the crucibles of Telluride, Denver, Cripple Creek, wherever the strikes were on. The ore was proving to be high grade.

CHAPTER X

"DEPORTATION OR DEATH"

THE Colorado Federation of Labor called a convention to be held in Denver. Three hundred and fifty delegates, representing all kinds of unions, gathered in the club building. There were delegates from the striking coal miners, from the striking miners of Telluride and the Cripple Creek district.

They discussed many things that had happened during the eight-hour struggle. They appointed a ways and means committee, the duty of which was to provide as much relief as possible for the many strikers and their families. A resolution was presented to the effect that the entire delegation visit Governor Peabody and demand the recall of the soldiers, the rescinding of the vagrancy order and the protection of all deported miners returning to their homes. It was finally decided that a committee should visit the governor with these proposals.

The committee met the governor in his office, a place that had become historic in the struggle of the miners. Governor Peabody blatantly informed them that no one had been deported except foreigners and rowdies. He could not see that in the committee were several who had been deported, among them Guy Miller, president of the Telluride Miners' Union, and he did not know that some of the best union men had been compelled to change their names in order to avoid the blacklist. He told the committee that all miners would be protected in their rights. Needless to say, the governor reserved the right of determining just what the miners' rights were.

The convention adopted the following resolution:

Whereas, organized labor in the State of Colorado is fighting a deathless battle for the right to organize and live; and

Whereas, the chief executive and the state administration have conspired and entered into collusion with the Mine Owners' Association, the smelting trust, the Colorado Fuel and Iron Company, and the commercial allies known as the Citizens' Alliance in defeating the political mandate of the people, as expressed at the polls in November, 1902; and

Whereas, the state militia has become corporate hirelings and resolved themselves into a military mob to annihilate organized labor, to train gatling guns upon the temple of justice, to defy the courts, to invade the sanctity of homes, to arrest without warrant or process of law, and incarcerate in a prison known as a military "bull-pen," men who have committed no crime save to clasp hands under the banner of unionism; and

Whereas, the governor of this state has declared martial law in Teller and San Miguel counties, and, with the power of armed might, deported law-abiding citizens and branded them as vagrants and outlaws; and

Whereas, to quote from the Declaration of Independence—"That to secure our rights, governments are instituted among men, deriving their just powers from the consent of the governed; that, whenever any form of government becomes destructive of these ends, it is the right of the people to alter or abolish it, and to institute a new government, laying its foundation on such principles and organizing its powers in such form as to them shall seem most likely to effect their safety and happiness. Prudence, indeed, will dictate that governments long established should not be changed for light and transient cause; and accordingly all experience hath shown that mankind are more disposed to suffer while evils are sufferable than to right themselves, abolishing the forms to which they are accustomed. But when a long trail of usurpations pursuing invariably the same object, evinces a design to reduce them under absolute despotism, it is their right, it is their duty, to throw off such government and to provide new guards for their future security." And

Whereas, free speech has been strangled, the press muzzled and the writ of habeas corpus suspended by military imperialism, backed by bristling bayonets; and

Whereas, the presence of an armed soldiery in Teller and San Miguel counties was for the sole use and benefit of the Mine Owners' Association in their warfare against organized labor, and not to preserve law and order, as neither was being violated; now, therefore, be it

Resolved, that the delegates and representatives of organized labor in convention assembled, condemn and denounce the assaults of the state administration upon the rights and liberties of citizenship by trampling under the iron heel of military despotism every principle of the organic law of the state,

Resolved, that we demand the immediate withdrawal of the troops, so that law and order may again prevail in Teller and San Miguel counties.

Resolved, that we are unalterably opposed to placing upon the shoulders of the tax-payers the expense incurred by the state militia while quartered in the strike regions during the years 1902-1904.

Resolved, that the membership of this convention, representing fifty thousand members of organized labor in Colorado, will vote for no candidate for the Fifteenth General Assembly who will not pledge himself, in the event of his election, to use his vote and influence against any and every measure looking to the payment of a single dollar of the expense referred to.

Resolved, that when the reign of military anarchy is at an end in this state, we urge the membership of organized labor throughout Colorado to come to the aid of the martyrs of "bull-pen" imprisonment, so that the wrongs and outrages from which they have suffered may be righted in the courts.

Resolved, that we commend and admire the gallant and unflinching battle of the Western Federation of Miners and the United Mine Workers of America, who have bared their breasts to corporate power, and who are now forcing greed to hoist the white flag.

Resolved, that we urge the membership of organized labor to establish coöperative stores wherever possible, in order that unionism may successfully measure steel with that band of brigands and pirates who have registered their names upon the roll of the Citizens' Alliance.

Resolved, that we call upon the membership of organized labor in every city, town and hamlet, and every liberty loving citizen of the state, to march to the polls in November, 1904, and bury the present administration so deep beneath an avalanche of ballots that a million blasts from Gabriel's trumpet will not be able to awaken it from political oblivion.

I was one of the thirteen signers of this resolution.

The miners were struck a hard blow when the Woods Investment Company declared that all men employed by them must sever their connection with the Western Federation of Miners. Woods met the miners as they were coming off shift at the Gold Coin mine, and later at the Economic mill, and submitted the proposition to them. They uanimously refused it. While this did not weaken the strike, it made hundreds of more members for whom we had to provide relief.

I had been having some difficulty with the relief committee of the Denver smelter men. At first we had been giving out relief at such a rate that I had to tell the chairman that he was providing the smelter men with more than they had had while at work. Then he cut down the rations until the wives of the smelter men began to complain that they were not getting enough to eat. Years later, when his letters were published in *The Pinkerton Labor Spy,* I discovered that the chairman of the relief committe was a Pinkerton detective, who was carrying out the instructions of the agency in his methods of handling the relief work, deliberately trying to stir up bad feeling between the strikers and the relief committee.

The American Labor Union had asked me to contribute to the *Voice of Labor,* its official organ. I wrote articles on the strikes and the mining industry, and aphorisms which became very popular— "Industrial Unionism is Socialism with its working clothes on," "The open union makes the closed shop," "A shorter workday makes a bigger payday," and so on; I used to hear "soap-boxers" using my maxims. At about this time I wrote a brief history of the Western Federation of Miners that had a wide circulation.

President Moyer was going to visit the unions at Ouray and other places in the southern part of the state. I suggested that it would be a good thing to take a traveling companion along with him, as he might run across gunmen from Telluride, and two men could do better than one against them. There was a member of the Western Federation from Cripple Creek who had come into the office a few days previously. He came again that afternoon and Moyer proposed that he should go with him to Ouray. I had asked Moyer if he knew him. Moyer told me that he had seen him in "the Creek," that he was an old-timer from the Cœur d'Alenes. It was Harry Orchard.

I asked Orchard if he had a gun with him. He had, and pulled a six-shooter a foot and a half long out of his pants. I said to him: "That's not a very handy gun; you'll have to pull your pants off to get it in action!" He looked as though he did not like the criticism, but he didn't say anything.

It was the second night after they had arrived in Ouray that Moyer was arrested by officials from San Migual county. He was charged with desecrating the flag and taken to Telluride. Orchard came back to headquarters and told me the details of Moyer's arrest, all of which I had already heard through telegrams and newspaper accounts. I didn't like the way in which Moyer had been arrested, with no resistance on the part of his supposed protector.

Orchard saw that I was angry and didn't stay more than a few minutes. Perhaps I was not so angry at Orchard as I was at the thought of Moyer's arrest for "desecrating the flag," as I knew that he had had nothing to do with that particular affair; he was not even in the office when the flag poster was made. Then I realized that it had his signature on it, which of course involved him as much as though he had written it himself.

I got word that there was also a warrant out for me on the same charge. As John Murphy was not in the city, I went to see the law firm of Richardson and Hawkins, to find out what I could do to avoid being taken to Telluride. Hawkins suggested that murder was a non-bailable offense, and if I should be charged with murder in Denver I could not be taken to another county. I thought that was a little too strong! Then he said:

"Well, why not be charged with desecrating the flag, right here in Denver?"

"But I want to avoid going to jail, and I want things so I can do my work in the office."

"Well," he said, "if you know a judge who will put you in charge of an officer while you look for bail, it can be done that way."

"I think I can fix that up with Billy Hynes," said I. "He's a union man."

"Let me know when the case is coming up," said Hawkins.

From his office I went to Pettibone's store and told George that I wanted to be arrested on the charge of desecrating the flag.

"Can you fix it up with one of the boys here?"

"Sure," he said, "Jake Wolf will swear out a warrant."

Then I went to Judge Hynes' court and told Billy the whole story. He made me no promises, but asked me if the case was coming up in his court. I told him I wanted to arrange it that way if I could. That afternoon the warrant was sworn out and served on me and the following morning the case came up for trial.

Mr. Hawkins said that it would take him some time to prepare the case and asked the judge to fix bond, which he did to the sum of three hundred dollars. I told his honor it would take me some time to get that amount of bond together. Calling one of the constables, he said:

"Connolly, you go with Mr. Haywood and stay with him until he gets the bond."

I left the court and took Connolly to the office. He stayed with me night and day, and when the time limit was up, we went back to the court and I asked the judge for more time, which he granted without hesitation.

When my case came up before Judge Hynes I came into court with all kinds of specimens of advertisements using the American flag. Unknown friends had sent me these in every mail. I must have had twenty or thirty samples; tobacco sacks, cigar boxes, labels from tomato cans, the flag of a colored men's political club with announcements written on the stripes, and the business card of the Pinkerton Detective Agency, with the all-seeing eye surrounded with flags, the principal among them being the Stars and Stripes. The case was dismissed. Some time later the use of the flag in advertising was prohibited by law.

But before my trial, Moyer had been released on bond and re-arrested two or three times, until finally the militia decided to hold him as a "military necessity." I got Attorney Richardson to apply to the state supreme court for a writ of habeas corpus, which was granted. Moyer was brought to Denver.

On the morning of his arrival the stenographers from our office wanted to go to the depot to see him come in. I asked Connolly, the constable who was guarding me, what he thought about us going too. He said he couldn't see any harm in it.

The girls had small copies of the flag poster pasted on their handbags, and I told them it might be just as well not to flaunt these in the faces of the soldiers. We went to the station and when the train pulled in a detachment of twelve soldiers got off first, then Moyer alone, then twelve more soldiers with officers following.

I stepped in and shook hands with Moyer and was walking along with him, hands clasped, when I felt a pressure on my shoulder, trying to force us apart. I looked around. There was Captain Bulkeley Wells, the same Wells who, a few months before, had entered into an agreement with us that would have brought about the peaceful settlement of the strike at Telluride. This thought flashed through my mind, and I wheeled and struck him full in the face.

It was a wild thing to do. In a flash the soldiers came to his rescue, and with the butts of their guns they struck me over the head and knocked me back between two cars. One pulled his gun down on me. I could see the hole in the barrel. I said, "Pull it, you son of a bitch, pull it!"

One of the officers knocked up the barrel and said sharply:

"Stand back, stand back!" Then addressing me, "Haywood, go along with Moyer!"

I went along with Moyer and we marched to the Oxford Hotel. I saw Constable Connolly in the line of people as we passed. He looked rather dejected. I have never seen him since. When we reached the Oxford Hotel we marched in and Moyer sat down. I was standing with my elbow on the counter, when Walter Kinley, the Telluride gunman, came up to me and said:

"Sit down!"

"I don't want to sit down."

He pulled out his six-shooter and made a swing at me, shouting: "Sit down, God damn ye!"

I hit him first and his gun did not strike me. Five or six soldiers rushed up and struck me several times, knocking me back against the wall. Kinley ran around to where he could get an opening, reached over and hit me on the head with the handle of his gun. About the same time a soldier made a jab at me, striking me on the cartilage just below the ribs. An officer came up swinging his six-shooter, shouting:

"Get back, you fellers, get back! How many does it take to handle this man?"

I could feel myself getting weak and I staggered to a chair where I sat awaiting further orders. I was bleeding like a stuck hog from blows on the head.

Soon I was taken upstairs and two gunmen were left in the room with me. One of them was Kinley, who was complaining about having broken the pearl handle of his gun on my head. It was only a few moments until the reporters appeared. I gave my keys and papers to John Tierney of the *Denver Times*. In a short time clean clothes came from home and I changed to the skin, all the time keeping a six-shooter which I had never attempted to use, and which had been somehow overlooked in their perfunctory search.

An army surgeon came and dressed the cuts in my head, sewing back my right ear, which required seven stitches. Then Ham Armstrong, the sheriff of the city and county of Denver, arrived and said, "I want you, Bill." I got up and remarked:

"That's good news!" and we started for the sheriff's office. As we were walking along, Armstrong said to me:

"You've got yourself in bad this time, Bill."

I asked him why. He said:

"They're going to take you back to Telluride."

"No, they won't!"

"Why, that's Sheriff Rutan, going over for you now, walking on the edge of the sidewalk," he told me. I looked at Rutan and then turned to Ham, saying:

"Well, I'm not going to Telluride."

When we got to the sheriff's office, Rutan came in and sat down. Armstrong said to me:

"Had I better call up Richardson?" I said, "I think so."

It happened that Richardson was the sheriff's attorney, as well as being attorney for the W.F.M. While I could hear only one end of the telephone conversation, I saw Armstrong's face light up. He hung up the phone and called me out into the corridor. There he told me that Richardson had instructed him to hold me in the county jail until Richardson told him to turn me loose.

Then I pulled out my gun, handed it to Armstrong and asked him to keep it until I called for it, saying:

"I told you I wasn't going to Telluride. They would do less to me for killing that sheriff in Denver than they would do to me in Telluride for 'desecrating the flag.'"

Ham stared at me and said: "Well, by God, do you mean it?"

"I certainly do," said I. "I would have killed him rather than go to Telluride."

Ham told a policeman to get a carriage and take me over to the county jail. On the way over, I bought cigars and smoking tobacco, thinking that there would be a lot of fellows in jail who might be short of smokes. When we got to the jail, the warden said:

"I'm sorry, Mr. Haywood, we can't make you as comfortable here as we'd like to!"

I was weighed and measured according to the rules, and as I stepped off the scales, little Billy Green, the "boss of Green county," came in through an inner door. He said:

"Hello, Bill! Just come this way, will you?"

I followed him, thinking that I was going to a cell, but he led me into an adjoining store room where thirty-five or forty rifles lay on a long table.

"Take your choice," he said, "and we'll have a man behind every one of the others, and if that God damned militia shows up they'll get the warmest reception they ever got!"

I swung a rifle up to my shoulder and remarked that we were pretty well barricaded here in the jail. Then we went back to the office where the sheriff said:

"Here's a desk that you can use, Mr. Haywood. You'll have connection with your office on the telephone, and you can bring your stenographers over here if you have any special work to do."

Pettibone and some others called that afternoon, and Pettibone went to my home to break the news of my arrest to my wife.

"Oh, that don't worry me at all! I'll know where he is every night now," said she. For months she had expected me to be brought home any night on a stretcher.

As soon as the union men of Denver heard that I had been taken into custody by the militia at the station, they had started to organize. They appointed captains to gather squads and armed them to prevent the militia from taking me out of the city of Denver. This was probably the reason that Governor Peabody issued orders that I should be turned over to the civil authorities.

The morning after I moved in, I was in the office of the jail alone when the doorbell rang. I lifted the shutter of the peep-hole and recognized D. C. Copley, a member of the executive board from Cripple Creek. I let him in, and he said:

"I thought you were in jail?"

"I am. In this much of the jail!"

He had come to bring me word that Moyer had been remanded back to Telluride.

After being in jail about two weeks, I telephoned to Richardson and told him I wanted to get back to the office. He said:

"You know you're liable to arrest as soon as you step out of jail. You've got your office there, haven't you?"

"Yes," I said. "I've got everything. But it's not like working at my own desk, and I'm willing to take the chance. I'd like you to fix it up with the sheriff."

He fixed it up, and I never again heard of that Telluride warrant.

One of the first approaches that was made to me in the way of a bribe did not come directly but through the attorney, Richardson, who told me that Cass Harrington, a lawyer for one of the Colorado coal companies, had said that if I would "quit this Socialist nonsense," I could have any office in the state. I told Richardson that Harrington had another guess coming.

We filed an application for a writ of habeas corpus for Moyer, this time in the Federal District Court at St. Louis, before Judge Thayer. A short time afterward Moyer was released. He seemed to be no longer a "military necessity." He was re-arrested, this time charged with murder, but as the warrant made no mention of the name of the person supposed to have been killed, nor of the date nor place of the murder, this charge would not hold water. Then he was arrested for complicity in the Vindicator explosion, which had happened some time before in Cripple Creek. This could not be fastened on him, and before the order was received from the Federal Court, he had been released.

While Moyer was in jail in Telluride, the 1904 convention of the Western Federation of Miners was held in Denver. Many of the men who had been arrested in different places were there as delegates. Pettibone got a letter from Moyer asking that Moyer's picture should be hung on the platform over the president's chair, and that when the photograph of the delegates was taken a vacant chair should be put in the president's place. Pettibone came to the hall with Moyer's enlarged picture, which was hung up as he had asked while the delegates were in session. It all happened without a murmur of applause from any one. Of course, the delegates didn't know that Moyer had requested it; they thought it was just a tribute on the part of Pettibone. So many of them had been in the bullpens or in jail that they didn't appreciate the impressiveness of Moyer's incarceration.

Many of the delegates gathered in the hall early on the morning of June the sixth. Some had newspapers grasped in their hands, others had the papers spread out before their eyes. A horror-stricken look was upon the faces of them all; they were reading about the explosion that had blown up the Independence Depot at Cripple Creek the night before.

As soon as the roll was called the explosion was taken up as a special order of business. There was not much that could be said, as no one knew anything except what they had read in the papers. It was decided to offer a reward of five thousand dollars for the arrest and conviction of those responsible for the frightful disaster, and to send a committee immediately from the convention to Cripple Creek, and to await their report before further action should be taken.

At Cripple Creek, Sheriff Robertson with his under-sheriffs went to the scene of the explosion at an early hour. They put ropes at some distance from the depot to keep the curious from treading on the ground, and immediately sent to Trinidad for bloodhounds.

When the committee returned they reported that conditions at Cripple Creek were unbelievable. They said that the terrible explosion had killed twelve or thirteen men and wounded many others, and that Sheriff Robertson had been called into a conference of bankers and mine owners and his resignation had been asked for. He emphatically refused to resign his office, until a rope was thrown at his feet and he was told that the crowd outside would be called in and he would be hanged if he did not resign at once. Robertson decided to quit. One of the mine owners' men was appointed in his place. This was the noon following the explosion.

The committee said that Marshal Mike O'Connell of Victor had appointed and armed a hundred or more union men as deputies to preserve order, and that he had tried to get the local militia to assist in dispersing a mob that was gathering on a corner of the main street. The militia refused to lend O'Connell any aid. The marshal was called into a conference of business men a few minutes later and dismissed after he had refused to resign. He then went and told the men he had deputized that he had been suspended.

When the bloodhounds arrived they were taken to the demolished railroad station. The first dog went direct to the home of one of the Citizens' Alliance detectives. On the second trial the bloodhound followed the same trail. Then they tried another dog which went direct to the powder magazine of one of the non-union mines.

A few days before the explosion, Carlton, the Victor banker, had met William Graham, the chief of police of Victor, and had said to him:

"Billy, you and I have always been good friends, and you've been a good officer. You haven't shown any partiality either for or against the Citizens' Alliance. But we're going to ask you to resign, as we don't want a neutral man in the position you are holding. Now I'll give you a hundred dollars and a ticket to Kansas City and you'd better get out as soon as you can. There is work to be done that you won't want to do."

Graham refused to resign.

Murphy, a boss of the Findley mine, was reported to have tried to hold back the men of that mine, telling them not to go to the depot for at least fifteen minutes. The men were anxious to get home and wanted to catch a train that was about due, so they broke away and ran to the station, many of them to meet their deaths. What did Murphy know?

The coroner's jury found that "members and officials of the Western Federation of Miners were responsible" for the Independence depot explosion.

The committee thought that every act of the atrocity had been premeditated by the Citizens' Alliance, as all the mines were closed after the explosion, and the scabs and thugs were gathered in Victor and armed for the occasion. Hamlin, the secretary of the Mine Owners' Association, addressed the great mob, violently condemning the W.F.M. for the explosion, saying that fifty union men should be shot down and as many more strung to telegraph poles, and the rest of them driven over the hills for the death of the brave men who had been blown up in the depot. One of the strikers asked: "Who do you mean by them?" Then the riot broke loose.

Several scabs and non-union men were killed, and many union men who had taken refuge in their hall were seriously injured by volleys of bullets that were fired in the windows and down the skylights. When the sheriff came to the hall, the union men surrendered and were taken to the armory, the quarters of the militia, which was afterwards called the bull-pen.

The furniture and fittings of all the union halls had been demolished. The hall of the engineer's union was a total wreck. On the blackboard was written this motto: "For being a union man, deportation or death will be your fate. Citizens' Alliance."

The committee told with some feeling about the wrecking of the union stores at Anaconda, Goldfield, Victor and Cripple Creek. Tons of goods had been carried away by the scabs. The bankers and prominent citizens took part themselves in the riot, played the devil with everything in the stores, poured coal oil over vast quantities of flour, sugar, meat and other foodstuffs, smashed the cash registers, the computing scales, and did all the damage they could.

The office of the Victor *Record* was again invaded, this time by strong-arm men who arrested all the staff and put them in the bull-pen. They smashed the linotype machines with big hammers and broke the presses, destroying everything to such an extent that the subsequent issues of the paper were printed on the presses of the

Cripple Creek *Star*. The publisher of the *Record* had had an editorial calling on the W.F.M. to declare the strike off, the morning that the plant was wrecked. The Citizens' Alliance probably thought that because of this people would think that union men had destroyed the plant. The publisher got four thousand dollars for the damage, and immediately reversed his former friendly attitude to us.

The miners at the convention were a mad lot of men when they heard of these countless outrages. During the following days many members from Cripple Creek came to Denver, and all had the same or worse stories to tell. The coroner's jury found a verdict in which the officers of the W.F.M. were implicated in the riot, and informations were filed against Moyer, the members of the executive board, myself and about forty others.

When the Cripple Creek authorities came to Denver with warrants, I got news of their arrival and went to the home of Colonel Irby, secretary to the mayor of Denver. I stayed there for a day or two. Meanwhile warrants had been served on Moyer and James Kirwin. They gave bail, but the authorities made no further attempt to arrest me.

The marshal of Victor, Mike O'Connell, who had deputized a hundred miners to disperse the mob after the explosion, was one of the first fifty deported. A few days after his arrival, he fell or was pushed out of a window, and was found dead in the alley below.

The militia closed down the Portland mine and a majority of the board of directors, over the protest of Jim Burns, decided to employ none but non-union men. However, to operate this big property, it was necessary to have many skilled engineers. The engineers refused to relinquish their cards in the W.F.M. The directors were compelled to allow the union engineers to work if they could get them. The district union wanted to retain a hold on the Portland mine, so decided that it would be best if the engineers remained at work. The Portland Mining Company filed suit against Governor Peabody for the damage they incurred when Adjutant General Bell closed down the mine. But when Sherman Bell found that the engineers in the Portland had not quit the union, he closed down the mine again. It was reopened shortly afterward under some agreement with the directors that they would make the changes in their force as soon as possible.

An employment card was adopted by the Mine Owners' Association, without which they intended that no man could work in the district. This card closely resembled the membership card of the W.F.M. A blacklist was instituted by the Citizens' Alliance against all the members of the Western Federation and of the American Federation of Labor, but when they found that this applied to the American Federation men who were working in the newspaper offices, they rescinded their action against the A. F. of L., and in its place put the American Labor Union. This happened without protest from the A. F. of L.

The Mine Owners' Association at Leadville introduced the employment card, although it was a violation of the injunction that had been issued by Judge Owers. The bosses expected this would be a means of wiping out the W.F.M., but to their surprise every member of the union took out a card and continued at work.

For many months the vicious outrages continued. Martial law was again declared and Adjutant General Sherman Bell appointed a super-court and a provost marshal for the district. Sixteen hundred men were arrested and put through the sweat box of the Citizens' Alliance. Two hundred and fifty of them were ordered deported, and forty-two were held for criminal trial. However, not a single member of the W.F.M. was convicted.

The commission of the super-court stated that all who were ordered deported were ore-thieves, gamblers and such-like bad characters. They knew that this report was a lie, as some of the best men in the district were among those deported. Many of them were men who owned their homes in Cripple Creek, and had lived and worked there for years. Their children had been born here in the mining camp. It was their home. Besides the miners there were some lawyers, a former attorney general of the state, a veteran of the Civil War, General Engley, and Frank Hangs, attorney for the W.F.M., who had lived a long time in the district; J. C. Cole, who had been county attorney; Judge Frost, and County Clerk Mannix. The Citizens' Alliance took this opportunity to get rid, not only of those active in the W.F.M., but also of any man they wanted to drive out of the district. Any scoundrel with an old score to settle could work through the Citizens' Alliance to get even with any one.

Brigadier General Bell by this time had swelled up until he thought that he was an officer of the Russian Czar, and the free people of Colorado his serfs. The orders he issued, exiling men from their homes to the adjoining states of Kansas and New Mexico, were carried out with the rigor of a despot. He said, "What steps I take as military commander concern nobody but myself and my commander-in-chief, the governor of the state. . . . I don't want these men in Colorado."

Beginning as one of Roosevelt's Rough Riders, he was affected with the same megalomania as his commander. He even had a habit of strutting around with his hand in the breast of his coat, like Napoleon. This was a matter of such common jest that the Denver papers cartooned him in his queer attitudes and demanded his removal on the ground that his mind was affected.

Harper, Parfet, Jenks and Hooten, the store managers of the district, had all been deported and came to Denver. Each of them was determined to return and open the stores again. When they went back to the district, Harper applied to General Bell for protection in opening the stores. Bell said that nothing would happen to them. It was but a short time afterward that the desperadoes invaded and robbed all the stores again.

The unions of Butte, Montana, were vitally interested in what was going on in Cripple Creek. They organized the Interstate Mercantile Company, sending two men from Butte to represent the organization and run the Cripple Creek stores. It was thought that a business incorporated in another state would not be interfered with.

When Hall and Heimerdinger arrived with their credentials I gave them letters to the district union and the store managers. They went at once to Cripple Creek and took charge of our stores there. The stores were reopened and restocked, and commenced to do business under the name of the Interstate Mercantile Company. This, however, was not a protection. The stores were again demolished and robbed. But as it was now a "foreign company," an injunction was sued out against Carlton, Hamlin, and many other prominent citizens of the district in the federal court of Denver. This was granted, and we suffered no further inconvenience except a boycott.

I got in touch with as many of the deportees as I could reach, and had them file personal claims against the state in sums ranging from five to ten thousand dollars. The aggregate amount was an enormous sum, to which we added a claim for damages done to the stores in the riots and raids. From the last claim, I learned later, sixty thousand dollars had been recovered by the Federation. I never heard whether any of the personal claims were paid.

I received a letter from Colonel Verdeckberg, telling me to send no more relief to the district, except through military channels, and enclosing a copy of a special order to that effect. This was an attempt to starve out the families of the strikers and deportees. Telegrams to President Roosevelt and to the Red Cross brought no action, and the relief work was carried on secretly by the brave women of the district. Eight of these women, members of the women's auxiliaries of the Federation, including Mrs. Hooten and Estelle Nicholls, were taken before Verdeckberg and instructed that they could not distribute relief in the Cripple Creek district. But the military order did not prevent these women from doing their work as they had always done.

Frank Cochran, the secretary of the Victor Miners' Union, was arrested, and when his office was searched a number of pictures of scabs were found, marked with a cross on the back. The military demanded of Cochran what these marked pictures were intended for. He explained that they were to be used for the scab posters that were circulated throughout the state. They tortured him in an effort to make him change his story, put a rope around his neck and threatened to hang him unless he would say that the marked pictures were those of scabs who were to be made away with. Cochran stood by the truth, and finally they let him go.

A committee of "white-cappers," who were sometimes called the Ku-Klux Klan, went to the home of George Seitz, and one of them walked into the kitchen where there was no one but Seitz and his two daughters. He ordered Seitz to come along with them, and to frighten him a shot was fired. But Seitz replied with a Winchester, and drove off the mob. The next morning the papers announced that two prominent individuals, naming them, had left the district and probably would not return. It was generally supposed that these two were members of the mob, and had been injured or killed by Seitz. That was the last case of invading homes. Seitz did a good job.

While all these fearful things were happening in Cripple Creek, the same mad rule of the gold barons was going on in San Juan district, and the coal barons of the southern part of the state were also doing their damndest to obliterate unionism.

At headquarters I was sitting tight, not knowing what atrocity would come next. There was a tremendous shock but the organization did not seem to be weakening anywhere. The strike in all its intensity had continued unbroken for over three years. The very first sign of weakness came with the discovery of gold in Tonopah and Goldfield, Nevada, coupled with a cordial invitation to the Cripple Creek miners from Governor Sparks of Nevada, who urged them to accept the hospitality of the "sage-brush state" and share its riches, adding that he would meet the Colorado miners at the border with a special train. There was no immediate exodus, but a good many of the miners left for Nevada, affected not so much by gold fever as a desire for peace, a chance to sleep without the overhanging thought of militia, gunmen, jails and bull-pens.

I was thinking about what could be done to strengthen the position of the Western Federation. The strategic fortresses of the mine managers were not altogether unassailable, but they were strong with the control of the supreme court and the state government. They, with the smelting and milling companies, had unlimited money for corruption as well as the support of the Rockefeller interests and the unscrupulous Citizens' Alliance, which apparently could resort to the most criminal atrocities with the assurance of military and civil protection. The barbarous gold barons—they did not find the gold, they did not mine the gold, they did not mill the gold, but by some weird alchemy all the gold belonged to them!

In a poster that I got out about this time, with the flaring headline, "Is Liberty Dead?" I recited many of the outrages that had occurred in Cripple Creek.

I had prepared a financial report for the year. Sam Gompers took occasion to criticize this report because, under the sum totals of expenditures, I had a large sum, thirty thousand dollars, I think, under the head of "miscellaneous." Sam seemed to be interested in what a miscellaneous expenditure of so large an amount could mean. But it is quite evident that he did not go through the report, because I had an itemized statement of the "miscellaneous" elsewhere. Gompers in this criticism was as bad as Walter Wellman. He jumped at the chance to try to tell our enemies—the enemies of labor—that we were using relief funds for something that could not be set forth plainly in the report.

The coal miners of Mystic, Iowa, invited me to speak at their

Labor Day demonstration early in September. I told them that I thought the United Mine Workers were making a mistake in their methods of dealing with coal companies, that I thought their position would be much stronger if their agreements terminated in November instead of on the first of April, when the demand for coal was declining. The supply of coal usually on hand in April was enough to run through the summer months, while in November the demand was on the increase, which would give the workers an advantage.

"But," I said, "why enter into an agreement with the mining companies at all—that is, a time agreement? Why not be in a position to strike at any time?

"Let me show you what an agreement really means. If a member of your union signed an individual agreement with the boss, you would say he was a yellow cur. But there are labor organizations which will enter into local agreements without considering the other workers in their industry. This only increases the size of the yellow dog. And the same is true of you as coal miners when you enter into an agreement including the entire industry. This agreement you regard as sacred and you feel that it compels you to work and provide coal, no matter what the conditions of the other workers may be.

"Take, for example, the locomotive engineers—they have never broken an agreement in the history of their organization. But they have scabbed on every big strike that has taken place in this country. So I say that even the workers in the entire industry have no right to enter into a time agreement, and this is true of the working class as a whole. We have no right to enter into agreements with the capitalist class, because it is the historic mission of the working class to overthrow the capitalist system. It is our only means of emancipation from wage slavery."

The Liberty League, organized by the Colorado State Federation of Labor, was active in the election of 1904. It had determined upon a labor party program, the main feature of which was the defeat of Governor Peabody, and its planks were nailed down with the slogan "Anybody but Peabody." This, of course, did not develop into a labor party, but into the support of the Democratic Party, which in its convention adopted the demands of the Liberty League. Roosevelt carried the state by a large majority, but Peabody was swamped. Alva Adams, Democratic governor-elect, was installed. The Republican Party, on behalf of Peabody, filed a protest with the supreme court, which in itself was so corrupt that it threw out the ballots of enough precincts and wards for the Republican legislature to declare that Peabody had been elected. He at once resigned, and the Republican lieutenant governor, Jesse MacDonald, took his place. Colorado had three governors in twenty-four hours.

CHAPTER XI

INDUSTRIAL WORKERS OF THE WORLD

AFTER a long and hard-fought battle in the southern part of the state, the United Mine Workers of this district called off their strike. The Colorado Fuel and Iron Company, with various other coal companies, continued to violate the eight-hour law, the anti-scrip law, which forbade the companies issuing their own money to the workers; the law that prohibited the companies from compelling the workers to trade at company stores, and other laws. Seven labor laws were being ignored with impunity. Not the least of them was the check-weighman law, by evading which the companies got thirty-eight hundred pounds of coal to the ton.

During this criminal lawbreaking the sniffling old profligate at the head of the Rockefeller interests was nibbling his hypocritical Baptist communion, wielding more power with his golf sticks than could the people of Colorado with their ballots.

When the legislature finally passed a new eight-hour law the smelter men of Denver declared their strike off after a struggle lasting twenty-one months, during which time, in spite of the work of the detective agencies, there were few desertions from the ranks.

Industrial unionism was rapidly developing. The 1904 convention of the Western Federation had outlined plans for the amalgamation of the entire working class into one general organization, and had instructed the executive board to carry out this program. There had been some informal conferences in Denver with Dan MacDonald of the American Labor Union and George Estes of the United Railway Workers, and we had had some correspondence with Clarence Smith, secretary of the American Labor Union. A secret conference was called to be held in Chicago on January second, 1905. The letter or invitation, which was sent to about thirty people, contained the following paragraph:

Asserting our confidence in the ability of the working class, if correctly organized in both political and industrial lines, to take possession

174

of and operate successfully . . . the industries of the country; believing that working-class political expression, through the Socialist ballot, in order to be sound, must have its economic counterpart in a labor organization builded as the structure of socialist society, embracing within itself the working class in approximately the same groups and departments and industries that the workers would assume in the working-class administration of the Coöperative Commonwealth . . . we invite you to meet us at Chicago, Monday, January second, 1905, in secret conference to discuss ways and means of uniting the working people of America in correct revolutionary principles, regardless of any general labor organization of past or present, and only restricted by such basic principles as will insure its integrity as a real protector of the interest of the workers.

Moyer, O'Neill and I were elected by the executive board to represent the Western Federation of Miners at this conference. We met in a hall in Lake street, often used as a meeting place by the Chicago anarchists, where Parsons and Spies had spoken to the workers. When the conference was called to order, I was elected permanent chairman, and George Estes permanent secretary. At these sessions we formulated the manifesto that brought into existence the Industrial Workers of the World, which read:

Social relations and groupings only reflect mechanical and industrial conditions. The great facts of present industry are the displacement of human skill by machines and the increase of capitalist power through concentration in the possession of the tools with which wealth is produced and distributed.

Because of these facts trade divisions among laborers and competition among capitalists are alike disappearing. Class divisions grow ever more fixed and class antagonisms more sharp. Trade lines have been swallowed up in a common servitude of all workers to the machines which they tend. New machines, ever replacing less productive ones, wipe out whole trades and plunge new bodies of workers into the ever-growing army of tradeless, hopeless unemployed. As human beings and human skill are displaced by mechanical progress, the capitalists need use the workers only during the brief period when muscles and nerves respond most intensely. The moment the laborer no longer yields the maximum of profits, he is thrown upon the scrap-pile, to starve alongside the discarded machine. A dead-line has been drawn, and an age-limit established, to cross which, in this world of monopolized opportunities, means condemnation to industrial death.

The worker, wholly separated from the land and the tools, with his skill of craftsmanship rendered useless, is sunk in the uniform mass of wage slaves. He sees his power of resistance broken by craft divisions, perpetuated from outgrown industrial stages. His wages constantly grow less as his hours grow longer and monopolized prices grow higher. Shifted hither and thither by the demands of profit-takers the laborer's home no longer exists. In this helpless condition he is forced to accept whatever humiliating conditions his master may impose. He is submitted to a physical and intellectual examination more searching than was the chattel slave when sold from the auction block. Laborers are no longer classified by differences in trade skill, but the employer assigns them according to the machines to which they are attached. These divisions, far from representing differences in skill or interests among the laborers, are imposed by the employers that workers may be pitted against one another and spurred to greater exertion in the shop, and that all resistance to capitalist tyranny may be weakened by artificial distinctions.

While encouraging these outgrown divisions among the workers the capitalists carefully adjust themselves to the new conditions. They wipe out all differences among themselves and present a united front in their war upon labor. Through employers' associations they seek to crush with brutal force, by the injunctions of the judiciary and the use of military power, all efforts at resistance. Or when the other policy seems more profitable, they conceal their daggers beneath the Civic Federation and hoodwink and betray those whom they would rule and exploit. Both methods depend for success upon the blindness and internal dissensions of the working class. The employers' line of battle and methods of warfare correspond to the solidarity of the mechanical and industrial concentration, while laborers still form their fighting organizations on lines of long-gone trade divisions. The battles of the past emphasize this lesson. The textile workers of Lowell, Philadelphia, and Fall River; the butchers of Chicago, weakened by the disintegrating effects of trade divisions; the machinists of the Santa Fe, unsupported by their fellow-workers subject to the same masters; the long struggling miners of Colorado, hampered by lack of unity and solidarity upon the industrial battle-field, all bear witness to the helplessness and impotency of labor as at present organized.

This worn out and corrupt system offers no promise of improvement and adaptation. There is no silver lining to the clouds of darkness and despair settling down upon the world of labor.

This system offers only a perpetual struggle for slight relief within wage slavery. It is blind to the possibility of establishing an industrial democracy, wherein there shall be no wage slavery, but where the workers will own the tools which they operate, and the product of which they alone will enjoy.

It shatters the ranks of the workers into fragments, rendering them helpless and impotent on the industrial battle-field.

Separation of craft from craft renders industrial and financial solidarity impossible.

Union men scab upon union men; hatred of worker for worker is engendered, and the workers are delivered helpless and disintegrated into the hands of the capitalists.

Craft jealousy leads to the attempt to create trade monopolies. Prohibitive initiation fees are established that force men to become scabs against their will. Men whom manliness or circumstances have driven from one trade are thereby fined when they seek to transfer membership to the union of the new craft. Craft divisions foster political ignorance among the workers, thus dividing their class at the ballot box as well as in the shop, mine and factory.

Craft unions may be and have been used to assist employers in the establishment of monopolies and the raising of prices. One set of workers is thus used to make harder the conditions of life of another body of workers.

Craft divisions hinder the growth of class consciousness of the workers, foster the idea of harmony of interests between employing exploiter and employed slave. They permit the association of the misleaders of the workers with the capitalists in the Civic Federation, where plans are made for the perpetuation of capitalism and the permanent enslavement of the workers through the wage system.

Previous efforts for the betterment of the working class have proven abortive because limited in scope and disconnected in action.

Universal economic evils afflicting the working class can be eradicated only by a universal working-class movement. Such a movement of the working class is impossible while separate craft and wage agreements are made favoring the employer against other crafts in the same industry, and while energies are wasted in fruitless jurisdiction struggles which serve only to further the personal aggrandizement of union officials.

A movement to fulfill these conditions must consist of one great industrial union embracing all industries,—providing for craft autonomy locally, industrial autonomy internationally, and working-class unity generally.

It must be founded on the class struggle, and its general administration must be conducted in harmony with the recognition of the irrepressible conflict between the capitalist class and the working class.

It should be established as the economic organization of the working class, without affiliation to any political party.

All power should rest in a collective membership.

Local, national and general administration, including union labels, buttons, badges, transfer cards, initiation fees, and per capita tax, should be uniform throughout.

All members must hold membership in the local, national or international union covering the industry in which they are employed, but transfers of membership between unions should be universal.

Workingmen bringing union cards from industrial unions in foreign countries should be freely admitted into the organization.

The general administration should issue a publication representing the entire union and its principles which should reach all members in every industry at regular intervals.

A central defense fund, to which all members contribute equally, should be established and maintained.

All workers, therefore, who agree with the principles herein set forth, will meet in convention at Chicago the 27th day of June, 1905, for the purpose of forming an economic organization of the working class along the lines marked out in this Manifesto.

Representation to the convention should be based upon the number of workers the delegate represents. No delegate, however, shall be given representation in the convention on the numerical basis of an organization unless he has credentials—bearing the seal of his union, local, national or international, and the signatures of the officers thereof,—authorizing him to install his union as a working part of the proposed economic organization in the industrial department in which it logically belongs in the general plan of the organization. Lacking this authority the delegate shall represent himself as an individual.

Adopted at Chicago, January 2, 3, and 4, 1905.

The signers of the Manifesto were:

A. G. Swing	Jos. Schmidt
A. M. Simons	John Guild
W. Shurtleff	Daniel McDonald
Frank McCabe	Eugene V. Debs
John M. O'Neill	Thos. J. DeYoung
Geo. Estes	Thos. J. Hagerty
Wm. D. Haywood	Fred D. Henion
Mother Jones	W. J. Bradley
Ernest Untermann	Chas. O. Sherman
W. L. Hall	M. E. White
Chas. H. Moyer	Wm. J. Pinkerton
Clarence Smith	Frank Krafft
Wm. E. Trautmann	J. E. Fitzgerald

Frank Bohn

On the back of the Manifesto was printed a chart classifying the industrial workers, with a statement of the requirements for an industrial organization of the workers:

A labor organization to correctly represent the working class must have two things in view.

First—It must combine the wage workers in such a way that it can most successfully fight the battles and protect the interests of the working people of to-day in their struggle for fewer hours, more wages and better conditions.

Secondly—It must offer a final solution of the labor problem—an emancipation from strikes, injunctions and bull-pens.

Study the chart and observe how this organization will give recognition to trade and craft divisions, yet provide perfect Industrial Unionism and converge the strength of all organized workers to a common center, from which any weak point can be strengthened and protected.

Observe, also, how the growth and development of this organization will build up within itself the structure of an Industrial Democracy—a Workers' Coöperative Republic—which must finally burst the shell of capitalist government, and be the agency by which the working people will operate the industries and appropriate the products to themselves.

One obligation for all.

A union man once and in one industry, a union man always and in all industries.

Universal transfers.

Universal label.

An open union and a closed shop.

Three secretaries were elected to attend to the distribution of the Manifesto, one for the East, one for the middle of the country, and myself for the West. Two hundred thousand copies of the Manifesto were distributed, and there was much correspondence and other work involved in preparing for the convention that we had decided upon holding in Chicago the following June. There was a general response to the Manifesto. It was gratifying to see the number of different trades and industries that took an active interest.

With the exception of the strike at the Standard Mill in Colorado City, and the strike in the Cripple Creek District, the strikes in Colorado had been settled or called off, with a decided gain for the workers in the metalliferous industry. After we had returned to the W.F.M. headquarters in Denver, we issued a circular to the workers in the mining industry, reminding them that the Cripple Creek strike was still on, and signed by Moyer and myself.

One day about this time I went home a little earlier than usual and found the house flooded with a crowd of laughing, romping children. I asked my wife what it all meant. She told me:

"I don't know! You'll have to ask Henrietta."

I could see seven-year-old Henrietta's red head bobbing up and down among the others in the dining room. When I could attract her attention I called her to me and asked her why all the children were there.

"Why," she said, "it's a party!"

"Well, why didn't you say something about it to your mamma or to me?" I asked. "Who do you think is running this house?"

"Well," she answered, looking up at me with flashing eyes, "I guess I'm running part of it!"

I looked at her. All at once I saw that she was no longer a baby. I said:

"I realize that. But you haven't made any arrangements to entertain all these children."

"I couldn't tell mamma. She can't keep anything to herself. And, besides, it's a surprise party on her."

"Well," I said, "let's go out and get some cakes and candy to feed all the guests."

After the other children had gone, I called Henrietta and Vernie to the couch where their mother was lying.

"This afternoon Henrietta told me she was running part of this house. Now, in that case, you children will have to take part of the responsibility. You must keep an account of the money you spend, and maybe with four of us running the house we can do it better than it has been done before." From that day the children did their share, and we talked things over with them.

The twelfth convention of the W.F.M., in 1905, was in Salt Lake City. In spite of the many strikes and the tremendous expense involved, it was the finest convention that we ever had held. There had been an increase of three thousand members during the previous year. There were delegates from the new camps in Nevada— Tonopah, Goldfield, Rhyolite and Bullfrog. Albert Ryan was a delegate from Arizona; the W.F.M. elected him to the first I.W.W. convention. Later he got mixed up in a shooting scrape and killed two gunmen who had been strike-breakers, and was sentenced to life imprisonment in San Quentin, California, where he served fifteen years before he was pardoned. The other delegates to the June convention of the I.W.W. were Moyer, Baker, McKinnon and myself. The W.F.M. had adopted the Manifesto and instructed us to install the Federation in the new organization.

After we returned to Denver from Salt Lake, it was only a matter of a few days until we went to Chicago for the first convention of what was to be the Industrial Workers of the World. Brand's Hall, on June 27, 1905, was packed with spectators and over two hundred delegates. Many of the delegates had come up on the platform, among them two old veterans, Mother Jones, the only woman who had taken part in the initial conference, and Gene Debs.

As I exchanged greetings with them, I turned over in my mind how I should open the convention. I recalled that during the French Commune the workers had addressed each other as "fellow citizens," but here there were many workers who were not citizens of the country, so that would not do. I didn't want to use the old trade union form, "brothers and sisters," so, picking up a piece of board that lay on the platform and using it for a gavel, I opened the convention with "fellow workers":

In calling this convention to order I do so with a sense of the responsibility that rests upon me and rests upon every delegate that is here. This is the Continental Congress of the working-class. We are here to confederate the workers of this country into a working-class movement that shall have for its purpose the emancipation of the working class from the slave bondage of capitalism. There is no organization, or there seems to be no labor organization, that has for its purpose the same object as that for which you are called together to-day. The aims and objects of this organization shall be to put the working-class in possession of the economic power, the means of life, in control of the machinery of production and distribution, without regard to capitalist masters.

The American Federation of Labor, which presumes to be the labor movement of this country, is not a working-class movement. It does not represent the working-class. There are organizations that are affiliated, but loosely affiliated, with the A. F. of L. which in their constitution and by-laws prohibit the initiation of, or conferring the obligation on, a colored man; that prohibit the conferring of the obligation on foreigners. What we want to establish at this time is a labor organization that will open wide its doors to every man that earns his livelihood either by his brain or his muscle. There is a great work to be accomplished at this convention, and every one of you must recognize the responsibility that rests upon you.

When the corporations and the capitalists understand that you are organized for the express purpose of placing the supervision of industry in the hands of those who do the work, you are going to be subjected to every indignity and cruelty that their minds can invent. You are also going to be confronted with the so-called labor leader, the man who will tell you and other workers that the interests of the capitalist and the workingman are identical. I want to say that a man who makes that assertion is a worse foe to the working-class than is D. M. Parry or August Belmont. There is not a man who has an ounce of honesty in his make-up but recognizes the fact that there is a continuous struggle between the two classes, and this organization will be formed, based and founded on the class struggle, having in view no compromise and no surrender, and but one object and one purpose, and that is to bring the workers of this country into the possession of the full value of the product of their toil.

Communications were read from many foreign countries; Pouget of the Confederation of Labor of France, Carl Legien of the German labor movement, and the secretaries of other countries had written, wishing success to the convention. There were letters from many in the United States. Ed Boyce sent his excuses for not attending, and there was a letter from Vincent St. John, later to become one of the leaders of the new organization, who signed his letter with an assumed name.

The convention was composed of several groups, the Western Federation of Miners being the dominant factor. Moyer, O'Neill and myself, with the other delegates that represented the W.F.M. as well as the individual miners and smelter men, were acting under the instructions of previous conventions and came to Chicago with clear-cut ideas as to the necessity of an industrial union of the working class.

The American Labor Union delegates were as definite in their purpose, though they had not had the same active experience in the strikes of the West as had the delegates of the W.F.M.

The Socialists who were in the convention with Debs realized that industrial unionism was the foundation of the socialist movement. None of the politicians of the Socialist Party, such as Berger, Hillquit, Spargo or Hayes, took part.

The Socialist Trade and Labor Alliance, DeLeon's organization, might be described as a sect which came to the convention not on account of its activity among the working class, but because of having read and absorbed the Manifesto that called the convention, while the few anarchists present felt that the new organization was a rejuvenation of the early days of the labor movement.

There were, besides these, metal workers and railroad workers representing small bodies which had been disillusioned by the A. F. of L. and the Railroad Brotherhoods. The individual delegates were people who were actively interested in industrial unionism. About 300,000 workers were represented at this first convention. I was elected permanent chairman.

The first important order of business was a discussion on the reasons for the Manifesto. Before the speaking began one of the delegates gave me a gavel. The discussion was opened by William

Trautmann, who had been the editor of the *Brewery Workers Journal,* and who made a scathing indictment of the American Federation of Labor. Other speakers followed who gave many examples of the corruption and inadequacy of the A. F. of L. When Debs arose to speak, there was on one side of him Mother Jones, and on the other Lucy Parsons, widow of one of the Haymarket martyrs. The three made a picture symbolic of the work we had undertaken. Debs said:

They charge us with being assembled here for the purpose of disrupting the union movement. It is already disrupted. And if it were not disrupted, we would not behold the spectacle here in this city of a white policeman guarding a black scab and a black policeman guarding a white scab, while the trade unions stand by, with their hands in their pockets, wondering what is the matter with union labor in America. We are here to-day for the purpose of uniting the working class, for the purpose of eliminating that form of unionism which is responsible for the conditions as they exist to-day.

The trade union movement is to-day under the control of the capitalist class. It is preaching capitalist economics, it is serving capitalist purposes. Proof of it, positive and overwhelming, appears on every hand. All of the important strikes during the last two or three years have been lost. . . .

There is certainly something wrong with that form of unionism which has its chief support in the press that represents capitalism; something wrong in that form of unionism that forms an alliance with such capitalist combinations as the Civic Federation, whose sole purpose is to chloroform the working-class while the capitalist class goes through their pockets. . . .

I believe that it is possible for the delegates here assembled to form a great sound economic organization of the working class based upon the class struggle, that shall be broad enough to embrace every honest worker, yet narrow enough to exclude every faker.

Sitting in front of Debs was Daniel DeLeon of the Socialist Trade and Labor Alliance, with badger-gray whiskers, a black spot on the chin. He had been eyeing his old antagonist, Debs, furtively and seemed charmed by what the leader of workingmen had to say. For years there had been a wide difference of opinion between Debs and DeLeon. They represented extremes in the socialist movement. I could feel what this difference meant when DeLeon began to speak; he was the theorizing professor, while Debs was the working man who had laid down his shovel on the locomotive when he took up the work of organizing the firemen. Debs' ideas, while not clearly developed, were built upon his contact with the workers in their struggle. DeLeon's only contact with the workers was through the ideas with which he wished to "indoctrinate" them, to use his own word. He said:

... I shall simply make a prophecy to Debs and to you that he will also become what the foe said I was—a fanatic; that as he sees the thing clearer to-day than he saw it when the American Railway Union was organized, he will find it also clearer who the foes of the labor movement are. . . . All I wish to go on record as saying is this: I can imagine nothing more pitiable from a man's standpoint than to aspire to an ideal that is unrealizable, and I have overhauled my position again and again answering this question, "Is this problem solvable?" and I have concluded that it is. . . .

If I were to be asked: What difference would you point out more basic than any other between the Socialist Trade and Labor Alliance and any other of the numerous economic organizations that are started with good purpose? I should say this: That the S. T. & L. A. stated what it was there for and stated it frankly . . . frankly and fully stated to the working class of America that they had to capture the public powers. Their belief is this: that you could not first take the men into the union under the false pretense that you were going to raise their wages, and afterward indoctrinate them. No, you had to indoctrinate them *first*, then bring them in. If the S. T. & L. A. had made any mistakes at all, it would be to imagine ten years ago that there were then enough such men in existence to join our ranks. . . .

This showed the strength and the weakness of DeLeon: on the one hand an understanding of the necessity of working-class seizure of power; on the other hand, a lack of understanding of the fact that only through the actual struggle can the working-class get its education for the seizure of power. DeLeon would have been politically sound if he had not been economically hollow.

I spoke on the reasons for the Manifesto:

It has been said that this convention was to form an organization rival to the A. F. of L. That is a mistake. We are here for the purpose of organizing a labor organization; an organization broad enough to take in all the working class. The A. F. of L. is not that kind of an organization, inasmuch as there are a number of international bodies affiliated with it that absolutely refuse to take in any more men. . . .

We recognize that this is a revolutionary movement and that the capitalists are not the only foes that you are to fight, but the most ardent enemy will be the pure and simple trade unionist. But there is only a few of him. He is not very well organized. You have got a tremendous field to work in. There are at least twenty million unorganized workers in the United States of America, to say nothing of Canada. This industrial union movement is broad enough to take in all of them, and we are here for the purpose of launching that union that will open wide its doors to the working class. . . .

The indictments that have been presented here against the International unions and against the A. F. of L. are not nearly as strong as they could have been made, but I think they are sufficient for the occasion. Every individual delegate on this floor knows the terrible corruption that exists in many of these international organizations. . . .

I am delighted to see the extreme political forces joining hands on this economic middle ground. This is what I regard as the basis of all political parties—a solid foundation on which an organization can be built, where the workers can come into a solid and grand formation; and just as surely as the sun rises, when you get the working class organized economically, it will find its proper reflection at the polls. . . .

After considerable debate a constitution was adopted, with the preamble which follows :*

The working class and the employing class have nothing in common. There can be no peace so long as hunger and want are found among millions of working people and the few who make up the employing class have all the good things of life.

Between these two classes a struggle must go on, until all the toilers come together on the political as well as on the industrial field, and take and hold that which they produce by their labor, through an economic organization of the working class without affiliation to any political party.

The rapid gathering of wealth and the centering of the management of industries into fewer and fewer hands make the trade unions unable to cope with the ever-growing power of the employing class, because the trade unions foster a state of things which allows one set of workers to be pitted against another set of workers in the same industry, thereby helping defeat one another in wage wars. The trades unions aid the employing class to mislead the workers into the belief that the working-class has interests in common with their employers.

These sad conditions can be changed and the interests of the working class upheld only by an organization formed in such a way that all its members in any one industry, or in all industries, if necessary, cease work whenever a strike or a lockout is on in any department thereof, thus making an injury to one an injury to all.

Therefore we, the working class, unite under the following constitution.

* This first preamble includes the "political action clause" on which the fight to make the I.W.W. an anarcho-syndicalist organization soon began.

During the convention I was a very busy man. I seldom left the chair during the sessions, and after the meetings were over I met with many of the different committees of which I was considered an ex-officio member. Sullivan, president of the Colorado state federation of labor, was on the committee on the preamble. I suggested some of the changes in the preamble that were adopted. It was Coates who proposed the change of the old slogan of the Knights of Labor, "An injury to one is the concern of all," and made it read, "An injury to one is an injury to all." In the convention it was the miners' delegates that decided every important issue. They had come with the definite purpose of organizing an industrial union. All of these miners' delegates were Socialists, but they fully appreciated the need of an economic organization as a foundation.

The first of May was adopted as the international holiday of the American working class. The general strike was recommended as the most effective weapon against capitalism. It was decided that only wage workers should be eligible to membership. The universal transfer of membership was adopted; any man coming to America with a paid-up card to any union in his own country was accepted into the I.W.W. The American unions at this time were demanding enormous initiation fees from foreign union men applying for membership.

A resolution was adopted for a labor press, a literature committee and a lecture bureau. Militarism was condemned, and any one who joined the army, the militia, or the police power was forever denied membership. This was, of course, at a time when there was no conscription in America.

A. M. Simons and a number of other delegates had referred in their speeches to the Russian Revolution of 1905, which was already an inspiration to the labor movement all over the world. Lucy Parsons spoke of the terror felt by the capitalists of Russia at the raising of the red flag in Odessa. Delegate Kiehn of the Longshoremen introduced a resolution on Russia:

Whereas there is in progress at the present time a mighty struggle of the laboring class of far-off Russia against unbearable outrage, oppression and cruelty, and for more humane conditions for the working class of that country; and

Whereas the outcome of the struggle is of the utmost consequence to the members of the working class of all countries in their struggle for their emancipation; and

Whereas, this convention is assembled for the purpose of organizing the working class of America into an organization that will enable them to shake off the yoke of capitalist oppression: now therefore be it

Resolved, that we, the industrial unionists of America in convention assembled, urge our Russian fellow-workmen on in their struggle, and express our heartfelt sympathy with the victims of outrage, oppression and cruelty, and pledge our moral support and promise financial assistance as much as lies within our power, to our persecuted, struggling and suffering comrades in far-off Russia.

The delegates visited Waldheim cemetery to see the graves of the Chicago martyrs.

When the officers of the new organization were elected, I was nominated by Guy Miller for president. Several other delegates spoke in support of the nomination when it was seconded, one of them saying that I was a man who would not be afraid to go to the bull-pen if necessary. "And lick the militia!" added Mother Jones. But I had to decline, as I had just been reëlected secretary-treasurer of the Western Federation of Miners, and my duties lay with them for the time being. Coates and Sherman were also nominated. Coates declining, Sherman was unanimously elected first—and last—president of the Industrial Workers of the World.

At the ratification meeting which followed, six delegates spoke, among them myself. I said in part:

The organization which has been launched recognizes neither "race, creed, color, sex, or previous condition of servitude." We came out of the West to meet the textile workers of the East. We men of the West are getting more wages per day than these men are getting. We recognize the fact that unless we bring them up to our condition they of necessity will drag us down to theirs. We propose that this industrial movement shall provide, for every man and woman that works, a decent livelihood. Is that something worth working for?

Now understand me—or rather, do not misunderstand me; I do not mean that this organization is going to improve the condition of purely the skilled workers, but I mean we are going to get at the mass of the workers and bring them up to a decent plane of living. I do not care a snap of my finger whether or not the skilled workers join this industrial movement at the present time. When we get the unorganized and the unskilled laborer into this organization the skilled worker will of necessity come here for his own protection. As strange as it may seem to you, the skilled worker to-day is exploiting the labor beneath him, the unskilled man, just as much as the capitalist is. To make myself better understood, the skilled worker has organized for himself a union, recognizing that in unity there is strength. He has thrown high walls around that union which prohibit men from joining the organization. He exacts that a man to become a member of the labor union must of necessity serve an apprenticeship to develop his skill. What for? For the benefit of the union? No, but for the benefit of his employer who is a member of the Citizens' Alliance and who is trying to crush out of existence the same union. . . . The skilled mechanic, by means of the pure and simple trade union, is exploiting the unskilled laborer. . . . There are unions in this country that exact an initiation fee, some of them as high as five hundred dollars. There is the glass blowers' union, to be specific. How long would it take a man working for a dollar or a dollar and a quarter a day and providing for a family to save up enough money to pay his initiation fee into the union? . . . The unskilled laborer's wages have been continually going down and the skilled mechanic through his union has been able to hold his wages at a price and upon a scale that has insured him, even at these high prices, a reasonably decent living, but the laborer at the bottom who is working for a dollar or a dollar and a quarter a day has been ground into a state of destitution. . . .

Now, don't get discouraged, you folks, you of the working class, because here in Chicago you have lost some strikes. Remember that you never could have lost those strikes if you had been organized industrially as the workers in Russia are organized—organized into an organization that takes every man, woman and child working in an industry. For instance, in the packing plants, the butchers' organization was one of the best in this country, reputed to be fifty thousand strong. They were well disciplined, which is shown by the fact that when they were called on strike, they quit to a man. That is, the butchers quit. But did the engineers quit? Did the firemen quit? Did the men who were running the ice plants quit? They were not in the union, not in that particular union. They had agreements with their employers which forbade them quitting. The result was that the butchers' union was practically totally disrupted, entirely wiped out.

Now, presuming that every man around the packing houses, from the printer to the pig stickers, belonged to one union; that when they went on strike the engineers, firemen and men who ran the ice plants all quit; that millions of dollars of produce were in a state so that it would rapidly perish, don't you believe those packing house companies would have capitulated?

Don't you believe that if to-day the organized workers in this great city would not go on strike, but would stay home for two or three days, that the teamsters would win the strike that they are engaged in? One union man is no better than another union man, and any union man that will stand back because a company has an agreement with him, and who will scab on his fellow union man, he may be a union man, but in my opinion he is a scab. . . .

DeLeon's opening speech had, to me, been flat and disappointing, but as the convention progressed he seemed to get into the swing of the work. He was elected on the Constitution Committee as a substitute for a delegate who was taken sick. Immediately after adjournment he delivered an excellent speech in Minneapolis on the Preamble of the I.W.W., which was later brought out as a pamphlet. Debs also took up the work of organization, and a speech of his at Grand Central Palace, New York, was gotten out as a pamphlet. These two speeches were of great propaganda value.

Sam Gompers, in an issue of the *American Federationist,* had tried to belittle the first convention of the I.W.W., but he paid the organization the great compliment of imitating some of its plans, that is, to the extent of establishing departments in the A. F. of L.

On our way back to Denver we talked over the work that had been done and the officials who had been elected. I expressed my confidence in the earnestness and ability of Trautmann, the secretary-treasurer of the new organization. Moyer and the other boys thought that Sherman, of the Metal and Machine Workers, who had been elected president, was a responsible man, and it looked to us, generally speaking, as though the work we had been instructed to do had been well done. There was no misgiving in my mind, at that time, of the possibility of mismanagement or any other kind of trouble arising within the new organization. The fervor and enthusiasm of the delegates were still with me. I felt that the Industrial Workers of the World had a great future before it.

CHAPTER XII

"UNDESIRABLE CITIZENS"

HUNDREDS of Cripple Creek miners had left for the new gold camps in Nevada, where strong unions had been organized at Goldfield, Tonopah and other places. The strike at Cripple Creek and Colorado City was dragging itself out, with nothing definite as to the future.

That fall there was a Mountain and Plains Festival in Denver, of which one of the features was a broncho-busting contest. My brother-in-law, Tom Minor, was one of the riders. I met many of the cowboys and invited them to the headquarters of the Federation, and suggested that their wages and conditions could be improved if they were organized. I said:

"It seems to me you fellows take a lot of chances riding in these contests. For this dangerous work you should get at least fifty dollars a day, and much higher wages than you get now while breaking bronchos on the ranch."

As the result of our meeting the Broncho Busters' and Range Riders' Union of the I.W.W. was organized. Harry Brennan, the champion rider, was elected president and Minor, secretary. Wages for riding in contests were fixed at fifty dollars a day, and fifty dollars a month for broncho busting and range riding on the ranch. They asked me to act as secretary until they were better organized or until Minor had a permanent address. The seal of the union was a cowboy on a bucking broncho which was branded on the hip B.B.R.R. I got out letter heads and envelopes with the same design, but with the cowboy throwing a rope around the return address, saying: "If not rounded up in ten days return to——." The union did not grow or even live very long, and I had but little time to devote to it.

One day I was sitting at my desk when Moyer came in and put down a telegram he had just received. I read it; it was from his wife, who was then in California, saying that she was very sick and asking him to come at once. He had put the telegram down without saying anything, and I picked it up and went into his office. As I handed it back to him I said:

"I'm sorry your wife is sick, Charley. I suppose you'll have to leave right away." He told me that he would, and made arrangements to go that evening. As he left the building I went back to his office.

There on his desk was a book of telegraph blanks, with the carbon paper on top. The thought struck me, why did he tear the copy off? I picked up the carbon paper, took it into my office, and read it in a mirror. It was a telegram from Moyer to his wife, telling her to wire him that she was sick and wanted him to come.

I was surprised at this subterfuge, as there was no occasion for it. If Moyer had told me that he was going to California, I would not have made any objection. When he returned he brought his wife back with him.

It was not long after this that the startling news was in the papers that ex-governor Steunenberg of Idaho had been killed by a bomb at his home in Caldwell. This was on the thirtieth of December, 1905. Shortly after this a man by the name of Hynes began to frequent our office. He spent considerable time in the editor's office. One day early in February he came to my desk and asked if I had the monthly financial report ready. I said, "Yes, I'll get you a copy," and went into the adjoining room, when it occurred to me that it was strange that he should ask for a copy of the financial report; no one had ever done that. I went back and told him it had not yet come from the printer. Then I went out and asked the janitor if he could spare a little time.

"Yes," he said, "what do you want me to do?"

"There's a man in my office," I told him, "a fat fellow. When he leaves I want you to follow him and see where he goes."

He did this and when he came back reported that Hynes had gone to the office of the Pinkerton Detective Agency in the Tabor Block.

I told O'Neill about it, and he wrote a short article about this detective for the next issue of the *Miners' Magazine*. A copy of the article, with the dick's picture, was sent to the Pinkerton office as a valentine.

I said: "There must be more of these skunks around, they probably do not work on one shift."

I had noticed a red-headed fellow hanging around across the street from the office. I said to Moyer: "Let's go to the cattle show." When we got on the street-car, Red-Head jumped on as it was about to move off. When we got to the stock-yards, without seeming to pay attention, we could see this dick dodging around in the crowd. We went back to the office, and from the window a little later we saw him go up to a man sitting on the back of an express wagon. We thought "that makes three of them." The next morning Moyer said that when he was coming out of his house he had seen a man leaning against a stone wall a short distance away. When he looked around he saw that this man was following him.

We soon found out what all these detectives meant. On the night of February seventeenth, Moyer, I, and George Pettibone were arrested; Moyer at the depot, where he was on his way to visit the Smeltermen's Union at Iola and other places in Kansas. Pettibone at his home, and myself at a rooming house near the office.

About eleven thirty in the evening there was a knock on the door. I got up and asked who was there. A voice replied:

"I want to see you, Bill." I opened the door, holding it partly closed when I saw a deputy sheriff whom I knew. He said:

"I want you to come with me." I asked him why.

He said: "I can't tell you now but you must come." I told him to wait a few minutes while I put on some clothes. We went down and got into a carriage. I asked where we were going. He told me, "To the county jail."

"Well," I said, "if you are arresting me why didn't you come with a warrant?"

"I have no warrant," he replied. "We've sent a messenger out for Richardson; we couldn't get him on the 'phone." Richardson being one of the attorneys of the W.F.M., I felt more at ease with this information.

When we got to the jail I was "measured in" as I had been on the previous occasion, when this place had been turned into an office of the W.F.M. Then I was told that Moyer and Pettibone were already arrested and in jail.

They put me in one of the Federal cells. The other boys were in the same quarters. A few minutes later the sheriff who had been elected to fill the place of my friend Ham Armstrong came around. I asked him what it all meant. He said:

"They're going to take you to Idaho. They've got you mixed up in the Steunenberg murder."

"Are we to have no chance at all? You can't arrest a man without a warrant and transport him to another state without extradition papers!"

"It looks as though that's what they are preparing to do," he admitted.

About five o'clock in the morning I was taken with Moyer and Pettibone into the office. There were a lot of strange men there, but among them was Bulkeley Wells. Some one said:

"The carriages are ready. We'll drive down to the hotel."

We drove along the quietest streets, each of us in a separate carriage with three guards. It was very dark. I could not recognize a building through the carriage windows. But when we stopped I found it was at the Oxford Hotel. After a short stop we were marched to the depot, deserted at that hour of the morning. A train was ready and waiting. We stepped aboard and were off for Idaho.

We had a car to ourselves except for the guards, one of whom was Bob Meldrum from Telluride. I have never seen a human face that looked so much like a hyena. His eyes were deep-set and close together. His upper lip was drawn back, showing teeth like fangs.

The deputy warden of the Idaho pentitentiary came up and spoke to us. In the course of his talk, he told us many of his exploits in arresting dangerous men. We listened for want of better entertainment. Later Bulkeley Wells came into the car with a bottle of whisky and asked us to have a drink, which we did, handling the glass rather awkardly on account of the handcuffs. We found out from him that we were on a special train and that we would arrive in Boise the following morning.

We were going at terrific speed. The engine took on coal and water at small stations and stopped at none of the larger towns along the route. When we arrived at Boise we were put into separate conveyances. At the depot a crowd had gathered. I saw among the people a storekeeper whom I had known at Silver City. He spoke to me genially.

We drove to the penitentiary. There was the sign over the gate, Admittance Twenty-five Cents, but as before, when I had come to see Paul Corcoran, I was admitted without charge. In the office we signed a paper authorizing the warden to open any mail that came for us, and I requested that a telegram be sent to John O'Neill in Denver, asking him to forward my personal mail to the penitentiary. I couldn't help noticing the look of surprise that went over the face of Bulkeley Wells at this; he could not have expressed more plainly in words his astonishment that I had nothing to hide in my personal mail.

After being searched in the office we were taken into the prison and put in the death cells. I have always thought that we were put in the death cells in order to condemn us in the mind of the public before we were tried. While we were there I was constantly under the eyes of the death-watch, who sat immediately opposite my cell. Many times I thought, "There are moments when one likes to be alone."

As we entered this corridor and our numbers were called out Pettibone quoted, "There is luck in odd numbers, said Barney Mc-Graw!" My number was nine, Moyer's eleven, and Pettibone's thirteen. Through the window that faced the rear wall I could see what I afterward learned was the death-house, where the condemned were hanged.

Here we were in murderers' row, in the penitentiary, arrested without warrant, extradited without warrant, and under the death watch! We had been kidnaped in the dead of night and did not know whether our lawyers were aware of our destination. Certainly no one could have expected that we would be put in the penitentiary without a hearing, without a trial, or even the semblance of an investigation. They held us there for nearly three weeks. We later found out that Governor Gooding had said that we would "never leave the state alive." This remark piled up a lot of tribulation for the governor. He got thousands of letters of condemnation from all over the world. One person contrived to mail him a letter from a different city every day in the year. We were told that he got six post-bags of mail in one day. But in spite of this he was later elected United States Senator.

On either side of my cell were men who had been condemned to death. Immediately in front of me was the death-watch with his chair propped back against the wall. He did not seem to be interested in the men he was put there to watch. He seemed to keep his venomous eye fastened upon me except when the cell was opened to take out the bucket, or at meal hours when he would turn the food over in the plates and then slip it under the door. It is difficult to realize that under these circumstances I could get news from outside. But the Boise penitentiary was no exception to prisons in general. The prisoners had a code language in which they could discuss almost anything. Messages came in and went out. I cannot tell you how, because there are men still serving time in Boise who were there when I was, twenty years ago.

One day I saw a strip of paper coming through the interstices of the front bars from the cell on my left. I got up and grabbed it, but pulling it too hard I tore it in two. I kept the part I had concealed in my hand until I could find a moment to read it.

The guard, who had probably turned his head away for a moment, thought that I had slipped the message to the other man. He called a "trusty" and sent for the warden. In a few minutes there was a general commotion. They dragged out the man and threw out his bedding and bunk, and examined everything minutely. Finally they pulled out the bucket, and found the charred remains of a bit of paper, a part of the message he had tried to slip me. The little bit of paper I got was blank.

The warden came up to my cell and said: "Haywood, while you're here you are under the rules of this pentitentiary. I do not want you to attempt to communicate with any one."

I replied: "You needn't be alarmed about that. I don't know whom you have got planted around here."

After awhile he came back with a box of cigars that had been sent to us from town by some friend. The cigars had been taken out, of course, and the box had been examined. He was going to hand them through the bars but I told him to give me a few and take the rest to the other boys.

When our lawyers got on the ground, they raised such a hullaballoo about our being in the penitentiary that we were transferred to the county jail at Caldwell. The morning we left for Caldwell we ate breakfast in the prison kitchen, with a guard at the elbow of each of us. It was the first meal we had eaten outside our cells.

On the train from Boise to Caldwell we rode in the day-coach. The other people in the car were reading newspapers. Across the headlines, in letters that could be read fifty feet away, were the names of Moyer, Haywood and Pettibone. In the seat in front of me a man had his paper spread out so that I read over his shoulder.

A Thiel detective who was acting as a guard said "You must not read that." I told him:

"There's nothing I'm more interested in. You fellows have kept us in the dark long enough."

The Caldwell jail was a small affair of four cells, in one of which we were locked up at night. In the daytime we were allowed the use of a large room where there was a cookstove. There were five or six short-time prisoners. Like all county prisons this jail had its "kangaroo court." The prisoners were inclined to let us off without trial, as we agreed to pay any reasonable fine that they might assess us, but we had an opportunity to see how the "kangaroo court" works, when a young fellow was put in the jail charged with rape. In Idaho there is an "age-of-consent" law, and it seemed that in this case the girl was not old enough to consent. The prisoners told this fellow that he was under arrest and that he would have to appear before the "judge," a young hobo who was then seated at the table. They asked him if he had a lawyer; he said no. Pettibone volunteered to act in that capacity. The judge told the prisoner before him that he was charged with breaking into the county jail, which he had done without the consent of the inmates, and asked the attorney what the prisoner had to say in defense. Pettibone made a plea. The prisoner was fined a dollar which was to be used for the benefit of all. Then they arrested Pettibone for having volunteered to act as lawyer, and fined him a dollar. The "kangaroo court" was conducted in much the same order and with quite as much regard for the law as the courts on the outside.

While we were in Caldwell we learned that a stone cutter from Chicago by the name of Billy Cavanaugh, and his partner, were cutting stone for the new court house that was being built in Caldwell. Cavanaugh sent word to us to know if there was any thing we would like to put in the cavity under the cornerstone. We could think of nothing better than a copy of the constitution of the Western Federation of Miners and my membership card, which we sent out by a trusty. Cavanaugh saw that they were deposited before the cornerstone was placed.

One of the prisoners, a bright young fellow, said that he would be going out within a few days, and if there was anything that we wanted him to do for us he would carry any message and bring back the answer either to the Caldwell jail or any other place that we might be moved to. He explained that he could break into jail at any time, and wouldn't do anything that would get him more than six months. We thanked him as best we could and told him that through our lawyers we could get all the news in and out that we required. It seemed that we were not without friends. Here was a man who was willing to do six months in prison for the privilege of bringing us a message! In the penitentiary was the man who had tried to slip me the note, who had been willing to take a chance to give us information, in spite of the fact that his days were numbered. There were others who risked punishment to help us.

While at Caldwell we were taken into the county court, Judge Smith presiding, given a preliminary hearing and remanded back to jail. By some hocus-pocus of the law, a change of venue for the state had been enacted by the legislature. We were transferred to Ada County jail, in the county in which our trial was to take place. Here we were confined at night in a little jail that had been built behind the main building. There were special guards outside, day and night. Sheriff Moseley was a man of some feeling who tried to show us that in his opinion we were not guilty until convicted. We were the only occupants of this little jail, and while our cells were not locked at night, there was a lock on the cage and on the door that led into the main prison.

The first day in the Ada County jail, when I went out for exercise, I was surprised to see that one of the guards was John Taylor, the man on whom I had called years before as one of the committee from the union at Silver City, and who had been compelled to leave the camp by the men of the Black Jack Mine. I couldn't help smiling at the irony of the situation. I never mentioned the incident; neither did he.

The executive board of the W.F.M. had voted me a vacation with five hundred dollars. I had been at the desk continuously for five years, and the members of the board thought that I was entitled to a rest. I never got that vacation. The eighteen months in prison could not be called a vacation.

In the daytime we had a special cell where we had our meals together, and each of us got out for an hour every day, to walk up and down in the sun or amuse ourselves as we pleased in the yard under close watch of the guards. I took excellent care of my health. We had a tub in which we could bathe at any time so I always had a bath at night and setting up exercises in the morning. I fasted several times, for two, three and once for six days. At the time of the trial I was as clear as crystal both physically and mentally.

This was the jail where the plans for the Western Federation of Miners had been talked over before the initial convention in Butte in 1893. Now Moyer and I, the officials of this organization, were imprisoned in this historic jail some fourteen years later. Pettibone had never been a member of the Western Federation.

One of the first bits of good news that we received from headquarters was about the spontaneous defense fund that was being provided for our trial. We had been arrested on February seventeenth. On the twentieth of the same month, Belleville local of the United Mine Workers sent five thousand dollars. This was before any appeal for funds had been made. Telluride Miners' Union sent a large contribution and said they would sell their hospital to increase the fund if necessary. Silverton, Colorado, sent five thousand dollars and guaranteed to raise thirty thousand by selling their hall if it was needed. Goldfield contributed six thousand dollars, so it was easy to see that we were going to have funds enough to secure counsel for our defense.

I made a poster which was printed at headquarters, with a picture of the kidnapers' train, Moyer's picture in the center just above it, Pettibone's and mine on either side, decorated with handcuffs and guns. Across the top was a slogan of Debs: "Arouse, ye Slaves! Their only crime is loyalty to the working class!" With this I gave a description of the manner of our arrest. The poster was distributed broadcast, and was probably the means of raising considerable money.

A part of the time I spent in the Ada County jail was the most quiet, peaceful period of my life. I have never enjoyed myself better than the first months I was there. It was my first real opportunity to read. There I went through Buckle's *History of Civilization*, and extended my acquaintance with Voltaire. I read many English classics, *Tristram Shandy*, the *Sentimental Journey*, Carlyle and others on the French Revolution, much revolutionary literature, Marx and Engels. *The Jungle* by Upton Sinclair kept me awake a whole night, I remember. In addition to this I took a correspondence course in law, John Murphy having arranged this for me. Murphy was always anxious for me to become a law partner of his, but before

I got out of prison my experience there, added to what I had observed about the law in Colorado and previously in Idaho, made me unwilling to become involved in a profession that was so crooked and so meaningless for the working class.

We had applied to the United States Supreme Court for a writ of habeas corpus. Our attorney sent for the circumstances of our arrest, and that with the connivance of the governors of the two states we had been transported from Colorado to Idaho without extradition warrants; that we had had no opportunity to see counsel. Habeas Corpus means that the body of the arrested shall be brought into court. As it is to prevent secret and illegal arrest and detention it is supposed to be acted upon promptly. But we were in jail from February until the following December. When the decision was handed down at last, refusing the writ of habeas corpus, eight of the august judges voted in favor of it, Judge McKenna being the lone dissenter. He declared that the kidnaping was a crime pure and simple, and said that "the states, through their officers, were the offenders." In his opinion this was not, as the majority tried to make out, a case of an individual kidnaping an individual. "No individuals could have accomplished what the power of two states accomplished; no individuals could have commanded the means and success; could have made two arrests of prominent citizens by invading their homes; could have commanded the resources of jails, armed guards and special trains; could have successfully timed all acts to prevent inquiry and judicial interference."

When we learned of this decision I got out another poster under the title of "Habeas Corpus be Damned; We'll give 'em post mortems." Adjutant General Sherman Bell had said this when he and Captain Bulkeley Wells had ignored the writ of habeas corpus that had been granted to Moyer at Telluride. They had been fined five hundred dollars each for contempt of court, which they never paid. But here was the United States Supreme Court itself upholding their criminal action. On this poster was printed the dissenting opinion of Judge McKenna.

When Maxim Gorky came to New York from Russia, one of the first things he did was to send us a telegram of greetings from the Russian workers. I replied to this telegram and told Gorky that our being in prison was an expression of the class struggle which was the same in America as in Russia and in all other capitalist countries. Immediately after this a howl went up against Gorky in regard to his wife, who had come from Russia with him. American moralists, among them Mark Twain, objected to the fact that Gorky had never been legally married to his wife, although they had lived together many years. It was strange that no one thought of this objection until after Gorky had telegraphed to us in prison. He was thrown out of hotels, viciously attacked in the newspapers, and finally forced to leave the country.

From the 1906 convention of the Western Federation of Miners we received resolutions of encouragement. A new preamble to the constitution was adopted, which I quote here:

1. We hold that there is a class struggle in society and that this struggle is caused by economic conditions.

2. We affirm the economic condition of the producer to be that he is exploited of the wealth that he produces, being allowed to retain barely sufficient for his elementary necessities.

3. We hold that the class struggle will continue until the producer is recognized as the sole master of his product.

4. We assert that the working class, and it alone, can and must achieve its own emancipation.

5. We hold, finally, that an industrial union and the concerted political action of all wage workers is the only method of attaining this end.

6. Therefore, we, the wage slaves, employed in and around the mines, mills, smelters, tunnels, open pits and open cuts, have associated in the Western Federation of Miners.

Senator Patterson wrote an editorial, devoting an entire page of the *Rocky Mountain News* to criticism of the W.F.M. for having referred to themselves as "wage slaves."

Theodore Roosevelt, then president of the United States, got into the game by declaring that we were "undesirable citizens." I answered this statement briefly, calling to the president's attention the fact that the laws of the country stated that we were to be considered innocent until proven guilty; that a man in his position should be the last to judge us until the case was decided in court. My statement had a wide circulation. Many people, and probably all the workers, agreed to what I had said.

I often thought over this charge of Roosevelt's, and on the public platform I have compared myself to this man who in his book about the battle of San Juan Hill openly declared that he had shot a fleeing

Spaniard in the back, adding: "It was not until the next day that I learned that my act was not unique, as a lieutenant had also killed another Spaniard in the same way."

In 1907, during the financial crisis, the gold mining companies of Nevada attempted to pay off their men with clearing house checks. James Kirwan, who was acting as secretary-treasurer of the W.F.M., wrote asking me to get out some sort of circular on the fake money that the mining companies were trying to impose on the miners. The workers were producing gold, and expressed their willingness to accept part of the product in return for their labor. I got out a draft of a circular for the campaign. The miners succeeded in getting their pay in money every month, but this exaction engendered hard feelings between them and the companies.

William E. Borah was at this time attorney for the Barbour Lumber Company, the president of which was in the Ada County jail. It seems that the lumber company had been fraudulently locating timber claims. It was intimated at the time that Borah would likewise be indicted, but the case blew over. When the president of the company was leaving the prison, he passed a window where I was standing and said, "I wish you luck!"

"Thank you," I replied, "I'd rather be where I am than where you are, although you are leaving the jail."

Through the inch-square holes of the flat-barred window of our day cell I could look out on the broad lawn where dandelions were scattered about like pieces of miser's gold on a green cloth, shaded near the fence by a giant maple tree. In the cell the setting sun cast checkered shadows on the floor.

One night while sitting in my cell I saw a tiny curved strip of silver at one of the small windows high up near the roof. I could not think what it was. It kept growing bigger and at last I realized that it was the moon. It soon covered the entire window. It was the first time I had seen the moon in fifteen months.

On one side of the Boise court house and jail were sixteen rose bushes. These afforded me much pleasure the first summer I was there. When I went out for exercise, I would walk up and down among these bushes and pick off all the roses whose petals were about to fall. Every day I carried a quantity into the cell, spread papers and dried the petals in the shade. I kept on doing this until I had a pile of rose leaves large enough to make a cushion. Then

I had Mrs. Moyer get me a cushion cover; she chose one of silk with roses embroidered on it. I had her buy me a little attar of roses to sprinkle over the leaves. I filled the cushion and sent it to my wife. She treasured it as her favorite keepsake.

Pettibone spent much of his time doing pyrography, or burnt wood work. He made some very fine specimens, using the tops and bottoms of cigar boxes for material.

Moyer devoted most of his time to reading.

The Socialist Party of Colorado nominated me as candidate for Governor in the elections of 1906. It was a most unusual proceeding, to nominate a man who was in prison in another state. I wrote a letter of acceptance, but I might remark that I didn't run; I just marked time. Still, after the elections the returns showed that I had something over sixteen thousand votes, which was not a bad endorsement in a state where the vote was as small as that of Colorado. In this election I ran neck-and-neck with Judge Ben Lindsey, the reformer who conducted the children's court in Denver.

We thought that Judge Lindsey was inclined to be friendly to the W.F.M. but we had had occasion at one time to take exception to his method of giving the children who came before him vacations. He had suggested that they should be sent out to work in the beetfields. O'Neill wrote a strong article in the *Miners' Magazine* against this proposal to work the children in the fields, and told Judge Lindsey that it would look better on his part if he would try to arrange real vacations for the children in pleasant places in the mountains. This suggestion was received favorably by the judge, who tried to put it into effect.

The second convention of the Industrial Workers of the World was held in Chicago in September, 1906. Acrimony developed in this convention between Charles Mahoney, then vice president of the W.F.M., and Vincent St. John, who had also come to the convention as a delegate. This feeling arose partially over St. John's antagonism to Charles Sherman, the president of the I.W.W.

Sherman was deposed and the office of president was abolished. Sherman had proved incapable, and if not actually dishonest, he had used an enormous amount of the funds for unnecessary purposes. Mahoney had joined forces with the metal workers, and St. John had the locals, formerly of the American Labor Union, behind him, as well as the few members of DeLeon's Socialist Trade and Labor Alliance who had joined the I.W.W. The St. John forces controlled the convention, but Sherman and Mahoney took possession of the office.

Two factions of the I.W.W. were established, the St. John faction with Trautmann as secretary, and the Mahoney-Sherman faction which had elected a man by the name of Hanneman. The last named faction soon liquidated for want of members. Through the manipulations of a Socialist lawyer, Seymour Stedman, the Socialist Party came into possession of the office fixtures, safes, desks, and so on. The W.F.M. stood aloof from both elements. While this bitter fight was going on we were behind the bars, powerless to do anything. I wrote a letter to the convention, a part of which I quote from Brissenden's *History of the I.W.W.*, with Brissenden's comments:

The jailing of Haywood, especially, one of the most aggressive and influential organizers of the I.W.W., deeply affected the members of that body and really substracted much from their strength. It was generally felt among laboring men and women that Moyer and Haywood were jailed because they were members of the Industrial Workers of the World, or because they were Socialists. A letter written by Haywood in the Ada County jail on the day that the second convention opened in Chicago indicates the active interest he continued to take in the organization even during his imprisonment. It is here given in part:

Ada County Jail, Boise, Idaho, Sept. 17, 1906.
To the Officers and Delegates of the Second Annual Convention of the Industrial Workers of the World.
Comrades and Fellow Workers:
While you have been in convention to-day I have devoted the hours to a careful review of the proceedings of the initial convention of the I.W.W. and of the conference that issued the Manifesto leading up to the formation of the organization which has . . . rekindled the smoldering fire of ambition and hope in the breast of the working class of this continent . . . (quoting here from his own letter to the fourteenth convention of the Western Federation of Miners). Organized industrially, united politically, labor will assume grace and dignity, horny hand and busy brain will be the badge of distinction and honor, all humanity will be free from bondage, a fraternal brotherhood imbued with the spirit of independence and freedom, tempered with the sentiment of justice and love of order; such will be . . . the goal (and) aspiration of the Industrial Workers of the World.
The message was received with boundless enthusiasm. It stimulated all to more determined efforts on behalf of the accused.

Bad feeling grew between Moyer and myself, and for nearly a year we were not on speaking terms. To the following convention of the W.F.M. I wrote a letter in which I strongly condemned the methods that had been adopted by Mahoney, the manner in which he had handled the affair at Chicago, and his employing strong-arm men for the defense of the I.W.W. office, Mahoney having seized the office and held it by force against the St. John faction. This letter was addressed to James Kirwan, who was acting in my place as secretary-treasurer. I concluded it by saying "I can have no friends among your enemies." I did not learn until a long time later that Kirwan read to the convention only that part of this letter of mine that referred to himself. He neglected to read the first part of the letter, in which I had criticized Mahoney. The letter, as he read it, appeared in the Proceedings of the W.F.M. convention.

The action of St. John and his supporters at this time was wholly commendable, and upon them rests the entire credit for the continuation of the Industrial Workers of the World.

Brissenden outlines the reasons for the slow growth of the I.W.W. at this time, and for the withdrawal of the W.F.M.:

Although the Moyer-Haywood trial and the final acquittal of the accused men made the I.W.W. somewhat more commonly known and understood among the working class throughout the country it was, on the whole, nothing less than a calamity for that organization. The I.W.W. did not even get publicity out of the Moyer-Haywood case. The Western Federation got all the advertising. It was a well-established labor organization with an eventful—almost a lurid—history. Its early activities were more or less related to the Moyer-Haywood-Pettibone affair and the general public very naturally thought of the Western Federation when they thought of the Haywood deportation. The I.W.W. was not popularly associated with the Boise trial at all. The organization was obliged almost completely to suspend its vital work of organization to raise funds for the defense. But this was not the most serious result. The Moyer-Haywood-Pettibone deportation was unquestionably one of the causes operating to split off the Western Federation of Miners. The imprisonment of Haywood certainly weakened that element in the Western Federation which backed the I.W.W., and strengthened the hands of those who were opposed to continued incorporation with it. This combined with the deposition of President Sherman, which yet further weakened the forces of the miners who supported the I.W.W., finally gave the I.W.W. knockers in the Western Federation the upper hand. The result was, first a decision by referendum vote of the Western Federation of Miners not to pay dues to either the Shermanite or the anti-

Shermanite factions in the I.W.W., and second, the formal withdrawal of the mining department and the reëstablishment of an independent Western Federation of Miners in the summer of 1907.*

It would be hard to describe my feelings at this time. I felt the work of a lifetime was being torn into shreds. The peace and quiet of the jail were dispelled. The poet who wrote "stone walls do not a prison make, nor iron bars a cage," was not like me, crowded with thoughts, with no chance for action. I was in prison, and every letter, every article that I read bearing upon this disruption increased my restlessness under restraint.

Many letters were coming to us from different organizations all over the country, with news of widespread demonstrations on our behalf. There had been a protest meeting on Boston Common, where it was estimated two hundred thousand people had gathered to voice their condemnation of our illegal arrest and kidnaping. Moyer-Haywood-Pettibone parades were being held everywhere. In Chicago fifty thousand union men and women marched in protest. In New York the parade was even larger. It was not hard for me to imagine that I could hear the marching millions shouting aloud: "If Moyer, Haywood and Pettibone die, millions of workers will know the reason why!" If the slogan "united front" had existed then, it would have applied to the solidarity of the workers in our case.

The workers of the little town of Boise were coöperating. One day we received a cake from a restaurant in Boise, and under the cake was a letter from the workers who had made it and other employees of the restaurant.

The second summer I was there, I cleared away a lot of lumber that was in the back yard of the jail and smoothed off a piece of ground for a garden. I had nasturtiums growing up over the woodpile and sweet peas against the little fence, sunflowers against the outer fence, that grew eight or ten feet high with immense blossoms. I had all kinds of garden truck, too, enough not only for ourselves but for the warden's family and the other prisoners.

I was out in this garden one day when two nuns passed by. Ras Beamer, a guard who was standing near me, said:

"By God! Did you see that?" I asked him what he meant.

"Do you know that nun nearest the fence?" he asked.

---

* Brissenden, *Loc. cit.*, p. 175.

"I don't think so. Why?"

"She turned right round and waved at you!" he said. I had not noticed her.

Moyer's and Pettibone's wives lived in Boise during our imprisonment. My family came just before the trial began, and usually I spent an hour with them every day, out on the lawn near the rose bushes. One day I was surprised to see my mother step out of a carriage that had driven into the back yard. She saw me and called out, "Come here, my son!"

When I got to her she met me with a warm embrace. Her health was not good, but she was in the courtroom until near the end of my trial, when she had to go to the hospital.

Lawyers came by ones and twos until we had a strong array of legal talent. John Murphy, the regular attorney for the W.F.M.; Darrow and Richardson, senior counsel; John F. Nugent, a lawyer from Silver City who afterward became United States Senator, an old-time friend of mine; Edgar Wilson, ex-congressman; Miller and Whitsell. Some of them came to the jail every day.

Darrow often came to the jail, down-in-the-mouth and worried. Pettibone would offer consolation, saying that we knew it would be hard on Darrow to lose this great case, but, he would add, "You know it's us fellows that have to be hanged!" I suggested to Darrow that when things got gloomy around the office he should come to the jail and we would cheer him up.

As the opening day of the trial came nearer, correspondents of many papers began to arrive; from the Associated Press, the United Press, the *Appeal to Reason,* this last a Socialist paper published in Girard, Kansas, with Debs as one of the editors. The *Appeal to Reason* got out many editions in connection with our case, one of them called the Kidnaping Edition, of four million copies; the like was never duplicated before or since. The *New York American,* a Hearst paper, also got out a special edition in which there was nothing except articles about the Moyer-Haywood-Pettibone case.

The prosecution decided to try my case first.

CHAPTER XIII

THE BOISE TRIAL

My trial began on the ninth of May, 1907. William E. Borah, who had been elected United States Senator by the previous legislature, the man who had prosecuted Paul Corcoran, was a special prosecutor in this case. James Hawley, a one-time miner who had been the lawyer for the Cœur d'Alenes prisoners when they had occupied the jail we now lived in, was also a special prosecutor. Hawley was the man who had suggested to the imprisoned miners that an organization should be formed comprising all the miners of the West. The Caldwell County attorney was one of the assistant prosecutors.

A suggestion was made that Eugene V. Debs should be invited to come to Boise to write up the trial for the *Appeal to Reason*. Debs was then at the height of his fame and was the spokesman for a vast number of working-class people, and a leader of the Socialist Party. This suggestion was discussed by Darrow, Richardson, my fellow prisoners and myself. Moyer and Pettibone were not interested in having Debs come to Boise, and Darrow raised vigorous objections, without giving any definite reason. His opposition could not have been because of Debs being a Socialist. I, too, was a Socialist, and Darrow himself, with Jack London and some others, had some time before issued a call for the organization of a society to promote an intelligent interest in Socialism among college men and women, which resulted in the formation of the Intercollegiate Socialist Society. I searched my mind for Darrow's reason for objecting to Debs' presence, and could think of nothing but his desire to be recognized as the most prominent person in the trial.

The attorneys for the defense sat at a table on the right of the courtroom. When my mother, wife and daughters came to the court, they occupied a place inside the railing. Correspondents of different newspapers were back of the attorneys on either side of the courtroom. Judge Woods presided, on an elevated platform behind the jury. I sat so near the first juryman in the front row that I could have touched him. My close contact with him during the weeks that we were together in the court formed an acquaintanceship. Although I never spoke to him until after the trial was over, I felt that I knew him.

A labor jury of Socialists and union men was seated among the audience. All the members of this jury attended every session of the court, and rendered a final verdict. The court was crowded every day.

At this time a writer in *McClure's Magazine* described me in the following words:

I place Haywood's name first; he is a man of force in the Federation. And a man who can rise to supremacy over such an organization must be endowed with not a few high qualities of leadership. Haywood is a powerfully built man, built with the physical strength of an ox. He has a big head and a square jaw. A leader is here judged by the very force of his impact. Risen from the mines himself, "from the bowels of the earth," as he describes it, this man has become a sort of religious zealot, and Socialism is his religion. He is a type of the man not unfamiliar now in America, equipped with a good brain, who has come up struggling and fighting, giving blows and taking them, who, knowing deeply the wrongs of his class, sees nothing beyond; whose mind, groping hopelessly for remedies, seizes eagerly upon a scheme like Socialism which so smoothly and perfectly solves all difficulties. Take a character like this, hard, tough, warped, immensely resistant, and give him a final touch of idealism, a Jesuitic zeal that carries the man beyond himself, and you have a leader who, like Haywood, will bend his people to his own beliefs. And we do not expect to find such a leader patient of obstacles, nor far-sighted, nor politic, nor withholding a blow when there is power to inflict the blow, nor careful of means when there are ends to be gained. What is a man, or a state, when a cause is to be served?

Everybody was on the *qui vive* about the confession which they knew Harry Orchard had made, although it had not been published. Steve Adams, a Cripple Creek miner, who had been arrested at his uncle's ranch in Oregon, had also made a confession which he later repudiated. While the people who crowded the court were eager, there was to be some delay, as the jury had still to be selected. The examination of the jurors was a broad education in the class struggle. In the panels selected, all the bankers of the county had been called as jurymen, but Darrow disposed of these in short order. He would begin by asking if they were acquainted with the case; if they read the newspapers; if they had formed an opinion; whether evidence would be required to change this opinion. Then he would show by his questions that there was little difference between a banker and a burglar; one worked in the daytime with interest and stock-juggling as the means of robbery, while the other worked at night with the jimmy and nitroglycerin. He would challenge them for cause. It was like killing snakes.

The regular jury when finally selected was composed almost entirely of farmers. The bankers and business men had been challenged by the defense; the few union men or Socialists called had been challenged by the prosecution. Another thing had happened to lower still further my estimation of the law; the legislature had enacted an ex-post-facto law which added to the number of jury challenges of the state.

The prosecution laid their foundation for the trial with the testimony of several minor witnesses. Then Harry Orchard was called to the stand. He was neatly dressed in a gray suit of the warden's, was clean shaven, with his hair combed smoothly over a head as round as a billiard-ball. I remarked his resemblance to MacParland the detective. Far from being the furtive weasel of a man that his story would lead one to expect, Orchard was well-set-up, bluff, with an apparently open manner. I kept my eyes on that man while he was on the stand, but he never met my gaze.

He was not questioned much by Borah, but was told to tell his story in narrative form. He related a blood-curdling tale, commencing with his life in Canada. He had left a wife and child in Ontario after burning down a cheese-factory there. He said his real name was Albert Horseley. The next exploit that he claimed to his credit was the lighting of one of the fuses that had caused the explosion that destroyed the Bunker Hill and Sullivan Mill in the Cœur d'Alenes. At that time he claimed to have been one of the owners of the Headlight group of mines near Burke, Idaho.

As a gambler and rounder he had made his way to the Cripple Creek district. There he seemed to have taken an active part in the union work for a time, in order to gain the confidence of the miners, and was at the same time the associate and employee of the Citizens' Alliance. It was at about this time that he had first come to the headquarters of the Federation, at the request, as we later discovered, of Detective Scott, by whom he was paid and to whom he reported. His next visit to headquarters was when he went to Ouray with Moyer. Beckmann and McKinley were his coworkers. These men, it will be remembered, had tried to wreck a train in Cripple Creek, which they said they were willing to do for five hundred dollars, though it might cost the lives of two hundred and fifty or more people. For this they had been employed by Scott and Sterling, both of whom now sat in the Boise courtroom listening to Orchard's story. Neither of them took the stand as witnesses in this case.

Orchard told of his connection with the Vindicator explosion, the Independence Depot explosion, and of many attempts on the lives of Governor Peabody, Judges Gabbert and Goddard, and McNeil, Hearn, Bradley and others. It was a revolting story of a callous degenerate, and no one will ever know how much of it was true and how much fabrication. He concluded his tale by telling how he had caused the death of ex-governor Frank Steunenberg.

From beginning to end he mentioned the names of Pettibone, Moyer and myself as having been the instigators of his murders; saying that either one or the other of us had instructed him in the commission of the work that he had engaged in. He varied little in his story under cross-examination, having been well drilled by his mentor, James MacParland, head of the Denver agency of the Pinkerton Detectives. This was the same man who had started his career long before by swearing away the lives of the Molly Maguires in Pennsylvania.

After the testimony of Orchard, the prosecution introduced old numbers of the Anarchist paper, the *Alarm,* which had been edited by Albert Parsons in 1886. Many articles were read to prove the theory and practice of the Western Federation of Miners twenty years later. Then they introduced copies of the *Miners' Magazine.* O'Neill had written an editorial describing the explosion which killed Governor Steunenberg, which was supposed to show the animus of the Federation. Perhaps the prosecution had expected us to mourn the governor's death.

Then they introduced the resolution I had written in the Florida tunnel, in Silver City, in which I had condemned Steunenberg for asking for federal troops and declaring martial law in the Cœur d'Alenes. Their next witness was Stewart, who had been master mechanic at the Blaine mine and mill when I was working there. He testified that I had said that "Steunenberg ought to be exterminated." He said he remembered these words, as he had always regarded me as one of the best citizens in the camp. When he made this remark it was decided that there was no need to cross-examine him.

It was thought that Governor Peabody would be an interesting witness; he had testified one forenoon and was to be cross-examined in the afternoon. During the noon recess, Darrow and Richardson talked over his testimony with me and decided there was nothing we wanted to develop through him. When court convened the governor took the stand and sat there for ten minutes, adjusting his necktie, smoothing his hair, pulling down his vest and straightening the creases in his trousers, the picture of nervousness and apprehension, catching at a lump in his throat when Richardson said, "That's all, Governor."

Ex-Governor Grant of Colorado, president of the Grant Smelter Company, was the next witness. He testified about the smelter men's strike, and on cross-examination denied that he had shed tears when he spoke to me after my speech on the condition of the smelter men's families, in the assembly chamber of the capitol building at Denver.

One of the victims of the Independence Depot explosion got on the stand with his crippled legs and testified as to the explosion and the injuries he had received. But he had such a hang-dog look that even the prosecution was digusted with the specimen they had brought for exhibition. He was no better as a witness than Governor Peabody had been.

During the progress of the trial I received several strange requests. One was from some person in Florida, who sent me a box of magnolias and asked me to wear a magnolia bud in my buttonhole every day during the trial. Another asked for the imprint of my hand in plaster, in order to read my palm. Through Darrow I received an offer from *McClure's* of three thousand dollars for a thousand-word story, or a thousand dollars for three thousand words—some enormous sum, I don't remember which! I complied with none of these requests.

As soon as Orchard's testimony was heralded over the country, telegrams began coming in from people he had mentioned, offering to come as witnesses to repudiate what he had said. Bill Davis and others came and demolished that part of Orchard's testimony that referred to them. Two men came from Mullan, Idaho, and testified that Orchard was playing poker with them in the rear of a cigar store in Mullan at the time of the explosion that destroyed the

Bunker Hill and Sullivan mill. A contractor and builder from San Francisco testified that the building from the roof of which Orchard claimed to have stepped to the Bradley home, had not yet been built when Orchard said he had been in San Francisco. A woman from Cripple Creek gave evidence about the many times that Orchard had visited the rooms of Stirling and Scott in her rooming house. Charles Moyer was a creditable witness, but to my surprise, when we returned to the cell where Pettibone was, he blurted out, "I hope that will please the Goddam revolutionists!"

Ed Boyce, former president of the Western Federation, was also a witness. He was severely cross-examined by Borah, but he never flinched. He stated that he had said in his report in 1896 that he "hoped to hear the martial tread of twenty-five thousand armed miners before the next convention," and that he was in earnest in this desire because of what had happened in the Cœur d'Alenes, Cripple Creek and Leadville. It gave me a thrill of the old days to hear Boyce testify.

Darrow, in this case as in others that he has defended, picked out a "goat" among the prosecution lawyers. In this instance it was Jim Hawley upon whom he concentrated his sarcasm. He was at times so venomous that Hawley's son threatened him with personal violence. Darrow was not always the smiling, suave, persuasive individual that he is sometimes described. His grandest moments were when he was in the attitude of attack. Some of the witnesses suffered severely. He tore the degenerate Orchard to fragments, and said, "It is this arch criminal that the prosecution is protecting!" to which Senator Borah took exception, saying with uplifted hand, "May my right hand wither if this man is not prosecuted!"

During the trial I had stretched out on my cot in the jail one night when I was taken with severe cramps that soon developed into convulsions. The jail was aroused, and before the doctor arrived I was suffering intense pain. By morning I had not recovered sufficiently to go into court, so the trial was delayed for a day.

When I went on the witness stand the examination was conducted by Darrow. I went over the history of my life, my connection with the Western Federation, my knowledge of Orchard, and everything that had happened with which I had anything to do, down to that hour. Borah in his cross-examination did not have things all his own way. He faced me with his bulldog expression and the deep dimple in his chin, and asked about the resolution that I had written in Silver City. He said:

"You felt very bitter against Governor Steunenberg?"

"Yes," I answered, "I felt toward him much as I did toward you and others who were responsible for martial law and the bull-pen in the Cœur d'Alenes."

"So I have understood," the senator remarked. Just what he meant I could not make out.

During his cross-examination the sun was sinking and shining through a window toward which I was facing. I said to the judge, "If your Honor please, will you kindly have the shutters closed on that window? The sun is shining in my face and I cannot see the senator's eyes."

It was not my intention to disconcert the senator, but I was told afterward that he said he had never heard of a man on trial for his life who was so anxious to see the prosecutor's eyes. He said, "It doubled me up like a jack-knife!"

One day when I was on the stand being cross-examined, the judge announced that there would probably be a night session. The senator protested, saying that he felt as if he had already done two days' work in one.

I was examined and cross-examined about Stewart's testimony that I had said Governor Steunenberg should be exterminated. I said that, to the best of my remembrance, I had said he should be eliminated.

Almost a hundred witnesses came to Boise for me at the trial; eighty-seven of them testified in my behalf, a few of them did not take the stand. These people were not subpœnaed, as most of them were residents of other states. Frank Schmelzer, a member of the executive board of the Western Federation, was killed as he attempted to step on a moving train at Denver on his way to the trial. Alva Swain, Denver editor of the Pueblo *Chieftain,* whom I have mentioned before, came to Boise twice before the opportunity came for him to testify.

When the defense rested, Borah opened the argument to the jury. He spoke long and forcibly.

I had been charged with killing Governor Frank Steunenberg, a man whom I had never seen, who was killed in a place where I had never been. I was more than a thousand miles away at the time of his death. He had been killed by a man whom I had not seen for eight months or a year, and from whom I had never heard during that time. It seemed to me impossible that Borah could expect a conviction; and in all his speech he did not ask that I be hanged.

He was followed by Richardson, who spoke for nine hours. The concluding address to the jury in my behalf was made by Clarence Darrow, who is not only a great lawyer but a keen psychologist.

When Darrow rose to address the jury he stood big and broad-shouldered, dressed in a slouchy gray suit, a wisp of hair down across his forehead, his glasses in his hand, clasped by the nose-piece. He began by tracing the history of the Western Federation of Miners, from the jail that had been our home for the past eighteen months, where the organization had been conceived. He pictured the isolated assemblies of the Knights of Labor and the efforts of these organizations to maintain a decent standard of living. He told of the Cœur d'Alenes strike of 1892 and the strike of 1899 which had been called an insurrection. He told about the calling of the Federal soldiers into the Cœur D'Alenes district at the time of these strikes, of martial law, of bull-pens, special prosecutions and imprisonments.

He went over in detail the many strikes that the W.F.M. had conducted in Colorado, showing that when the eight-hour law for which the organization had fought was passed, the unions were compelled to strike in order to enforce the law. He spoke of the effect of martial law on the people of a state or district where it prevailed, and of the suffering and worry that it entailed upon all who lived under such conditions.

He went over the testimony of the various witnesses for the state and then drew a comparison between them and the people who had given testimony for me. He told again of the illegal arrest, the kidnaping, the special train and military guard, showed that the prosecution would have shrunk from nothing in order to implicate me in this murder.

To kill him, gentlemen! I want to speak to you plainly. Mr. Haywood is not my greatest concern. Other men have died before him. Other men have been martyrs to a holy cause since the world began. Wherever men have looked upward and onward, forgotten their selfishness, struggled for humanity, worked for the poor and the weak, they have been sacrificed. They have been sacrificed in the prison, on the scaffold, in the flame. They have met their death, and he can meet his if you twelve men say he must. But, gentlemen, you short-sighted men of the prosecution, you men of the Mine Owners' Association, you people who would cure hatred with hate, you who think you can crush out the feelings and the hopes and the aspirations of men by tying a noose around his neck, you who are seeking to kill him, not because it is Haywood, but because he represents a class, don't be so blind, be so foolish as to believe you can strangle the Western Federation of Miners when you tie a rope around his neck. Don't be so blind in your madness as to believe that if you make three fresh, new graves you will kill the labor movement of the world. I want to say to you, gentlemen, Bill Haywood can't die unless you kill him. You have got to tie the rope. You twelve men of Idaho, the burden will be on you. If, at the behest of this mob, you should kill Bill Haywood, he is mortal, he will die, and I want to say that a million men will take up the banner of labor at the open grave where Haywood lays it down, and in spite of prisons or scaffolds or fire, in spite of prosecution or jury, these men of willing hands will carry it on to victory in the end. . . .

The legislature, in 1902, was asked to pass that law which the Constitution commanded them to pass, and what did it do? Mr. Guggenheim and Mr. Moffatt and the Mine Owners' Association and all the good people in Colorado who lived by the sweat and blood of their fellow men—all of those invaded the chamber of the house and the senate and said: "No, you must not pass an eight-hour law; true, the Constitution requires it; but here is our gold, which is stronger than the Constitution." The legislature met and discussed the matter. Haywood was there; the labor organizations were there pleading then, as they have always pleaded, for the poor, the weak, the oppressed. . . .

"What is the Constitution for except to let the rich rob the poor?" asked Darrow. He described Supreme Court Justice Goddard as the dirtiest political skate in Colorado. . . .

If you kill him your act will be applauded by many; if you should decree Haywood's death, in the great railroad offices of our great cities men will sing your praises. If you decree his death, amongst the spiders and vultures of Wall Street will go up paeans of praise for those twelve good men and true who killed Bill Haywood. . . .

In almost every bank in the world, where men wish to get rid of agitators and disturbers, where men put in prison one who fights for the poor and against the accursed system upon which they live and grow fat, from all these you will receive blessings and praise that you have killed him.

But if you free him there are still those who will reverently bow their heads and thank these twelve men for the character they have saved. Out on our broad prairies, where men toil with their hands: out on the broad ocean, where men are sailing the ships: through our mills and factories: down deep under the earth, thousands of men, of women, of children, men who labor, men who suffer, women and children weary with care and toil, these men and these women and these children will kneel to-night and ask their God to guide your judgment. These men and these women and these little children, the poor and the weak and the suffering of the world, will stretch out their hands to this jury and implore you to save Haywood's life. . . .

He had spoken eleven hours. While he spoke he was sometimes intense, his great voice rumbling, his left hand shoved deep in his coat pocket, his right arm uplifted. Again he would take a pleading attitude, his voice would become gentle and very quiet. At times he would approach the jury almost on tiptoe. This speech was, I think, one of Clarence Darrow's greatest.

A part of the instructions that were read to the jury by Judge Woods was written by John Murphy in his sick-bed at the hospital. The case went to the jury on the night of June twenty-seventh.

That night I went to bed at about the usual time, and slept undisturbed until they aroused me in the morning with the news that the verdict had been brought in. There was no hint as to what the verdict might be.

When I came into the court the room was filled with people. The jury was called and the judge asked if they had come to a verdict. The foreman answered that they had and briefly added, "Not guilty."

There was some commotion as the jurymen began to step from their places. At the request of Richardson they were called back and polled, each one answering formally as he was called upon, "Not guilty."

I had been surprised as the jury came in at the appearance of a juryman named Gilbert; his face was ashen gray.

One of the jurymen, with long whiskers, pulled a small American flag out of his pocket and said, "Haywood, I'd like you to sign your name on this flag." I laughed and reminded him of the trouble I had already got into in Denver, writing on the flag. But I signed my name and he got his souvenir.

The labor jury's verdict of "not guilty" had already been announced. I received many congratulations from friends in the courtroom and from all my lawyers, shook hands with the jurymen, and was invited by the foreman to visit his home before I left town.

As I went down the back stairs to the jail, I saw the penitentiary wagon just driving out of the yard. The warden had been waiting for me. The guard unlocked the cell. Moyer and Pettibone had already heard the news; Pettibone shook hands with me, but Moyer did not rise from his seat, although my acquittal had assured the probability of his. He only remarked laconically, "That's good." I gathered up my books and papers, and went into the night cell to get the rest of my stuff.

There were a number of members of the Federation waiting at the back door of the jail, among them Bill Davis and John Harper, who had been manager of the Victor coöperative store. They were warm and spontaneous in their congratulations. Some of them went with me to the house where my wife was living. She and the girls had gone there immediately after the verdict had been announced. I was surrounded by a happy crowd.

From there I went to the hospital where my mother was waiting for me. She reached up her arms to me from the bed and said, "I knew you were coming!" I could not stay long with her because I had to go to see Murphy at the other hospital, but before I left she told me that she would get well right away.

Murphy was lying on a cot on the veranda. A nun was sitting beside him. When he saw me he sat up. I came up to his bed and he threw his arms around me and said, "Bill, in this hour of great triumph, be humble!"

That afternoon I went to the home of the foreman of the jury. He wanted to tell me the story of how the verdict had been reached. He said that there were many ballots cast, the first few being ten for acquittal, one for conviction and one blank. He added that it was he who cast the blank ballot. "I wanted to find out who it was that was voting for conviction," he said. "In the discussion that followed, I learned that it was Gilbert. From then on the ballots were eleven for acquittal and one for conviction. Gilbert thought I had been won over and it was only a little while before we arrived at a verdict." It was Gilbert I had seen coming into the courtroom with a gray face. I wondered whether this Gilbert had made some promise to the prosecution which he found impossible to carry out with the pressure of the other jurymen against him. The foreman had used a clever method, I thought. I tried to express my gratitude, then I went home.

When I got home, several packets of telegrams had arrived. I started the folks to opening and reading them. There were nearly a thousand messages of congratulations from different organizations, members of the Western Federation and other individuals throughout the country.

We decided to return to Denver the next night. On the following morning I took a walk with Darrow, who tried to dissuade me from returning to Denver with my wife and children. He told me that I should go somewhere up in the mountains for awhile; he seemed to feel that it was important to me to keep out of the public eye for a time, but his arguments had no weight with me. Darrow had been employed as a lawyer and not as a mentor. I told him that I should probably be called upon to go out to raise funds for the defense of Moyer and Pettibone.

I went to the hospital and brought my mother home, then to the other hospital to see about taking Murphy back to Denver with me. John was in the last stages of consumption, and we knew he would not live long. He was in his room at the hospital. The nun who answered the door was not the one who had been with him the previous day, but as I entered I saw two others gliding along the corridor like upright coffins. One of these was the sister I had seen the day before. She went with me to Murphy's room. He was ready and anxious to leave that night. I told him I would come for him with a carriage.

When I was leaving the nun asked me if I would not like to see the conservatory of music connected with the convent. From the music rooms she took me over to the academy and introduced me to the other nuns, who all congratulated me on my acquittal. The mother superior was away at a convention of mothers.

While she was showing me over the building, the little nun told me she had seen MacParland in church, sitting directly below her place in the gallery. She said that she felt like throwing her prayer-book at his old bald head. Then she told me it was she who had turned and waved at me when I was working in my garden in the prison yard.

On the street corner, as I left the convent, I met Robertson, who was the oldest man in the jury. He said, "Well, my son, how are you?"

"First rate, thank you," I answered. He continued:

"William, they could have bleached my old bones before they could have convicted you. Now you be quiet awhile." Then he wished me a safe journey home.

That afternoon Moyer was released on twenty-five thousand dollar bail, furnished by the Butte Miners' Union. I went to the jail and bid Pettibone good-by. The date of his trial had not yet been fixed. Some of the witnesses were going to remain for his trial, or at least until the date was set.

When the news of my acquittal was received in the mining camps of the West there was a general jubilation. Perhaps tons of dynamite were exploded in the celebration. In Goldfield when I went there later they showed me the dents that had been made in the mahogany bars in the saloons by the hobnails of the boys who had danced to celebrate their joy at my release. There is no way of estimating how much whisky was drunk for the occasion. Drinking whisky was the miners' way of celebrating.

That night I drove with my wife and mother to the depot, where the train was already made up. I helped my mother on board, and carried my wife to her berth. Then I went to get Murphy. As I picked him up in my arms he whispered to me, "Let Charley help you, Bill." Moyer was there visiting Murphy. He and I put our hands together and made a "chair" to carry Murphy to the carriage.

The first town of importance that we came to was Pocatello. There was a big crowd at the station, and at the request of a committee I spoke to the crowd, standing on a freight truck. The weather was sultry, and my invalids were worn and tired when we got to Salt Lake. We stopped there two days, my wife and daughters staying with my sister Maud. Murphy went on to Denver with a friend. In Salt Lake I was overwhelmed with the congratulations of relatives and members of the labor organizations.

Darrow accompanied us on part of the journey. He seemed peevish and sulky, but I knew of no reason for this except my refusal to retire to the mountains as he had advised me.

When we got to Leadville, though it was very early in the morning, there was a delegation to meet the train. I was still in bed, but some of the boys handed in a bottle of whisky from the platform in honor of the occasion.

The train made a record trip; it got to Denver on time for once. There was a tremendous crowd awaiting its arrival. Outside the Union Depot in Denver there was an arch with the word WELCOME in electric lights, to greet travelers arriving in the city. The sign was dark; I was told that the authorities, under the influence of the

Citizens' Alliance, had had the light put out. But the sign was nothing to me; I could see the light of welcome in the eyes of the thousands of workers who had come to meet me.

I put my wife in a chair and rolled it to the carriage that was waiting, and we moved through cheering throngs to the Albany Hotel. I carried my wife to her room, then went back to the carriage and spoke from the seat to the people gathered in the street, thanking them for what they had done for me, and asking them to continue their support until Moyer and Pettibone stood beside me, free men. When I started back into the hotel, there were crowds of friends who shook my hand, among them Emma Langdon, who had written the history of the Cripple Creek strike, and who had been assistant secretary of the first I.W.W. convention. She planted a kiss on my lips, which made a ripple of excitement among the reporters, who wanted to find out who she was.

My work began at once, as I had many hundreds of telegrams to answer, and letters of congratulation were coming in every day. I replied to them all. One of especial importance was a resolution from the Socialist Congress then in session in Stuttgart:

The International Congress sends William Haywood the congratulations of the Socialist movement of the world in view of the magnificent fight he put up in the interests of the organized workers of the United States. It condemns emphatically the attempt of the mine owners to have an innocent person punished by law only because of his services to the cause of the organized workers. The Congress sees in the legal proceedings and in the systematic campaign of slander carried on by the entire capitalist press against Haywood the expression of the class policy of the bourgeoisie of America, which is coming more and more to the fore, and of the bourgeoisie's total lack of tolerance and sense of honor in all occasions when its profits and its power are threatened. The Congress also congratulates the Socialists of the United States on the enthusiasm and solidarity with which they resisted this attack. The class conscious proletariat of Europe looks upon the enormous strength manifested by this act of solidarity as a guarantee of unity for the future and hopes that the American proletariat will show the same solidarity and determination in the fight for its complete emancipation.

Among the communications was a letter from Daniel DeLeon, written before he had left for Stuttgart, and delivered to me some time later.

Such, I know, must have been the shower of congratulations that poured upon you at your acquittal that I purposely kept in the rear lest my voice be drowned in the multitude. . . . I am about to leave for Europe for the International Socialist Congress. Things in America remain in a disturbed and disordered condition. Nevertheless, it is a state of disorder and disturbance from which your acquittal is calculated to bring speedy order and harmony. The capitalist class has again wrought better for the Social Revolution than that class is aware—it has, through your now celebrated case, built you up for the work of unifying the Movement upon solid ground. Those who have been early in the struggle have necessarily drawn upon themselves animosities. However undeserved, these animosities are unavoidable; and what is worse yet, tend to disqualify such organizations and their spokesmen for the work of themselves speedily effecting unification, however certain the soundness of their work may make ultimate unification. Important as their work was in the past, and will continue to be, not through them could a short cut to victory, through united efforts, be made. The very value of their work in one direction interferes with their power in another. As I said, the capitalist class, through this late persecution of you, has "produced" the unifier—the Socialist who understands, as the Socialist Labor Party does, that, without the ballot, the emancipation of the Working Class cannot be reached; and that, without the industrially economic organization of the workers, the day of the workers' victory at the polls (even if such victory could be attained under such circumstances), would be the day of their defeat; last, not least, the Socialist who is unencumbered by animosities inseparable from the early stages of the struggle. We are again in the days when the old Republican Party was organized out of warring free-soil and abolitionist, and of up to then wavering elements. Thanks to your own antecedents, your celebrated case, the unanimity of the Working Class in your behalf, and your triumphant vindication, the capitalist class has itself hatched out the needed leader. The capitalist class has thrown the ball into your hands. You can kick it over the goal. . . .

Men who are incapable of appreciating straight-forward and consistent action have long been pronouncing the S.L.P. dead, more lately also the I.W.W., and myself as merely anxious to "hang on to something." The soundness of the S.L.P. principle, coupled with the power of its press, insures it against any such death. As I stated in the course of the recent debate, "As to Politics," so long as its mission remains unfulfilled, the S.L.P. will hold the field unterrified; the day, however, when the I.W.W. will have reflected its own political party, in other words, the day when the vicious nonsense of "pure and simple political Socialism" will be at an end, it will be with a shout of joy that the S.L.P. will break ranks. . . .

This letter I did not answer. First, because DeLeon was not in the country at the time, and second because I was becoming more and more convinced that the Socialist Labor Party was so completely dominated by DeLeon's prejudices that it could not lend strength to any movement with which it became associated. Whether right or wrong, DeLeon always insisted that he was right. He made it impossible for any except his devotees to work with him. One able man after another had to leave him.

To DeLeon the Industrial Workers of the World was a recruiting ground for the Socialist Labor Party. The S.L.P. had agreed at the first convention that the I.W.W. should be organized on the economic and political fields without affiliation to any political party; this left the I.W.W. free to develop in time its own political reflection, a party of the working class.

The history of the I.W.W. has shown the significance of political action. While there are some members who decry legislative and congressional action and who refuse to cast a ballot for any political party, yet the I.W.W. has fought more political battles for the working class than any other labor organization or political party in America. They have had one battle after another for free speech. They have fought against vagrancy laws, against criminal syndicalism laws, and to establish the right of workers to organize. They have gone on strike for men in prison. It is to the ignominy of the Socialist Party and the Socialist Labor Party that they have so seldom joined forces with the I.W.W. in these desperate political struggles.

The trial was now a thing of the past. Although Orchard had testified to my being a party to the Independence Depot explosion, the Vindicator explosion, and all the other diabolical deeds in Colorado to which he had confessed, and although I had been charged in the courts of Cripple Creek district with some of these crimes, no word was ever raised against me after my return from Boise, and no move was ever made to revive these charges. The mine owners were whipped in their attempt to wreck the train, they were whipped in the Boise trial, and they knew they would be whipped again if ever they attempted to try any of us for these crimes, of which they themselves had indubitably been guilty.

CHAPTER XIV

THE WORLD WIDENS

MANY big offers of money came to me from different parts of the country, for lectures and vaudeville appearances after my acquittal at Boise. The Tuileries Gardens of Denver offered me seven thousand dollars for a week's appearance. Zick Abrams of California offered fifteen thousand dollars for forty lectures. The Star Circuit wanted to give me four thousand a week for eight weeks.

I talked over the various offers with my wife and my friends and while I could see that there was an opportunity to make a large sum of money, I told them that if I took these offers from capitalist concerns, the price would fall from month to month and my prestige would be lessened every day. If I limited my lectures to working class organizations every step I made would be upward in the estimation of the workers. In vaudeville I should be speaking to mixed audiences, not carrying the message to the working class.

I was called to meetings in Chicago and Milwaukee under the auspices of the labor organizations and Socialist Parties of these cities. In Chicago the first meeting was at Luna Park, where there were forty-five thousand paid admissions, before the crowd broke down the fence and filled the field where I spoke. Later there was a meeting at Riverside Park, arranged by the Socialist Party, where there were sixty thousand paid admissions. At Milwaukee there was an audience estimated at thirty-seven thousand, if I remember correctly; at any rate it was a vast assemblage.

I went back to Chicago and was for a few days the guest of Anton Johansen, organizer for the Wood Workers' Union. He and Matt Schmidt, who is now in San Quentin Penitentiary, took me for an automobile ride through the beautiful parks and boulevards. The monument of the policeman with his club was then still standing in Haymarket Square. I recall the revulsion of feeling that filled me when I looked at this symbol of working-class oppression. Then they drove me out to Waldheim Cemetery. When I realized that I was standing at the foot of the monument to the workers who had been hanged twenty years before, I burst into tears. The remembrance of these men had grown closer to me than a blood relationship, since the time when, as a boy, I had followed the details of their trial and execution.

After going back to Denver, I returned to Boise, where Pettibone's trial was about to begin. Pettibone was then in the hospital. I think his illness had been caused partly by his loneliness after we left the jail.

Darrow was suffering from mastoiditis. He was so ill that he had to remain seated in the courtroom. About two weeks after the trial opened, when the jury had been chosen, he had to go away for an operation on his ear. We then put Judge Hilton of Denver in charge of the case, Richardson having withdrawn after my trial.

Pettibone's trial began like a repetition of my own. He himself did not take the stand because of his ill health, and it was finally decided to submit the case to the jury without argument. The jury acquitted him. Moyer was never tried; the case against him was dismissed soon after Pettibone's acquittal.

Pettibone died shortly after his return to Denver. John Murphy, too, died at about the same time, of consumption. The Western Federation put up monuments to them both, but I was on a speaking tour and could not attend their funerals.

In the fall of 1907 the executive board of the W.F.M. asked me to go to Goldfield, Nevada, in behalf of Preston and Smith, who were serving life sentences in Carson Penitentiary.

Preston and Smith had been convicted of killing a restaurant keeper in Goldfield. Preston was a miner, and all the workers in Goldfield were organized, the town workers in the I.W.W., the miners in the W.F.M. There had been some commotion in front of a restaurant against which a strike had been declared. The boss rushed out with a gun in his hand, and either fired at or threatened Preston, who shot and killed him. I do not remember Smith's connection with the affair, but it was the general consensus of opinion that these men had been railroaded to the penitentiary, and I was sent there to see what could be done about securing their release.

At about the same time, Grant Hamilton, an American Federation of Labor organizer and a Mason of high standing, was sent to Goldfield by Gompers to try to organize the A. F. of L. in that camp. Hamilton was quartered at the Montezuma Club, the head-

quarters of the mine owners. A short time later a group of restaurant workers, members of the A. F. of L., were brought to scab
on the I.W.W. strike in Goldfield.

Bitter feeling was growing up between the staunch I.W.W.'s and
the reactionists in the W.F.M. Vincent St. John had gone to Goldfield from the Cœur d'Alenes and was active in affairs there. Some
difficulty arose between St. John and Paddy Mullaney. The two men
met in the street one day and Mullaney whipped out his gun. Before
St. John had a chance to draw, Mullaney shot him through both
arms. When I got to Goldfield, St. John was in the hospital and
Mullaney was in jail. I went to see St. John. He was in bed, his
right arm badly injured. Although the hand was saved, he was
permanently crippled.

After speaking at a meeting of Goldfield Miners' Union, telling
the members the purpose of my visit, and urging them to stand
closer together, to avoid the outbreaks that were likely to occur
among the members if contention continued, I went to Carson City.
The attorney general, whom I saw there, spoke favorably about en-
dorsing a parole for Preston and Smith.

The boys in the penitentiary were glad of my coming. I told them
that I felt the chances were good for a pardon. Out in the yard,
which I have already described, with its prehistoric footprints, I
saw old One Arm Jim, the Indian from Willow Creek who was
serving a life sentence for killing Andy Kinniger.

From Carson City I went to Reno. Senator George Nixon, who
had been a friend of mine in Winnemucca years before, sent to
the hotel for me, and I went to his office. We talked over the
situation in Goldfield, where there was much bitterness developing
between the mine owners and the union. There was some talk about
soldiers being called for. There were already many gunmen, a private
army, as it were, employed by the mine owners. I wanted, if possible, to prevent a recurrence of what had happened in the mining
camps of Colorado, and asked the senator to use his influence against
the employment of soldiers in Nevada. This he promised to do,
or at least he would notify me at headquarters if an attempt was
made to bring in federal soldiers. He evidently forgot his promise;
I never heard from him, and soldiers were sent to Goldfield by
President Roosevelt a short time later.

On my return to Denver I found that the spirit of intrigue at headquarters was more than I could overcome. Moyer, Mahoney, Kirwan and O'Neill were definitely opposed to the I.W.W., or at least to that faction of it to which St. John had been elected general organizer. Although I never had a word of contention with them, I could feel the hostility that was brooding in their breasts.

St. John went to Chicago from Goldfield at about this time. There he took up his work as general organizer of the I.W.W.

One day in the W.F.M. office the men were discussing the Cripple Creek strike. The terrible financial crisis had caused a very great unemployment, and the officials of the Federation seemed to fear that the old-timers would drift back to Cripple Creek as scabs. The thought that seemed to prevail among them was that the strike should be called off. I asked why they didn't submit a resolution to the unions of the district Number 1 and let them decide it themselves. I hurriedly scratched off the resolution that called off the great Cripple Creek strike. I do not know whether it was referred to the unions of the district for their consideration, but later a letter of remonstrance came to the office, which said that if I had been on the job nothing of the kind would have been done.

Early in January, 1908, a meeting had been arranged for me in Grand Central Palace, New York. It was my first visit to the great metropolis. When I arrived I was met at the train by the secretary of the Socialist Party, U. Solomon, who took me to a hotel near the station. Solomon left me there, and I roamed around the streets of New York alone, more lonesome than I had ever been in my life.

The Grand Central Palace was in a side street, but a short distance from the hotel. Early in the evening I went past the building and wondered what the great crowd that was standing around meant. No committee came to the hotel to take me to the hall, so when I thought it was time I went along and attempted to make my way through the crowd which had greatly increased. I was told I couldn't get in, as the auditorium was already packed. As I was making my way toward the front entrance, some one recognized me and a small group hustled me around to the back door, coming in with me. Some one directed me to the platform. While I was climbing up, there was a tremendous burst of applause. When I realized that this applause was for me, it warmed the cockles of my heart, and relieved me of the chilly feeling of neglect that I had been carrying around with me all afternoon. Solomon told me that the time of my arrival in the city had not been publicly announced as they were "afraid that there would be too big a crowd at the station." Remembering the Denver and Chicago demonstrations, I couldn't understand this timidity.

The audience of ten thousand was wildly enthusiastic. I was greeted by hundreds after the meeting. One little woman threw her arms round my neck, kissing me repeatedly. When I got a chance to look at her face, I found that it was my sister Mary, who was then living on Staten Island.

After this meeting, I arranged to make a tour of the country with Luella Twining as manager. Comrade Twining had been a delegate to the initial convention of the I.W.W. She accompanied me as far as Denver, where there was a convention of the W.F.M.

When I rose to speak at this convention, Moyer got up from his chair and walked out of the hall. The atmosphere was permeated with antagonism. There were many stanch old-time workers among the delegates, but a rift had taken place in the organization. I felt it would take time to heal the breach.

In Los Angeles, after the meeting there, a good-looking young woman came up and introduced herself to me as Mrs. Smith. I told her that was not an unusual name. "But," she said, "I'm Judge Smith's wife from Caldwell." This was the judge before whom our preliminary hearing had been held in Idaho. She told me that Billy Cavanaugh, the stone-cutter who had put the constitution and membership card of the W.F.M. under the cornerstone of the new Caldwell courthouse, was living in Venice, a seaside resort in Los Angeles. We went to see him the next day.

Olaf Tvietmoe, editor of *San Francisco Labor*, took me to see the big trees of Calaveras, which are one of the wonders of California. We went from there to San Francisco, where I addressed a large meeting in Dreamland Rink, and later the Central Labor body. From there I went by boat to Eureka, one of the large lumber camps of northern California.

A meeting had been arranged in the tabernacle of some evangelist in Portland, Oregon, still farther north. The day after the meeting I went to see Ed Boyce, who was then manager of the Portland Hotel. My visit with him was pleasant enough. He took me out to his home, where I saw Mrs. Boyce, who was as lively and entertaining as ever. She told me that they were not as happy with all their money as they had been during the time they lived in my house in Denver. I looked at Boyce in his beautiful surroundings, and thought of him as the petty manager of a hotel. It seemed to me that he had lost all the imagination he had ever had, that the contact with money had destroyed his vision. I knew him to have been an earnest revolutionist. But now in a few years he had become musty and was vegetating in his prosperity.

From Portland I went by boat to Seattle. In the dining saloon a man sitting opposite me said, "I beg your pardon, but you put me in mind of that lawyer—what is his name?—who defended those fellows in Idaho." "You probably mean Darrow," said I. "Yes, that's it. Are you Darrow?" "No," I answered, "I'm not Darrow. I'm the fellow he defended." He looked very much chagrined. "Well, well," he said, "is that so?" The conversation languished.

There was a fine meeting in Seattle, and from that city I had dates across the state of Washington. At Yakima I was arrested —for smoking cigarettes. After all the indictments I had been subjected to, this was my first conviction. It was repeated in a string of other towns in Washington, where there was a law against cigarette smoking. There was also a law against giving tips; if I was not arrested for this, it was not because I did not violate it! My persecution and the publicity that followed it caused the repeal of the anti-cigarette law.

When I arrived at Wardner, Idaho, I was almost worn out. I went to bed until it was nearly time for the meeting, and when the comrades came for me, I got up and had a drink and started for the hall with them. On the way I told them that they would have to find some one to speak in my place, as my head was in such a whirl that I knew I could not deliver a speech. They objected— "You've had a good rest. You didn't have more than one drink, did you?" "No," I said, "but there's something the matter with me. I can't speak to-night." When we got to the hall I went on the platform long enough to apologize to the audience, and ask one of the comrades to speak. Then I went back to the hotel and to bed. This was the only time, of the many hundreds of meetings I have held, that could be called a miss. I never missed a meeting, I never missed a train in all my travels. I liked speaking; I liked the way I could handle an audience, the way they responded.

Up in British Columbia, in Canada, I spoke at a meeting under the auspices of the Rossland Miners' Union. Casey, the secretary of the union, told me of the disadvantage I was putting myself under by drinking so much.

"That is exactly what Moyer likes to see you do," he told me. "At the last convention I know that Moyer gave members money and told them to go out and have a good time with Bill; get him good and drunk."

I said, "Is that so?" Casey replied, "Sure. It's a fact."

I had a bottle of Canadian Scotch in my grip. As the train moved along the next morning, I got to thinking about what Casey had said. I told myself, "If Moyer wants me to drink, it's a thing I shouldn't do." My friends and family had often begged me to stop drinking; I had made many promises which I knew I wouldn't keep. But now I was mad; mad clear through, under the eyes, deep down in the stomach.

I took out that bottle of whisky, walked out on the platform of the moving train, and dropped it down between the cars. I did not touch intoxicating liquor after that for many years.

Stopping the drink so suddenly caused a violent reaction which was hard to endure for a time. But I had a reason now that was greater in my mind than the desire to drink. I began to renew my energies and threw myself into my work with my old-time vim and more pleasure than I had felt in many months.

I was in Chicago during this trip, in the early spring of 1908. Mahoney came there to see me and proposed that I should publish an announcement in the *Miners' Magazine* to the effect that I was not lecturing under the auspices of the Western Federation of Miners. He did not explain why he proposed this, and I could see no reason why I should do it. Shortly after this a notice appeared in the *Miners' Magazine*:

Notice. To whom it may concern: This is to inform you that the Executive Board of the Western Federation of Miners has decided to terminate the services of William D. Haywood as a representative of the Western Federation of Miners in the field, the same to take effect on the eighth day of April, 1908.
C. E. Mahoney, vice-president, W.F.M.

When Mahoney had left me in Chicago, it seemed to be in a friendly spirit. I could understand that the poisonous animus of Moyer against me had percolated through the executive board. But why Moyer had not signed the notice instead of Mahoney I never found out. The W.F.M. had withdrawn by this time from the I.W.W., and Moyer had announced that "if to be conservative meant to stay out of prison, he was going to be conservative." They had probably gone over the reports of my speeches on the trip, and had found that they were too revolutionary for their liking.

Although I was no longer an official, I did not at this time sever my relations with the W.F.M. But I was certain that this would happen eventually if Moyer continued as president of the organization.

The convention of the Socialist Party that met in Chicago in May, 1908, adopted a platform that rang clear. The class struggle was its foundation. This was the most revolutionary period of the Socialist Party in America.

At this time the party had recovered from its early colonization schemes and measures previously adopted for the purchase of mining lands in the Cripple Creek district, and it had not yet degenerated to its later vote-getting policy of opportunism.

Many of the delegates suggested to me that I should run for the nomination as candidate for president. This I declined in writing, mentioning the fact that I was in favor of Eugene V. Debs, who was nominated by the convention as the party's candidate for president. That year a whirlwind campaign was inaugurated and a train was chartered, called the "Red Special," to tour the country with speakers. It was estimated that Debs and the group traveling with him spoke to eight hundred thousand people on this trip, which lasted about three months.

Tom Mooney, who is doing a life-sentence in San Quentin, framed up after the San Francisco Preparedness Parade bomb, was one of the literature agents on the Red Special.

At the end of the campaign I went from Chicago to Racine on the Red Special, spoke at the meeting there, and at the closing meeting of the tour at Terre Haute, Indiana, Debs' home.

The publicity value of the Red Special could not be overestimated. At every town and city crowds visited the train, and wherever stops were made the crowds were addressed from the rear platform. There was an appreciable increase of votes but it was the educational value of the campaign that counted most.

During this vital period of the Socialist Party's existence the

American Federation of Labor was kowtowing, silk hat in hand, before the United States government officials. It was about this time that Gompers, Mitchell and Morrison of the A. F. of L. had been convicted of violating an injunction. The judge scathingly rebuked the A. F. of L. and its principal officers, sentencing them to six months or a year in prison. This they never served. The A. F. of L. was a part of the National Civic Federation, an alliance of capital and trade union leaders for the purpose of class collaboration. Gompers was at one time acting president of the National Civic Federation for eight months following the death of the president. But this close connection with capital did not prevent the many failures of the A. F. of L. to secure the passage of laws beneficial to labor. The A. F. of L. presented "Labor's Bill of Grievances" to the President of the United States, the Vice-President, and the Speaker of the House of Representatives. A part of the Bill follows:

We present these grievances to your attention because we have long, patiently and in vain waited for redress. There is not any matter of which we have complained but for which we have in an honorable and lawful manner submitted remedies. The remedies for these grievances proposed by labor are in line with fundamental law, and with progress and development made necessary by changed industrial conditions.

Labor brings these grievances to your attention because you are the representatives responsible for legislation and for the failures of legislation. The toilers come to you as your fellow citizens who, by reason of their position in life, have not only with all other citizens an equal interest in our country, but the further interest of being the burden bearers and wage-earners of America. As labor's representatives we ask you to redress these grievances, for it is in your power so to do.

Labor now appeals to you, and we trust it may not be in vain. But if perchance you may not heed us, we shall appeal to the conscience and support of our fellow citizens.

This humiliating attitude of the labor leaders brought them nothing from the politicians in Washington.

I had been elected to the National Executive Committee of the Socialist Party, and served for some time in that capacity. When the massacre of the Lena River gold miners occurred in Siberia, the National Executive Committee passed a resolution that I had introduced, condemning the Czar and the British gold mining companies for the murder of the miners who had gone on strike to improve their working conditions.

The Socialist Congress of the Second International was held in Copenhagen in 1910. Much to my surprise I was elected a delegate by a larger referendum vote than any other delegate elected. The others were John Spargo, Morris Hillquit, Victor Berger, Robert Hunter, May Wood Simons and Lena Morrow Lewis.

I had covered the United States from coast to coast, and here was an opportunity to cross the ocean. The thought of the trip, and the chance it gave me to get acquainted with comrades from foreign countries and to take part in the work of an international congress, gratified me deeply.

Our passage was booked second class on the *Lusitania*. When we landed in England we transferred to a boat that went direct to Copenhagen.

Copenhagen was at that time under a Socialist administration. I had never seen anything to equal the congress. There were red flags everywhere, crowds and demonstrations. I met comrades whose names I knew and whose writings I had read, such of them as had been translated into English.

I was given a choice of serving either on the war or the labor commission. I chose the latter. Berger and Schlueter, editor of the *New Yorker Volkszeitung,* and Olive Johnson of the Socialist Labor Party were on the same commission. Hjalmar Branting of Denmark was the chairman.

When the time came, I spoke on the labor organizations of the United States, and described in detail the American Federation of Labor, its high initiation fees, its limited membership, its time agreements with the employers. I referred to its relationship with the National Civic Federation. I showed the growth toward the idea of industrial unionism shown in the formation of the Industrial Workers of the World.

When I had finished, Branting said something to the interpreter which, of course, I didn't understand. There was an altercation between them, and the interpreter picked up his chair and sat down with his back to Branting. Finally he turned around and gave my speech at length. He told me afterward what had happened. Branting had told him to cut my speech short, but he had replied that it was perhaps the most important speech that would be made

in that commission, and he proposed to give it as nearly as possible
as it had been spoken.

Lenin was in Copenhagen at the head of the Russian delegation.
I don't remember what name he was going under at this congress,
and of course I did not realize that he was to become the greatest
leader of the revolution. When I came to Russia, Lenin reminded
me that we had met at the Copenhagen congress.

Rosa Luxemburg and Georg Ledebour were two of the delegates
I met; I remember the castigation Ledebour gave Ramsay Mac-
Donald. Jaurès came from France, and Keir Hardie from England, and many others of whom I had heard in the socialist and
labor movement.

What might have become an important resolution was the
Vaillant-Hardie resolution on war, but its main clause, the general
strike, was eliminated chiefly through the action of the German
delegation, which was the dominant factor in this convention. Victor
Berger supported their position, and I asked him at the time
whether he was representing the American or the German working class. He might have answered "neither" quite truthfully.

I spoke at several meetings in Copenhagen at which Clara Zetkin
and Alexandra Kollontay interpreted for me. Speaking at many
union meetings, I became acquainted with the form and methods of
organization. I learned, for instance, that the typographical workers were one hundred per cent organized, but when I inquired who
was their president, they told me that he was a man who was running
a shop of his own, employing over a hundred workers. Then I
learned that the typographical union had a nine-year contract with
the employers. I used this fact in speeches, and asked why the
workers didn't sign up for ninety years or nine hundred years while
they were about it, thus eliminating the class struggle from their
span of life!

When I investigated the coöperative system of Denmark, it was
to learn with much regret that the splendid farms and dairies were
carried on at the cost of the blood and sweat of emigrants brought
over every year from Poland, Austria and Hungary, who were paid
a krone a day—twenty-eight cents—for harvest work, and fed on
cow-peas, small potatoes and sour milk.

A bird's-eye view of Denmark reminded me of a children's playground; it looked as though Noah's Ark toys had been set down in-

discriminately. I saw the statue of a man on horseback in the middle of a hayfield. And one time in a quiet little village a company of toy soldiers came marching down the street and whirled around a corner. I went with a comrade to his home in a little town which I was delighted to learn had been the home of Hans Christian Andersen.

Then I traveled through Sweden, speaking at Malmo and Stockholm, where I met the secretary of the Swedish miners.

From Stockholm I went to Gothenburg, and from there to Christiania, now Oslo. There was a strike in the curtain and carpet factories. The employers had stolen the girls and boys from their homes and were making slaves of them, and were using their friends and relatives, the young men of Norway, as police and soldiers to defeat the strikers. When my speech was translated, the audience answered with a sob.

Lee and Inkpin, whom I found at the office of the Socialist Party in Maiden Lane, London, had arranged a tour of Great Britain for me. My first meeting was in Memorial Hall in London. Ben Tillet was chairman. I had heard the English people described as being cold and phlegmatic, but I found that this was far from the truth. This audience was one of the most attentive, responsive and enthusiastic that I have ever spoken to in my life. They followed my speech for two hours, and then stood up and cheered.

After the meeting I met George Bernard Shaw, who told me of the many invitations he had had from the United States. I told him that I thought a speaking tour there would be an ovation for him "Oh," he said, "I shouldn't like that!" He mentioned some society woman in New York who had had the nerve to offer him twenty-five hundred dollars to appear first in her drawing-room.

While I was in London the Socialist Party gave me a dinner in Soho, at which Socialists, labor men, Fabians, and artists were present.

Glasgow had a tremendous meeting. The fact that the city of Glasgow owned the tramways, waterworks, and a large number of workers' houses had not materially improved the condition of the toilers there. The slum quarter was as bad as I have ever seen, and I saw more drunken women on the streets the Saturday night I was there than I have ever seen anywhere before or since. From Glasgow I went to Lanarkshire, where I spoke to the coal miners.

In Lanarkshire I saw an appalling sight. On one side of the street was a four-story ramshackle brick building, in which lived about five hundred laboring men. They did their own cooking in a greasy kitchen. There was a slimy bath house. They slept in dirty wards. This was called, for some reason that I was never able to fathom, the Model House. Across the street from it was a sheer blank wall, as high as a penitentiary wall. Behind the blank wall was a great mansion with hundreds of rooms, in which lived one man, the Duke of Hamilton.

I went to see the mausoleum of this noble family. One of the tombs was of black basalt and had been brought from Egypt. These aristocratic grave-robbers had dumped out the original owner, and had brought the sarcophagus to Scotland. When the Scot died, they found that his body was too long for the coffin. As it was impossible to lengthen the stone coffin, they had to double up the occupant's legs in order to crowd him in. There he rested as comfortably as such a crooked man could.

I went to visit the homes of some of the coal miners. They were rabbit-warrens, built back to back in long rows, with one door and one window apiece. One room to a family, never more than two rooms at most. A bed was built into the wall, like a hole, where pots and pans were piled in the daytime, and dumped out on the floor at night to make room for the sleepers.

This town was the birthplace of Andy Carnegie, and was marked with one of his libraries.

Robert Smillie, leader of the coal miners, took me to his home which was little more than a "butt and ben." He drove me around to the various mining camps and to Lead Mills, one of the oldest mining towns in Britain, with the oldest circulating library in the country. At the mine there was a big old water wheel that for generations had operated the lift in the mine.

After splendid meetings in Edinburgh, Cambushlang, and other places in Scotland, I went down into the black country in England, to speak at Manchester and Salford.

At Burnley Tom Mann, William Hyndman and I spoke at the same meeting. Mann was a vigorous speaker and a fine propogandist. He was at that time much interested in the syndicalist movement and was attempting to federate the transport workers along the lines which he thought the syndicalist movement of France followed.

However, syndicalism was not what Mann really wanted. Industrial unionism was nearer to what he was striving for.

Pottstown is the center of the manufacture of pottery, porcelain, enamel and similar wares. Here, when the weather is murky, the smoke from hundreds of stacks settles down on the towns like a blanket. I had some good meetings, and visited some of the factories, where I saw the workers dipping the wares into the lead glaze that, after firing, makes chinaware white. These men, after a very few years, become so poisoned with the lead and its fumes that their teeth fall out and their joints are locked as if with the worst attacks of rheumatism. I was told that these workers did not live longer than from twenty-eight to thirty-three years old. The sacrifice of their lives was only one of the demands of capitalism.

I went to the coal fields of South Wales, Rhondda Valley and Merthyr Tydvel, speaking at Tonypandy in the Royal Theater a night or two before a strike was declared on the mines of that vicinity. I told the coal miners how the Western Federation was organized, with every man who worked around the mines belonging to the same union, and that when we went on strike every man quit at one time. I said that when the pump men were pulled off, as the water came up in the mine the spirits of the owners went down in the office. The miners of Tonypandy seemed to think that this was good advice. When the strike started they pulled out the engine drivers, the pump men, the pony drivers and stable tenders underground, and the mine owners were in a real dilemma.

In the course of a day or two the King of England sent a telegram inquiring whether the mine ponies were still alive. He did not inquire after the health and welfare of the miners and their wives and children.

There were a few scabs during the strike; they call them blacklegs in England. The women dealt with them. They got hold of them, stripped them, and put white shirts on them, with a sign written on each shirt-bosom—"I am a blackleg." Then they put ropes around the men's necks and led them through the streets.

At Liverpool I spoke in St. George's Hall. Ramsay MacDonald preceded me. After I had concluded, members of the audience, especially those in the gallery, rose with a great shout, and throwing up their caps, they cried, "Hurrah! You've saved the meeting, Bill!"

An industrial syndicalist conference took place in Manchester, which endorsed direct action, formed the Industrial Syndicalist Educational League, and started a paper called the *Syndicalist*. Tom Mann did much active work under the auspices of the League.

After speaking at local meetings of the Dock Workers' Union, I was made an honorary member, and given an engraved charter as a membership card.

In Paris at the headquarters of the Confederation of Labor, I met Charles Marck, who was the treasurer of the organization and who spoke English fluently. On his desk was a pile of postcard pictures, showing the victims of the Spokane free speech fight of the I.W.W.

Jouhaux, secretary of the Confederation, said that they were trying to get the Saturday half holiday. They were following closely in the footsteps of the British trade union movement. I came to the conclusion that the union movement of France was built on about the same lines as the A. F. of L. It was a little more radical because its members were more class conscious.

In Paris I met William Z. Foster, who had attended the International Labor Congress that had met in Buda-Pesth, where he had gone as a delegate from the I.W.W. He had not been seated, because of the antagonism of James Duncan, who was representing the A. F. of L., but he formed a friendship with the French delegates and became very much imbued with the idea of syndicalism, which he thought should be introduced in America.

When Foster returned to the United States he wrote some articles on syndicalism for the I.W.W. papers, and he ran for office as editor of one of the papers in which he was defeated. He later started the Syndicalist League and a paper.

Many people have imagined that syndicalism and industrial unionism are one and the same thing. But they are two distinct schools of thought in the world labor movement. The I.W.W. had been organized independently and separate from the movement in France. The two movements differed in theory, and the I.W.W. was as revolutionary in practice as the Syndicalists. It conceived the idea of organizing the working class along the lines actually existing in industry instead of in various crafts and trades, and in uniting industries into one comprehensive union. The syndicalists simply coordinated the different trades and crafts, as is done in the building trades of America.

After a short trip to Italy I returned to England. Crossing the

Channel on the same boat were Jaurès and Vandervelde. I shook hands with the former, but did not make the acquaintance of the so-called Socialist from Belgium.

From England I sailed on the *Mauretania* for home.

CHAPTER XV

THE LAWRENCE STRIKE

A MEETING had been arranged by the I.W.W. in New York, for my homecoming. Elizabeth Gurley Flynn was the chairman and in her opening remarks she said the meeting was to welcome me back home. I told the audience that, while I fully appreciated the splendid reception they were giving me, I had really not been away from home. In all my travels I had been with the working class in different countries. I told them of the labor movement in France, England, the Scandinavian countries and Italy. I did not neglect to mention the effect of long-time contracts on the typographical workers of Denmark, and also explained the difference between the syndicalist movement of France and industrial unionism in America.

In its early years the I.W.W. had shared the history of the Western Federation of Miners; it was now writing history of its own. The free speech fight in the West had excited the imagination of the working class throughout the country. The organization was growing in New York as elsewhere. The steel workers in the East and the lumber and agricultural workers in the West were being organized by the I.W.W. Small groups of workers who had become imbued with the spirit of industrial unionism were organized on the east side in New York. Workers who had been overlooked in other organizations found their place under industrial unionism.

Joseph Ettor, one of the most successful organizers of the I.W.W., was responsible for most of the eastern organization, in which he was ably assisted by Elizabeth Gurley Flynn. Many shoe workers had been organized in Brooklyn. The United Shoe Workers of the A. F. of L. had a few members in different shops. They had there, as elsewhere, signed a contract with the manufacturers, and were working for less wages than the I.W.W. or the individual workers. To prevent their pay being reduced to this level, the I.W.W. called a strike.

An amusing incident occurred in this strike. A former member of the I.W.W. had been severely injured in a street car accident and had lost his leg. The I.W.W. had paid his hospital expenses and had bought him an artificial leg. During the strike he continued to work. One day a group of strikers came into the office, one of them carrying an artificial leg over his shoulder. Some one called out, "What have you got there?"

"We've got that leg we bought for Dan Ritter. If he wants to scab he can hop to it, but he can't do it on our leg!"

I was called from New York about this time to Chicago during the strike of the clothing workers. The I.W.W. had organized about eighteen thousand clothing workers, and they framed the demands. But before the demands were presented to the manufacturers, Hart, Schaffner and Marx, the leading firm involved in the strike, granted even more than the strikers had demanded, and the strike on that firm was immediately settled. For a short time it had looked as though the clothing workers would become a part of the I.W.W., but they were organized as the Amalagamated Clothing Workers, with which most of the clothing workers later united.

I had planned another tour of the country, and was at Allentown, Pennsylvania, when I got a telegram telling me that my mother was dying. I canceled all dates and hurried westward as fast as possible, hoping to arrive at her beside before she died. But I was too late; she had passed away the night before I got there. I felt very deeply the loss of my mother. Her death took with it a love I would never know again. She had always been a great pal with me; as a boy I had often taken her to the theater or the lake or on other outings, in preference to girl companions. As I grew older, she sympathized with my ideas, and approved of the work I was engaged in.

After the funeral I returned to Pennsylvania where a cousin of mine lived. He had been the architect of the Vandergrift Steel Mill. I was anxious to make a study of a steel plant, and asked my cousin if he could arrange for me to go through the plant. He said, "Why, certainly—" and proceeded to tell me about some labor organizers who had been in Vandergrift but a short time before, who had been run out of town and had to swim the river to escape from the mob led by county officials. But my coming to Vandergrift had been unannounced, and no one knew of my presence there except my cousin.

When he had secured a permit for me I went through the great plant on two separate nights. I learned that the rollers, benders and trimmers were the highly paid men of the plant, and owned the fine homes that made up this model little town. They had automobiles, pony carriages for their children, pianos and phonographs for their wives. They associated with the townspeople and the business element, and held their heads high. When I came to inquire where the mass of the workers lived, I found that it was in a little town built on the river-bottom called Rising Sun. Floods made their houses uninhabitable every spring. The skilled workers got more money than the foremen and superintendents, but the great bulk of the workers received very small wages. This was a place that badly needed organization.

From Vandergrift I went to McKees Rocks, where the I.W.W. was conducting a strike against the Pressed Steel Car Company. This strike was handled so well that the steel trust was compelled to give in. It was the only strike of the lower paid workers that has ever been won against the steel trust. A striker was killed by the Pennsylvania Mounted Police, whom the strikers called the Black Cossacks. After this murder, the strikers notified the police that for every striker killed they would get three Cossacks. When I was there some of the members of the I.W.W. were in jail, among them Ben Williams, editor of the *Solidarity,* the official organ of the I.W.W., at that time a weekly. I went to see them, and contributed the proceeds of the meeting at New Castle to their defense.

On this trip I went through Tennessee, Kentucky, the southern parts of Ohio and Indiana, to Chicago. In Chicago I made arrangements to go down South into Louisiana, Arkansas and Texas to confer with the lumber workers. The Timber Workers' Union was having a convention at Alexandria, Louisiana.

I knew that the lumberjacks and mill workers of that part of the country were both black and white, and when I went to the convention hall in Alexandria, I was very much surprised to find no Negroes in the session. When I inquired as to the reason, I was told that it was against the law in Louisiana for white and black men to meet together. The black men were meeting in some other hall.

I said, "You work in the same mills together. Sometimes a black man and a white man chop down the same tree together. You are meeting in convention now to discuss the conditions under which you labor. This can't be done intelligently by passing resolutions here and then sending them out to another room for the black men to act upon. Why not be sensible about this and call the Negroes into this convention? If it is against the law, this is one time when the law should be broken."

The Negroes were called into the session without a murmur of opposition from any one. The mixed convention carried on its work in an orderly way, and when it came to the election of delegates to the next I.W.W. convention, black men as well as white were elected.

There was to be a mass meeting at the Opera House in Alexandria, at which I was to speak. I said that in this meeting as in the convention, we would have to make it known that the Negroes would come on the same terms as the white men, take part and sit where they pleased. There was to be no segregation of the Negroes in the top gallery, as the law provided. This was the first time that such a meeting had ever been suggested in Alexandria. The members did not know what might happen, but they were determined that the meeting should be held as we had planned. The Opera House was crowded from pit to roof. While many Negroes went up to the gallery, probably from habit, many others sat downstairs among the white workers. There was no interference by the management or the police, and the meeting had a tremendous effect on the workers, who discovered that they could mingle in meetings as they mingled at work.

I visited several of the southern lumber camps. At one of them, Graybow, offices, warehouses and post office were enclosed in a high lumber fence. The company store which provided all the supplies of the workers did business on the scrip basis; that is, the company issued its own money, made of paper and brass, called "batwings" and "cherryballs," which was not good anywhere else.

In spite of all the surveillance at Graybow, a strike was declared against the Long-Bell Lumber Company, which rapidly spread to other mills and lumber camps. At Graybow some of the guards and company men were killed, as well as some of the strikers. Seven white and five black strikers were put in jail and held for several months, but none of them were convicted.

I was told of almost indescribable conditions that prevailed in the turpentine camps, where some of the workers were short-time prisoners who had been literally purchased from the county in which they were convicted. These men were subjected to inhuman treatment, often terribly beaten. It was in such a camp that Martin Tabert, a seventeen-year-old boy, was beaten to death only a few years ago.

The turpentine and lumber companies fastened their hold on some of the workers, both black and white, more securely than by the steel bands of chattel slavery. They have deliberately cultivated the narcotic drug habit among the workers. At every company store cocaine, morphine and heroin are sold. The workers, once addicted, cannot think of going away from their sure source of supply, even if they could scrape together enough money to pay for the journey. These workers move about from camp to camp, but never get away from the district.

The companies had women who lived in the camps in little shacks. The men moved from camp to camp, staying perhaps a few months, perhaps a couple of years, but the women stayed in the shacks and took the newcomers as husbands for the duration of their stay in that camp. I was at many of the married workers' homes, rough lumber shacks, but kept as neat as a woman's attention could make them. The boarding houses were like other lumber camp boarding houses, with the exception that the hogs rooting around the doorsteps were here of the razor-back variety, slab-sided bony creatures. In Texas I spoke for the Farmers' Educational League, which was also a mixed organization.

On my return to Chicago I agreed with the Kerr Publishing Company to work with the *International Socialist Review,* and went on a tour. Each local for which I spoke sold tickets which included a subscription to the *Review.* I went through Duluth, Minneapolis and St. Paul, and had a splendid meeting in Butte, Montana. At Anaconda, a smelter town, such an air of mystery prevailed everywhere that I dubbed the place the "City of Whispers." The workers seemed to be afraid to open their mouths for fear of being fired.

At Spokane there was a fine meeting. The workers there were still imbued with the spirit of the free speech fight which had been carried on by the I.W.W. the previous year. The Spokane authorities had attempted to crush the I.W.W. and the spirit of its members, by crowding them into the county jail. For a time the jail was so crowded that the inmates had no room to lie down, but had to take turns snatching a few minutes' sleep. The windows of the corridor in which they were confined were closed and the steam was turned on. The heat became unbearable and for a while they thought they were going to be suffocated. This was only one of many free speech fights the I.W.W. was compelled to make throughout the country. But in each fight there was some unique development that gave the organization wide publicity and cultivated in the minds of the young migratory workers a sense of their importance and the strength of organization. They would no longer permit themselves to be driven from pillar to post by the police, and if they were arrested without cause, the branch to which they belonged always came to their rescue.

When a free speech fight began, every footloose worker that heard about it headed toward the town where the fight was on, crowded the jails and made it so generally uncomfortable for the officials that the right to speak was established. In Sioux City the I.W.W.'s filled the jails. The authorities sent for some carloads of granite which they expected the I.W.W.'s to break for macadamizing the roads. But instead of going to work the I.W.W.'s went on hunger strike. When they were brought into court, the judge said to one young fellow, "You're a worker, are you? Let me see the calluses on your hands." The young fellow replied, "Take down your pants, judge, and let me see where your calluses are!"

After the Portland meeting I got on the boat to go to Seattle. Fred Moore, a lawyer who had worked for the I.W.W., was on the boat. He came as a messenger from Clarence Darrow, who was acting as chief counsel for the MacNamara brothers, then under indictment for murder in connection with the Los Angeles *Times* explosion in California, which had killed a number of scabs.

My engagements were to take me through California, and Moore's message from Darrow was to ask me not to come into California until the MacNamara trial was over. As Moore put it to me, Darrow was afraid that my lectures in California would have a bad effect on the MacNamara case. I had been speaking everywhere on behalf of the boys, and the I.W.W. was working for them. Organized labor generally was inflamed over the manner of their kidnaping, which was a duplication of the method adopted when Moyer, Pettibone and myself were taken from Colorado to Idaho. I had no desire to do anything that would be detrimental to the MacNamara brothers, and after considering the situation carefully, I decided to cancel all my dates in California. Moore told me that Darrow had said that I should have no financial loss, but I replied that the financial end of it would be my contribution to the prisoners' defense.

I reversed my route and went to Canada. As I crossed the line the customs officer asked me if I was coming into the country only on a short trip. I said, "Only a matter of a few days." I did not tell him that it was my intention to tour the country, but on that trip I went from Vancouver to Cape Breton, from coast to coast, speaking at all the towns along the road. I hope that other workers will have the opportunity to see all the gorgeous beauty that I saw on this journey among the Canadian Rockies. I was fascinated by the lakes and the glaciers.

The train passed over the site of the town of Frank, which had been buried by a falling mountain. This had been a mining camp where hundreds of members of the W.F.M. had lived and worked, and had lost their lives in the disaster. Not a splinter of the town remained; we crossed a desolate stretch of bowlders under which the town lay buried.

On this trip I had a wide range of material to talk about. There had been my recent trip to Europe, there was the MacNamara case, and industrial unionism, which had taken hold of the imagination of the workers everywhere. I came down the eastern coast to New York, speaking at different towns.

A short time after I arrived in New York, I took part in a debate in Cooper Union arranged between Morris Hillquit and myself, on the Socialist Party and the Industrial Workers of the World. The Socialist Party had then veered away from the industrial program of 1908, and had definitely adopted a platform of opportunism. The election of a congressman was then, to the mind of the leading Socialists, one of the greatest achievements of the party. During this debate I read the amended preamble of the I.W.W. The words that referred to political action had been eliminated and other changes introduced, and the I.W.W. now stood as a revolutionary economic organization. As amended the preamble now read:

The working class and the employing class have nothing in common. There can be no peace so long as hunger and want are found among millions of working people and the few, who make up the employing class, have all the good things of life.

Between these two classes a struggle must go on until the workers of the world organize as a class, take possession of the earth and the machinery of production and abolish the wage system.

We find that the centering of the management of industries into fewer and fewer hands makes the trade unions unable to cope with the ever-growing power of the employing class. The trade unions foster a state of affairs which allows one set of workers to be pitted against another set of workers in the same industry thereby helping to defeat one another in wage wars. Moreover, the trade unions aid the employing class to mislead the workers into the belief that the workers have interests in common with their employers.

These conditions can be changed and the interests of the working-class upheld only by an organization formed in such a way that all its members in any one industry, or in all industries if necessary, cease work whenever a strike or lockout is on in any department thereof, thus making an injury to one an injury to all.

Instead of the conservative motto, "A fair day's wage for a fair day's work," we must inscribe on our banner the revolutionary watchword "Abolition of the wage system." It is the historic mission of the working class to do away with capitalism. The army of production must be organized, not only for the every-day struggle with capitalists, but to carry on production when capitalism shall have been overthrown. By organizing industrially we are forming the structure of the new society within the shell of the old.

Knowing therefore that such an organization is absolutely necessary for our emancipation, we unite under the following constitution.*

I pointed out that although the I.W.W. would not affiliate with any political party, this action did not make them anti-political; that I was as much a Socialist as any other member of the Socialist Party. I remember that after the meeting, Hubert Harrison, a colored man, said to me that while Douglas had won the debate, Lincoln had carried the country. I took this to mean that Hillquit had won the debate, but the workers of the nation were with me.

This meeting was attended by many leading members of the I.W.W. Ettor, Giovanitti, Gurley Flynn, and Jim Thompson were there. Ettor had just received a telegram from the Italians of Lawrence, Massachusetts, asking him to come there, as there was going to be a strike of the textile workers. Ettor left for Lawrence at once and in a few days I got a telegram from him asking me to come and help him with the strike.

When I got to Lawrence, Ettor had the situation well in hand.

---

*Although Haywood may have remained at this time a political actionist, the change in the preamble was brought about at a general convention of the I.W.W. dominated by a new group, the migratory workers, "the overalls' brigade," organized and brought to the convention by anarchist leaders. From that time on the I.W.W. has been militantly anti-political in practice, though the phrase meant really "anti-parliamentary."

There was a General Strike Committee organized, composed of one or more members from every mill or large department of the mills that were on strike.

The legislature of Massachusetts had passed a law reducing the hours of labor in the textile industry from fifty-six to fifty-four a week. The cotton and woolen companies announced that when this law went into effect wages would be reduced in proportion. The workers declared that wages were already lower than they should be. The average weekly wage was eight dollars and seventy-six cents, the women getting an average of only seven dollars and forty-two cents. This was the average for all workers, including the skilled. The average for the workers who conducted this strike was six dollars a week. These wages were only for time at work; there were no vacations, and all the holidays were deducted from the weekly pay. It was impossible to bring up families on such wages. The workers went on strike.

It was a strike against all the mills, and every worker, except a few of the most skilled, took part in the struggle. The strikers demanded a fifty-four hour week, a fifteen per cent increase in pay, double pay for overtime, abolition of all bonus or premium systems, and no discrimination against workers for activities during the strike.

The Lawrence strike grew until by the latter part of January, 1912, there were twenty-five thousand workers taking part in it. They were of about twenty-eight different nationalities and spoke forty-five different dialects. The entire textile industry of Lawrence and vicinity was closed down tight.

On my arrival in Lawrence a reception committee met me, composed of ten or fifteen thousand strikers. A parade was formed as we marched to the common, as the public park of every New England town is called. This, the Lawrence *Tribune* said, was the greatest demonstration ever accorded a visitor to Lawrence. On the common I spoke to the strikers.

I spoke many times to the strikers, and left Lawrence to go out and raise funds and create sympathy for the strike, until on February second, Ettor and Giovanitti were arrested under a framed-up charge of murder. Anna LaPiza, an Italian girl striker, had been killed by a policeman, but the charge was laid against the leaders of the strike. I returned at once to Lawrence and became chairman of the strike committee, which was composed of fifty-six members. Back of these were another fifty-six members ready to take the places of the strike committee if any arrests were made.

A writer in the *Outlook*, a conservative weekly which reported the strike, said:

Haywood does not want unions of weavers, unions of spinners, unions of loom-fixers, unions of wool-sorters, but he wants one comprehensive union of all textile workers, which in time will take over the textile factories, as the steel workers will take over the steel mills and the railway workers the railways. Haywood interprets the class conflict literally as a war which is always on, which becomes daily more bitter and uncompromising, which can end only with the conquest of capitalistic society by proletarians or wage workers, organized industry by industry.

Haywood places no trust in trade agreements, which, according to his theory, lead merely to social peace and "put the workers to sleep." Let the employer lock out his men when he pleases, and let the workmen strike when they please. He is opposed to arbitration, conciliation, compromise; to sliding scales, profit sharing, welfare work; to everything, in short, which may weaken the revolutionary force of the workers. He does not ask for the closed shop or the official recognition of the union, for he has no intention of recognizing the employer. What he desires is not a treaty of industrial peace between the two high contracting parties, but merely the creation of a proletarian impulse which will eventually revolutionize society. Haywood is a man who believes in men, not as you and I believe in them, but fervently, uncompromisingly, with an obstinate faith in the universal goodwill and constancy of the workers worthy of a great religious leader. That is what makes him supremely dangerous.

To the Legislative Committee which came to Lawrence I showed pay envelopes of the workers—six dollars and ninety-nine cents, five dollars and forty-five cents, six-thirty, and so on. I showed them, printed on the envelope marked five forty-five, advice about saving money, and the advertisement of the local bank. Five forty-five for a week's work—and advice about saving thrown in free! This was adding insult to injury indeed! The old man who had given me this particular envelope was an old-time employee of the mill, who should have been pensioned long before, after a life-time in the mill. Instead he had been reduced and reduced as he grew less active, until he was plugging along as a wool-sorter on five dollars and forty-five cents a week.

I knew the investigation would result in nothing; but it was good publicity.

After the arrest of Ettor and Giovanitti a demand was made for their release on bail. These men had been charged with being accessories to the death of Anna LaPiza, although nineteen witnesses had seen Policeman Beloit murder the girl. Ettor and Giovanitti were refused bail and held in jail for seven months.

Elizabeth Gurley Flynn, the leading woman organizer of the I.W.W., gave splendid service at Lawrence, speaking to the strikers, and also at meetings outside the strike district, raising money for the relief fund and for the defense of prisoners.

We were sending the children of strikers to sympathizers in other cities, to be cared for during the strike. Some of the groups of children were large and attracted a good deal of attention and sympathy. One day when a group was to be sent away, the militia formed a cordon around the depot and the police attempted to prevent the children getting on the train. When one of these big burleys would lay his hand on a child, of course it would scream, and its mother would fly to the rescue of her captive young. There was a turmoil in the station between the policemen and the fighting women. They stopped the children leaving this day, but they never attempted it a second time.

One morning on the picket line a Syrian boy, who belonged to the strikers fife and drum corps, was stabbed in the back with a bayonet. He died soon after being taken to the hospital.

Not only the local police force was used against the strikers, but police from other cities, the state police, and the state militia had been called in. These organized forces used the mills as their barracks.

The women strikers were as active and efficient as the men, and fought as well. One cold morning, after the strikers had been drenched on the bridge with the firehose of the mills, the women caught a policeman in the middle of the bridge and stripped off his uniform, pants and all. They were about to throw him in the icy river, when other policemen rushed in and saved him from the chilly ducking.

We appealed to Congressman Victor Berger for an investigation of the Lawrence strike, and through this Socialist congressman's efforts, a hearing was arranged before the Rules Committee of the House, in Washington, D. C. When we got news of this, the General Strike Committee decided to send sixteen witnesses to Washington, all boys and girls under sixteen years of age. One of them was a little girl whose hair had been caught in a machine and her scalp torn from her head. These child workers from the mills were able to picture their working conditions and their home life, and we felt convinced of their ability to explain why they and twenty-five thousand others were striking in the textile center of Lawrence and adjacent towns. Margaret Sanger, who afterward became famous for her campaigns for birth control, went with the children to Washington.

On the day of their arrival there, the boys and girls appeared before the Rules Committee. Samuel Gompers was present presumably in the interests of the A. F. of L. He was called as a witness, and condemned the strike and its leaders. Suddenly a childish voice rang out:

"You old son-of-a-bitch! You're telling a god-damned lie!"

It was a Polish boy who had interrupted Gompers. The chairman of the Committee rapped vigorously with his gavel and, looking sternly at the boy, said:

"Young man, that sort of language will not be tolerated here. Do not attempt it again!"

"It's the only kind of language I know," answered the boy, "and I'm not a-goin' to let that guy lie about us and get away with it!"

This incident is not reported in Gompers' *Seventy Years of Life and Labor.*

A newspaper reporter at the hearing remarked that "here was presented the old and the new of the labor movement."

When the committee in Lawrence heard that Gompers was taking part in the hearing, they decided to send me down to Washington to help the children who were representing the strikers, if they should need help. But the children had told everything about conditions in the mills, even to being compelled to buy drinking water.

The arranging of this hearing was not the only time that Victor Berger had responded to requests of the I.W.W. On a previous occasion I had appealed to him, when Federal Judge Hanford of Seattle had denied men citizenship because they belonged to the I.W.W. Hanford lost his job as a result of Berger's investigation.

The newspapers had a staff of reporters in Lawrence to cover the strike. Many of them were of the usual type; one told me that he was the man who had concocted the scheme for my arrest in

Yakima, in order to test the anti-cigarette law and to make a good story that he could sell.

Gertrude Marvin was reporting for the Boston *American*. She came to me for an interview and got it. When the story was finished, she thought she had something good for her paper, but the managing editor remarked, as he threw it in the wastebasket:

"That big two-fisted thug has put it all over you!"

Miss Marvin resigned and went to work for the I.W.W. in Lawrence, doing publicity work for the strike. Later she was engaged by the United Press to assist Marlen Pew. The stories these two sent out about the strike were so thoroughly appreciated by the papers subscribing to the United Press that these papers sent hundreds of letters from all over the country commending the stories. I saw these letters posted up all over the walls of the United Press' New York office.

The managing editor of the Boston *American* finally came to Lawrence and asked Gertrude Marvin to arrange an interview with me. After a long talk with me, he told her that he knew that he had made a mistake in throwing away that story.

I was speaking one night to a meeting made up almost entirely of Polish workers, when two Italian women came into the hall and were brought to the platform. The younger of the two said to me, "To-morrow morning man no go on picket line. All man, boy stay home, sleep. Only woman, girl on picket line to-morrow morning. Soldier and policeman no beat woman, girl. You see—" turning to her companion, she said, "I got big belly, she too got big belly. Policeman no beat us. I want to speak to all woman here."

I presented her to the assembled strikers and told them what she had said to me. Then she spoke herself, in plaintive voice reciting her message, and all agreed that next morning no men or boys should be on the picket line.

The women were out in full force, many of them pregnant mothers. Horrible to relate, the little Italian woman who had organized the women pickets, and another woman, Bertha Crouse, were so terribly beaten by the police that they gave premature birth to their babies and nearly died themselves.

Later a gang of gunmen was brought in. One night they went to the room of Jim Thompson, I.W.W. organizer and prominent figure in the steel strike. When he opened the door the crowd pushed in. Several shots were fired, but Thompson, a big man, was able to force his way out of the room, and ran naked to an adjoining harness shop. He had severe contusions on the head, but no other injuries. A stranger's gun and hat were found in his room, but there was no effort made by the Lawrence police to discover the culprits; they probably knew who they were.

Besides the mass picket line every day, there were many parades. One day sympathizers from Boston joined with the strikers in parade, carrying a banner inscribed:

"Arise! Slaves of the World!
"No God! No Master!
"One for all and all for one!"

This was answered by a parade called by the mill owners, which included some of the priests and ministers, the business men, and most of the public school children, although their parents were strikers. Across the principal street a banner was stretched, reading:

"For God and Country!
"The stars and stripes forever!
"The red flag never!"

A protest against the I.W.W., its principles and methods! A mad wave of patriotism came over the business element, and for a time they all wore little American flags in their buttonholes to the great satisfaction of the flag-manufacturers.

The mill owners were becoming desperate, and they resorted to the trick of planting dynamite where it would be found and charged to the strikers. But being on the alert, the workers discovered that the dynamite had been planted by the coroner of the county. This coroner, tool of the textile trust, was arrested, convicted, and fined five hundred dollars. Later a high official of the American Woolen Company committed suicide. It was rumored that he, too, had had something to do with the planted dynamite.

There were many hundreds of workers arrested during the strike. The United States Commissioner of Labor, in his report on the strike, cites three hundred and fifty-five arrests, but this makes no mention of the many hundreds thrown into jail and held for a time, and then released without a hearing or record. A man by the name of Caruso had been arrested later, on the same charge as Ettor and Giovanitti.

The United Textile Workers which belonged to the A. F. of L., and the Loom Fixers, most of them having no work on account of the strike, decided to go on strike themselves. They started a relief fund and sent out appeals. It has always been my opinion that most of the money, clothes and other supplies that they gathered in were intended by the donors for the great mass of the strikers. These skilled workers received the same proportional increase in pay, in the settlement, notwithstanding the fact that they had been scabbing during the early part of the strike, and grafting during the later. The I.W.W. was active in every textile center that we could reach. The blaze in Lawrence had spread, and when the strike was settled, two hundred and fifty thousand other textile workers received a small increase in wages.

The strike committee had its last meeting after a sub-committee had gone to Boston and made a settlement with William Wood of the American Woolen Company. The report of the sub-committee was received with long cheers. The strike was off, if the settlement should prove satisfactory to the majority of the workers of all the mills involved, and there was no reason to suppose they would not be satisfied. I appealed to the committee and the strikers that filled the hall, to hold their union together, as there would be a time when they would have to strike again, if Ettor and Giovanitti were not released from prison. I helped twenty-three members of the strike committee to climb up on the platform. They were all of different nationalities, and we sang the *International* in as many different tongues as were represented on the strike committee.

When the strike was settled, early in March, it was a sweeping victory for the workers. Hours of labor were reduced, wages were increased from five to twenty per cent, with increased compensation for overtime, and there was to be no discrimination against any person who had taken part in the strike. The strike had been a magnificent demonstration of solidarity, and of what solidarity can do for the workers.

Jim Thompson, Grover Perry, Gurley Flynn, Bill Trautmann, and other I.W.W. organizers, including myself, went on the road to raise funds for the approaching murder trial of Ettor, Giovanitti, and Caruso.

CHAPTER XVI

"ARTICLE 2, SECTION 6"

THERE was thunderous applause at the protest meeting in Cooper Union in New York, on behalf of Ettor and Giovanitti.

It was the rumble of just such applause, I said in my speech, that gave me courage and strength when I was in the same position as the men in whose behalf we are appealing to you to-night. I feel that my life must have been preserved by you for such occasions as this, and I feel now that it is not me to whom you are giving this magnificent reception, but the principles for which I stand. Your applause is but an echo of your hearts, but an echo of your own desires, and you realize that the men who are in jail in Lawrence are in jail because they are fighting your battles. I felt that when I was in jail in Boise. And I know that without the united action of the workingmen and women of New York City, of the state of New York, of the United States of America and of the world, instead of appealing to you here to-night on behalf of Ettor and Giovanitti, my comrades and I would have been judicially murdered by the authorities of the state of Idaho. The mine owners of Colorado had determined to bring about our death, even as these vultures of capitalism intend to make horrible examples of Ettor and Giovanitti. . . .

The police killed Anna LaPiza. The picket line was out that morning, 23,000 strong, an endless chain of pickets. And the police began to crowd them, crowded them up Common street, up Union street, down Broadway, until they were massed in so thick that they could not move back any further. Then the policemen began to club them. Some of the sympathizers threw coal from the windows. The strikers themselves threw snowballs and chunks of ice at the policemen. And one of the policemen was hit with a chunk of coal or a chunk of ice on the leg. It was the sergeant. He ordered the policemen to pull out the guns. And as they did, they fired. And officer Benoit is said to have fired the shot that killed Anna LaPiza. Nineteen witnesses saw him fire the shot. Anna LaPiza died, the second martyr to the Lawrence strike.

The second day after she was killed, Joseph J. Ettor and Arturo Giovanitti were arrested for being accessories to her murder. Ettor or Giovanitti would willingly have laid down their lives to have saved the life of Anna LaPiza. It was they who shed tears when they learned that Anna LaPiza had been killed. They were two miles away at the time, speaking at the German meeting. To-day they are in jail.

Of the management of the strike, I said:

It was a wonderful strike, the most significant strike, the greatest strike that has ever been carried on in this country or any other country. Not because it was so large numerically, but because we were able to bring together so many different nationalities. And the most significant part of that strike was that it was a democracy. The strikers handled their own affairs. There was no president of the organization who looked in and said, "Howdydo." There were no members of an executive board. There was no one the boss could see except the strikers. The strikers had a committee of 56, representing 27 different languages. The boss would have to see all the committee to do any business with them. And immediately behind that committee was a substitute committee of another 56 prepared in the event of the original committee's being arrested. Every official in touch with affairs at Lawrence had a substitute selected to take his place in the event of being thrown in jail.

All the workers in connection with that strike were picked from material that in the mill was regarded as worth no more than $6 or $7 a week. The workers did their own bookkeeping. They handled their own stores, six in number. They ran eleven soup kitchens. There were 120 investigating cases for relief. They had their own finance committee, their own relief committee. And their work was carried on in the open, even as this socialist meeting is being conducted, with the press on hand, with all the visitors that wanted to come, the hall packed with the strikers themselves. And when this committee finally reduced itself to ten to make negotiations with the mill owners it was agreed before they left that they must meet the mill owners alone.

You will remember now that when the strike was declared, it was to prevent a reduction of wages of 30 cents. When the strike was organized the strikers demanded the reduction of hours, a reinstatement of the 30 cents, and a general increase of 15 per cent. In the course of the negotiations the adjustment was finally made on the basis of five per cent for the highest paid, and 25 per cent for the lowest paid, those who needed it most, time and a quarter for overtime, readjustment of the premium system, and no discrimination against any man or woman or kid for the part that they took in the strike. You know, at the time of the great anthracite strike of 1902, John Mitchell, "the greatest labor leader that the world has ever known," said that in all great battles there are some soldiers that must fall. That is, he said, in effect, that there can be a limited blacklist established. But the Lawrence strikers, the "ignorant workers," said, "We will have no fallen soldiers, not in this battle." Out of their own wisdom they said there would be no blacklist. And there was no blacklist. . . .

Another enthusiastic meeting was held in Carnegie Hall where much interest was aroused and a large sum of money raised for the defense fund. After the meeting a group, among whom was Jack London, went to a restaurant, where I spent a pleasant evening with the famous author.

The second strike at Lawrence was about to take place. A meeting was arranged on the Boston Common. Special trains had been chartered from Lawrence, Lynn, Haverhill and other towns surrounding the Hub. I was to be one of the speakers at this meeting but an indictment had been issued for me at Lawrence and a warrant was out for my arrest. It was almost certain that if I went to Boston by train I would be arrested at the station and prevented from speaking at the meeting. So some of the Fellow Workers came for me in an automobile. We drove to Boston from Providence and when we got there went direct to the State House, which stands above the Common, and drove into the arch of the building where we waited until my time came to speak. I walked down through the crowd to the platform. As soon as I was in the body of the people it was impossible for the police to reach me.

After my speech was concluded some one indicated the direction where the automobile was standing and I asked the crowd to make a pathway for me. I walked hurriedly through this great throng of people to where I thought the automobile was standing. Some one said, "This way, Bill." I got into a car. I said to the chauffeur, "Step on the gas." Then I found that I was in the hands of police officers. They took me to the police station, where my friends immediately gave bail and I was turned loose.

This arrest interfered somewhat with my plans as it was necessary for me to go to Lawrence to plead.

When my case came up in the court there, after the indictment was read, the judge said, "Guilty or not guilty?"

My reply was, "Guilty of nothing except trying to help the workers of Lawrence get a little more bread."

The judge flared up and said, "Mr. Haywood, we want no speeches in this court. If it occurs again you'll be guilty of contempt. Answer the question that is asked of you, 'Guilty or not guilty?'"

I said, "Not guilty."

The judge mentioned a date on which my trial would be set. But this, like several other perfectly good indictments, went down in history. I was never tried under it. I returned to Massachusetts when Ettor and Giovanitti's trial came up at Salem. The first thing I did was to try and have our lawyers establish the rights of the prisoners by having them seated in the court room somewhere other than the cage in which they were impounded according to the custom in Massachusetts. The law provided that a man was presumed to be innocent until found guilty. I contended that these men seated in the cage, built in the center of the court room, were surrounded by all the evidence of guilt even before the trial began.

The trial ended with the acquittal of Ettor, Giovanitti and Caruso. A great demonstration was held in Lawrence as a reception for the prisoners when they were released. Ettor and Giovanitti spoke at this meeting.

Shortly following the Lawrence strike the textile workers of Little Falls, New York, went on strike, and made a set of demands which they submitted to the manufacturers of that place. Ben Legere and Matilda Rabinowitz were the chief organizers. When I arrived there Legere and others were in jail, and Matilda was acting as chairwoman of the strike committee. She was a little thing but filled the position with much credit to herself. The strike was a miniature repetition of the great Lawrence strike.

In 1912 the Socialist Party held a convention at Indianapolis. The delegates were of an altogether different caliber than those who went to make up the convention of 1908. The class struggle meant nothing to many who were there supposedly representing the working class. There were seventeen or more preachers who could scarcely disguise their sky-piloting proclivities. There were many lawyers and some editors.

A meeting was arranged for me in Tomlinson Hall. In describing the Lawrence strike, in my address, I neglected to mention the fact that to Congressman Victor Berger was due the credit for the investigation of the strike that took place before the Rules Committee of the House of Representatives in Washington, D. C. Victor Berger was sore to the bone. Hillquit, too, had not gotten over the fact that his offer to act as a lawyer for the men on trial for murder in Lawrence had not been accepted.

To these leaders and their henchmen in the convention the time seemed opportune to amend the constitution of the Socialist Party, which they did with Article 2, Section 6, providing that:

Any member of the party who opposes political action or advocates crime, sabotage or other methods of violence as a weapon of the working class to aid in its emancipation shall be expelled from membership in the party.

It was Reverend W. R. Gaylord who introduced the resolution against sabotage, direct action and violence. He said, "We do not want any of it. We don't want the touch of it on us. We do not want the hint of it connected with us. We repudiate it in every fiber of us."

Victor Berger expressed himself as follows:

I desire to say that articles in the *Industrial Worker* of Spokane, the official organ of the I.W.W., breathe the same spirit, are as anarchistic as anything that Johann Most has ever written. I want to say to you, Comrades, that I for one do not believe in murder as a means of propaganda. I do not believe in theft as a means of expropriation nor in a continuous riot as a free speech agitation. Every true Socialist will agree with me when I say that those who believe that we should substitute "Hallelujah, I'm a Bum" for the "Marseillaise" and the "International" should start a "bum organization" of their own.

It was a base, libelous, uncalled-for charge made by Berger against the *Industrial Worker*. He knew that the I.W.W. had never advocated murder as propaganda, he knew that it had never advocated theft as a means of acquiring the capitalists' property, he knew that the organization which he was slurring was Marxian in its concept. He had had a chance to learn something of its methods and tactics in conducting strikes, he knew the merits of the Lawrence strike, he had heard the children when they testified in Washington, he knew that the strike had been a great victory for the workers, and he knew that at the time he was speaking Ettor, Giovanitti and Caruso were in prison charged with murder. His speech in the convention in support of Article 2, Section 6, was a covert stab in the back at the men who were facing trial. Berger, if he ever saw a song book of the I.W.W., knew that with the satirical song, "Hallelujah, I'm a Bum" were also printed the "Marseillaise," the "International," and many other revolutionary songs.

If these songs were of American production the chorus of the "Marseillaise" would chill the blood in Berger's veins.

Compare the Article 2, Section 6 amendment to the Socialist Party constitution, the forerunner of the Criminal Syndicalism laws, with a typical criminal syndicalism law:

The Forerunner

Any member of the party who opposes political action or advocates crime, sabotage or other methods of violence as a weapon of the working class to aid in its emancipation shall be expelled from the membership in the party.

Existing Law

Criminal syndicalism is hereby defined to be the doctrine which advocates crime, violence, force, arson, destruction of property, sabotage, or other unlawful acts or methods, or any such acts, as a means of accomplishing or effecting industrial or political ends, or as a means of effecting industrial or political revolution.

A bill, introduced in the United States Senate, declares to be unlawful any association:

One of whose purpose or professed purpose is to bring about a governmental, social, industrial or economic change within the United States by the use, without authority of law, of physical force, violence or physical injury to persons or property, or by threats of such injury, or which teaches, advocates, advises or defends the use . . . of physical force, violence or physical injury to person or property, or threats of such injury, to accomplish such change or for any other purpose, and which, during any war in which the United States is engaged, shall by any such means prosecute or pursue such purpose or professed purpose, or shall so teach, advocate, advise or defend. . . .

The Criminal Syndicalism laws have been upheld by the United States Supreme Court and hundreds of men and women have been sent to the penitentiaries though not one of them had committed any offense except that of holding an opinion or being a member of the Industrial Workers of the World. It is under such a law that the Communists were tried in Michigan and C. E. Ruthenberg, Secretary of the Workers Party, convicted and sentenced to ten years in the penitentiary. The many who have been persecuted can thank the traitors of the Socialist Party who adopted Article 2, Section 6 against the working class.

This amendment was followed by a resolution of the National Executive Committee, of which I was then a member, directed against me, charging me with being an advocate of direct action, violence and sabotage.

It was submitted to a referendum vote and I was recalled from the National Executive Committee. I had been a member of the

Socialist Party since its inception, but had paid no dues into the organization since I had been recalled as a member of the National Executive Committee.

At a later date Berger testified before the Federal Court in Chicago that he was the man responsible for Article 2, Section 6, the clause in the Socialist Party constitution against violence, sabotage and direct action.

Berger went on record in the United States Congress on July 18, 1912, when asked, "How are you going to change the present economic basis? Give us a concrete statement of that proposition."

Berger replied: "That is easy enough. We surely could get the trust properties in the same way the trusts got them. The trusts paid for their properties almost entirely in watered stock, preferred and common. We can give the best security in existence to-day— United States bonds."

Had Berger been as well acquainted with "Imperial Washington" as was the late Senator Pettigrew he would have known that the trusts had not paid for the property that they own but that they had robbed the American people of their heritage. Congressman Berger, who was elected on a Socalist ticket, was willing to eliminate the class struggle and perpetuate the exploiting class by providing them with the world's best security—United States bonds!

These were not the tenets of the revolutionary Socialist Party in which the working class of America was becoming interested. It would seem needless for me to say that the Socialist Party began to retrograde from the date of the Indianapolis convention until now it has lost whatever influence it had.

The politicians at that convention were a slippery, desperate crew, who ignored the elementary principles of Socialism. The Communist Manifesto of Marx and Engels meant nothing to them. They cast aside its primary teachings which concluded with these inspiring words:

The Communists disdain to conceal their views and aims. They openly declare that their ends can be attained only by the forcible overthrow of all existing social conditions. Let the ruling classes tremble at a Communistic revolution. The workers have nothing to lose but their chains. They have a world to gain. Workers of the world, unite!

CHAPTER XVII

THE PAGEANT

PATERSON, the silk city of America, is built near the mosquito-infested swamp lands of New Jersey. It is a miserable place of factories, dye-houses, silk mills, which are operated by from 20,000 to 25,000 workers. There is not a park in the workers' quarter for the children to play in, no gardens or boulevards where mothers can give their babes a breath of fresh air.

Into this town there had thundered weekly a silk train from the West bringing the raw material from Seattle, where it had been shipped from Japan.

The mammoth Doherty mill, owned chiefly by Japanese capitalists, and the other mills, the dye-houses and the factories were all closed down by the great strike of 1913.

The workers were on strike for better conditions and to prevent the companies from increasing the number of looms that they should operate. Among these workers, as in Lawrence, were many nationalities—Italians, Syrians, Armenians, French, Germans, Jews from all countries, and many others.

Daily meetings of the strikers were held in Turn Hall and other places. We often had great mass meetings in the adjoining town of Haledon where we spoke from the veranda of a house occupied by a Socialist.

While this strike was on I learned something of the methods of producing silk. After the cocoons were unwound and the silk was whipped into skeins it was dyed with the glorious colors seen in this costly fabric. All of it went through a process called "dynamiting" where it was loaded with metals of different kinds—lead, tin and zinc. From a fourth to a third of the weight of the silk was of these adulterants, which shortened the life and durability though temporarily adding to the gloss and weight of the finished goods. The owners of silk garments could not understand how a folded or hanging gown would rust and break in the creases until this expose was made by the strikers. The metropolitan press ran stories about the "dynamiting" process, much to the embarrassment of the silk mill owners.

During the strike the mill owners and flag manufacturers attempted a patriotic stunt like that pulled off at Lawrence. Here in Paterson the silk weavers and others who were on strike produced the flag cloth. They allowed the flag sentiment to get a fairly good hold. All the mills were bedecked with flags, some of the stores were decorated with the colors and "patriots" were wearing flags on their lapels. But the strikers were alive to the situation. One day in a big parade every striker and his family wore a flag under which was printed:

"We weave the flag.
"We live under the flag.
"We die under the flag.
"But damn'd if we'll starve under the flag."

The patriotic wind raised by the manufacturers soon died down. The big flags that were flapping about in the wind and rain were removed and the flag waving became a mere incident of the strike.

The strikers of Paterson felt that "life without labor is robbery, labor without art is barbarity." They proceeded to produce the greatest labor pageant ever held in America.

At a small gathering in the home of a New York friend of mine it was suggested that it would be an excellent idea to stage the strike in New York City. I conveyed this suggestion to the strikers and it met with their approval.

At this time Jack Reed, who was then the dramatic editor of the *American Magazine,* came to Paterson and got interested in the strike. It was Jack's first venture in anything like a revolutionary movement. I introduced him at a meeting of the strikers where he spoke and later he taught the strikers a song which when sung by 25,000 people made an impression that cannot be realized without hearing such a great crowd give vent to their full voice. Booes like those of Lawrence were now used by the strikers of Paterson against the police. The sound of 25,000 people shouting "Boo, boo, boo" was like the blast of Gabriel's trumpet that shook down the walls of Jericho. These thunderous choruses will never be forgotten by those who took part in them or heard them sung.

On the day of the Paterson pageant 1,200 strikers crossed the Hudson river. From the dock we marched to Madison Square Garden, which for a week previous had every night been lighted by an electric sign of giant proportions with the letters "I.W.W." in red lamps. We had enlisted the services of 80 or 90 people with radical tendencies in New York. "Bobby" Jones, now a leading scenic designer, with Jack Reed, drew the poster—an heroic figure of a worker rising out of the background of factories, smokestacks and chimneys. A great stage had been erected in Madison Square Garden and scenery painted depicting the silk mills. Jack Reed acted as stage manager of the pageant.

When the doors were opened there were many queues. One was reported as 28 blocks long. That night the strikers were to disclose a part of their lives in Paterson to a tremendous audience of interested people, with music that had been composed to new songs written by the strikers.

The first scene showed the mill alive, working. Lights shone through hundreds of windows. The workers with spirits dead, walked down the street—the center of the great auditorium—in groups, singly and by twos,—an occasional one glancing at a newspaper, another humming a song, some talking, all with small baskets, buckets or packages of lunch in their hands or under their arms. The mill whistles blow. The thump, chug, rattle and buzz of machinery was heard. Then the wide aisle—the street—was deserted. All were at work. Two hours were supposed to elapse, when voices inside the mill were heard shouting "Strike! strike!" The workers came rushing out pell-mell, laughing, shouting, jostling each other. They burst out into glorious song—the "International"—joined by the audience.

In Scene Two the mills were dead—no lights, not a sound. They stood like monstrous specters. It was the morning following the strike. The workers were coming on massed picket duty. They sang their strike songs. One, an exuberant Italian, gayly strummed his guitar. A few policemen mingled with the laughing, singing crowd parading in front of the mills. Without warning the police began to club and beat the strikers. A fight ensued. Shots rang out. A striker fell. The police had killed one. Another limped out of the crowd wounded. The dead man was carried away. The strikers followed the body to its home. The day was done.

The third scene was the burial of the murdered striker. A coffin was carried on the shoulders of the pallbearers, followed by marching strikers singing the "Funeral March." The coffin was set down near the center of the stage. The strikers marched onto the stage, one on either side, placing a twig of evergreen and a red carnation on the coffin. The tributes pile high as the strikers formed in a group to the rear. Elizabeth Gurley Flynn, Carlo Tresca and I spoke, as we really did at the graveside of the dead striker in Paterson, impressing the listeners and again pledging the strikers to battle onward until the infamous system of exploitation is overthrown and the workers come into their own.

In Scene Four striking parents sent their children to other cities while the strike was on. A pathetic scene of filial devotion portraying the human reason for the strike—it was for the children. These same children had gone on a school strike because the teachers had called the striking silk workers and their organizers "Anarchists and good-for-nothing foreigners." The children who were bidding their parents good-by were decked out in red ashes. They departed singing the "Red Flag." They were then with new-found friends—their strike parents—to stay until the strike was ended.

The last scene was a strike meeting in Turn Hall, Paterson. The strikers came to the meeting down the main aisle. A platform had been made at the rear of the stage around which the strikers gathered with their backs turned to the audience, transforming the setting into a vast meeting. I addressed this great gathering as earnestly and as vigorously as one could whose heart was in the cause and inspired by thousands of sympathetic listeners.

The great pageant was ended with the crowd standing again singing the "International."

Many entertainments were held in behalf of the strike fund. Bob Fitzsimmons, one of the world's greatest fighters, gave an exhibition. Bertha Kalich, a noted actress, gave a reading at one of these entertainments.

While the Paterson strike was on there were other strikes of the I.W.W. throughout the country, the most important of which numerically was the strike of the rubber workers at Akron, Ohio. Among the organizers there were Jim Cannon, Jack White, Bill Trautmann and George Speed, who was in charge of the strike. These organizers had appealed to St. John at headquarters in Chicago to have me come and help them out with the strike. Two or three demands were made by wire when St. John telegraphed me to go to Akron, if possible. I started at once.

When the train pulled into the depot I saw 35 or 40 men with long yellow ribbons pinned on the lapels of their coats. I thought to myself, "That's a strange decoration for a reception committee." Then I saw that each man had a long, hickory club fastened to his wrist with a thong. When I stepped down from the coach two or three men came up to me and asked: "Are you Mr. Haywood?"

I said: "Yes, that's my name."

He added: "The chief wants to see you."

I asked: "Where is he?"

He said: "Right here."

I stepped over to where the chief of police was standing and he accosted me with: "Mr. Haywood, you realize that the situation in this city at the present time is very tense. I want to notify you that while you are here you are treading on very thin ice."

I said: "I know there is a strike here, and in all strikes the feeling is tense." Then I asked him if he had a warrant for me.

He said: "I have no warrant. I just wanted to warn you about the situation."

I remarked: "If that is all, step aside. I'm going this way."

Speed and the other organizers, with thousands of strikers, were on the bridgeway overlooking the depot. At the head of a great procession we marched through the streets of the town to the home of Margaret Prevey, where the strike committee was holding a session.

That afternoon we had a great meeting in Rainbow hall. My address was "A Lesson in Rubber." I took up the conditions of the rubber plantations of Congo, Africa, which were owned by King Leopold of Belgium in conjunction with American capitalists. I told of how the Congo slaves were compelled to gather a certain quota of rubber and if they did not they were not only beaten themselves but they were further punished by having the hand or foot of one of their children amputated. I traced the blood-stained rubber to Akron, where it was manufactured into automobile tires and other things. But the function of rubber was not complete until it became smeared with the blood of some innocent little child that was run over and killed in the street.

I told the rubber workers that the reason they got so little was because they gave the bosses so much, that they were compelled to work long hours because the bosses did not work at all. It took the Firestones, the Goodriches, the Seiberlings, all their time to spend the money that the workers piled up for them.

These companies, among the richest in America, were at the same time the bitterest exploiters of labor. They had in their employ hundreds of detectives furnished by the Corporation Auxiliary Co. and other detective agencies.

I made two or three trips between Paterson and Akron, where the work done among the rubber workers by the I.W.W. organizers was of permanent propaganda value. The companies learned that a strike was possible in spite of the finks and detectives that they employed.

I was going to Paterson one morning from New York when I was arrested on the train, taken off and driven by automobile to the county jail at Paterson. No charge had been made against me, no warrant was read. I was put into that poisonous hole.

All the prisoners were compelled to bathe in a foul tub. The cells were rusty and rank. I had been in two days when Jack Reed came down the stairs to the day cell where the prisoners sat gossiping, reading and writing.

I went up to him and said: "What's your assignment, Jack?"

He replied: "This is no assignment. I'm a prisoner, the same as the rest of you fellows."

I asked him why he had been arrested.

He said: "I was watching the parade, standing under the porch of a house, when a policeman came along and told me to move. That I refused to do and he put me under arrest."

We weren't there long before we were released on bail. I never learned just why I was arrested, as I was never put on trial in this as in so many other cases.

On another occasion the strikers had arranged a meeting to be held on the baseball grounds. When I went to the grounds a big crowd of strikers had gathered. A police officer came up to me and said: "Mr. Haywood, you'll not be allowed to speak here to-day." I looked at him. I was indignant, and turned to those who were with me and asked what they proposed we should do.

"Oh," they said, "let's go to Haledon," which was only a short distance away.

I replied: "All right, send out runners to notify the crowd." We started for our old speaking ground. We were almost outside the city limits when a patrol wagon rushed up and several of us were arrested and taken to the city jail.

The vicious cruelty of the police authorities was an outstanding feature of the Paterson strike. More than 1,800 arrests of men, women and children were made while the strike was on.

The sense of humor among the strikers could not be broken. The nights in the city jail were made stormy by the prisoners building a "battleship." This was done by creating as much noise as possible, slamming down the bunks on their chains, hammering against the bars with tin cups, rattling the doors and making as many other kinds of noises as possible.

About three o'clock in the morning a policeman came to my cell and said: "Get your clothes on, the chief wants to see you."

I went with him to a large room where the chief was seated behind a desk on one side. Along the wall of the other was a row of plainclothes detectives. I had been brought in for inspection.

The chief said: "Walk down to the other end, now back. I guess that will be all."

I don't think there was a dick in the gang who didn't know me as I had been speaking at strike meetings in Paterson for several months. I was only in a night or two when bonds were furnished and I was released to go on trial later.

A woman was arrested one morning on the picket line. She indignantly told the policeman: "I can't go to jail and leave my children." She picked up five of her six little ones and put them in the patrol wagon, saying to one of the other strikers: "If you see Freddie, tell him to come to jail."

I had been arrested when coming into Paterson. I was now to be tried for going out of Paterson. There were several witnesses who testified, one of them a policeman who said that a great crowd was following me.

Judge Minturn asked: "Was that the reason for your arresting him?" The judge added: "Other prominent people have visited our city. Crowds may have followed them. Did you arrest them for it?

Crowds follow a circus. Do you arrest the circus? The case is dismissed."

The silk strike extended to many other places. We found silk mills tucked away in the mining camps of Pennsylvania and elsewhere. When a strike broke out at Hazleton we sent Jessie Ashley and Margaret Sanger there as organizers. I spoke at meetings in many silk and textile centers—Passaic, Hazleton, Hoboken and surrounding towns.

The American Federation of Labor came to Paterson during the strike and held a meeting. It has always been my opinion that it was to break the ranks of the strikers, if possible. Sarah Conboy, an organizer of the United Textile Workers, a "perfect lady," but somewhat too fat, said, when addressing the meeting: "If that Bill Haywood gives me any back talk I'll scratch his other eye out."

The Socialists of New York offered a plan of settlement to the Paterson strikers. They had selected a commission, one of whom was Jacob Panken, who became a Judge in 1918. But the strikers could not see from the outline given what place they were going to have in the settlement, so the suggestion was not accepted.

Through the management of the Doherty mill the strikers were approached with a plan of settlement on the basis of the strikers taking over the mill and guaranteeing the stockholders five per cent interest on money invested. This proposition would have involved discussion about watered stock and other questions that the strikers did not feel they were competent to handle.

In the early period the strike was scarcely noticed by the New York papers but after the pageant they gave us more attention. One time the strikers wanted to put a half-page advertisement in the New York Call, official daily newspaper of the Socialist Party, but for some unknown reason the advertisement was questioned and not published. The man with the strongest influence with the New York Call was Morris Hillquit. I remembered then what he had said in our debate the year previous about how he would fight on the barricades for Socialism. But that meant only that he would fight if the Socialists were counted out at the ballot box. We came to see that he did not even mean that. When ten Socialists were elected to the New York Assembly, several years later, they were illegally dispossessed of their seats in the assembly. It was then that Morris Hillquit mounted a barricade of law books and fired well-worded briefs at the capitalist enemy, which proved of no avail.

At a strike meeting one day at Haledon it was raining. I spoke to a great audience which stood sheltered under umbrellas. When I asked the strikers to indicate their feeling by raising their right hand, up went that multitude of umbrellas. It looked as if the earth itself were rising up through the mist of the rain. There were many meetings of the strikers' children. One big meeting was held in Turn Hall to discuss the school strike. While the children were framing their demands one little lad sang out: "No home work, Bill. Put that in."

These children got together, organized a strike committee, appointed their speakers, elected a treasurer and collected money to be used for their needy members.

To these children and to others throughout the United States I used to tell a story about "Kids' Town." I did not know then that I would see a kids' town in real life or a children's home conducted by themselves as I have seen in Russia. The story I told was about a city where the people were all children. There were no grown-ups to keep telling them: "Don't, don't, don't." I told the children that the world is young and ever-changing, explaining to them the elemental forces continuously at work, the glaciers ever moving, the effects of earthquakes, volcanoes and cloudbursts, the erosion of the earth's surface and the reaction of heat and frost. That these great things, with the assistance of microbic life, were always making new out of the old. This is true of everything on the earth. I told them that the hardest thing to change is the minds of old people, and some people become old while young in years. It is they who make the world seem old. It is they who fasten on the people besotted governments, bigoted religions and frightful diseases. Generation after generation they precipitate disastrous wars. All of these terrible things the old give as a heritage to the children of the world.

The story about "Kids' Town" to me grew bigger and more interesting every time I told it because the children with their bright, keen imaginations lent many original and attractive ideas. Their young minds could readily grasp the advantages of communal life. But quite as important were the things they did not want in their city. No boy would think of being a policeman and soldiers wouldn't be needed. They were not going to fight with other children. They thought they could get along without prisons or banks, and none of them said anything about churches.

The children of Paterson knew who made the tools and machinery, who built the houses, who grew all the foodstuffs, who made all the clothes, and they knew, too, who enjoyed the use of all these things produced by the working class. And they would answer contemptuously, when asked: "Why, the bosses?"

One thing of interest was that the children everywhere wanted cities as close to nature as possible. They expressed their love of the green grass, the flowers, trees and singing birds. Often they made the suggestion that instead of common shade trees that the trees of their city should answer the double purpose of shade and good things to eat—fruit and nut trees. Instead of hedges of briary bramble they would have berry bushes.

The educational worth of the strikes of the Industrial Workers of the World more than repaid for everything that the speakers, organizers and organization put into them.

The deportation of the striking miners from Johannesburg, South Africa, took place during the Paterson strike. I then wrote the following greeting:

You, O Men of Africa, Greeting!
Greeting to you who are on the high seas,
You who have been exiled.
You who are on strike.
You who are fighting as only noble men can fight.
You who are ready to sacrifice your lives for the cause you love.

You who have been beaten.
You who have been imprisoned.
You who are separated from your loved ones.
You who grieve for your Comrades who have been murdered.

You, O Men of Ireland and of the Empire, Greeting!
You who have had your homes invaded.
You who have been maltreated.
You who have been duped by priests and politicians.
You who have been clubbed.
You who have been denied the right to organize.
You who have been bereaved by death.
You who have been evicted from miserable homes.
You who have been robbed of your heritage.

You, O Men of Europe, Greeting!
Slavs, Latins, Orientals, Teutons and Norsemen.
You who have been pitted against each other like beasts in bloody war.
You whose comrades have been massacred.
You who are conscripts of a monarch's army.
You who are denied voice in a nation's council.
You who give the themes of discourse and art.
You who build palaces and temples and live in hovels.
You whom churches and kings would use as puppets.
You who have been lashed with scorn.
You whose voices cannot be silenced with threat of bullet or gallows.

You, O Men of the Americas, Greeting!
You of the East, the West, the North, the South.
You who have been driven to take up arms against your oppressors.
You who have been hunted like wild animals.
You who have been blacklisted.
You who have lost your loved ones in disaster.
You who have been crippled.
You who have had your women violated.
You who are living under martial laws.
You who have been bullied and browbeaten.
You who have been deported.
You who have been in bull pens.
You who have been robbed of every civil and constitutional right.

You, all Men and Women and Children of Labor.
Greet each the other.
You who are white, black, brown, red or yellow of skin.
You who have been denied the sunlight of life.
You who have been denied knowledge.
You who have been denied love.

You who have never known independence.
You who are wage slaves in the mart.
You whose drops of blood turn the wheels of all industries.
You who fill the warehouses and granaries of the world.
You who have made all invention possible.
You who feed, and clothe, and shelter, and succor the peoples of the
    world.
You who have had the resources of the earth and machinery of
    production within your grasp.
You who are compelled to die of starvation amidst plenty.
You can start and stop every wheel.
You must rise in revolt against the inhuman master's control.
You must strip the rich of all power, save the strength to work.

You must feel that an injury to the least is an injury to all your class. You must know as individuals you cannot avoid the iniquities and tortures you have suffered.

You, O Men and Women and Children of Labor, you can end forever the wrongs your class has endured.
You have but to think within yourselves.
You have but to act within your class.
You must organize as you work together.
Think, Organize, Act Together.
Industrial Freedom Will Come to All.

Tom Mann, who had been in South Africa, came to the United States about this time on a speaking trip. Fred Merrick, then editor of *Justice*, published in Pittsburgh, had arranged a kind of patched-up tour for Mann. I think it proved anything but a successful venture. Tom could have had a magnificent speaking tour under the auspices of the I.W.W.

During the long strike at Paterson I was suffering from ulceration of the stomach, but I never missed attending a meeting and often spoke several times a day. I lost over 80 pounds in weight during the strike. When the strike was declared off I went with some friends to Provincetown, Massachusetts.

At the earnest invitation of a friend, I went to Paris. In France I was to take a vacation and a much-needed rest, the first of the kind that I had ever had. We visited the Louvre, the Luxembourg and, most important, Pere Lachaise cemetery—where I fastened a button of the I.W.W. on the wall where the Communards were shot.

While in Paris I met all the leading lights of the syndicalist and socialist movement—Jean Longuet, Rosmer, Pierre Monatte. The latter took me to see Guillaume, who had been secretary of the International Workingmen's Association. I had an interesting talk with the old man and he promised to give me the complete record of the First International. He said there would be seven volumes of the record. Whether it was printed before the death of Guillaume I do not know. I never received a copy.

I had been in Paris not more than a week when I got a telegram from the *Daily Herald* in London asking me to come and speak in behalf of Jim Larkin, who was then in Mountjoy Prison. I went to see the officials of the Confederation of Labor and told them I was going to England in behalf of Jim Larkin and the Dublin Transport Workers' strike, and that I would like a testimonial from France to the Dublin strikers—something that the strikers could use. They gave me a check for a thousand francs, a large contribution considering the condition of the workers of France at that time.

When I arrived in London a meeting was arranged in Albert Hall. Larkin was released from prison in time to speak at what proved to be a wonderful meeting. Twenty-five or thirty thousand people, more than could get in the hall, had gathered. Some students attempted to disrupt the meeting but the stewards or ushers were well organized and ejected the noisy bunch in quick order. A son of George Lansbury came over the railing of the first balcony and dropped into a struggling group which was fighting to get into the aisle.

The speakers were Lansbury, Cunningham-Graham, Dyson, Larkin, myself and others. Jim Larkin is a big bony man with a shock of iron-gray hair and marked features such as are appreciated by the sculptor or cartoonist. He is a vigorous speaker and this meeting was the beginning of a crusade that he called the "Fiery Cross." I have never spoken in any meeting with more satisfaction than in this auditorium. On the stage sat Hyndman, the man who had spoken with me at Burnley in 1910. He was very much put out with the things I said in Albert Hall, and remarked that he wondered the people were not angry enough to pull me limb from limb. I had strongly condemned war and was not choice in my remarks about the army and navy. The things I said met with much applause. I learned later that Hyndman was living on the dividends of stock that he owned in an arms and ammunition factory.

I went to Dublin where I met Jim Connolly, the martyr who was taken in 1916 from his sick bed and executed, after being court-martialed by the British for his leadership in the Easter uprising. I had known him in the United States. We reviewed the Citizens' Army on a piece of land that had been purchased by the Transport Workers' Union.

There was a splendid meeting of the strikers in front of Liberty Hall. A cordon of police had been formed on one side. In the course of my speech I referred to the then recent strikes in America and told what the workers could do with solidarity among themselves. I described how the workers booed the police and asked the Irish workers to try it with me once, saying: "Now altogether, as loud as you can, 'Boo, boo, boo.'" It was but a few minutes afterwards that the police formed in ranks and marched away.

Liberty Hall was a good building owned by the union. In the auditorium I saw a big sign with the familiar letters: "I.W.W." I learned later that these letters stood for "Irish Women Workers."

Connolly asked me to go to Belfast where he said a big meeting could be arranged. Peter Larkin, a brother of Jim, was there at the time. But I was already billed for Liverpool and returned there to speak to an enthusiastic crowd. After the meeting with Larkin I visited the Clarion and Anarchist clubs. The next day on the train Jim spent much of his time reading Rabelais. At Manchester we had a fine meeting in Free Trade Hall. After the meeting we went to the Clarion Club. There I described the Paterson pageant to some of the people who had gathered. This description seemed to interest the hearers as much as my speech of the evening. After speaking in several other cities in behalf of the Dublin Transport Workers I returned to London, where Larkin spoke at the Trade Union Congress, addressing the delegates as "Human beings."

After my return to America I devoted considerable time in behalf of Ford and Suhr, who had been arrested in California in connection with the hop pickers' strike of 1913, on the Durst ranch at Wheatland. The Durst Brothers' hop ranch was the biggest in the state of California. Twenty-eight hundred men, women and children had been engaged there to pick hops. These workers had been gathered together by lying advertisements from the unemployed of the cities and mining camps, as well as some people from mountain towns. The Dursts, through this advertising all over California, and parts of Oregon and Nevada, brought more pickers to their ranch than they could possibly employ.

There was no shelter for the workers excepting a motley collection of tents, lumber stockades and gunny-sack stretched over fences. The tents were rented by the Dursts at 75 cents a week. A great many had no blankets and slept on piles of straw thrown on the ground under the tents. One group of 45 men, women and children slept packed close together on a single pile of straw. Among the workers were many groups: Syrian, Mexican, Japanese, Spanish, Lithuanian, Italian, Greek, Polish, Cuban, Porto Rican, Swedish and American. For the accommodation of all these people Durst had built eight rough toilets which soon became too filthy for use. These vile toilets, the manure piles and garbage of the camp were the breeding places for millions of flies that carried intestinal microbes that poisoned the camp. This, added to the lack of water for the workers in the fields, caused epidemics of diarrhea, dysentery, malaria and typhoid fever.

No water was provided for the workers picking hops in the fields. All they had to drink had to be carried from a mile away. The temperature on this ranch at the time was from 106 to 110 Fahrenheit in the shade. Workers told of carrying water in the fields which they gave to little children prostrated with the heat. Lemonade was sold by Durst for five cents a glass which was proven to be made from citric acid. A cousin of the Dursts had this concession, which accounts for the lack of a supply of water.

These were the accumulated grievances when the workers met in protest meeting to demand better conditions. Richard Ford and Herman Suhr, members of the I.W.W., were the leaders of this movement. "Blackie" Ford had just taken a baby from its mother's arms and was holding it before the eyes of the workers, saying: "It is these children that we want to save." At this moment automobiles loaded with armed county officials drove up and fired into the meeting. A Porto Rican Negro and an English boy were shot and killed, and many of the strikers were seriously wounded. Some of the strikers replied with bullets, killing District Attorney Manwell and Deputy Sheriff Riordan. When he attempted to arrest "Blackie" Ford, the sheriff of the county was kicked into insensibility by the workers and the rest of the posse fled. The militia was ordered to the hop ranch the following day by the governor of the state.

The facts recited here were all testified to by the hop pickers themselves at the trial of Ford, Suhr, Beck and Bagan at Marysville. Ford and Suhr were convicted and sentenced to life imprisonment in Folson penitentiary. They had been there more than 12 years when Richard Ford was pardoned, and when he was released he was met at the gate by a sheriff with a warrant sworn out against him by the son of Attorney Manwell. Ford was again brought to trial but through the activities of the General Defense Committee of the I.W.W. and the International Labor Defense he was acquitted.

While the silk workers were on strike in Paterson, Jack Reed left for Mexico. He was with General Villa as a correspondent and wrote some articles for the *Metropolitan Magazine*. About the same time most of the members of the I.W.W., belonging to the Brawley and Imperial locals of Southern California, crossed the line and joined forces with the Mexican revolutionists.

During the years 1912-1913 there were many free speech fights carried on by the I.W.W. I was never personally involved but recognized their tremendous importance, and the bravery and endurance of those who took part in the battles for free speech. Long hunger strikes were often a part of their tactics. They endured the brutal cruelties imposed by "Citizens' Committees" as well as the elected officers of city, county and state. An investigator appointed by the governor of California said that "it was hard for him to believe that he was not sojourning in Russia (of the Czar) conducting his investigation there instead of the alleged 'land of the free and home of the brave.'" The human vultures acting as editors of local papers were bitterly hostile. One said: "Hanging is none too good for the I.W.W.'s. They would be much better dead, for they are absolutely useless in the human economy; they are the waste material of creation and should be drained off in the sewer of oblivion, there to rot in cold obstruction like any other excrement."

In Denver, Mayor Creel said to an I.W.W. committee: "Go ahead, boys, speak as much as you like. There's just one favor I'm going to ask. I wish you wouldn't spout directly under army headquarters. They are not important but they're childish. They'll make lots of bother if you do." There was no free speech fight in Denver at that time.

The decentralizing question arose in the organization and caused much internal dissension. It finally wore itself out after serious damage had been done because of the lack of organizing work among those taking part in the discussion to the exclusion of everything else. The decentralizers demanded that the executive board be abolished, that the conventions be discontinued, etc., etc. This, like other things that have marred the growth of the I.W.W., while detrimental for the time, was of much educational value. The organization came together later much stronger than ever.

I was elected General Organizer, but my work for a time was limited on account of ill health.

Long years of association with the metal miners caused many members of the Industrial Workers of the World who had belonged to the Western Federation of Miners to take a keen interest in everything that the metal miners, smelter men and mill men were doing. They had had a strike against the Utah Copper Co. in Bingham Canyon, Utah. This strike was against the old enemies of the W.F.M.—McNeil and Penrose of Colorado City. Nothing serious developed during this strike and no decided gains were made by the miners and smelter men.

An important strike occurred on the Upper Peninsula of Michigan involving all the copper miners of that district. By this time the Western Federation of Miners had died, with the blade of conservatism plunged deep into its heart. The name of the organization had been changed, and it was now called the International Union of Mine, Mill and Smelter Workers. They had become affiliated with the American Federation of Labor. The prestige of the W.F.M. was a thing of the past. Its revolutionary preamble had been changed for one emasculated of all revolutionary pretense, the last clause of which is: "To endeavor to negotiate time agreements with our employers and by all lawful means establish the principles embraced in the body of this constitution."

CHAPTER XVIII

THE U. S. INDUSTRIAL RELATIONS COMMISSION

At the time about which I write, around 1915, thousands of members of the Industrial Workers of the World had been imprisoned in the class struggle. Some men and women had been killed and at least three were now on their way to serve sentences of life imprisonment in the penitentiaries. They were Cline, Ford and Suhr.

But in spite of this splendid working-class record the supercilious DeLeon continued his slanders against the I.W.W. Nothing better than the "Bummery" or the "Overall Brigade" did he find in his lexicon to call the organization and its members.

During the Spokane free speech fight DeLeon said in a letter to Olive M. Johnson quoted in *Daniel DeLeon: A Symposium:*

When you say you hope the Spokanites may stop "before they make another '86" (the Chicago Haymarket bomb tragedy), you touch upon a thing that has given me not a little worry. I have all along been apprehensive that some of those Knipperdollings would throw a bomb. . . . Hence it is that I have been hitting so hard. I have been trying to keep the S.L.P. skirts clean against such an eventuality. Indeed I take the flattering unction to myself that the *People* has, at least, contributed towards rendering such an eventuality less likely. I notice with pleasure that some of the Spokane capitalist sheets are quoting the *People* on Spokane. So that they know there are Socialists who spurn I-am-a-bummism, and all that thereby hangs.

What caused DeLeon to fear that some of the I.W.W.'s would throw a bomb is something that will never be known. The thought was an aberration of his own mind, a mind so warped that it took unction from the fact that capitalist papers quoted his criticism on the free speech fight at Spokane.

Keeping step with DeLeon was the vituperative O'Neill, who spurted his venom through the columns of the *Miners' Magazine,* saying:

Since the Western Federation of Miners repudiated by referendum vote the aggregation of characterless fanatics who make up the official coterie of the International Workless Wonders, the officials of the Western Federation of Miners have been assailed by every disreputable hoodlum in the I.W.W. . . . . The time has come when the labor and Socialist press of America must hold up to the arclight these professional degenerates who create riots, and then, in the name of free speech, solicit revenue to free the prostituted parasites who yell "scab" and "fakiration" at every labor body whose members refuse to gulp down the lunacy of a "bummery" that would disgrace the lower confines of Hades.

Again he said: "Industrial unionism will not come through soup-houses, spectacular free speech fights, sabotage or insults to the flags of nations."

Even the genial Eugene V. Debs took a hard slam at the fighting organization. He said: "It is vain to talk about the I.W.W. The Chicago faction, it now seems plain, stands for anarchy. So be it. Let all who oppose political action and favor sabotage and the program of anarchism join that faction."

DeLeon had lost what little knowledge he had of industrial unionism. O'Neill was explosive for no other reason than jealousy of the progress being made by the I.W.W. It was harder to understand the attitude of Gene Debs, as he had always been friendly and was afterwards friendly to the I.W.W. as an organization.

An economic crisis was about to take place which was only averted when war was declared. Unemployment was growing in every section of the country. In San Francisco hundreds of men were herded into vacant buildings where they slept in rows on the floor with no bedding but newspapers. From San Francisco and other cities they started a march to Sacramento to make an appeal for aid to the legislature. They were met by citizens who were armed with pickhandles, and they were drenched with the firehose and driven to the outskirts of the city. In New York City the unemployed were organized by the I.W.W. They installed a soup kitchen and went to the churches to sleep but were told by the priests and ministers that the churches were not domiciles. Many of them were arrested and served time in prison.

Joe Hill, an I.W.W. song writer, was arrested in Salt Lake City, Utah, and charged with murder. I got out the first appeal in his behalf in which I described the method of execution in Utah, which Joe Hill would suffer in the event of his conviction. Joe thought I didn't remember him and wrote me that he "rattled the music box" (played the piano) when I spoke in San Diego. Some of his songs entertained the crowd at that meeting.

After the trial Joe wrote me that he had not had a square deal. He said: "The right of a fair trial is worth any man's life much more than mine." I sent Judge Hilton of Denver to Salt Lake City to assist in Joe Hill's defense. A new trial could not be secured and in spite of all that we could do Hill was sentenced to be executed. In Utah the law had not been changed and a man could select the means of his death—either by shooting or hanging. Joe Hill chose to be shot.

President Wilson made a request of Governor Spry for a respite and the Swedish government protested against the execution of Joe Hill.

All of Joe Hill's songs breathe the class struggle and are fine propaganda. I do not think that Joe ever wrote anything in verse that did not at some time find its way into the I.W.W. song book.

Among the songs written by Joe Hill were "What We Want," "Don't Take My Papa Away From Me," "Scissor Bill," "The White Slave," "There Is Power in a Union," "Casey Jones—the Union Scab," "Hallelujah, I'm a Bum," "Mr. Block," and "Should I Ever Be a Soldier."

Ralph Chaplin wrote a poem to Joe Hill from which I quote:

> Singer of manly songs, laughter and tears,
> Singer of Labor's wrongs, joys, hopes and fears.
>
> Though you were one of us, what could we do?
> Joe, there were none of us needed like you.
>
> Utah has drained your blood, white hands are wet,
> We of the "surging flood," NEVER FORGET!
>
> High head and back unbending—"rebel true blue."
> Into the night unending, why was it you?

When the war broke out I was struck dumb. For weeks I could scarcely talk. I spent much time in the libraries, the chess club and at Udell's little book shop on North Clark Street in Chicago. I could not concentrate my mind on chess, but at least there was no conversation as I watched the game. I could not read, as my mind was fixed on the war. I never felt any doubt about the United States becoming involved. Wilson had been reëlected to the Presidency the second time because "he kept us out of war." I knew that when the magnates of Wall Street pushed the button that the OYSTER FROM BUZZARD'S BAY would swell up as flamboyantly as the BUZZARD FROM OYSTER BAY did during the Spanish war.

When I was elected General Secretary-Treasurer of the Industrial Workers of the World, headquarters were located at 166 West Washington Street. At one time the office force was Matt Schmidt's sister, Katherine Schmidt, who was stenographer and bookkeeper, and myself. I had been in the office only a short time when I received a letter from Elwood Moore, a member, saying that he had inherited a small legacy and asking how it could be used to the best advantage of the organization. I told him of the financial straits of 'Solidarity' and suggested that he send $1,000 to that paper and the balance to headquarters, as we had decided to start a campaign to organize the agricultural workers. Also that I was anxious to get to work in other basic industries, especially metal mining, lumber, oil and the packing industry of Chicago and elsewhere.

The Agricultural Workers' Organization was formed in Kansas City and we began to develop the job-delegate system. The name was soon changed to Agricultural Workers' Industrial Union, which more nearly conformed to the plan of the organization. Walter T. Nef was secretary and the main office was in Minneapolis. The union grew very rapidly. My next move was to organize the metal mine workers. I sent Grover H. Perry as secretary of the Metal Mine Workers' Industrial Union to Phœnix, Arizona. Between these two unions I kept up a good-natured competition by writing to Nef about the growth of the Metal Miners and to Perry about how the Agricultural Workers was increasing.

We moved headquarters to a three-story building at 1001 West Madison Street. We put the print shop on the ground floor of the adjoining building and installed new machinery, moved Solidarity from Cleveland and printed other papers in many different languages, including Bohemian, Bulgarian, Croatian, Finnish, German, Hungarian, Italian, Jewish, Lithuanian, Russian, Slavonian, Spanish and Swedish.

The One Big Union Monthly and Tie Vapauteen, a Finnish monthly, were also published in Chicago. Other papers in various languages were published in other cities throughout the country, including the *Industrial Worker,* English official organ in Seattle, Washington, and a Finnish daily in Duluth.

The I.W.W. Work People's College was also located in Duluth. A thorough Marxian course was given in this college as well as excellent courses in public speaking, in English for workers of foreign and American birth, and in bookkeeping and organizing. The I.W.W. had much reason to be proud of its school, which has graduated many efficient organizers, and also of its papers and journals. Pamphlets were published by the hundreds of thousands, and leaflets and stickers by the millions. The propaganda of the I.W.W. was widespread and never-ending.

In 1913 in Colorado, the old battle ground of the Western Federation of Miners, a horrible massacre took place at Ludlow. The coal miners on strike there had been evicted from their homes. They were living in a tent colony. One day when most of the men were picketing the mines a company of militia passed the colony. A young miner was killed by a lieutenant who crushed his skull with the butt of a rifle when he approached the soldiers with a white flag of truce. The brutes then fired into the tent colony, killing women and children, and then set the colony afire and burned the bodies to a crisp. The news of this massacre horrified the workers from coast to coast.

John D. Rockefeller, Jr., in an article in the *Atlantic Monthly,* said: "Any situation, no matter what its cause, out of which so much bitterness could grow, clearly required amelioration," adding to this the contemptible lie: "It has always been the desire and purpose of the management of the Colorado Fuel and Iron Co. that its employees should be treated liberally and fairly."

Again, in speeches made in the state of Colorado, he reiterated the nonsense about capital and labor being partners, and with a lie on his lips spoke of the protection afforded to labor against oppression and exploitation, at the same time presenting an industrial plan that gave the Colorado Fuel and Iron Co. a strangle hold on all the workers it employed.

This industrial plan was framed by Mackenzie King, later prime minister of Canada, who, it is asserted, at one time said that "labor in Canada must come down to a lower standard of living nearer to that of the Chinese workers."

Rockefeller said: "The common stockholders have put $34,000,000 into this company in order to make it go, so that you men will get your wages, you officers have your salaries, and the directors get their fees, while not one cent has ever come back to them in these fourteen years."

This parasite must have thought the reader a damn fool to believe that the stockholders of any industry invest their money to pay the workers' wages. He knows and most people know that all industries are run for profit.

I was called to Washington to give testimony before the Industrial Relations Commission. This commission was formed by an act of Congress under the Roosevelt administration but did not come into existence until Woodrow Wilson was elected president of the United States, when he appointed the members comprising it with Frank P. Walsh, a lawyer of Kansas City, as chairman. The reason for this commission was the industrial unrest of the period: the woolen and cotton strike at Lawrence, the silk strike at Paterson, the textile strike at Little Falls, the rubber strike at Akron, the strikes in Colorado, the lumber strikes of the Northwest and the South, the Wheatland hop pickers' strike and other strikes in California, the strike of the copper miners in Michigan, the widespread free speech fights, as well as the condition of the workers in the South.

The commission was exhaustive in its investigation, though little or nothing came from Congress as a result of its report in eleven large volumes. The power of this commission insofar as investigation was concerned was extensive. The industrial magnates were compelled to testify, and to submit to the severest cross-examination. Among them was John D. Rockefeller, Jr., of whom it was said by one of the commissioners that he was "turned inside out."

I was on the stand for the better part of two days. I was first questioned by Chairman Walsh, and went over briefly many things that I have recounted in this book, adding:

This clearly portrays a condition that this commission should understand, and that is that there is a class struggle in society, with workers on one side of the struggle and the capitalists on the other,—that the workers have nothing but their labor power and the capitalists have the control of and the influence of all branches of government—legislative, executive and judicial,—that they have on their side of the question all of the forces of law,—they can hire detectives, they can have the police force for the asking or the militia, or the regular army.

There are workers who have come to the conclusion that there is only one way to win this battle. We don't agree at all with the statement that you have heard reiterated here day after day—that there is an identity of interests between capital and labor. We say to you frankly that there can be no identity of interests between workers, who produce all by their own labor power and their brains, and such men as John D. Rockefeller, Morgan, and their stockholders, who neither by brain nor muscle nor by any other effort contribute to the productivity of the industries that they own. We say that this struggle will go on in spite of anything that this commission can do or anything that you may recommend to Congress, that the struggle between the working class and the capitalist class is an inevitable battle, that it is a fight for what the capitalist class has control of—the means of life, the tools and machinery of production. These, we contend, should be in the hands of and controlled by the working class alone, independent of anything that capitalists and their shareholders and stockholders may say to the contrary. . . .

A dream that I have in the morning and at night and during the day is that there will be a new society sometime in which there will be no battle between capitalist and wage earner, but that every man will have free access to land and its resources. In that day there will be no political government, there will be no states, and Congress will not be composed of lawyers and preachers as it is now, but it will be composed of experts of the different branches of industry, who will come together for the purpose of discussing the welfare of all the people and discussing the means by which the machinery can be made the slave of the people instead of a part of the people being made the slave of machinery or the owners of machinery.

I believe there will come a time when the workers will realize what the few of us are striving for and that is industrial freedom.

Commissioner Weinstock, a merchant of Sacramento, California, was one of the commissioners who questioned me.

He asked me about the I.W.W. literature, saying: "Now I am going to read here some quotations from I.W.W. authenticated literature."

I wanted to know who was the author.

Commissioner Weinstock: The I.W.W. literature placed in the hands of the commission teaches militant action whenever such action may be deemed necessary. In a pamphlet published by the I.W.W., entitled *The I.W.W.—Its History Structure, and Methods,* written by Vincent St. John, the following statement appears:

"As a revolutionary organization the Industrial Workers of the World aims to use any and all tactics that will get the results sought with the least expenditure of time and energy. The tactics used are determined solely by the power of the organization to make good their use. The question of 'right' and 'wrong' does not concern us."

In the I.W.W. song book appears the following:

> "To arms, to arms, ye brave!
> The avenging sword unsheath!
> March on, march on, all hearts resolved
> On victory or death."

In a leaflet issued by the I.W.W., entitled *An Appeal to Wake Workers, Men and Women*, by E. S. Nelson, the following appears:

"In case of a capitalist injunction against strikers, violate it,—disobey it,—let the strikers and others go to jail, if necessary. That would cost so much that the injunction would be dispensed with. Final, universal strike, that is, to remain within the industrial institutions, lock the employers out for good as owners and parasites, and give them a chance to become toilers."

That is fairly representative, Mr. Haywood, of the attitude and propaganda of the I.W.W.—these extracts from these I.W.W. pamphlets and articles I have read?

To which I replied: Yes, in so far as you have quoted from the I.W.W. pamphlets. You have a number of pamphlets that were not written by members of the I.W.W. The first that you quoted is the National Song of France, the "Marseillaise." What you read advocating the taking of food was said in this city by Abraham Lincoln during war time, when speculators and gamblers in foodstuffs ran the prices of provisions up to 600 or 700 or 800 per cent, and the people came to Abraham Lincoln and asked him what to do, and he said, "Take your pickaxes and crowbars and go to the granaries and warehouses and help yourselves," and I think that is good I.W.W. doctrine. I do not see much there I would take issue with.

Commissioner Weinstock: Well, then, summing up we find that I.W.W.ism teaches the following:

(a) That the workers are to use any and all tactics that will get the results sought with the least possible expenditure of time and energy.

(b) The question of right or wrong is not to be considered.

(c) The avenging sword is to be unsheathed, with all hearts resolved on victory or death.

(d) The workman is to help himself when the proper time comes.

(e) No agreement with an employer is to be considered by the worker as sacred or inviolable.

(f) The worker is to produce inferior goods and kill time in getting tools repaired and in attending to repair work,—all by a silent understanding.

(g) The worker is to look forward to the day when he will confiscate the factories and drive out the owners.

(h) The worker is to get ready to cause industrial paralysis with a view of confiscating all industries, meanwhile taking forcible possession of all things that he may need.

(i) Strikers are to disobey and to treat with contempt all judicial injunction.

If that is the creed of the I.W.W. do you think the American people will ever stand for it?

Answer: There are many things I would like to explain to you, that is, as to the tactics and the results. Do you know the results we are hoping for? We hope to see the day when no child will labor. We hope to see the day when all able men will work, either with brain or with muscle,—we want to see the day when women will take their place as industrial units,—we want to see the day when every old man and every old woman will have the assurance of at least dying in peace. Now you have not got anything like that to-day. You have not the assurance, rich man as you are, of not dying a pauper. I have an idea that we can have a better society than we have got,—and I have another idea that we cannot have a much worse one than it is at present.

After I had answered Commissioner Weinstock's other questions regarding the teachings of the I.W.W., he submitted the last:

(i) Strikers are to disobey and treat with contempt all judicial injunction.

I answered: I have been plastered up with injunctions until I did not need a suit of clothes, and I have treated them with contempt. . . .

Commissioner Weinstock: If I was to come in and take possession of your property and throw you out, would I be robbing you?

Answer: You have a mistaken idea that property is yours. I hold that property does not belong to you,—that what you as a capitalist have piled up as property is merely unpaid labor, surplus value. You have no vested right in that property.

Commissioner Weinstock: You believe in the adoption of the methods advocated by the I.W.W.?

Answer: Can you conceive of anything that workers cannot do if they are organized in one big union? If labor was organized and self-disciplined it could stop every wheel in the United States to-night— every one—and sweep off your capitalists and state legislatures and politicians into the sea. Labor is what runs this country, and if the workers were organized, scientifically organized,—if they were class conscious, if they recognized that one worker's interest was every worker's interest, there is nothing they could not do. . . .

Commissioner Weinstock: I have been asked to submit this question to you if you care to answer it: "What would you do with the lazy man and those that would decide which job each man should take, and what each particular man should do under your system?"

Answer: I would give the lazy man the kind of work he would like to do. I don't believe any man is lazy. . . .

Commissioner Weinstock: Let me make sure, Mr. Haywood, that I certainly understand the objective of I.W.W.ism. I have assumed,— I will admit that I have assumed in my presentation to you—that I.W.W.ism was Socialism with a plus,—that is, that I.W.W.ism in—

I interrupted at this point, declaring that: I would very much prefer that you would eliminate the reference to Socialism in referring to I.W.W.ism, because from the examples we have, for instance, in Germany, Socialism has, or at least the Social Democratic Party, has been very much discredited in the minds of workers of other countries. They have gone in for the war, and those of us who believe we are Socialists are opposed to war. So if you don't mind we will discuss industrialism on its own basis.

Commissioner Weinstock: There is a radical difference between the I.W.W.s and the Social Democrats, Mr. Haywood?

Answer: Yes.

Commissioner Weinstock: The Social Democrat wants the state to own all the industries?

Answer: Yes.

Commissioner Weinstock: And the I.W.W., then, as you now explain it, proposes to have those industries not owned by the state but by the workers.

By the workers, I repeated.

Commissioner Weinstock (continuing): Independent of the state?

Answer: Independent of the state. There will be no such thing as the state or states. The industries will take the place of what are now existing states. Can you see any necessity for the states of Rhode Island and Connecticut, and two capitols in the smallest states in the Union?

Commissioner Weinstock: Except that of home rule.

Answer: Well, you have home rule, anyhow, when you place it in the people who are interested, and that is in the industries.

Commissioner Weinstock: Well, then, will you briefly outline to us, Mr. Haywood, how you would govern and direct the affairs under your proposed system of a hundred million people, as we are in this country to-day?

Answer: How are the affairs of the hundred million people conducted at the present time? The workers have no interest, have no voice in anything except the shops. Many of the workers are children. They certainly have no interest and no voice in the franchise. They are employed in the shops, and, of course, my idea is that children who work should have a voice in the way they work, in the wages they should receive—that is, under the present conditions children who labor should have that voice.

The same is true of women. The political state, the government, says that women are not entitled to vote—that is, except in the ten free states in the West,—but they are industrial units,—they are productive units. My idea is that they should have a voice in the control or disposition of their labor power, and the only place where they can express themselves is in their labor union halls, and there they express themselves to the fullest as citizens of industry, if you will, as to the purpose of their work and the conditions under which they will labor. Now, you recognize that in conjunction with women and children.

The black men of the South are on the same footing. They are all citizens of this country, but they have no voice in its government. Millions of black men are disfranchised, who if organized would have a voice in saying how they should work and how the conditions of labor should be regulated. But unorganized they are helpless and in the same condition of slavery as they were before the war.

This is not only true of women and children and black men, but it extends to the foreigner who comes to this country and is certainly a useful member of society. Most of them at once go into industries, but for five years they are not citizens. They plod along at their work and have no voice in the control or use of their labor power. And as you have learned through this commission there are corporations who direct the manner in which these foreigners shall vote. Certainly you have heard something of that in connection with the Rockefeller interests in the southern part of Colorado. You know that the elections there and in many other places were never carried on straight. These foreigners were directed as to how their ballot should be placed.

They are not the only ones disfranchised, but there is also the workingman who is born in this country, who is shifted about from place to place by industrial depressions,—their homes are broken up and they are compelled to go from one city to another, and each state requires a certain period of residence before a man has the right to vote. Some states say he must be a resident one year, others say two years,—he must live a certain length of time in the county,—he must live for 30 days or such a matter in the precinct before he has any voice in the conduct of government.

Now, if a man was not a subject of a state or nation, but a citizen of industry, moving from place to place, belonging to his union, wherever he went he would step in the union hall, show his card, register, and he at once would have a voice in the conduct of the affairs pertaining to his welfare. That is the form of society I want to see. Understand me, Mr. Weinstock, I think that the workingman, even doing the meanest kind of work, is a more important member of society than any judge on the supreme bench or any other useless member of society. I am speaking for the working class. I am a partisan of the workers.

Frank P. Walsh, Chairman of the Commission, put some questions to me: I have some questions that I have been requested to ask you that have been sent up, and I wish that you would answer them as briefly as you can.

One is, Do you not consider the exploitation of children in industry under the present system a form of violence of a very insidious and brutal sort?

Answer: I most certainly do. It is only one of the terrible violences that are practiced by the capitalist class.

Chairman Walsh: Then there is another question: Will I.W.W.ism do away with crime and criminals? If not, how will you organize your society to protect the well-behaved many against the vicious few?

Answer: Industrialism will do away with crime and criminals, as 95 per cent of the crime to-day is crime against property. Abolishing the wage system—abolishing private property—will remove 95 per cent of the crime. . . .

CHAPTER XIX

RAIDS! RAIDS! RAIDS!

The strike of the iron miners of Minnesota in 1916 was a great event in the history of the Industrial Workers of the World, though one thing occurred during this strike that caused an indelible black mark against the organization. This was the conviction of three of the strikers on a charge of murder. I will describe the affair later.

The strike began at the Silver Mine at Aurora, which was an iron property where the conditions under which the miners were working became unbearable. For example, there were places underground where the miners were compelled to drag timber through places so small that they had to get down on all fours in the slush and mud and drag the heavy timber to the places where they were working. Demands were made for improvements, and the strike began. It rapidly extended to the Mesaba, the Cayuna and Vermilion iron mining districts. Some 16,000 men were involved in the strike.

This was at a time when the United States Steel Corporation was flooded with war orders from all countries engaged in the carnival of murder.

The first move of the Steel Trust was to call out the guards and gunmen of the company. Then the Governor of the State sent the militia into the iron districts for the purpose of breaking the strike.

Governor Burnquist issued an order that there were to be no parades, processions, or demonstrations of the strikers. This would have deprived the men of one of their strongest means of agitation. The order was ignored.

A Finnish worker by the name of John Alar was killed while sitting on the porch of his house with his babe in his arms. This murder occurred at Eveleth. The dead miner's funeral was the occasion of a great demonstration of miners from all the different ranges. Those who went from the town of Virginia carried a streamer at the head of the procession upon which was inscribed: "An eye for an eye, a tooth for a tooth." The organizers of the I.W.W. were at the head of this parade followed by a band of music. As they marched along, gunmen and guards lined the sidewalk. When the funeral speeches were being made at the graveside, this old Biblical oath was adopted by the miners of several different nationalities by uplifted right hand.

This fact was later used in a trial when the organizers of the I.W.W. were arrested, charged with the murder of a gunman, one of a gang which organized in Duluth to go up on the range and clean up or drive out the leading men of the strike. They went to the home of a miner by the name of Masonovitch with whom two other miners were boarding, Geogorovitch and Orlanditch. A fight was started and the shots that were fired killed two men, one the driver of a grocery wagon, a Finnish worker named Latvala, and the gunman Myron.

This skirmish was immediately followed by the arrest of Masonovitch and the other two miners as well as of the organizers of the I.W.W., Joe Schmidt, Sam Scarlett and Carlo Tresca. The men were all put in prison in Duluth, and held there without bail.

I at once started a campaign for their defense. I sent to Denver for Judge Hilton, whom we had previously employed on behalf of Joe Hill and who took the place of Clarence Darrow in the defense of George Pettibone at Boise, Idaho. I also sent for a young lawyer by the name of Whitsell, who had worked for the Western Federation of Miners during the Boise trial. We employed local counsel in Minnesota, and felt that we were well prepared to defend not only the organizers who were facing the terrible charge of murder, but also the striking miners who were involved.

Joe Ettor, who was then the general organizer of the I.W.W., had been doing some work in Scranton, Penna., and vicinity. He had not been very active since the Lawrence strike. He arrived on the ground shortly after the strike began and also started collections for the defense. What with his work and that of the general headquarters, a large sum of money was raised.

When the case came to trial, I got word through the press of the conviction of the three miners. At once I wired Ettor to file an application for a new trial. I was dumbfounded to learn from him that the miners had pleaded guilty and had been sentenced from one to twenty years in the penitentiary. I telegraphed him at once to come with the organizers who had been released to headquarters.

With them came Elizabeth Gurley Flynn, who had also been working in the strike.

In going over the situation carefully, it developed that the arrangement for a plea of guilty on the part of the miners had been made in the Duluth prison. It was agreed that the miners would plead guilty and get a sentence of one year, while the organizers of the I.W.W. were to be released and the charge of murder against them quashed. The scene in the court was a farce. The miners who were not conversant with the English language found that they had pleaded guilty to second-degree murder and were sentenced to from five to twenty years.

Joe Schmidt, a Polish organizer, said to me at the conference at headquarters: "It was wrong, Bill, wrong from beginning to end. Those men should never have been sent to prison." Scarlett substantiated the words of Schmidt. I then looked to Ettor, Flynn and Tresca for an explanation. I did not expect much from Tresca, as he was not a member of the organization, though he had done effective work during the Lawrence strike in Massachusetts. Ettor and Flynn said it was the best that could be done. I told Ettor in plain language that when he was being held for murder in Lawrence, the organization would not have permitted him to plead guilty to anything, not even to spitting on the sidewalk.

The three of them knew that an injustice had been done to the convicted miners who were now on their way to the penitentiary. Their part in the affair terminated their connection with the I.W.W. Ettor and Flynn had long been connected with the I.W.W. and were earnest and vigorous workers. They should not have allowed themselves to be entrapped by lawyers who would rather "fix" a case than try it.

During the strike, Governor Burnquist sent a commission to the iron ranges to look into the condition of the miners. Later there was an investigation and a hearing before the Minnesota legislature. When the Governor's commission made its report, the miners returned to work, and, strange to say, every demand that had been made was granted by the Steel Trust without a conference, a settlement, or an agreement of any kind. The miners got an increase in wages, an eight-hour day, and better working conditions generally. This was the second time that the great steel corporation had granted demands made by the I.W.W., while the officials and members of the organization were no better acquainted with the officers of that concern than they had been before the strike began.

These facts are a lesson, a "Golden Rule" that the compromising officials of labor might well learn to the advantage of the membership of their organizations.

The industrial magnates of the United States realized that a victorious Germany would be a strong contender for the markets of the world. They were fearful of the inventive genius of this great nation that created ships like the *Deutschland* that came across the ocean under the water, and invented Zeppelins that could cross over the seas, made guns that would shoot 75 miles, invented a specific that could cure syphilis, and were proud to mark their products "Made in Germany." The United States was anxious to turn its batteries upon this growing industrial competitor. The ravage of Belgium by the "Huns" had slipped by. The destruction of the *Lusitania* was not enough for a declaration of war. The people of the United States, especially those of the Middle West and the western part of the country, were decidedly against the nation becoming involved. So it was necessary for Uncle Sam, personified by the imperialists of Wall Street, to start a preparedness campaign. First they secured control of all the most influential newspapers of the country. Then the commercial clubs, manufacturers' associations, etc., began their preparedness parades. These demonstrations were held in many of the large cities. The loans to the allied governments were, of course, the greatest factor in determining America's entrance into the war.

In San Francisco, two days previous to the preparedness parade, a great meeting was held in Dreamland Rink, protesting against the United States going into the war. At this meeting one of the speakers advocated as a means of ending the war that the soldiers shoot their officers and go home. The success of this meeting was guaranteed by the publicity of the *Bulletin*.

The following day letters of warning were sent to all the papers, telling them that "something would happen that would be heard around the world."

Something did happen on the day of the parade. An explosion occurred which killed many people and injured many others. Tom Mooney, Warren Billings and others were arrested and charged with this crime.

Tom Mooney had a short time previously led a strike of street car men in San Francisco. During this time he had written me to send some members of the I.W.W. to help him in the strike. It was for Mooney's vigorous and successful conduct of this strike that he was arrested, charged with being one who caused the explosion. Mooney and Billings were convicted and sentenced to death. Later this sentence was commuted to life imprisonment. They would have been murdered in the same cold-blooded manner as Sacco and Vanzetti, were it not for the fact that a committee of Russian workmen waited on Ambassador Francis in Petrograd and told him that their brother, Tom Mooney, in America, must not be hanged. Francis wired the United States in behalf of Mooney and Billings.

It must be said to the credit of Freemont Older, editor of the San Francisco *Bulletin,* that when he learned the facts of the Mooney and Billings case, he gave them the strongest support of the paper of which he was the editor.

At this time the I.W.W. was doing much propaganda work against the war, everywhere pasting up stickers which read "Don't be a soldier, be a man. Join the I.W.W. and fight on the job for yourself and your class."

The Convention of the I.W.W. in 1916 adopted the following resolution which was formulated from the Lenin resolution at the Zimmerwald Conference. It was headed "A Declaration."

We, the Industrial Workers of the World, in Convention assembled, hereby reaffirm our adherence to the principles of industrial unionism, and we dedicate ourselves to the unflinching, unfaltering prosecution of the struggle for the abolition of wage slavery, and the realization of our ideal in industrial democracy. With the European war for conquest and exploitation raging and destroying the lives, class consciousness and unity of the workers, and the ever-growing agitation for military preparedness clouding the main issues and delaying the realization of our ultimate aim with patriotic and, therefore, capitalistic aspirations, we openly declare ourselves the determined opponents of all nationalistic sectionalism, or patriotism, and the militarism preached and supported by our one enemy, the capitalist class. We condemn all wars, and for the prevention of such, we proclaim the anti-militarist propaganda in time of peace, thus promoting Class Solidarity among the workers of the entire world, and, in time of war, the General Strike in all industries. We extend assurances of both moral and material support to all the workers who suffer at the hands of the capitalist class for their adhesion to these principles and call on all workers to unite themselves with us, that the reign of the exploiters may cease and this earth be made fair through the establishment of the Industrial Democracy.

I had a leaflet made of this resolution with a red border which we printed alongside of a resolution which was adopted by the American Federation of Labor, bordered in black, under the caption "A Deadly Parallel." These were circulated in vast numbers throughout the country. This "Deadly Parallel" was also published in a pamphlet which we called "The Last War."

Spruce lumber was an important war material which the Lumber Trust was supplying to the warring nations, and later to the United States government, at a price increased from $33 a thousand to $110 a thousand. The lumber workers, members of the I.W.W., felt that they were justly entitled to better working conditions, better living conditions, shorter hours, and an increase in wages. They were making great efforts to organize the lumber workers, mill hands, and others employed in the production of lumber. But in many places they met with the opposition of the county authorities, all of whom were under the influence of the great lumber companies.

This was true at Everett, Washington, where the sheriff continued to arrest the organizers and speakers of the I.W.W. and disrupted the meetings. The Seattle branches of the organization decided to send a number of their members to Everett to establish free speech and the right to organize. On Sunday, November 5th, 1916, they chartered the vessel *Verona* and a sister ship, and started for Everett. When the *Verona* reached the wharf, the workers aboard the ship were met with a volley of rifle shots fired by deputy sheriffs and gunmen from an ambush. Five members of the I.W.W. were killed and many wounded. Though their fellow members had been cruelly murdered, a large number who were aboard the *Verona* were arrested and compelled to stand trial for murder, as some of the officers on the land had been killed by volleys returned from the ship. After long imprisonment, when tried, they were released.

The work of organizing went on with the lumber workers until a strike was declared and carried on with much energy until, for the lack of funds, it became necessary to strike on the job. The men returned to work and quit when they had put in 8 hours. This angered the superintendent and foreman, who repeatedly told the men they would have to work 10 hours, as the place was a 10-hour camp.   The workers replied that they knew that when they took the job, but that they were 8-hour men and would work no longer. They compelled the companies to install beds instead of the muzzle-loading bunks that were in use, they got shower-baths, washing facilities, and better grub.   On May 1st, 1917, all the lumber workers burned all their vermin-infested lousy blankets.

The conditions in the oil fields of Oklahoma, Texas and California were very bad.   The Oil Workers' Industrial Union determined that something must be done for the workers employed around the oil wells and in the camps that were prospecting for oil.

Tulsa, Oklahoma, was the place decided upon for a beginning. One night some members of the Commercial Club, with a body of policemen, invaded the I.W.W. hall and arrested all the members that were there, and took them to jail.   But they had not thought of a charge to put against the men, so they were taken out of jail and put into automobiles, driven outside the city limits, where this mob tied them to trees and beat them with blacksnakes until their bodies were dripping with blood.   They then poured hot tar on their lacerated bodies and sprinkled them with feathers.   They turned them loose, and told them to go and never come back to Tulsa again, if they did not want to meet with worse treatment.

Charles Kreiger, a member of the I.W.W., a machinist, was arrested in Tulsa on some framed up charge and held there many months before he was finally tried and acquitted.

It was during this busy period that I received a telegram from my daughters, then in Denver, telling me that their mother had died. While I felt very badly, I realized that she was released from her long sufferings.   From the small equity that we owned in a little home in Denver, my daughters arranged to take their mother's body back to Nevada where she is buried near her father and mother at McDermitt, which is still a wild frontier country.

For a long time there were special agents watching every meeting of the I.W.W. and every action insofar as they could of the membership.   In January, 1916, it is said that there were 75 to 100 men detailed to this work.   They had the support and assistance of all State, municipal and county officials.   There was little for the finks to do as all meetings were open and there was nothing for us to hide in our work.

Following the announcement of a state of war by President Wilson in February, 1917, the surveillance by the government of the I.W.W. and of all radicals became more intense.

In the monthly bulletin for April, 1917, I wrote:

Since the last *Bulletin*, President Wilson has proclaimed a state of war against the Imperial Government of Germany. A volunteer army has been called for, and, possibly, conscription measures will be passed by the United States Congress. All class conscious members of the Industrial Workers of the World are conscientiously opposed to spilling the life blood of human beings, *not for religious reasons*, as are the Quakers and Friendly Societies, but because we believe that the interests and welfare of the working class in all countries are identical. While we are bitterly opposed to the Imperialist Capitalistic Government of Germany, we are against slaughtering and maiming the workers of any country. In many lands, our members are suffering imprisonment, death and abuse of all kinds in the class war which we are waging for social and industrial justice.

The I.W.W. had extended its activity to far off Australia. There the members were carrying on a campaign against the war. Twelve were arrested in Sidney, tried, and sentenced to 14 years' imprisonment. Our paper, *Direct Action,* was suppressed, and the editor, Tom Barker, was deported.

In the July *Bulletin,* I reported to the Industrial Unions and general membership as follows:

At Rockford, Illinois, over 150 men, members of the I.W.W. and Socialists, gave themselves up voluntarily to the authorities for evading the Registration Act. They were treated with unusual brutality. When they objected to being isolated in groups in other jails and determined to stand together, they were clubbed unmercifully by the sheriff of the Rockford jail and his deputies. When their trial came, they were taken before a judge who is notoriously unfair, a judge who in a recent speech before the trials took place, had made a statement that "He was sorry he could not go to the war to fight, but since he could not go, he could at least stay at home and fight the men who were fighting the soldiers here." This judge, Kenesaw Mountain Landis by name, has a son in the army, so one can imagine how fair he would be to men who were opposed to registration and did not believe in wars or armies. As was expected, the "Honorable" (save the mark) judge, simply "kangarooed" the boys, giving all but a few the limit, and in order to make their sentence harder, sentenced them to the Bridewell in Chicago, where, as he said, "The work is much harder than in the Federal Prison." He also took advantage of their helplessness to deliver an insulting speech to them in which he called them coward and "whining, belly-aching puppies" because they would not register to fight for Morgan and his loans.

In June, 1917, just three years from the date of the blowing up of the Miners' Hall in Butte, Montana, a horrible disaster occurred in the Speculator mine of that camp. A fire broke out from some unknown cause on the 2,400 foot level. It caused the death of 194 men. The victims could not get out of the mine, nor could they make their way to the adjoining mines, as concrete bulkheads had been built that could not be dug through without blasting. The men, who were without tools, scratched and dug to escape until their fingers were worn to the bone. Those who were not actually burned to death were smothered by the smoke. Some frightful stories were told about what was done at the morgue with the charred remains and unidentified bodies. These were sold for $12 apiece, probably for dissecting purposes in the medical college.

The fire in the Speculator mine was quickly followed by a general strike in all the mines of Butte. This strike was conducted by a new union that had been formed called the United Metal Mine Workers. Former members of the Western Federation of Miners and members of the I.W.W. were the officials.

I received the information that the government intended to make overtures to the I.W.W., the same as they had done to the American Federation of Labor. But the officials who intended to approach us were apprised of the fact that the I.W.W. would not enter into any contract or agreement with any employer.

A lawyer by the name of "Judge" Kerr * employed by the United Mine Workers of Illinois is said to have gone to Washington to intercede on behalf of the International Mine, Mill and Smelter Workers' Union (formerly the Western Federation of Miners). This organization received the support of the government, the same as all other internationals of the A. F. of L. during the war.

---

* Judge Kerr was a permanent member of Frank Farrington's staff for many years. He had his office in the U.M.W.A., District 12 headquarters at Springfield. He directly represented the district administration as an assistant prosecutor in the framed-up prosecution of the Ziegler boys, for murder. He died in 1927.

The International Mine, Mill, and Smelter Workers' Union made little progress even with the support of the A. F. of L. and the government. Moyer paid lip service to Gompers at a Pan American Conference. He did the incredible thing of thanking Gompers for what he had done in our behalf when we were on trial in Idaho. The fact was that Gompers did nothing, did not even raise his voice, though unions affiliated to the A. F. of L. helped financially and gave us real earnest support.

Debs bitterly criticized Moyer for his lying kowtowing, and he did not forget to lambast Gompers for what he did not do.

Moyer was finally removed from the presidency of the Mine, Mill and Smelter Workers' organization.

After the declaration of war in 1917 I was told by Robert Bruere, who was then writing a series of articles called "Following the Trail of the I.W.W.," that the organization was to be raided. He told me that to this end Sam Gompers had gone to Newton Baker, then Secretary of War, and had presented to him a plan to annihilate the I.W.W. Baker refused to take the suggestion of Gompers seriously; the latter then went to the Department of Justice, where he met with more success.

An extremely bitter stream of publicity had been started by the press, charging the I.W.W. with receiving vast sums of German gold. It was said that we intended to poison the canned goods used by the army, and that we were responsible for the spread of the hoof and mouth disease that was raging and had killed great herds of cattle.

The work of organizing by the Mine Workers' Industrial Union was extending to the different mining regions of the country and was especially strong in the state of Arizona where the membership had determined to demand an increase of wages. The Copper Trust had increased the price of copper from 11 cents a pound to 33 cents a pound without giving a thought to the conditions of the men who produced the ore. The infamous Citizens' Alliance was resurrected, and under the name of Loyalty League began its inhuman atrocities.

Early in the morning of July 10th, 1917, gunmen of the United Verde Copper Company at Jerome, Arizona, belonging to ex-Senator William Clark, rounded up the miners of that camp, and, selecting

70 militants from among them, loaded these on cattle cars and sent them to California. The California sheriff refused relief, and drove them back across the Arizona line, the group breaking up at Kingman, Arizona.

On July 12th, 1917, the miners of Bisbee, Arizona, were taken unawares by the gunmen of the mining companies, and the business element, who composed a Vigilance Committee. They went in the small hours of the morning to the homes and boarding houses where the miners lived, and routed them out of bed. The men were marched to the baseball park near the depot, and when 1162 of them had been herded together, they were loaded into cattle and freight cars and shipped to the desert of Hermanas. There they were unloaded and left without food or water.

As soon as I got word of this desperate outrage, I telegraphed to President Wilson at Washington, demanding that the miners be returned to their homes in Bisbee, and there protected from the fury of the mob. I received no answer to the wire I sent, and a day or two later learned that the men had been moved to Columbus, New Mexico. Again I telegraphed to the President, and received no reply.

The members of the I.W.W. were indignant at the outrage imposed upon their fellow workers, and began to agitate earnestly for a general strike in the industries where they had control or enough influence to cause the desired action by the workers. This agitation brought bitter retaliation on the part of the employing class and the government. Arrests and deportations of the I.W.W. took place in many parts of the country.

At a meeting of the General Executive Board held in Chicago in July, 1917, the war was discussed from different points of view, but no definite action was decided upon other than what was being done by the organization, though it was agreed that a statement would be issued to the membership. After the meeting of the Board, Ralph Chaplin, then editor of *Solidarity*, published the following in the issue of July 28th:

WERE YOU DRAFTED?
Where the I.W.W. Stands on the Question of War.
The attitude of the Industrial Workers of the World is well known to the people of the United States and is generally recognized by the labor movement throughout the world.

Since its inception our organization has opposed all national and imperialistic wars. We have proved, beyond the shadow of a doubt, that war is a question with which we never have and never intend to compromise.

Members joining the military forces of any nation have always been expelled from the organization.

The I.W.W. has placed itself on record regarding its opposition to war, and also as being bitterly opposed to having its members forced into the bloody and needless quarrels of the ruling class of different nations.

The principle of the international solidarity of labor to which we have always adhered makes it impossible for us to participate in any and all of the plunder-squabbles of the parasite class.

Our songs, our literature, the sentiment of the entire membership —the very spirit of our union, give evidence of our unalterable opposition to both capitalism and its wars.

All members of the I.W.W. who have been drafted should mark their claims for exemption, "I.W.W., opposed to war."

After the meeting of the Executive Board, Frank Little, a Board member, went to Butte, Montana, to assist in the strike there. He was hobbling around on crutches with his leg in a plaster cast, as it had been broken just before he left Arizona. But he felt, in spite of this handicap, that he could do something to help the miners who were then on strike in Butte. He was an energetic worker, part Cherokee Indian, black-eyed, hot-blooded, and reliable.

He addressed several meetings in Butte and it was charged that he made remarks in contempt of the United States troops.

While in Butte, Little lived in a Finnish boarding house near the I.W.W. hall. At 3 o'clock in the morning, August 1, 1917, an automobile load of thugs went to the building where Little had his room. They got into his room, and either dragged or carried him with his broken leg down to the automobile.

They fastened a rope around his neck and must have dragged him part or all the way to a railroad bridge where they hung him up by the neck. They pinned to his shirt a card "3-7-77." * Bill Dunne, then editor of the Butte *Bulletin,* Tom Campbell and one or two others, got cards with this deadly warning 3-7-77 of the bloody-handed Vigilance Committee.

---

* "3-7-77" meant a grave according to specifications in Montana: 3 feet wide, 7 feet long, 77 inches deep.

When Frank Little's body was found, it was taken in charge by
the mine workers and a huge funeral was held in the graveyard on
the flat below Butte.

A motion picture was taken of the ceremony. But this, as well as
the motion picture of the funeral of Joe Hill, was taken from headquarters by a photographer named George Dawson, who lived near
Pittsburgh, Pa., and who has since proven to be a Federal agent.

So-called independent unions, the railroad organizations and the
American Federation of Labor were definitely for the war, and in
every division of trade and industry they had secured real personal
benefits in the way of an increase in wages, and in some places a
reduction of hours with extra pay for overtime. And they worked
overtime whenever they could. The I.W.W. adopted the slogan:
"Overtime is scab time, any time there are some who are working
no time."

The country was going mad about the war. On the 5th of September, 1917, the secret agents of the Department of Justice swooped
down on the I.W.W. like a cloud of vultures. The organization was
raided from coast to coast, from the Great Lakes to the Gulf of
Mexico. The general headquarters, the main offices of the industrial
unions, the industrial union branches, and the recruiting unions were
in the hands of the government. Even the homes of the members
were invaded. And all of this took place without a search warrant
of any kind.

The books in which were recorded the transactions of the organization, the literature, the furniture, typewriters, mimeograph machines,
pictures from the wall and spittoons from the floor were seized as
evidence and sent to Chicago. Tons upon tons of the property of the
Industrial Workers of the World were there piled in the Federal
Building. The letters and correspondence were most carefully investigated by the prosecutors of the Federal government. Special
men of the judiciary were assigned to this work.

An indictment of five counts was found against the officers and
members of the Industrial Workers of the World. The laws that
we were charged with violating were all passed after the declaration of war. They were emergency measures which were to become null and void after the war was over. The indictment was the
cause of another general raid upon the I.W.W. on September 28,
1917.

This time the arrest of the officers and members of the organization was general. Thousands of them were crowded into jail in all parts of the country. There were three groups that were held, one in Sacramento, Cal., one in Wichita, Kan., and the larger one in Chicago, Ill. Members were dragged from their homes and families, single men from their living places, brought to Chicago, shackled and handcuffed. The arrests were not a surprise, but no man had left his post, though it would have been easy for many to have escaped across the border line into Canada or Mexico. The arrests were to have been all at the same hour, and they practically occurred that way, though in Chicago the warrants had not been prepared.

When the Federal officers surrounded the general headquarters, 1001 West Madison, Chicago, Taro Yashiharo and I were in a barber shop a short distance from the office when some member rushed in and told me what was taking place. As soon as we got shaved we went back to see what was going on. As I opened the door I saw several deputy marshals. I was acquainted with most of them, as they had been in the office several days during the time of the previous raid. One of them said to me: "Mr. Haywood, just step in this machine." There were several automobiles lined up along the curb. I got in one and we were driven to the Federal Building, and there taken up into the office of the Secret Service Department.

Hilton Claybaugh, superintendent of the secret agents, asked me to come into the adjoining room. When I was seated he began to question me about the whereabouts of members of the organization. I told him I had no information to give him.

Pagan, a special prosecutor who had been brought from Washington to formulate the indictment, came from another room. He had a copy of Pouget's *Sabotage* in his hand. Claybaugh introduced him to me. He said: "Hard lines, Mr. Haywood, but I wish you the best of luck." The other fellow workers were brought into the room where I was, Marshal Bradley read to us the warrant that should have been served upon each man when he was arrested. This was another of my strange experiences with the law.

From there we were taken into the subway of the building, loaded into patrol wagons and driven to Cook County jail. We went into the rear entrance and were put into a small cell, there to wait until our names were entered on the books. Chaplin used the time to draw an emblem of the I.W.W. on the wall.

This was the same jail in which the Haymarket martyrs were imprisoned for eighteen months and where they were hanged. I did not learn the numbers of the cells that they occupied, but it is certain that some of us lived in those cells while we were in the place.

When our records were taken, we had to give our names, our birth place, age, religion, etc. Some of the boys, when asked about their religion, answered: "The Industrial Workers of the World." The guard said: "That's no religion." "Well," they replied, "that's the only religion I've got." Another question that was asked was— "Who is your best friend?" One member said: "Bill Haywood." The guard said: "He can't do you any good, he's in here with you." The answer was: "That's all right, he's my best friend."

The jail is in the heart of Chicago on the corner of Austin Avenue and Dearborn Street. It is a forbidding and filthy old structure built of gray granite. The cell houses are in a quadrangle. Long barred windows, like gashes in a cliff, face the street. The bottom of the windows are high up from the street. The glass had long lost its transparency because of years of accumulation of dust and cobwebs. The cells were built in tiers, back to back, barred doors face the outside walls. The cells were painted black and were dirty with dust and tobacco spit. A rusty iron basin and toilet stood in the corner behind the bunks. The heat and water pipes were slimy and rusted red. Three narrow bunks, one over the other, occupied more than one-half the space. In each bunk were old papers and a dirty mattress of straw, old and lumpy. The scanty bedding was filthy, reeking with vermin and disease. It was three paces from the rear wall to the door. To take these three steps one had to put all the furniture, which consisted of one stool, on the bed. I had the lower bunk. In looking up at the old newspapers on the bottom of the bunk above me, I saw a picture of myself. I got the paper out. It was an old issue of one of the Chicago dailies. There were no lights in the cells except the little that trickled through the bars from the screened electric globe outside the door. All the prisoners were kept locked in these cells for twenty hours a day. To read was difficult on account of the dim light. Two hours in the forenoon and two hours in the afternoon, the prisoners were let out for exercise, and walked in a slow measured pace around and around the corridor, called the bull-pen. It was always gloomy, and the floor upon which the sun had never shone was wet and slippery with spit and slime. The laws of the country made no distinction between criminal and political prisoners.

In the morning we were aroused by the raucous voice of the runner, calling "Cups out, cups out." We held our cups through the bars, one trusty filled them with a noxious fluid, a substitute for coffee, another gave us some chunks of bread. For dinner and supper the meals were more substantial, but often the food was unfit to eat. One day they brought in corned beef and cabbage. The beef was rotten and filled the prison with a vile stench. All the men shoved their plates off the galleries onto the floor below, the air was filled with cabbage and strips of beef.

In this terrible prison over one hundred members of the I.W.W. were held over a year until their trial was finished.

A newspaper was started among us called "The Can-Opener" which afforded some of the men an opportunity to pass away the time.

A man whose father had been hanged in this prison by mistake had a concession of a little store. He had two cells and sold pie, tobacco, cigarettes, newspapers, and other things that the prisoners needed.

Visiting days were Tuesdays and Fridays. We were separated from those who came to see us by two half-inch screens, two feet apart. This place was a disease distributor, if ever there was one, as every one stood against the screen talking to those who had come to see us who were behind the other screen. One got no satisfaction out of a visit at this screen, as the medley of many voices made it almost impossible to hear what was being said to one.

The hospital and bathroom were a disgrace to a civilized community. This prison had many times been condemned, but it is still filled with the unfortunates of society.

Every week we held a meeting, at which members selected by a Program Committee would make speeches, recite original poems, or tell stories. One Sunday I told a story which I called "The Monkey Strike in California." It was to give an idea of the ends to which the exploiting class would resort. I began:

The fruit-growing landowners of the golden state had determined to rid themselves of members of the I.W.W. The first move on their part was to introduce Japanese workers in the orchards and vineyards. Some of the little yellow men joined the I.W.W. which, unlike many labor unions of America, admitted them the same as white or men of any other color.

But the Japanese were not satisfied to work for small wages under the miserable conditions imposed by the members of the Fruitgrowers' Association, so they formed coöperatives, saved their money, and began purchasing land for themselves, becoming serious competitors of their former employers.

Fearful that the Japanese would buy the entire fruit-growing section of California, having already bought most of the land in the Vaca Valley, laws were passed by the legislature forbidding the sale of land to Japanese, and a Federal law was passed at Washington restricting their immigration to the United States. There was already a law restricting the immigration of the Chinese.

The fruitgrowers were again compelled to employ migratory white labor, until a wonderful idea developed at one of the conventions of the Fruitgrowers' Association. One of the delegates got up and suggested that it would be possible to train monkeys to pick and pack fruit. This was decided upon without hesitation, and steps were taken at once to get a lot of monkey fruit pickers.

The Chimpanzee breed was decided upon as the most intelligent.

Splendid little houses, all nicely painted, were built and equipped for the monkeys. They were actually fed and taught what they were to do.

When the fruit got ripe, the owners brought their friends from the city to see how ingeniously they were solving the labor problem.

The monkeys were restless in their houses, as the air was aromatic with the ripened fruit. When they were turned loose, they hurriedly climbed the trees. But instead of doing as they had been taught—to bring the fruit down and put it in a box, the mischievous little rascals would dart about, selecting the choicest fruit, take a bite or two, throw the rest away, and go after more.

Before the day was gone, and the monkeys with paunches full had gone back to their houses, much damage was done.

The wise fruitgrowers had to seek another method. The next day each monkey had a muzzle put on.

They went up into the trees rapidly enough, but none of them would pick any fruit. They were busily engaged in trying to rid themselves of the frightful contrivance that prevented them from eating and enjoying themselves.

The fruitgrowers were in an awful predicament with so many monkeys to feed which would do no work in return. They appealed to the Governor of the State, who regretfully replied that as the offenders were not men, they were not amenable to the law. If they were I.W.W.s, he could have them imprisoned and perhaps have the leaders shot, but over monkeys he had no jurisdiction.

The Society for the Prevention of Cruelty to Animals, who had never interested itself on behalf of the I.W.W. or the Japanese, learning that the monkeys were being neglected, threatened to prosecute the fruitgrowers if the little animals were not properly taken care of.

The Chimpanzees came to be disliked as much as the I.W.W. Some of the fruitgrowers owned cotton plantations in Imperial Valley on which they had trouble in getting white and black wage slaves sufficiently docile for the work of picking cotton. It occurred to them that the monkeys could be made to pick cotton, and there would be no trouble about them trying to eat it.

So all the monkeys were shipped to the new location. Strange to say, they could pick cotton and at a speed that made their owners happy. Here was the solution of the labor problem as far as picking cotton was concerned. But their satisfaction was short-lived.

One day, while all the monkeys were at work, chattering while they gathered the white bolls of cotton, a gentle breeze wafted a white tuft from a monkey's hand. It amused him to see it floating through the air. He tossed up another bit, and another. The other monkeys, catching the spirit of the fun, began to do the same. At first little bits and then handfuls, till the air was full of fleecy cotton. It looked as though the first snowstorm had struck southern California.

The overseers were alarmed.

There was no way to stop the monkeys in their eager playfulness, which, before they had tired themselves out, had almost destroyed the entire crop of that particular plantation.

In some peculiar manner the monkeys on other plantations learned of the fun, and their pranks caused the same disastrous result.

The fruit and cotton growers were at their wits' end. They knew not what to do with the monkeys, until deportation was finally decided on, and the Chimpanzees were shipped back to the forests of Africa, where they now gather together and the eldest, with a grin on his face, hanging by his tail, tells the younger generation how they won the strike in California.

This story met with great approval, as a tale with a moral should, and the next Sunday Dick Brazier reproduced it in verse which decidedly improved the original.

From my cell, No. 275, I could look down into the end of the corridor, and could picture the scaffold that had been built there when it was the death scene of Parsons, Spies, Engel and Fisher. Their words seemed to reverberate throughout the prison. Their silence spoke an undying tongue. I remember the inscription on their monument.

When the news of the Russian Revolution of March, 1917, was heralded throughout the United States, the nation throbbed with a spirit of jubilation. It seemed that every one was satisfied with the overthrow of that cruel monarch, the Russian Czar, every one was glad that he and his lecherous family had been cast into oblivion.

A call came from Russia for the return of all exiles and immigrants who had been forced to leave on account of pogroms and other bitter persecutions. The editor of our Russian paper, Vladimir Lossieff, was working in behalf of Russian political emigrants with the Russian consul in Chicago, who provided transportation for a number of Russians who wanted to return to the land of their birth.

When the Soviet revolution occurred on the 7th of November, the sentiment of the people changed. Their opinions seemed to have been formed by the monied interests of Wall Street. There was a feeling of hostility against Russia now, except on the part of those who were radical enough to appreciate what the Workers' Dictatorship meant.

The Russian ship *Sitka,* the crew of which revolted with the Russian workers, landed in Seattle. They had much difficulty with the authorities of that port, but the sailors from the vessel were entertained by the I.W.W. They made the hall their headquarters, and at meetings held for them told what they knew about the revolution. The ship was finally cleared without serious trouble.

Early in the spring of 1918, I was released on bail.

In Chicago the Russian members of the I.W.W. were active in getting up a big meeting which was held in the West Side Auditorium. I was one of the speakers. I expressed the hope that the revolution that had overthrown the Czar would prove to be a working-class victory.

Jack Reed was then touring the country on behalf of Russia. When he came to Chicago he lived with me. A fine meeting was arranged for him at the Chicago Theater. From Jack I got much interesting news of what had happened in Russia. I read his book *Ten Days That Shook The World* while in the Leavenworth Penitentiary, referring to it at the time as the "Minutes of the Russian Revolution." The book was generally circulated among us.

The general strike in Seattle in which all the members of the

I.W.W. of that city took part, was among the I.W.W.'s chiefly to prevent the further shipment of amunitions and supplies to the Koltchak forces in far eastern Siberia. When I later went to Seattle I saw many hundreds of tons of freight piled along the shore that had not been loaded.

CHAPTER XX

THE I.W.W. TRIALS

WHEN the Criminal Syndicalism Law was passed in California, Jack Gaveel, a Hollander, and one of the Fly-By-Night organizers, signed a call to take action on the infamous legislation. The slogan was: "Fill the jails." Gaveel was one of the first to be sent to the penitentiary for from one to fourteen years. The possession of an I.W.W. membership book or song book was sufficient evidence to send a man to the state prisons, either to Folsom or San Quentin. Persecution sent more than one hundred men and one or more women to the prisons of California.

Andrew Furuseth, President of the International Seamen's Union, and other leaders of the A. F. of L. joined with the other reactionaries to exterminate the I.W.W., which they called a "red menace." The authorities paid some traveling witnesses who went from place to place to testify against the I.W.W. One of these was named Jack Diamond, another was Ralph Coutes. These agent provocateurs testified at many trials; though they were criminals with long records, their evidence has been used to send I.W.W.'s to the penitentiary.

In some instances no evidence was necessary. Men were called to testify in behalf of their fellow workers on trial. When they acknowledged on the witness stand that they were members of the I.W.W. their arrest and conviction immediately followed on the ground that mere membership in the I.W.W. violated the criminal Syndicalist Law. Their persecution did not end when they reached the prison doors with sentences of from one to fourteen years, and some with a double sentence of from two to twenty-eight years. The Warden gave them the hardest and dirtiest work that he could find. This treatment resulted in many revolts and hunger strikes, which were punished by imprisonment in the Black Hole on bread and water.

There was the case of Tom Connors, secretary of the California

District Defense Committee. He had sent out an appeal throughout the state on behalf of members who were to go to trial. By chance one of these appeals reached a citizen who was later called as a juryman. Connors was arrested and convicted of attempting to tamper with the jury, and sentenced to prison from one to fourteen years.

One I.W.W. was murdered in San Quentin. The prisoners were going across the yard in file when one man stooped as if to pick something up from the ground. He was shot dead by one of the guards.

Under the Criminal Syndicalism Law many men were sent to prison in other states, notably Washington, Idaho, Oregon and Kansas, where some are yet confined.

At headquarters we were continually pestered with the representatives of the government in the drive to sell Liberty Bonds. They wanted to post their placards on the windows of the office, announcing the sale of war stamps, Liberty bonds, and other war notices. This I never permitted. I got out an issue of Freedom Certificates and Defense Stamps in which we were much more interested.

Five groups were in prison under indictment or waiting to be indicted in the different cities—San Diego, Sacramento, Omaha, Wichita, and Chicago. The Wichita and Sacramento prisoners were really the worst sufferers on account of the condition of the jails in which they were confined. The Sacramento jail was infected with Spanish influenza. Several members of the I.W.W. died in that prison awaiting trial. The lack of medical attention, nurses, and food, undoubtedly caused the death of these men, some of whom were weakened by long hunger strikes.

The Silent Defense of the Sacramento group stands as a record, a scathing denunciation not to be expressed by words, of judicial procedure.

At the time of the trial, influenza was an epidemic. The Judge, the prosecutors, the guards, policemen and audience were all wearing masks as flu preventives. But no masks were provided for the defendants.

After they had been convicted and sentences of long terms in the Federal penitentiary had been imposed upon them, there in the court room they broke their silence by singing the "International." *

At Wichita, Kan., one jail in which the prisoners were held

---

* For a list of those convicted at Sacramento see Appendix I.

awaiting trial, is what is called a Paula revolving jail, a terrible contrivance that can be compared to a gigantic squirrel cage. One of the members went crazy while in prison there and cut his throat, another went insane while being held in the Newton County jail.

In the state of Kansas over thirty men had been imprisoned for nearly two years in some of what are reported to be the worst jails in the United States.* I issued a statement on their behalf, beginning:

IN JAIL TWO YEARS—FOR WHAT?

Workers of America! Do you know that twenty or more innocent workingmen are now being slowly tortured to death in the Bastilles of Kansas? The men in question are those that have been held for two years *without trial,* on what is known as the Wichita indictment. The charges of conspiracy against these victims are so vague that to the average fair-minded individual it seems incredible that such an injustice can be imposed. But the fact of the matter is that this group is undergoing the most vindictive persecution known in the history of American labor. Never before has a group of men undergone such a rigid ordeal.

The despicable forces back of this damnable outrage, are determined to have the blood of these men. The scurrilous sheets, called newspapers, spout their venom with fury. The oligarchy of Kansas and Oklahoma are set upon crushing out every semblance of unionism. That is the reason why they are so intolerably insisting in slowly murdereing these men, so as to hold them up as examples in frightening other workers into submission and keep them from organizing. The Right to Organize belongs to every man! Keep it! . . .

When the Kansas prisoners were finally convicted, it was a relief to them, and every man was glad because they were being released from the hellish places known as county jails, though they were going to serve long terms in the Federal prisons.

The government was not content with its bitter persecution for alleged violation of war measures, but everything possible was done to prevent us from raising funds for our defense. Appeals that we sent through the post office or the express companies were confiscated and destroyed. Our speakers were arrested. Meetings were broken up.

After speaking in Sioux City and Minneapolis, under threats from the Legion, I went to Superior where the Lumber Workers and Iron Miners had a defense picnic outside the city. The rostrum was

---

* For a list of those convicted at Wichita see Appendix II.

here the rear end of a truck. I was just getting warmed up to the occasion when the sheriff and some deputies came up and said that the meeting could not proceed as they were afraid of bloodshed. The lumberjacks and miners circled around him and asked, "What's that you say?" Some of them adding: "We've got guns, appoint us as deputies. We'll prevent any trouble." The sheriff turned on his heel and walked away, saying, "We've done all we can, let 'em go to hell with their meeting." I recall that at the time of the interruption I was speaking about the Russian Revolution.

THE CHICAGO TRIAL

The preliminary hearing in the Chicago case came up on December 15th, 1917. We all gathered in the Federal Building, those from the county jail as well as those of us who were out on bail. Ettor, Flynn and Tresca came on from New York City, but the cases against them were dismissed. They were never tried. When Arturo Giovanitti demanded to know why his name had not been read by the clerk, he was informed that the case against him was dismissed. He entered a protest and demanded that he be tried with the rest of the defendants. But this was not allowed.

All the rest of us pleaded "Not Guilty."

The big trial began on April 1st, 1918. Judge Kenesaw Mountain Landis was the umpire of the District Court of the U. S., Northern District of Illinois, Eastern Division. There was a strong array of legal talent against us consisting of Charles F. Clyne, district attorney of Chicago, Frank K. Nebeker, formerly attorney for the Utah Machinery Co. at Salt Lake City, and Claude R. Porter of Iowa. We had for counsel George F. Vanderveer of Seattle, who had ably and successfully conducted the defense of the Everett case, Otto Christensen of Chicago, William B. Cleary of Bisbee, Arizona, and Caroline Lowe, who was also one of the counsel in the Wichita case.

The court room in which we were tried was white marble decorated with gilt. The Judge's bench was on an elevated platform at the right of the door which we entered. There was a big desk behind which Judge Landis sat. At his left were the witness stand and the jurors. The prosecutors sat at a table near the Judge, the attorneys for the defense had a table immediately back of them. There was a long press table inside the railing that separated the spectators from the arena. At this sat newspaper and magazine reporters from different parts of the country as well as a few from foreign lands. At the end of the table nearest the prosecutors sat a person named Karm, supposedly a labor reporter, who enthusiastically played the rôle of informer by prompting our prosecutors with suggestions and documents. The prisoners sat behind the press table along the railing, and some of us at the table with our lawyers. A panel of 200 veniremen had been called.

Attorneys for the defense questioned the veniremen on socialism, social science, industrial unionism, and industrial conditions. Then a question would be asked: "Is the industrial system involving the exploitation of society by a few individuals, the best possible scheme of things?" "Can you conceive of a society owning and controlling the means of production, communication and exchange, and the coöperative carrying on of production for use instead of profit?"

Vanderveer challenged the government when he said, "It is the social system that is on trial." He asked:

Are you aware that 2 per cent of the population of the United States own 60 per cent of the wealth? Do you know that prostitution is caused because women in industry do not get living wages? Do you know the number of children under 16 years of age now employed in the industries of this country? Do you believe in slavery—whether it be chattel slavery where the master owns the worker body and soul or whether it be industrial slavery? Have you never read in school about the American Revolution of 1776 or the French Revolution that deposed a king and made France a republic, or the Russian Revolution that overthrew the autocracy and the Czar? Do you recognize the right of people to revolt? Do you recognize the idea of revolution as one of the principles of the Declaration of Independence upon which this nation is founded? Do you believe in the right of people to govern themselves and to have a voice in this government? Do you believe this applies to industry as well as politics? Would it prejudice you if it should appear that these defendants believe that all industries should be owned by the people and operated for the benefit of the people?

Three jurymen had been accepted by both sides. The defense had used but one of the ten peremptory challenges. The prosecution had exhausted three of their six. At this time things looked a little favorable for the I.W.W., when we were met with the surprising charge that we had been trying to tamper with the prospective jurors. It was said that a member by the name of Russell had held a conversation with a relative of one of the prospective jurymen. The Judge took the high-handed method of discharging not only the jurymen that had been selected, but the entire remaining number of the panel. This was not, in my opinion, done on the sole initiative of the Judge, but because of a letter from Attorney-General Gregory at Washington giving instructions as to the kind of a jury that must be secured. We were informed that this letter had been received, by one of the secret agents who offered to get it for us for the sum of $1,000. But we did not think it would be of any particular use, as the jury had already been discharged.

The trial proved to be a protracted propaganda meeting lasting nearly six months. Two members of the I.W.W. had gone insane in Cook County jail. One of them was a defendant in this case. Both had to be removed to a hospital for the insane.

When the new venire came in, District Attorney Clyne was removed, though nothing was said about it in the press. Nebeker took the chief part as prosecutor. The duel between him and Vanderveer in the examination of the jury was even more keen than it had been with Clyne.

Nebeker asked prospective jurymen:

Have you any sympathy with any organization that seeks to overthrow the institutions of this country or to violate its laws? Do you believe that free speech gives any one the right to advocate the breaking of the law? Do you believe in the right of individuals to acquire property? Do you believe it right for any body of men or organization to take that property away by force or other unlawful means? Do you believe any one has the right to stir up rebellion or revolution? Do you believe in the wage system and in the social system as it is organized at present? Were you heartily in favor of the declaration of war against the Imperial German Government? Are you in favor of the various appropriations made to insure the successful prosecution of this war?

And then Vanderveer, the defense attorney, would come back with such questions as:

Do you believe in the right to strike? Do you believe in the right to peacefully picket? Do you believe in the right of free speech?

After a careful examination in which the class struggle was clearly portrayed, the responsibility rested upon the jurymen. Nebeker, the chief prosecutor, took more than five hours to tell what he knew and what he didn't know about the Industrial Workers of the World. He charged us with offenses that we had never dreamed of. But he knew the structure of the organization, and told of the recruiting union, the shop branches, the branches of industrial unions, how the industrial unions were connected with the general administration. He said that Bill Haywood was the uncrowned king in a swivel chair, backed by the Executive Board; that we were striving to build a government within the government. He told how this organization with its 200,000 members had closed down the copper mines of Arizona and Montana, and were contriving to call a strike on the lead and copper mines of Utah. He recited the efforts that were being made to shut down the lumber industry, and of the efforts of the Finnish workers to close the iron mines, adding that it was our intention to hamper the farmers in the gathering of the harvest.

Nebeker read many editorials from the pages of *Solidarity*. From one, entitled, "We are dissatisfied," he read, "A revolutionary body testifies to complete dissatisfaction with the existing order of things. And this is the first reason and main reason for the existence of the I.W.W. We are absolutely and irrevocably dissatisfied with the present system of society. We consider it a useless system, and we mean to destroy it. . . ."

From the I.W.W. Song Book, Nebeker read with vibrant voice the parody on that religious hymn, "Onward Christian Soldiers," which ends:

> Onward Christian soldiers! Blighting all you meet.
> Trampling human freedom under pious feet.
> Praise the Lord whose dollar sign dupes his favored race,
> Make the foreign trash respect your bullion brand of grace.

This and many other songs read by Nebeker were a decided relief after the hundreds of routine letters and bulletins that had been read to the jury. He added that the Finnish miners of the Mesaba range had declared a strike against conscription. It was true that the Finnish miners were making a hard fight against the war and against being conscripted as soldiers and later one of the Finnish workers had his eyes scraped out because of his opposition to war. This terrible punishment was inflicted upon him by a patriotic mob.

Nebeker, a Mormon lawyer, the mouthpiece of capitalism, told the jury what he seemed to think was a remarkable thing. It was that I had had the effrontery to telegraph President Wilson demanding that the Bisbee deportees be returned to their homes and there protected from further mob violence.

The first witnesses for the government were the stenographers, filing clerk and bookkeeper from the office of the General Headquarters, and the official accountants of the government who had investigated the finances and books, and who testified that the accounts were well kept and that there was no German money ever received by the Industrial Workers of the World.

Their next witnesses were sheriffs and gunmen from the coal fields of Pennsylvania who testified to the arrests of members and to the fact that they had disrupted meetings of the I.W.W. without authority, sometimes at the request of the United Mine Workers of America and again on a verbal order from the court. There were other sheriffs and gunmen as witnesses from different parts of Arizona, Montana and Washington. There were some farmers who told of working their employees sixteen hours a day, lumber bosses, mine owners and one or two renegade members, with a horde of secret service agents.

It was developed that the company for which one witness was superintendent had raised the price of spruce lumber from $33 a thousand to $110 a thousand.

With other witnesses of similar character, Nebeker finally turned to the Judge and said: "Your Honor, the Government rests."

George Vanderveer, chief counsel for the defense, a lawyer of exceptional ability, began the opening statement for the defense in a cool, calm manner, but before he had proceeded far, his eyes were blazing as he told the jury about the class struggle:

This case is unusual. It is supposed to be a case against William D. Haywood, James P. Thompson, John Foss, and a great number of other men whom you never heard of before, but—it is a charge of "conspiracy" wherein the prosecution claims these defendants have conspired to violate certain laws of the United States and for which alleged crime the prosecution here purposes to send these defendants to prison. Yet in reality, it is the purpose of the prosecution to destroy the organization with which these men are connected and to break the ideal for which their organization stands.

You are told that this case is of great importance to the nation; yet it involves more than the nation—it involves the whole social order.

There are five counts in the indictment which recites numerous "overt acts" supposedly committed in furtherance of the "conspiracy"; one of these acts is the circulation of the Preamble of the I.W.W. Constitution; and an editorial stating that "the present industrial system is useless and we mean to destroy it." It is the function of the defense to explain this to you. We want you to notice especially that the purpose of this organization is not to destroy government but to control industry—two things which ought to be separated.

It is manifestly impossible for me, gentlemen, within the limit of time allotted to me to attempt it—to tell you all that these hundred or more defendants have said or done, and all that they have had in their minds.

They classify themselves, however, into two classes. Some have had something to do with strikes—not unlawful as such—and which become unlawful only when accompanied by a certain sinister, unlawful purpose which is attributed to them in these various counts of the indictment.

Some of these men, again, have had no direct connection with any strike, but they have engaged during the period of supposed conspiracy in organizing men on various jobs—or have gone out as lecturers, or have carried the gospel of the organization in whatever manner to the workers.

I am not clear, in my own mind, upon what theory counsel seeks to hold here men who have had nothing to do with strikes, men who have had nothing to do with war activities. It may be counsel's contention that their activities as members became unlawful by reason of the unlawful character of the organization. Again the question whether or not it is lawful or unlawful in its character must be determined by its purpose.

Now, in every issue of *Solidarity*, about which you have heard a great deal here—on the top of the front page you will find these words: "Education—Organization—Emancipation." What do they mean? What do they mean standing alone or taken in connection with other things which you will find stated as part of the philosophy of the organization?

For instance, what do they mean in connection with the statement that the two classes in our society have nothing in common, the working class and the employing class?

I want to state to you what these men have said, what they have done, and what their intention has been in doing these things.

His Honor has struck out my reference to the Industrial Relations Commission Report. I do not want to repeat. You will remember—how the vast majority of our common laborers in the basic industries from which this organization recruits its membership, are unable to earn the barest living for themselves and their families. It has been the function of these men to tell these facts to the working people, in order that, understanding their conditions, and the causes of their conditions, they may more intelligently and efficiently go out and find and apply the remedy. It is a sad commentary on our system that 79 per cent of the heads of our working class families are utterly unable to support their families and educate their children on a plane of civic decency. Nobody can right the wrongs of the past. All we can do is to concern ourselves with the future and prevent, if possible, further development and growth of a system which brings these things about. . . . Why political action? This thing was not reared by law. It grew because some men by combining in trusts and corporations within industry got power to exploit labor. And it will quit growing just as soon as labor organizes and gets the power to stop its being exploited. "But you use sabotage," says counsel. Yet out of the thousands of lumber mills in Washington, he brings only two which had saws broken by something not proven and a few threshing machines out of hundreds testified about here by witnesses. We will bring witnesses—not the kind you have seen here, I hope—but reputable farmers, who have been dealing with the I.W.W. for years in the places best organized by it, who will tell you they never had better workers than the I.W.W. . . .

Coming to Butte and the Copper Trust, with its blacklist and recklessness of miners' lives, Vanderveer told how the strike, which was charged against us as a crime, occurred:

On the 8th of June there was a fire, known as the Speculator fire, and if you have never seen a mine fire no man can picture it to you. It simply surpasses description. The people who went to this mine found the gates locked and the property barred. Wives and children could not go there to see whether or not their husbands and fathers were burned to death. The women went up on that hill with all the horror in their hearts that experience has taught all miners' wives, crying and weeping. And finally the bodies came out; and with the men who had found them came the damnable story of how it happened! These poor people saw the bodies lined up, 175 of them, 68 burned so black they were never identified. They were told that underground, in order to prevent the spread of fire which might do some damage to property, they had built concrete bulkheads without a manhole, and there the bodies were found, piled in one charred heap.

Then there was another strike down in Arizona, said Vanderveer, on July 12, 1917, in Bisbee, 1186 men were taken at the point of machine guns, loaded into cattle cars six inches deep in manure; hauled out through a blistering Arizona desert to a place called Hermanas, shuffled back and forth between there and Columbus, New Mexico, where they were finally taken in charge by United States troops. But a curious thing happened that day; every man approached was asked, "Will you go to work or be deported?" While all this was going on, wives and children were left at home to starve, without money, without food, without anything in the world.

Nearing conclusion, Vanderveer said, "If patriotism means to wave flags from the housetops and then profiteer, then the I.W.W. is unpatriotic. If patriotism means that one must believe in war as the best way of settling things—that the wholesale slaughter of innocent people—is right, then again I say the I.W.W. for years has been in that sense unpatriotic; because the I.W.W. has not believed and does not believe in war."

Many witnesses had come to Chicago to testify on behalf of the I.W.W. We were able to prove that hundreds of members of the organization had fought forest fires and had saved the timber of Washington, Idaho and Montana. There were farmers who took the witness stand and said that the I.W.W.'s were the best workers that they had employed upon their ranches.

One of the victims who had been tarred and feathered at Tulsa, Oklahoma, told of the manner in which this deed was done by a patriotic mob. Miners who had escaped from the Speculator Mine at the time of the terrible underground fire in that property told of having climbed up 200 feet to another level where they went in and built a bulkhead of boards and planks, stuffing up the cracks with their clothes, where they stayed for 36 hours. They had but little air and no water.

The defense began with James P. Thompson, an old-time organizer, a splendid specimen of manhood with mind as clear as a bell. His picture, painted by one of America's artists, is now hung in the hall of the Irish Workers in Dublin.

Jim started his testimony with a reference to the report of the Industrial Relations Commission which had been barred out by Judge Landis. But Jim was permitted to use the report as he had testified before the Industrial Relations Commission.

He concluded his evidence by saying: "The very people who are abusing the I.W.W. to-day, if they had lived in the days of our forefathers would have been licking the boots of King George. They would have said of the boys fighting barefooted in the snow at Valley Forge, 'Look at them! They haven't got a shoe to their feet and they are talking about Liberty!' The people who are knocking the I.W.W. are the same type who dragged William Lloyd Garrison through the streets of Boston with a halter, who killed Lovejoy and threw his printing press into the Mississippi River; it is the same type who murdered Frank Little!"

Nebeker rose to object, to be met with a hot rejoinder, "I do not mean to be personal," said Thompson. "This is what I said in my lectures, but if the shoe fits—wear it."

A blackboard had been placed on an easel for the convenience of the jury. J. T. (Red) Doran used it to illustrate the lectures he was in the habit of delivering to the workers of Seattle and vicinity.

Bill Dunne, an electrical worker, then editor of the Butte *Bulletin*, testified to the lynching of Frank Little, the martyr of the Copper Trust. He mentioned the fact that Little was on crutches with a broken leg, that he was suffering from a double rupture which he got from being manhandled by a mob in Wisconsin, that he had only one eye, and that the murderers who killed him had pinned on his body the death warrant of the Vigilance Committee—"3-7-77." Dunne himself had received a similar notice.

One after another of the defendants testified for themselves and the organization to which they belonged. There were the secretaries of the industrial unions, the editors of the English language papers, the monthly magazine, and the various foreign language papers.

Among the last of the witnesses, I was called. Again I had to go over my life and work, my connection with the Western Federation of Miners, the launching of the Industrial Workers of the World, the aim and purpose of the organization. I was on the stand four days, being directly examined by Vanderveer and cross-examined by Nebeker.

Vanderveer read excerpts from *Labor Disturbances in Colorado*, the report of Carroll D. Wright's investigation, written by Walter B. Palmer. When Vanderveer questioned me about the contents of that report, there were objections from Nebeker on the part of the government which were finally overruled by Judge Landis because of the fact that I had endorsed the report before it was printed. A truth that was not developed was the fact that I had written the brief statement in the report about the first convention of the Western Federation of Miners.

When questioned about the World War, I replied: "Mr. Vanderveer, I don't want the jury and I don't want these defendants to get the idea that I am in favor of war. I am very much opposed to war, and would have the war stopped to-day if it were in my power to do it. I believe that there are other methods by which human beings should settle any existing difficulty. It is not only the murdering of the men, it is the suffering of the wives and children. And it is what this war means to society after this war is over. Somewhere in the files here is jotted down on a piece of paper what is meant by the aftermath of the war. Nothing for a hundred years but war, war, war. Nothing to follow but war cripples, war widows, war orphans, war stories, war pictures and war everything. That is the terrible part of this war. I hope, if it be necessary, that every man that is imbued with the spirit of war will fight long enough to drive the spirit of hate and war out of his breast. That this may be the last war that the world will ever know."

Vanderveer asked me if I, with the other defendants, were conspiring to interfere with the profits of certain people who were engaged in the manufacture of munitions supplies. I answered: "We are conspiring. We are conspiring to prevent the making of profits on labor power in any industry. We are conspiring against the dividend makers. We are conspiring against rent and interest. We want to establish a new society, where people can live without profit, without dividends, without rent and without interest if it is possible; and it is possible, if people will live normally, live like human beings should live. I would say that if that is a conspiracy, we are conspiring."

Nebeker, the chief prosecutor, was a smooth individual, a slimy creature, even more foxy than he tried to prove me to be. He questioned me at great length about the literature of the organization, about the strikes of the iron and copper miners, lumber workers, my telegrams to the President and official relations with various members of the organization.

While I was on the stand being cross-examined by Nebeker, Karm, the stool pigeon, handed the prosecutor a pamphlet. It was *As to Politics*, by Daniel DeLeon. After Nebeker had looked over this pamphlet, he gave it to me saying that he would question me about it later. I had made some notes on the margins of the pages. When Nebeker asked me for it, I handed it back. He never questioned me about it further.

When I was called to the witness stand the court room became suddenly crowded and a feeling of drama was in the air. Doubtless it was drama, to listen to the story of labor's struggles for the past 30 years. For hours every one remained immovable. The jurors leaned forward to catch my words. Even the judge forgot the passing hours and the bailiff had to remind him that it was after the closing hour.

I told of the contrast of wealth and poverty existing side by side in the richest country of the world, the life of misery of the wealth producers in the mines of the West, the mills of the North, the turpentine camps of the South and the textile factories of the East. I compared the security, such as it was, of the Negro chattel slaves of the South with the terrible insecurity of life of the wage slaves of to-day. I showed a chunk of life as it is borne by millions who go hungry in periods of hard times, to prove that the solicitude the master had for his slave, when the slave represented an investment of hundreds of dollars, has no parallel in the relations of employers and their wage slaves to-day.

In the town of Fall River, I told how women and children toil long hours for starvation wages, their pinched and miserable lives, where underfed mothers are so unable to nurse their babies that infant mortality was the incredible proportion of 400 per thousand born into the world. And right across the river from that hell-hole of capitalism is Newport, where the "unemployed" capitalists flaunt their orgies of idiocy and sensuality, where they amuse themselves with monkey dinners and dog weddings—the wedding of two poodle dogs attended by such parasites as Mrs. Penrose, Mrs. Frank Heath and Mrs. MacNeil, the Penrose and MacNeil families owners of copper mines where the I.W.W. was striking.

Where the prosecution had tried to prove that the I.W.W. expelled men who joined the army, I proved that there was no record of such expulsions nor any clause in the constitution to that effect, although many labor organizations deny membership to militiamen.

Nebeker had objected to the introduction of photographs depicting workers blown to pieces in mines, lynched and tortured by mobs of bosses and businessmen, etc. Nebeker said they were "gruesome," and I replied that conditions were gruesome. The camera only recorded the truth.

Also, I told how our witnesses were being interfered with and intimidated, our defense mail held up and those who collected money for our defense arrested, even those who contributed to our legal defense were arrested wholesale. It was proven in court that witnesses subpœnaed to testify, were visited in their hotel rooms at Chicago and threatened by detectives connected with the prosecution.

When the evidence was all in, Nebeker made the first argument to the jury. He spoke for less than one hour. To the amazement of prosecutors, the attorneys for the defense decided to submit our case without argument. This prevented the prosecution from having the closing argument to the jury. Judge Landis read his instructions. The jury was out one hour. Their verdict was completed and read to the court: "Guilty, as charged in the indictment."

The jury had listened to scores of witnesses. There were hundreds of exhibits to examine. There were 17,500 offenses to consider. There were 40,000 pages of typewritten records, some of which could have been examined. But the jury's verdict was given within an hour. It was no surprise to any of us; the verdict was a foregone conclusion.

When the sentences were pronounced, the defendants were called to the bar in groups. One or two of the defendants were discharged, Meyer Friedkin and Charles Roberts were sentenced to 10 days in the county jail. A small group to one year in the Federal penitentiary. A larger group to five years in the penitentiary. Another, not so large, to ten years. And for some unknown reason, the fourth group was sentenced to five years. The last group was sentenced to an aggregate of 38 years on the four counts, the longest term was 20 years, and the sentences were to run concurrently. Before we were sentenced, we were asked by the Judge if we had anything to say as to why sentence could not be passed upon us. Many of the boys made brief speeches. I told the Judge that I thought the trial was a farce and a travesty upon justice.

When the prisoners started to leave the court room, the Judge asked Vanderveer if it was the intention to apply for a new trial. Vanderveer said that it was. The Judge then called back all the defendants and placed a fine from $20,000 to $30,000 on each man.

Pontius Pilate or Bloody Jeffreys never enjoyed themselves better than did Judge Landis when he was imposing these terrible sentences upon a group of working men for whom he had no feeling of humanity, no sense of justice.*

Ben Fletcher sidled over to me and said: "The Judge has been using very ungrammatical language." I looked at his smiling black face and asked: "How's that, Ben?" He said: "His sentences are

---

* For a list of those convicted at the Chicago trial and the sentences imposed on them, see Appendix III.

much too long." At one time previous to this during the great trial in a spirit of humor, Ben remarked: "If it wasn't for me, there'd be no color in this trial at all." I might explain that he was the only Negro in the group.

Our bail was cancelled, and we were taken from the court room to the subway under the building, loaded into patrol wagons, and driven to Cook County jail.

We were trying to have our bonds continued while the application for a new trial was being considered by the District Federal Court. I was taken one day to the marshal's office which occupied the top floor of the Federal Building. The post office was on the ground floor of this massive granite structure, which occupied an entire block in the congested center of the city.

During a recess I went with two deputy marshals down the elevator and across the street to a basement lunch room. After we had had something to eat, we returned to the building and up to the marshal's office.

I had been granted permission to have a stenographer and had just started to dictate to Elizabeth Serviss when the air was rent with a rumbling blast. A tremor ran through every one in the room. Momentarily they appeared petrified. Then we heard a heavy shower of glass falling on the pavement below. It was some minutes before we learned what had happened.

A bomb, supposedly of T.N.T., had been placed near the entrance through which we had just come as we returned from the restaurant. When the bomb exploded a woman and two men were killed, several were badly injured. Some little damage was done to that side of the building.

The explosion happened in the early afternoon. I was held in the marshal's office until after 6 o'clock. When we went down in the elevator, it did not stop at the main floor but went to the subway below where the mail wagons were loaded. There was a procession of patrol wagons, seven in all, if I remember rightly, all loaded with policemen. I was told to get into the middle wagon. With this parade of seven "black marias" I was escorted back to Cook County jail.

My fellow workers in prison soon learned of my return and that I was uninjured. Many of them thought that I had been the victim of treachery, that the explosion which every one in the prison knew about had, in the opinion of some, been concocted for my personal benefit, and had missed me by minutes only. It was said at the time that such a T.N.T. bomb as was alleged to have been used, could be obtained only from government sources.

This midday explosion happened on a bright September day, 1918, with many people going in and out of the busy building in which the United States Marshal, the Department of Justice, and the United States Secret Service were quartered. No arrests were made of any one who knew about the explosion. No cause was assigned for the explosion. It caused one to wonder whether the conjecture of my prison comrades was not correct.

Detectives went to the house where I lived, and arrested Minnie Wyman. They also arrested J. W. Wilson of the General Defense Committee. Both of them were soon released.

Enough to say, no bonds were granted for any of us. The Chicago Post Office explosion is one of the ghastly mysteries of the world's most criminal, most imperialistic government.

CHAPTER XXI

THE PRISON

THE word was passed around that we were going to Leavenworth. I was then in a cell facing the back wall. I could hear the grating of the keys, the slamming of the cell doors as the men were being taken out. I could also hear other prisoners saying, "Good-by, good luck!" I was left until the last.

I did not know anything about the place I was going to, but together with the others I was glad to be leaving the gloomy, dank surroundings of the Cook County jail.

Jim Rowan was just ahead of me, and when we reached the jailer's office, Davies, the jailer and hangman, put the handcuffs on Rowan and me. My blood almost curdled when his fingers touched my wrist. I thought of the many men whom he had hanged. His hands had put the rope around the necks of 58 men.

As I was stepping into a patrol wagon, a big burly policeman standing near, said: "I would like to put a bullet through that fellow." I did not hear the remark myself, but one of the fellow workers told me on the train.

The long procession of patrol wagons started for the LaSalle Street depot. We drove around to the baggage platform and were loaded on a special train.

William Bross Lloyd, who had been one of my bondsmen and who had just arrived on another train, shouted a farewell greeting.

The ninety-five prisoners and numerous guards filed into the coaches.

Jerry Soper, the heaviest man in our coach, was released from his handcuffs to act as runner. St. John was handcuffed to my left wrist.

The guard who was in charge of our coach was going to chain Jim Rowan to the seat. That would have released my right wrist, but St. John protested. He told the guard that in the event of a wreck a man chained to the seat would have no chance at all.

The guard replied: "If you can stand it that way, I can."

Ben Fletcher, to while away the time, held a mock court. His imitation of Judge Landis was laughable. He sat on the back of the seat looking solemn and spitting tobacco juice up the aisle. He had taken off his shoes, collar and tie, and his coat and vest as far as he could get them off. He grabbed at his pants to keep them from falling down as the Judge had done one day in the court. Judge Landis was not a grave, black-robed individual such as judges are sometimes pictured. During the hot summer of our trial he stripped down as far as decency would permit. Fletcher gave a good imitation of the Judge's antics. He swore in the prisoners as a jury; calling the guards and detectives up to him he sentenced them without further ado to be hanged and shot and imprisoned for life.

After a night and a better part of a day's run across the prairie, we got a glimpse of the Leavenworth penitentiary in the distance. When we arrived there, the train pulled in to a high brick-walled corridor. The big iron gate to the outside world was closed.

When we got off and lined up, the handcuffs and shackles were taken from our wrists and thrown into a pile, which, when they were all gathered together, would fill a wheelbarrow.

We marched through the inside gate to the chapel. On our left were the hospital and the cell houses which filled one side of a 10-acre square. The carpenter shop, boiler house and machine shop were to the left. A brickyard was down in the right-hand corner, also the stone yard.

In the chapel the Warden introduced to me the reporters of the Kansas City newspapers. I had little to say to them.

The Warden told us that "there we would be treated as individuals," that "every man was in the first grade," that "we should be careful to save our good time." With these few words we were turned over to the guard and everything was taken from our pockets, and a list made of each man's valuables.

Many of us dropped our cigarettes and tobacco on the floor, knowing that other prisoners would pick them up.

Two by two, we went to the dining room, a large spacious hall with many windows and long aisles running through rows of little narrow tables. On the front of each there were three seats that swung down on a hinge. All prisoners sat facing the music stand and kitchen. The dining hall looked attractive with the tables all scrubbed clean, a white china cup and plate with knife and fork and two red tomatoes at each place. It was an unexpected touch of color.

All of us were conducted to "B" cell house. As we passed "D" cell house, the prisoners could see us from the windows and sent up a great cheer of welcome. I heard a voice sing out: "Hello, Bill!" As we entered "B" cell house, strains of the "International" rang out. A Socialist, who was a member of the band, had taken his instrument to his cell and was greeting us with his flute.

The first night I had a cell with Charles Ashleigh on the fifth tier. We were tired, as we had had no sleep the previous night, and were just going to get into bed when a man climbed over the railing in front of our cell and asked us if we'd like a smoke. I could think of nothing I would have liked better. He handed us some tobacco and cigarette papers, saying: "I almost got shot getting up here." I learned later that to be "shot" meant to be reported, which would mean he would have a "court call" in the morning, have to go before the Deputy Warden and would be put into the Black Hole or lose some days of his "good" time. He divided up his tobacco as far as it would go.

The next morning, after a breakfast of oatmeal, bread, molasses and coffee, we were taken to the clothing room and there measured for shoes and clothes, and gave the size of our hats. We were asked whether we wanted to store, destroy, or give away the clothes that we wore when we came in. From there we went to the bath house, and when we stripped, our clothes were put in separate piles. After a shower bath, "Darky" Chase, a trusty, held out to each of us a big can of blue ointment, saying: "Take some of this, rub it under your arms, on your breast, between your legs." It was an exterminator of lice and other vermin.

We then went to the barber and, stretched out on a chair made of boards, got shaved while we were still naked. Then we got our prison clothes, rough cotton flannel underwear, a striped hickory shirt, and a pair of blue overalls. We were also given two pairs of socks, two handkerchiefs, a winter suit of gray cloth, a coat with brass buttons, and a cap of the same kind of material. We were permitted to wear our own shoes. With our extra clothes on one arm, we went to the Deputy Warden's office. There we were to be assigned to our work and cells.

The Deputy Warden said to me: "Haywood, the cells are small and would be close quarters for two big men. Is there any one of the small men you would like for a cell mate?"

I said: "Yes, I can pick out one."

"Let me know his name as soon as you can."

Vladimir Lossieff was sitting just opposite me. I asked him how he'd like to live with me for the next twenty years.

He said: "That would be fine!"

We were sitting in the corridor when I was called into the Warden's office. He said: "Have you got a cell mate?"

I said: "Yes, Vladimir Lossieff."

"You will have cell No. 200 in 'D' cell house."

The Deputy Warden inquired as to what I had worked at, and I told him that for seventeen years I had been most of the time in an office or on the lecture platform. He put me to work as assistant bookkeeper in the clothing room. My duty there was to keep track of all clothing that was dispensed to the prisoners.

The cells were small. In the one in which Lossieff and I were confined for nearly a year I could stand with my shoulder against one wall and with arm outstretched could touch the other wall with the tips of my fingers. It was about 10 feet long. I slept on the upper bunk.

At 9 o'clock at night taps were sounded by a bugler and the lights were turned out. In the morning we were aroused at 6:30 with the bugler's notes of reveille. At noon hour we were lined up in long rows ready to go into the dining room, when we were surprised with the music of a brass band. We marched in long files down the aisles, the first taking the rear seats. In a few minutes all were seated facing the music. Then the waiters came in with huge trays of bread, of which a man could have as much as he wanted. Other waiters with soup or stew; boiled potatoes aplenty. The kitchen was arranged with big copper boilers and practically all of the food except the bread was steam cooked, a method that seemed to make everything taste alike.

Our numbers were already stamped on our prison clothes across the shoulders of the shirt and across both knees. Mine was 13106. Our records were not yet complete. The next day we were photographed with our numbers on, our heads measured by the Bertillon system, and fingerprints of both hands were taken.

Then we had an interview with the Chaplain. In my brief conversation with the prison sky-pilot I told him that three institutions in the country used bars and locks. One of them was a prison to confine a man's body. One was the church to imprison his soul, if he had one. And one was the bank that kept his money guarded. Our almost united opposition to churches or religions of any kind resulted in an order being issued that men who did not want to attend chapel on Sunday morning should remain in the cells. But many men, though not interested in the Chaplain's sermon, wanted to get out of their cells, so they went to church. The following day we were all taken to the hospital, where we were stripped and weighed, vaccinated, and had our teeth examined.

Now it might be said that we began our prison life. A big gang of men were working in the "A" cell house which had not been completed. Jim Thompson was given the job of foreman over a gang of concrete men, many of whom were members of the I.W.W. One day a colored prisoner asked one of our boys "if that big feller Thompson was an I.W.W." He was told that he was.

But the colored man said: "Ah doan think he's an I.W.W. He doan act like an I.W.W. Why's he hurrin' round for all de time? Ah tell you, feller, Ah got a little sab cat up in mah cell, an' if that feller Thompson doan quit hurryin' round like that, Ah's goin' to turn that sab cat loose."

One morning Thompson and his gang went into the cell house to their work. The night before they had filled a form, that is, planks set up and bolted together with the liquid concrete in between. They had left this form to set during the night, but the nuts were not on the bolts and the concrete spread the boards apart and flowed all over the floor. It was set, as hard as concrete could set.

The guard reported the matter to the Deputy Warden, who issued a court call for Thompson, and the next morning he answered at the office. When the Deputy Warden read him the law against sabotage, what it meant in the way of fine and imprisonment, he asked Thompson: "Is there any one in your gang who has got it in for you?"

Thompson said he didn't think so.

The Deputy Warden then asked: "Well, how did this thing happen, then?"

Thompson could only reply that he didn't know.

He went back to his job somewhat crestfallen. One of the boys said to him: "Well, why did you want to assume the responsibility of foreman? Your job's no better than mine, you don't get no more money than I do, and I don't get any! You better quit this job of foreman." Thompson quit. A black fellow took the job, and there was no more trouble with the sab cat.

A group of the I.W.W.'s were working in the stone yard. St. John was foreman of this gang, but he wasn't hurrying around any. It was the guard that seemed to think that there wasn't enough work being done, and had begun to exert his authority. One day the guard was talking threateningly in a rather loud voice to one of the boys when some one knocked him on the head with a hammer. He dropped unconscious. An investigation was made but no one had seen any one hit him, so the matter was dropped but not forgotten. He recovered with nothing worse than a sore head.

"C" cell house was for Negro prisoners. There were some hundreds of them, among them men who were serving life sentences for a so-called mutiny in the army at Houston, Texas. I got acquainted with many of these ex-soldiers who had formerly been quartered at Brownsville, Texas. Among them were some who were in the army at the time the soldiers were sent to the Cœur d'Alenes strike in 1899. They were honest enough to regret that they had been compelled to guard the miners who were then in the bull pen.

My sight became so bad that I could not work longer on the books, so I was put in charge of the dressing out department. This was where the prisoners who had served their time and were being released got their new clothes. A suit, hat, shoes, underclothes, shirt, collar and necktie with a new handkerchief were given to every man departing from the prison. The whole outfit cost less than $13. I called the place where I worked the "Happy Corner." It was the last place the prisoners came to before they left the penitentiary. It was the only place where one could see a real happy smile.

There were comparatively few guards in this big institution. The prisoners did all the work. The records in the office of the main building, the Bertillon system, photographs and finger prints, all were taken by the prisoners. The filing clerks were prisoners. Typists and bookkeepers were prisoners. The print shop, shoe shop, clothing shop, carpenter shop, the rock shed, laundry, the brick mill, machine shop, kitchen, dining hall and hospital were all conducted by the prisoners themselves.

Aside from the guards, there were other civilians employed in the prison. One, a member of the Department of Justice who was supposed to look after the records; a physician, the steward, the boss tailor, the Chaplain, and there may have been one or two others.

There were several escapes from the prison while I was there. After the count and discovery was made that a prisoner was gone, they would blow the wild-cat whistle, the siren at the boiler house. As soon as the wild-cat would begin to blow, a terrible yell would go up from the prisoners in the different cell houses, though none of them knew who it was who had escaped, they would sing out in a mighty voice: "Good-by, good luck, good luck! Don't come back! Go it! Go it! you son of a bitch!"

In the department with me was a life timer known as "Red" Spain. His work was to store the clothes and other effects of incoming prisoners. Spain had been a soldier in the regular army and fought in the Philippines. He told me how proud he had been of his soldier's uniform. When he first put it on he took a walk down the streets of Cleveland, Ohio, where he had enlisted. He passed a Salvation Army barracks, outside of which there was a sign "Dogs and Soldiers NOT ALLOWED." He said his idea of a soldier began to dwindle from that time on.

This penitentiary was a little different from others. Here the prisoners did not wear the usual black and white convicts' stripes, and the terrible silent system was enforced only at certain hours and places. But like all prisons, it was a vicious place. Prisons have been called "The Universities of Crime." This was such a university with many post-graduates. There were men who were 2, 3 and 4 time "losers." "Blacky" had been in the Ohio State Penitentiary where he knew Bill Porter, who afterwards was known as O. Henry, the famous short story writer.

There were times when two or three trusties would gather in our work room and relate their past experiences. I heard "Whitey" tell of a time when he and some others blew a safe in some town near Pittsburgh. He said to Townes: "You boosted me up on the dry goods boxes that we piled in a pyramid under the second story window."

Townes said: "I don't remember that." I looked at him in surprise. Here was a man who had blown open so many safes that there was one instance he had entirely forgotten.

One night Lossieff and I both got a court call. We were not certain, but felt that for some reason or other we had been "shot." The next morning we went to the Deputy Warden's office, and he told me that I was reported for talking in the dining room, that this time sentence would be suspended, but that the offense called for a loss of "good" time or time in the hole. Lossieff got the same reprimand.

One day the gang that was doing roustabout work were ordered to unload a couple of car loads of coal. They had just had their baths that morning, and to shovel coal would mean that they would get grimy and have to stay that way for a week. They made a kick and demanded that they be taken to the Deputy Warden. He immediately put them in their cells and told them they would either shovel coal or stay there on bread and water and be chained to the bars during working hours.

The dining room was the principal place where the silent system was in force. There, when a man wanted a crust of bread he would hold up his clenched fist. If one wanted the salt he shook his hand palm down; pepper, he wiggled his fingers.

One day the dining hall was the scene of a near riot. The prisoners' band was furnishing us music. But from the kitchen, for the third day in succession, they sent in baked parsnips. The cry went up from many prisoners: "Take that damn music out of here and give us something to eat!"

Some one had dared to speak out loud in the dining room! The sound of angry voices caused some commotion among the guards. There was a clatter of broken plates as they were flung on the floor.

The Deputy Warden came in and some plates and cups were shied at his head. He ordered the Negro prisoners, who were seated in front, to their cells. They did not obey his first command, then got up and marched out, followed in turn by the rest of us.

The next morning there were many court calls. Some were sentenced to isolation. That night two Negroes, who were protected with baseball masks and armed with clubs, were told to go into the isolation cells and "beat hell out of those rowdies." There was no one killed, no bones broken, but the boys were roughly handled. Manuel Rey told me afterwards that it was a bloody night. Two white prisoners, defaulting bankers from South Dakota, took a hand in the affair, and afterwards said that the I.W.W.'s got just what was coming to them.

The dining hall in the winter months was converted into a school every evening. Thirty-four members of the I.W.W. were teachers of various classes which ranged from running a motor car to the study of foreign languages.

Court calls were not unusual, as there were daily violations of the rules of the institution. But there were many things that were done by the prisoners that the guard did not see or hear, though there were "snitches" everywhere. The office workers and those employed in the dining room and hospital all wore white jackets. These were called snitch jackets" by the mass of prisoners, though by no means all who wore them were informers.

Stills for making whisky were operated in different parts of the penitentiary. From the large amount of supplies used in an institution of this kind, it was easy enough to get potatoes, rye, or corn, and many times raisins, in quantities enough to make a good supply of moonshine whisky. A still in full operation was one day discovered up in the unused smokestack, which carried off the telltale smell. How long this bootlegging joint had been running no one knew.

The town of Leavenworth was found to be flooded with counterfeit coin one time. When the Department of Justice got on the job, they traced the counterfeit money to trusty prisoners in the penitentiary. Two counterfeiting plants were discovered within the walls. One of them was down in a sewer tunnel. Here some prisoners had been melting all the nickel, copper and babbitt metal that they could get hold of from the printing shop, making it into money. The trusties who were working outside had a chance to spend their counterfeit money and brought their purchases into the prison every day after work.

A visit to the bakeshop was unusual for a prisoner not employed there, but I had occasion to go there one day. Charlie Lambert was a baker and working at his job. He said to me: "Bill, do you want a pie?"

I said: "There's nothing that would suit me better."

"How can you carry it?" he asked, holding out a big juicy apple pie, baked for the prison officers.

"Give it to me, I'll carry it."

I lifted my coat tails and slipped it under my suspenders, buttoned up, and started out. When I got to the clothing department, the pie was there, but the juice had run all down my legs. The boys who got a piece thought the pie was good, but said it would have been better if I hadn't lost all the juice.

One day Charlie Plahn, a five-year man of our group, who was working with the road gang outside the walls, got separated from the men he was working with. It was just about quitting time, and they had gone into the prison. Plahn looked around. He could see none of them. When he came to the prison gate, it was locked. Not content with being on the outside, he knocked and hollered for admittance. When the story was found out, all the boys joked him about breaking into the penitentiary.

Herbert MacCutcheon was one day told to go to work with the rock gang. He had been employed in the carpenter shop. He protested against the change of work and asked for the privilege of seeing the Deputy Warden. The Deputy Warden was not in the frame of mind to argue the question, and he told MacCutcheon that he'd have to do as he was ordered or he would put him in the hole. MacCutcheon told the Deputy Warden that he could do with him what he would, but he couldn't make him break rock. Herbert was put into the black hole on bread and water, every third day regulation food, and chained to the bars eight hours every working day. He stood this torture for months. He was kept in this condition until I was released on bail and secured bond for him.

One day the order came: "All you fellers go up to the parole room."

We walked out and every man of the clothing department, storage, and dressing room were lined up. We went up to the parole room, a large cell where there were 20 or more beds, and stayed there not knowing what was going on where we had been at work. We were held there for an hour or more.

There was a guard at the door, and how the word got in I could never tell, but it was noised around that guns had been found in my department.

Shortly after we were returned to our work. The place looked like a hurricane had struck it. The lockers had all been opened, bags, suitcases and bundles were opened, the suits of clothes thrown around. It took us some time to get things straightened up. Then I learned that some six-shooters with cartridges had been found in the locker used by "Blacky," "Red" Spain, and myself. I was left to conjecture what it was all about.

All the other prisoners were saying: "That will mean the hole for them fellers."

I had been reading *The Star Rover* by Jack London, and could appreciate how easy it would be to frame up on a prisoner, or how some unthinking person might drop a word about dynamite. It would be just as easy to bring dynamite into the prison as six-shooters. In fact, the thought of high explosives had already entered the minds of the guards. When they were emptying the lockers, one dropped a bag from some height to the floor, when another said: "For Christ's sake, don't throw the stuff around like that! You don't know what them fellers may have stored around here."

The next morning I was called into the Deputy Warden's office. He opened the conversation by saying that there was one thing they always expected the prisoners to try to do, and that was to escape. He got up from his chair and walked to a corner to the rear and picked up a short-handled shovel.

He said: "We've just found out that some of the prisoners were trying to dig out under the wall. You know that some guns were found in your locker."

I said: "Yes. I heard of it."

He said: "Did you put them there?"

"No, I did not," I replied, trying to catch his eye, which was a difficult thing to do. The Deputy Warden, whose name was Fletcher, was a shifty-eyed person.

"Do you know who did?"

"No, I do not," was my answer.

"I guess that will be all, to-day," he said.

I went back to my place of work. The prisoners asked me as I passed them: "What happened, Bill?"

I said: "Nothing, so far."

I worried a good deal about those guns being in my locker, until one day the man who put them there told me about it, and said with a grin on his face: "As I was carrying them across the yard, the paper with the cartridges in it broke, and I was dropping them at every step. Had to go back and pick them up. I don't know how any one found out I had those guns, but there are snitches in every corner."

Members of the I.W.W. were tortured in the Leavenworth penitentiary. Some of them were in isolation in the prison within a prison. Some were in the black hole. Others were being strung up to the bars every day during working hours. Many of them had been cruelly beaten.

It was in this hour of stress that the Mexican delegates at the Pan-American Labor Conference at Laredo, Texas, raised their voices for the release of all political prisoners. Samuel Gompers, backed by other A. F. of L. officials, including Charles H. Moyer, one time President of the Western Federation of Miners, rejected the appeal of the Mexican workers.

CHAPTER XXII

WITH DROPS OF BLOOD

In behalf of those of us who had been convicted in Chicago an application for a new trial was filed in the United States Circuit Court of Appeals for the 7th Circuit. It was supported by a voluminous brief and argument by Vanderveer and Christensen.

Judge Landis in the meantime made a visit to the Leavenworth penitentiary. We never knew just why he came, unless it was to gloat over his victims. The I.W.W. case was the last one of note over which Landis presided, as he shortly after resigned the judgeship to act as baseball commissioner at $45,000 a year, which has since been increased to $60,000 a year. They put the dollar sign on him and he quit.

Our trial had been a great hardship on the Judge, because during that season his time was much occupied and he could not go to as many ball games as had previously been his custom.

When Landis was at Leavenworth, he did not take a place in the gallery over the music stand where the visitors usually sat, but stuck his head in the door and looked furtively over the prisoners. He probably wanted the satisfaction of seeing for himself that we were really there.

Five Socialists had been convicted in his court at Chicago. They were Berger, Germer, Tucker, Engdahl and Kruse. They had each been sentenced to 20 years in Leavenworth, but the Judge had fumbled when he refused to grant them a change of venue. His decision was reversed by the Appellate Court and they were never tried again. It would have been the irony of fate if Berger had landed in the Leavenworth penitentiary under a 20-year sentence, there to mingle with the I.W.W.'s whom he had so brutally traduced at his own trial in patent effort to escape conviction.

The monotony of prison life was bearing down heavily upon me. I was beginning to realize what was meant by "prison blues." In me it was caused largely by lack of satisfactory reports from headquarters. I had but few visitors, and we were only allowed to write one letter a week. I never went to chapel on Sunday morning nor did I attend school during the winter months.

Dan Buckley, Secretary of Construction Workers' Union Number 573 contrived a decoration for the mess hall on St. Patrick's Day. He had a wheelbarrow loaded with brick rampant on the table with a hod, shovel and hoe couchant, all nicely draped with Erin's favorite color. Tacked to the wheelbarrow was a sign: "No. 573." Buckley's symbol was appreciated by the members of the I.W.W., though most of the other prisoners did not know what it meant.

The baseball games on Saturday afternoon and the freedom of the yard on Sunday were of no particular interest to me other than the chance it gave me to talk over the situation with some of the other members.

The monotony was broken for a time when the boys from Sacramento, Cal., arrived and I had the opportunity of talking with them about the manner in which their trial was conducted. This group, who had made a silent defense, had not been in Leavenworth long when one of their number, Connors by name, attempted to make an escape.

His temporary absence was cause enough for the wild-cat whistle, but they found Connors in a tool box in the baseball yard from which he intended to try to get over the wall in the darkness of the night.

The "prison blues" sometimes deranged men. At any sign of insanity they were put "in quarters," that is, confined in certain cells of the ground floor in "B" cell house. For severe cases there were insane cells in the hospital, and if there was no recovery, the prisoner was sent to an asylum at Washington, D. C.

The General Defense Committee was endeavoring to raise bail and many personal friends were exerting their efforts to get bond for me, which was finally secured, and I was released pending the finding of the Circuit Court on the application for a new trial.

I left the Leavenworth penitentiary on July 28th, 1919. It was the anniversary of my acquittal in Idaho. I did not have a chance to say a word of farewell to many of my fellow workers, but I had made up my mind to work as hard as I could in their behalf during the time that I was out on bail.

When I got out, the labor movement was astir with big issues. The split between the right and left wings of the Socialist Party was ripening, following the formation of the Third International in March. In September it was to come to a head at Chicago. In the same month the great Steel Strike began. There were mine strikes in the air. Meanwhile, we of the I.W.W. were being attacked on all sides.

As I walked out the front gate of the penitentiary, a machine drove up. The guard who was with me introduced the driver as the editor of a local paper published in the town of Leavenworth. He invited me to get in, saying that he was going back to town. On his way he remarked that we were on the old Continental Highway. I told him that over this road my mother had gone West with her family in a covered wagon with an ox team; my father had also gone westward when a boy. Both of them had traveled over this road.

While in Kansas City I went to see Fred Moore, attorney in the Wichita case. He had fixed up a little office and Caroline Lowe was getting out a circular appeal.

When I got to Headquarters in Chicago I found many changes had taken place. The general office had been moved to the top floor. Things seemed to me to be rather cluttered up. I called a conference of the secretaries of the industrial unions, the manager of the print shop, the general secretary-treasurer—Tom Whitehead of Seattle, the editors of the different papers. At this conference I spoke of the need of reorganizing the General Defense Committee, because during the year that we had been in prison only a little over $7,000 had been raised for the general defense. I told them that if I went on a lecture trip I could raise more than that myself in a few months. This conference decided to elect me as secretary-treasurer of the General Defense Committee.

I went to work at once; got the addressograph set up, found one of the mimeograph machines in the cellar, rusty and covered with mud, got it cleaned and repaired. I wrote to the general membership asking their coöperation in reviving the work of the General Defense Committee.

My first appeal was a letter "In Memoriam," heavily bordered in black, which said in part:

Fellow Workers and Friends:

This letter is in remembrance of R. J. Blaine, Ed. Burns, H. C. Evans, James Nolan and Frank Travis, all of whom died in prison at Sacramento, California, while waiting trial under the blanket indictment, the original of which was framed at Chicago, Illinois—and likewise in memory of James Gossard, who died in jail at Newton, Kansas, while waiting trial under a similar indictment.

This is also to remind you that there are hundreds of members of the Industrial Workers of the World languishing in penitentiaries and jails, some serving long sentences, some yet to be tried. In the State of Kansas there are thirty-three men who have been imprisoned for nearly two years in some of what are reported to be the worst jails in the United States. On two occasions these men have answered to indictments that would not stand. The third indictment has been returned; the trial has been set for next September. . . .

I sent this letter out in a black-bordered envelope, and when I learned that our mail was being tied up in Chicago, I resorted to shipping trunks full of letters to Minneapolis, Milwaukee, Detroit, Cleveland, and other cities where I had them mailed. The first month's receipts was over $9,000.

I wrote other letters to the members appealing for their help in arousing public interest in the Wichita, the Chicago and the Sacramento cases, as well as in many cases pending throughout the country.

The Wichita trial, resulting in a conviction, took place in December. I had secured the services of a first-class lawyer in Kansas City to work in conjunction with Fred Moore. This lawyer went to New York with Fred Moore. Then he went to Washington in connection with the case. While in New York, Fred Moore disappeared for a few days. They found his baggage, brief case and all the documents at his room in the hotel. The Kansas City lawyer dropped the case after his visit to Washington, D. C.

We filed an application for a new trial on behalf of the men convicted at Wichita. But for some reason, Moore neglected to make the application in time.

I again called a conference at headquarters and had Moore there to explain this apparent neglect. I demanded of him that he cite in a letter to the Judge the full reason why he, as counsel, had not made the application for a new trial within the required time.

Moore said that to do that would be "committing hari-kari." I then told those who were at the conference of other delinquencies committed by Moore during the Ettor and Giovanitti trial at Salem, and the Everett trial at Seattle. While these had not been so serious as the present negligence, the organization must protect itself.

Moore at this time was the attorney for the defense of Charles Kreiger at Tulsa, Okla. Kreiger demanded that he be continued as his lawyer. Moore handled the Kreiger case successfully, but that terminated his relations with the I.W.W. He was later employed by the Workers' Defense Committee in the defense of Sacco and Vanzetti.

I went to New York City, where I spoke at several defense meetings. The night I left I was standing on one of the platforms at the Pennsylvania Station when a young man dressed in an army uniform walked up to me. Before he spoke, the thought flashed through my mind—"Now, what's up?" He said: "You are Mr. Haywood?"

I replied: "Yes, that's my name."

He said: "I'm Corliss, don't you remember me? I'm a son of Sheriff Moseley's. Don't you remember me out in Idaho?"

I remembered him as a little boy. He used to come to our cell door nearly every day. I said: "You're in the army now?"

"Yes. I first joined the Medical Corps and then I took up aviation. You saw the porter carrying in that silver thing? That's a trophy that I won at Mineola to-day for fast flying. I came very close to the world's record. This is my friend, Lieutenant Streete. He is the man who recently made the flight to Nome. If you come to Washington I would be glad to take you up. There's no danger," he said, "not nearly as much as there is with an automobile. I've taken up my mother and my sister."

I said: "I might be glad to go up with you some time. Are you going on this train?"

He replied: "Yes."

"Well," I said, "I'll be traveling in fast company."

I got off at Philadelphia, and the following night spoke in the Labor Assembly Hall. I was leaving the next afternoon. Before I got on the train I got the Philadelphia and New York papers and read of the terrible explosion in Wall Street, New York, which had killed 29 people and injured 200.

Without a scrap of evidence the charge was deliberately made that Communists or other radicals had planned to kill some of America's greatest capitalists.

Somewhere along the road I was able to get the Chicago paper where I found in big headlines that Haywood was wanted in connection with the Wall Street explosion. The story went on to say that the authorities were searching for me. I determined in this instance not to surrender myself, but to avoid arrest as long as possible.

When I arrived in Chicago I went to the office of Otto Christensen, a lawyer employed by the I.W.W., and with him went to Grace Bay, a summer resort where I enjoyed the hospitality of the caretaker of a summer home belonging to one of the Chicago capitalists.

It is not difficult to imagine the influence that the Wall Street explosion had on the minds of the Judges of the Circuit Court, the judicial body before which our application for a new trial was pending.

When I went back to Headquarters, I decided to draft another appeal. I went to Maurice Becker, who was then working for the organization as cartoonist, and asked him to draw me a drop of blood. What he drew looked much like a pearl or a grape. It was anything but what I wanted. I dipped a pen into a bottle of ink and held it up until a drop fell on the paper. I said: "That's what I want."

Becker said: "Well, why not have the cut made of that?"

This I did, and used it on the appeal I wrote entitled: "With Drops of Blood the History of the Industrial Workers of the World has been Written." The first words were printed in red, with the drop of blood on the first and fourth pages. The appeal recounted the persecution of the I.W.W., the imprisonment and murder of members, raiding of halls, denial of right to exist and function as a labor organization.

There was a generous response to the appeal. For the month of November over $22,000 was received for the general defense. Liberty Bonds and cash contributions were sent in for bail. During the trials there was an aggregate of $400,000 received for general defense, and a half million dollars for bail.

The black bordered letters that were returned by the Post Office I made use of by having them distributed in street cars, theaters, restaurants and by dropping them here and there on the streets. Curious-minded people were certain to investigate a letter with a black border, for the purpose of finding out who was dead.

The letter with drops of blood created a decided sensation. It was printed in England, Russia and other countries. The National Security League used the drops of blood on a circular issued by that organization when they were after the scalp of Winthrop D. Lane, who had used the letter With Drops of Blood in an article that was not derogatory to the I.W.W. Lane had visited me while I was in the penitentiary. I gave him what information I could.

There were many others who wrote favorable articles in support of the organization and the men in prison.

The American Civil Liberties Union took up our case and issued several pamphlets in our behalf, or rather, as the members of that organization would say, in behalf of justice and civil liberty.

In September, 1919, the expelled Left Wing Socialists met in Chicago to form the Communist Party. Unfortunately there was a division of opinion among this group, and a part of them seceded, and there were two parties formed, one the Communist Party and the other the Communist Labor Party. The last named organization held its sessions in the I.W.W. hall at 119 Troop Street. I was invited to address the Communists gathered there, but wrote a letter saying it was my intention to go on a lecture tour and that I hoped to have the opportunity of meeting them at the meetings that I would hold. Jack Reed was the chairman at the convention of the Communist Labor Party.

Twelve prominent lawyers, several of whom were professors at the Harvard Law School, issued a report in which they bitterly condemned the Department of Justice for resorting to under-cover methods and the agent provocateurs working for the government, in which, after describing the state of affairs, they said:

... These acts may be grouped under the following heads:
(1) Cruel and Unusual Punishments.
(2) Arrests without Warrant.

(3) Unreasonable Searches and Seizures.
(4) Provocative Agents.
(5) Compelling Persons to be Witnesses against Themselves.
(6) Propaganda by the Department of Justice.

The Exhibitions attached are only a small part of the evidence which may be presented of the continued violation of law by the Attorney General's Department.

Since these illegal acts have been committed by the highest legal powers in the United States, there is no final appeal from them except to the conscience and condemnation of the American People.

R. C. Brown,
  Memphis, Tenn.
Zachariah Chafee, Jr.
  Cambridge, Mass.
Felix Frankfurter,
  Cambridge, Mass.
Ernst Freund,
  Chicago, Ill.
Swinburne Hale,
  New York City.
Francis Fisher Kane,
  Philadelphia, Pa.

Alfred S. Niles,
  Baltimore, Md.
Roscoe Pound,
  Cambridge, Mass.
Jackson H. Ralston,
  Washington, D. C.
Frank P. Walsh,
  New York City.
Tyrrell Williams,
  St. Louis, Mo.
David Wallerstein,
  Philadelphia, Pa.

Then came the Palmer raids. The government had set its net for a new school of radicals. They caught in the drag many thousand members of the Communist parties and several hundred I.W.W., I being among the number. The following are examples of secret documents issued by government authority:

To All Special Agents and Employees:
I have already transmitted to you two briefs prepared in this department upon the Communist Party of America and the Communist Labor Party with instructions that these briefs be carefully examined and studied for the purpose of familiarizing yourself and the agents under your direction with the principles and tactics of these two respective organizations.

You have submitted to me affidavits upon various individuals connected with these respective organizations, stating that these persons are aliens and members of the organization referred to. I have transmitted to the Commissioner General of Immigration the affidavits submitted by you with the request that warrants of arrest be issued at once. This action is now being taken by the Bureau of Immigration and warrants of arrest are being prepared and will shortly be forwarded to the immigration inspector of your district.

Briefly the arrangements which have been made are that the warrants will be forwarded to the immigration inspector who will at once communicate with you and advise you of the names of the persons for whom he has received warrants. You should then place under surveillance, where practicable, the persons mentioned and at the appointed time you will be advised by me by wire when to take into custody all persons for whom warrants have been issued.

At the time of the apprehension of these persons, every effort must be made by you to definitely establish the fact that the persons arrested are members of either the Communist Party of America or the Communist Labor Party. I have been reliably informed that instructions have been issued from the headquarters of each of these organizations to their members that they are to refuse to answer any questions put to them by any Federal officers and are to destroy all evidence of membership or affiliation with their respective organizations. It is, therefore, of the utmost importance that you at once make every effort to ascertain the location of all the books and records of these organizations in your territory and that the same be secured at the time of the arrests. As soon as the subjects are apprehended, you should endeavor to obtain from them, if possible, admissions that they are members of either of these parties, together with any statement concerning their citizenship status. I cannot impress upon you too strongly the necessity of obtaining documentary evidence proving membership.

Particular efforts should be made to apprehend all of the officers of either of these two parties if they are aliens; the residences of such officers should be searched in every instance for literature, membership cards, records and correspondence. The meeting rooms should be thoroughly searched and an effort made to locate the charter of the Communist Party of America or the Communist Labor Party, under which the local organization operates, as well as the membership and financial records which if not found in the meeting rooms of the organization will probably be found in the house of the recording and financial secretaries, respectively. All literature, books, papers and anything hanging on the walls should be gathered up; the ceiling and partitions should be sounded for hiding places. After obtaining any documentary evidence, the same should be wrapped up in packages and marked thereon, the location of the place, and the name of the persons obtaining the evidence and the contents of each package.

Violence towards any aliens should be scrupulously avoided. Immediately upon apprehending an alien, he should be thoroughly searched. If found in groups in meeting rooms, they should be lined up against the wall and there searched; particular attention being given to finding the membership book, in which connection the search of the pockets will not be sufficient. In no instance should money or other valuables be taken from the aliens. All documentary evidence taken from an alien should be placed in an individual envelope, provided for the purpose, which envelope should be marked showing the contents contained in the same, whether they were found in possession of the alien or in his room, and if in the latter the address of the house should be given as well as the name of the alien and the officer who obtained the evidence. At the time of the transfer of the alien to the immigration inspector, you should also turn over to the immigration inspector the original evidence obtained in the particular case, plainly marked so that there may be no complaint by the immigration officers as to the manner in which evidence has been collected by the agents of this Bureau.

I have made mention above that the meeting places and residences of the members should be thoroughly searched. I leave it entirely to your discretion as to the method by which you should gain access to such places. If, due to the local conditions in your territory, you find that it is absolutely necessary for you to obtain a search warrant for the premises, you should communicate with the local authorities a few hours before the time for the arrests is set and request a warrant to search the premises.

Under no conditions are you to take into your confidence the local police authorities or the state authorities prior to the making of the arrests. It is not the intention nor the desire of this office that American citizens, members of the two organizations, be arrested at this time. If, however, they are taken into custody any American citizens, through error and who are members of the Communist Party of America or the Communist Labor Party, you should immediately refer their cases to the local authorities.

It may be necessary, in order to successfully make the arrests that you obtain the assistance of the local authorities at the time of the arrests. This action should not be taken, unless it is absolutely necessary; but I will appreciate that where a large number of arrests are to be made it may be impossible for the same to be made by special agents of this Department, in which event you are authorized to request the assistance of the local police authorities. Such assistance should not be requested until a few hours before the time set for the arrests, in order that no "leak" may occur. It is to be distinctly understood that the arrests made are being made under the direction and supervision of the Department of Justice.

For your own personal information, I have to advise you that the tentative date fixed for the arrests of the Communists is Friday evening, January 2, 1920. This date may be changed, due to the fact that all the immigration warrants may not be issued by that time. You will, however, be advised by telegraph as to the exact date and hour when the arrests are to be made.

If possible you should arrange with your under-cover informants to have meetings of the Communist Party and the Communist Labor

Party held on the night set. I have been informed by some of the bureau officers that such arrangements will be made. This, of course, would facilitate the making of the arrests.

On the evening of the arrests, this office will be open the entire night and I desire that you communicate by long distance to Mr. Hoover any matters of vital importance or interest which may arise during the course of the arrests. You will possibly be given from seven o'clock in the evening until seven o'clock in the morning to conclude the arrests and examinations. As pointed out previously, grounds for deportation in these cases will be based solely upon membership in the Communist Party of America or the Communist Labor Party and for that reason it will not be necessary for you to go in detail into the particular activities of the persons apprehended. It is, however, desirable that wherever possible you should obtain additional evidence upon the individuals, particularly those who are leaders and officers in the local organization. The immigration inspector will be under instruction to coöperate with you fully and I likewise desire that you coöperate in the same manner with the Immigration Inspector at the time of the arrests, as well as following the arrests. At the hearings before the Immigration Inspector you should render any and all reasonable assistance to the immigration authorities, both in the way of offering your services to them and the services of any of your stenographic force. It is of utmost necessity that these cases be expedited and disposed of at the earliest possible moment and for that reason stenographic assistance and any assistance necessary should be rendered by you to the immigration inspectors. An excellent spirit of coöperation exists between the Commissioner-General of Immigration and this Department in Washington and I desire that the same spirit of coöperation between the field officers of this Bureau and the field officers of the Bureau of Immigration also exist.

I desire that the morning following the arrests you should forward to this office by special delivery marked for the "Attention of Mr. Hoover" a complete list of the names of the persons arrested, with an indication of residence, or organization to which they belong, and whether or not they were included in the original list of warrants. In cases where arrests are made of persons not covered by warrants, you should at once request the local immigration authorities for warrants in all such cases and you should also communicate with this office at the same time. I desire also that the morning following the arrests that you communicate in detail by telegram "Attention of Mr. Hoover" the results of the arrests made, giving the total number of persons of each organization taken into custody, together with a statement of any interesting evidence secured.

The above cover the general instructions to be followed in these arrests and the same will be supplemented by telegraphic instructions at the proper time.

Along with these general orders went "Instructions to Agents" who were to do the dirty work. These were numbered, and Number 5, showing official instructions were issued at Washington to violate constitutional rights, is proven by this clause which said:

Person or persons taken into custody not to be permitted to communicate with any outside person until after examination by this office and until permission is given by this office.

I had been invited to eat New Year's dinner with Ben Schrager. I left his home to go north to the Swedish I.W.W. Hall. I had stepped back into one of the rear rooms when one of the fellow workers came in and told me that there were two detectives in the buffet at the front.

I said: "I'd better get out of here," as the boys had already showed me one of the evening papers with flaring headlines: "The I.W.W. Raided Again." I went to the home of Mary and Leslie Marcy, where I stopped that night.

The following evening, Jack Johnstone, who was then organizer for the stockyard workers, sent his car with an invitation to go to a place that they had selected on Ontario Street near Michigan Boulevard. There I remained for a couple of days. When I went to Christensen's office they were surprised when they saw me, and asked: "Haven't the police got you yet?"

I said: "Not yet."

They informed me that every one at Headquarters except the stenographers was under arrest. That afternoon I went with William Bross Lloyd to Judge Pam's court. There Lloyd gave bond for me for the sum of $10,000. Ed. Nockles, secretary of the Chicago Federation of Labor, was in the court room. I said to him: "It's hell, Ed, that the I.W.W. should get pinched for the things the A. F. of L. does." He smiled knowingly and said: "There's some truth in what you say."

Of the thousands rounded up in these "red raids," some hundreds were deported to their native lands, a whole shipload leaving the "land of liberty" on the steamer *Buford*.

Twenty-eight Communists who had been arrested in the January 1st raid in Chicago were convicted and sentenced to the Joliet penitentiary of the State of Illinois, where they were held ten days and then pardoned.

The Seattle branch of the General Defense Committee was doing good work in raising bail and money. When they had got their first $10,000 they had a drawing. Manuel Rey was the name first pulled out of the sack, but as his bond was for a larger amount, they made a second selection, Red Doran.

CHAPTER XXIII

THE CENTRALIA TRAGEDY

WE were now to learn some facts about the war. Woodrow Wilson, who was then President, said: "This is an industrial and commercial war." He might have added that the stake won by the United States in this war was $30,000,000,000.

The press and the politicians were telling the people that it was a "war to make the world safe for democracy." It was a war that made a $6,000,000,000 debtor nation into a $24,000,000,000 creditor nation. It was a "war to end war," but the Wall Street birds of prey had hatched out a big flock of war millionaires, who are preparing for another war.

The Armistice did not settle the war in the United States.

This knowledge was violently hammered into the I.W.W. by the tragedy at Centralia, Washington, on Armistice Day, November 11, 1919. To lay this tragedy at the door of a department of the Federal Government and to charge William B. Wilson, ex-secretary of the United Mine Workers of America, then Secretary of Labor in Wilson's Cabinet, with the responsibility would seem far fetched, but this is what has been done by investigators, not members of the I.W.W., but appointed by the University of Washington. The Secretary of Labor was told that the chief among the lumber workers' troubles was the failure of their leaders, and that to be really informed, the Secretary must make a thorough attempt to understand the motives and methods of the I.W.W.

The Secretary of Labor, being merely a governmental representative of the A. F. of L., literally raised his hands in holy horror and told the investigators and the rest of the Commission that there was no such organization as the I.W.W.

Secretary of Labor Wilson had, so far as was in his power, outlawed the I.W.W.

The Lumbermen's Association and the press knew and cared only that Secretary of Labor Wilson had in effect termed the I.W.W. a disloyal and outcast group, and they proceeded with a campaign of suppression and violence under the guise of law, secure in the knowledge that they had the sanction and approval of official Washington.

Secretary of Labor Wilson made the Centralia outrage possible.

Throughout the West, hundreds of I.W.W. halls had been raided and property destroyed. The first Centralia raid took place in April, 1918. The occasion was a Red Cross parade.

The *Hub* and the *Chronicle,* two lumber trust papers in Centralia, were bitter in their denunciation of the I.W.W. and spoke of them in the identical terms used against the abolitionists before the Civil War.

In this Red Cross parade, the Chief of Police, the Mayor, and the Governor of the State were given places of honor at the head of the procession. There was Company G of the National Guard, but the members of the Elks Club made up the main body of the parade. This was the vicious reactionary element, and when they got in front of the hall, they cried out: "Let's raid the I.W.W. Hall." They stormed the building with stones and clubs, every window was shattered, every door was smashed. The sides of the building were torn off by the mob in its blind fury. Inside the rioters tore down the partitions, broke chairs and pictures. The union men were surrounded, beaten and driven to the street, where they were forced to watch furniture, records, typewriters and literature demolished and burned before their eyes.

A victrola and desk were carried to the street with much care. The gramophone was auctioned off on the spot for the benefit of the Red Cross. The owner of a glove factory won the machine, and still boasts of its possession. The desk was carted off to the office of the Chamber of Commerce.

The mob surged around the men who had been found in the Union Hall; with kicks and blows they were dragged to waiting trucks where they were lifted by the ears to the body of the machine and knocked prostrate one at a time. Like all similar mobs, this one carried ropes which were placed around the necks of the loggers.

"Here's an I.W.W.," some one yelled, "What shall we do with him?"

"Lynch him! Lynch him!"

Some of the union men were taken to the city jail and the rest were dumped across the county line.

The I.W.W. had not attempted to defend their hall in this raid, but it was different on Armistice Day.

The Lumber Workers' Industrial Union had not been crushed. It was growing stronger. The Employers' Association of Washington likewise redoubled its efforts, and continued a bitter campaign against the organization.

The following are a few of the suggestions offered in its bulletin to the members:

April 30th, 1919: "Keep business out of the control of radicals and I.W.W. . . . Overcome agitation. . . . Suppress the agitators. . . . Hang the Bolshevists. . . ."

May 30th, 1919: "If the agitators were taken care of we would have very little trouble. . . . Propaganda to counteract radicals and overcome agitation. . . . Put the I.W.W. in jail."

July 2nd, 1919: "Educate along the line of the three 'R's' and the Golden Rule, Economy and Self-Denial. . . . Import Japanese labor. . . . Import Chinese labor. . . ."

July 31st, 1919: "Deport about ten Russians in this community. . . ."

October 31st, 1919: ". . . Businessmen and taxpayers of Vancouver, Washington, have organized the loyal Citizens' Protective League; opposed to Bolsheviki and the Soviet form of government and in favor of the open shop. . . . Jail the radicals and deport them. . . . Since the Armistice, these radicals have started in again. . . . ONLY TWO COMMUNITIES IN WASHINGTON ALLOW I.W.W. HEADQUARTERS!"

On October 19th the Centralia *Hub* published an item headed: "Employers Called to Discuss Handling of 'Wobbly' Problem." This article urged all employers to attend, stating that the meeting would be held in the Elks' Club. On the following day, October 20th, three weeks before the shooting, this meeting was held at the hall of the Benevolent and Protective Order of Elks—the now famous Elks' Club of Centralia. The avowed purpose of this meeting was to "deal with the I.W.W. problem."

The I.W.W. issued a leaflet, appealing to citizens against use of violence against them.

Among the men in the Centralia union was Wesley Everest, an overseas veteran of remarkable courage, who was said to have won more medals for valor in France than Sergeant York. He had returned to the work he was interested in as a lumber worker, organizing and educating his fellow workmen. He was selling literature when Elmer Smith, a lawyer with a conscience, told a meeting of union men they had a legal right to defend the hall against attack.

On November 11th, 1919, a parade of American Legion men and assorted patriots was held. At the meeting to "deal with the I.W.W." mentioned above, a secret plot was concocted among the Lumber Trust leaders to mob the I.W.W. Hall, leading the paraders into the attack.

At the moment agreed upon, the leaders cried out upon signal from a man on horseback, "Let's go-o-o! At 'em, boys!" and the door of the hall was smashed in, some entering, when a rain of bullets came from within, halting the attack and leaving two attackers dead and several wounded. Some of the mob carried ropes, evidently ready to lynch the union men. One fellow who died said before he cashed out, "It served me right." That was Warren Grimm.

But the hall was surrounded and the attackers gained entrance in force, seizing the few workers there, with the exception of one man, Wesley Everest. Leaving the hall by the rear door he broke through the mob and made for the river, rifle bullets of his prepared assassins zipping around him. With little ammunition, he stopped to reload, reached the river and tried to ford it. Failing because of its depth, he came back to shore and shouted his readiness to surrender to any constituted authority.

The mob paid no attention and came on, firing as they came, until Everest saw there was no hope of ceasing the fight and resumed firing. This halted the mob but one man came on, armed and firing. With his last cartridge Everest shot this fellow, Dale Hubbard, nephew of the chief conspirator. Everest was seized by the mob.

On the way to the jail he was beaten, kicked and cursed. With a rifle-butt his front teeth were knocked out. A rope was thrown round his neck, but with characteristic defiance he told them, "You haven't got the guts to lynch a man in the daytime."

Night came. Maimed and bleeding in a cell next to his fellow workers, lay Everest. At a late hour the lights of the city suddenly were extinguished. The jail door was smashed. No one tried to stop the lynchers. Staggering erect, Everest said to the other prisoners: "Tell the boys I died for my class."

A brief struggle. Many blows. A sound of dragging. The

purring of high-powered cars. Again the lights came on. The autos reached the bridge over the Chehalis River. A rope was tied to the steel framework and Everest, with a noose around his neck, was brutally kicked from the bridge. After a pause he was hauled up, and it being found that he had some life left, a longer rope was used and the brutal process repeated. Again hauled up, the ghouls again flung the body over. An auto headlight was trained on the body, disclosing that some sadist, more degenerate than the rest, had ripped Everest's sexual organs almost loose from his body with some sharp instrument during the auto trip to the bridge.

Finally, after riddling the body with bullets, it was cut loose and let fall in the river, later to be found, a sodden, ghastly thing, taken back to the jail where it was placed in view of Everest's friends there in prison and at last buried in an unmarked grave.

Four union loggers were taken out of jail to do the work of burial under a heavy guard of soldiers. Some kind of a farcical inquest was held.

In the hall that day, besides Everest, were Bert Faulkner, Roy Becker, Britt Smith, Mike Sheehan, James McInerney and Morgan. The latter broke down under the torture all were put through. The terror continued for nine days. Loren Roberts, 19 years old, was driven insane.

A reign of terror existed throughout the Northwest. More than a thousand men and women were arrested in the State of Washington alone. Union halls were closed, labor papers suppressed, and many men were given sentences of from one to fourteen years for having in their possession copies of papers that contained the truth about the Centralia tragedy.

From the headquarters of the Employers' Association came many bulletins, among others one dated December 31, 1919: "Get rid of all the I.W.W.'s and other un-American organizations. . . . Deport the radicals or use the rope as at Centralia. . . . Until we get rid of the I.W.W. and radicals we don't expect to do much in this country. . . . Keep cleaning up on the I.W.W. . . . Don't let it lie down. . . . Keep up public sentiment. . . ."

George F. Vanderveer, attorney for the I.W.W., was then in Chicago. As secretary of the General Defense Committee, I talked over with him the situation at Centralia. This was the most important case in which the I.W.W. had ever been involved. While there were not so many men to be tried, yet it was a case of life and death and was different from all other cases because the men at Centralia were indicted for murder, when in fact they had done nothing but protect their lives, their bodies and their property from a mob whose hands were reeking with blood. He rushed across country to take up the defense of the eleven men who had been arrested at Centralia.

Lewis County and the Lumber and Employers' Associations had provided special prosecutors for this trial. There was a heavy array of these mouthpieces of capitalism and they were backed up by all the authority of the State. The Governor had sent the militia to the town of Montesano where the trial was held, and the Congressman had sent word that the members of the American Legion who were employed as deputy sheriffs, could wear their uniforms in the court room with a red chevron to designate past service in the army. Against this force which the timber wolves had employed, Vanderveer stood alone. He was a lawyer with a heart, as dangerous as a workingman with brains.

With everything against them, witnesses intimidated, the court room packed with soldiers in uniform and every possible thing done, even to threaten the defense attorneys with death and jurymen overawed, the verdict was a foregone conclusion.

The jury was out a total of 22 hours and 20 minutes. In their verdict, Eugene Barnett and John Lamb were found guilty of manslaughter, or murder, in the third degree. The Judge refused to accept this verdict, and sent the jury back to change it, and the final verdict was "guilty of murder in the second degree—Eugene Barnett, John Lamb, Britt Smith, Bert Bland, Commodore Bland, Roy Becker and John McInerney. Acquitted: Mike Sheehan and Elmer Stewart Smith."

They judged Loren Roberts insane and irresponsible.

Bert Faulkner was released during the trial.

A part of the jury's verdict, forced as it was by an atmosphere of terror, neverthless said:

We, the undersigned jurors, respectfully petition the court to extend leniency to the defendants whose names appear on the attached verdict. Signed and sealed.

A "labor jury" was elected from the A. F. of L. unions of Washington state who attended the trial.

The verdict of the labor jury was "Not guilty," voting to give their report to the press. It was signed by Theodore Meyer of the Everett Central Labor Council and John O. Craft of the Seattle Metal Trades Council.

John M. Wilson was the Judge presiding at this trial. Vanderveer told him in open court: "There was a time when I thought your rulings were due to ignorance of the law. That idea will no longer explain them."

Judge John M. Wilson sentenced the seven convicted men to terms of from 25 to 40 years in the Walla Walla penitentiary. Though the jury had asked for leniency, the Judge gave the men the limit of the law. These men are still in prison and there is a movement on foot for their release.

Five of the regular jurymen have since sworn to affidavits saying that the verdict was unjust. One told of a preliminary ballot unanimously for acquittal.

I tried to get each member of the I.W.W. who had been released from the penitentiary on bond to make a lecture tour in behalf of himself, his fellow workers, and the organization generally. It was upon my suggestion that Ralph Chaplin went to the Northwest. While there he gathered material for his splendid pamphlet, *The Centralia Conspiracy.*

CHAPTER XXIV

FAREWELL, CAPITALIST AMERICA!

OUR application for a new trial had been denied by the United States Court of Appeals, though that court overruled one of the counts under which we were convicted and eliminated the fines that had been imposed upon us by Judge Landis.

It is evident, however, that the Court did not review the testimony. As for example, Clyde Hough, a young machinist from Rockford, Ill., was convicted with us though he was in prison at the time the Espionage Law was passed and remained there until finally sent to Leavenworth. He had had no chance to violate the law under which he was convicted, even had he wanted to. Then there was Walter T. Nef, who at the time of his arrest was secretary of the Marine Transport Workers at Philadelphia. Nef was a Swiss by birth, and felt a bitter antipathy towards the Kaiser and everything German. He was a protagonist of the war and had never hesitated to say how he felt about it. His appeal, like that of the rest of us, was denied.

Our next move and last hope was to take the case to the United States Supreme Court, where it was pending when I left the country. The decision of this august body would determine whether or not we should return to Leavenworth prison, and with those who were still there, whether we should serve out the time of our sentences.

I learned that President Harding was interviewed by Meyer London, Socialist congressman from the State of New York, and was told by the President that the I.W.W. members would be pardoned with the exception of Haywood, whom they were going to hold.

It was good news when I learned in 1924 of the downfall of William J. Burns, the Director of the Department of Justice, who had been handling the affairs of this government Department in the interests of his private detective agency.

The I.W.W. "came into possession" of personal documents of William J. Burns, which they printed in their official organ. As a result of the exposure, Burns was dumped out on the dung heap where he properly belonged, and several detectives and agents provocateurs were discovered and expelled from the I.W.W. by the General Executive Board.

When the reactionaries wanted to cast opprobrium upon the I.W.W. they would call us "Bolshevists." We were sometimes hailed with approval as "Bolsheviki" by the others.

Immediately after the Russian Revolution, Harrison George began a pamphlet entitled *Red Dawn.* He vividly portrayed the historic development of the Russian Revolution. I had it published in February 1918. Many thousands of copies were distributed. But when the new administration took over the headquarters in 1920, it reflected the opposition which had developed in the I.W.W. against the state character of the Soviets, and the remainder of George's pamphlet was destroyed.

About this time a lengthy letter reached us addressed to the I.W.W. by the Communist International. This letter spoke of the situation of capitalism after the imperialist war, outlined the points in common held by the I.W.W. and the Communists, warned of the coming attacks on the workers, pictured the futility of reformism, analyzed the capitalist state and the rôle of the dictatorship of the proletariat and told how the Soviet state of workers and peasants was constructed. Such basic questions as "political" and "industrial" action, democratic centralization, the nature of the social revolution and of future society were gone into thoroughly. After I had finished reading it, I called Ralph Chaplin over to my desk and said to him: "Here is what we have been dreaming about; here is the I.W.W. all feathered out!"

The receipt of this letter was a momentous circumstance in my somewhat eventful life. While it was addressed to the I.W.W. as an organization, I felt, as I knew many other members did, that it was a tribute to ourselves, as each had helped to build this class conscious movement.

On July 4th, 1920, I spoke at Renton Park, Seattle, where an enormous crowd had gathered. After the meeting I was introduced to one of Wesley Everest's closest friends. He had served with Everest in the trenches and had been so badly injured in the back that it was impossible for him to move without assistance. The income from the Seattle meeting was something over $6,000.

From Seattle I went to Portland, Ore., where another large meeting was held. George F. Vanderveer, the attorney, was the chairman. At this meeting considerable over $1,000 was raised for the defense.

As soon as the consolidation of the Communist Party in the United States was effected, I became a member. John Martin was elected secretary of the General Defense Committee.

I came on to New York City and there urged members of the Central Executive Committee and other leaders who were known to me that some effort must be made to get the Party or an organization representing it out from underground, giving it as my opinion that little would be accomplished until we could freely publish our papers and take a place on the public platform.

I spoke at several meetings for the defense, the last of which was held in the Rand School. At this meeting two of my codefendants, who were out on bail, George Andreychine and Charles Ashleigh, were also speakers.

The suggestion had been made to me that I should go to Russia. There was little hope entertained of a favorable decision from the United States Supreme Court, and my friends thought it would be an unnecessary sacrifice for me to spend the rest of my life in prison. When I was told that I should go to Russia, I said: "It may not be so easy for me to get away, but I will make the effort."

I was booked with other friends on the S.S. *Oscar II*, which had been Henry Ford's "peace ship." After bidding my friends farewell, I stopped in the home of a Lettish family—my last night in the United States. From there I went early in the morning to a hotel in Hoboken where I had breakfast. I then went to the wharf and direct to the boat where I showed to the inspector what purported to be a passport. I went aboard and down into the hold where a berth had been reserved. I remained there until the ship was under way. When I came on deck we were passing the Statue of Liberty. Saluting the old hag with her uplifted torch, I said: "Good-by, you've had your back turned on me too long. I am now going to the land of freedom."

One of the stewards, who recognized me, was an I.W.W., and we were able to get better fare than is usually served to steerage passengers.

We traveled to Riga through battle-scarred country, marked with cemeteries, trenches, deserted fortifications and endless miles of barbed wire entanglements.

At Riga we were loaded into box cars. The train was guarded by Latvian soldiers until we reached the border. As we crossed the Russian line, there was a mighty burst of cheers and singing of the "International." The train moved along like a red flame. Red bunting, red banners, and red kerchiefs were flying to the breeze.

When we landed in the ancient city of Moscow, now again the capital of Russia, we were met at the station with automobiles and driven at once to the hotel. Michael Borodin asked me if I would like to go to the Kremlin to meet Lenin. I was suffering from diabetes and very tired after the long trip, and I told him I first needed a rest.

Some days later an interview was arranged for me with Comrade Lenin. It is not my purpose to describe here his personality or our meeting. I will just mention one phase of our conversation before closing this book.

I asked Comrade Lenin "if the industries of the Soviet Republic are run and administered by the workers?"

His reply was: "Yes, Comrade Haywood, that is Communism."

CHAPTER XXV

HAYWOOD'S LIFE IN THE SOVIET UNION *

READERS of "Bill Haywood's Book" will have learned from his own narrative that he was seriously ill before he left America. Undoubtedly his illness either arose from or was made worse by his imprisonment. All who knew him after his release noted his state of ill health. While in New York before his departure, he was very sick and constantly under a doctor's care. While he improved considerably after he arrived in the Soviet Union, as time went on his health gradually declined. This interfered greatly with the writing of his book and prevented him from writing additional chapters in which he planned to tell of his life and work in Soviet Russia.

Haywood was welcomed by the Russian masses and by the leaders of the Communist Party as befitted an old fighter of Labor's struggles. He was received everywhere with eager acclaim and decorated as a Revolutionary Hero with a medal which he wore with pride and which lay upon his breast when he at last reposed in death.

He regarded himself as a political refugee, "pending the revolution in America," and carefully followed every development in the American labor movement with great interest. He wrote articles for the press, and Moscow papers called upon him repeatedly for his opinion of the meaning of American events. His room, in a comfortable Moscow hotel, was a center of attraction for all American workers visiting Moscow, with whom he would discuss their problems and spend hours of comradely conviviality, often until the early Russian dawn began to appear over the gilded domes of the ancient city. Haywood's room was also a center for the children who romped about the corridor near his door, and often a young one

---

PUBLISHER'S NOTE: Haywood's death on May 18, 1928, prevented him from completing his memoirs. The publishers therefore requested a friend and co-worker of Haywood to write a short account of the latter's sojourn in Soviet Russia.

would be found spending an afternoon with "Bolshoi Bill," regaled with dainties and with stories in Russian, which he learned but never mastered. He married a Russian office worker and lived calmly in Moscow, often much amused to read accounts of American papers of his "persecution by the Reds" and "flight across snowy steppes" to Turkey.

Always a man of action, he wished to take a hand in the reconstruction of industry shattered by war and counter-revolution, and in 1921, shortly after his arrival, he participated in the Organizing Committee of the Kuznetz Colony. This project had as its aim the reopening and operation of industry in the Kuznetz Basin, about a thousand miles east of the Urals near the city of Tomsk. This area holds enormous coal deposits, and the Soviet Government turned over this district, the mines and deserted chemical plant, the only chemical plant in Siberia, to the autonomous Kuznetz Colony, which brought in American skilled labor, imported tractors for its farms and reopened the plant and the mines. Haywood took a place on the Management Board in 1922 and spent several months in the colony, later returning to Moscow where he worked at the colony's office until late in 1923. In the general reorganization of Soviet industry, the government took over the administration of the Kuznetz area in 1925.

Haywood felt very deeply the persecution of labor men in the United States, and following his connection with "Kuzbas," began a period of activity with the "MOPR," the Russion section of the International Organization for the Relief of Revolutionary Fighters with which the International Labor Defense in America is affiliated. He made several speaking trips through the Soviet Union for this organization, spreading the stories of Mooney and Billings, the Centralia victims, the I.W.W. and other criminal-syndicalist law prisoners.

While, as a refugee, he maintained his affiliation with the American Communist Party, and his interest in the American labor movement never waned, he was ever ready to boast, almost as of a personal accomplishment, of the advance of Soviet economy, pointing out to visitors the busy coöperative and government stores, the humming factories and new buildings, and contrasting this with the famine and ruin which he saw on his arrival. He would listen courteously, as he always did to any worker, to followers of Trotsky in the latter's conflict with the Russian Communist Party, some of these old fellow workers of his in the American I.W.W. who were prone to conclude from some bureaucratic abuse that Russia was "going back to capitalism," and at the end would remind them of the greater issue of the growth of socialist economy contending against world imperialism and scoldingly tell them they had lived too long in the Soviet Union and should "go back where they came from" to get a fresh taste of capitalism. Not long before he died he transferred to the Russian Communist Party.

In March, 1928, Haywood was preparing to attend the Fourth Congress of the Red International of Labor Unions, as he had done on previous occasions. He was regretting that the opening session was to take place on March 17, as he was assigned by the Communist Party to speak that night in commemoration of the Paris Commune, when both of these activities had to be put aside. He was overcome by a paralytic stroke the night of March 16, and was taken to the Kremlin hospital, where he received the best care by eminent physicians.

His wonderful vitality and the treatment given him enabled him to return to his home, as he wished, after about three weeks. But he was obviously weak, though able to walk about. His mind was again busy with the labor movement. He received many of the R.I.L.U. congress delegates who were still in the city, and discussed the problems of the congress. But suddenly he was again taken ill, and although removed at once to the Kremlin hospital, passed away on May 18, 1928.

His funeral was attended by the whole group of American workers in Moscow, delegations from the Russian Communist Party and the various international organizations, as well as personal friends. Flowers were piled high over his coffin, which was taken to a crematorium as he had desired. His ashes, as he had directed, were divided into two parts. One was buried under the Kremlin wall at a great demonstration in the Red Square. The other half of Haywood's ashes lies, by his request, in Waldheim cemetery, Chicago, near the graves of the Haymarket victims, whose story so profoundly influenced his life.

THE END

APPENDIX I

LIST OF I.W.W.'S CONVICTED IN THE SACRAMENTO CASE

Edward Anderson
Elmer Anderson
Pete de Bernardi
Harry Brewer
Edward S. Carey
Joseph Carroll
Felix Cedno
Robert Connellan
Roy P. Connor
Mortimer Downing
Godrey Ebell
Frank Elliott
Frederick Esmond
Robert Feehan
Otto Fisher
A. L. Fox
John Grave
H. Gray
Harry Hammer
Joseph Harper

William Hood
H. A. LaTour
Chris. A. Luber
George O'Connell
Phil McLaughlin
Frank Moran
James Mulrooney
John L. Murphy
J. Potthast
James Price
Edward Quigley
James Quinlan
Frank Reilly
Vincent Santilli
Myron Sprague
Herbert Stredwick
Caesar Tabib
J. Tori
George F. Voetter

APPENDIX II

LIST OF I.W.W.'S CONVICTED IN THE WICHITA CASE

C. W. Anderson
Albert Barr
A. M. Blumberg
E. M. Boyd
J. Caffrey
F. J. Callagher
Jim Davis
Harry Drew
S. Forbes
W. Francik
O. E. Gordon
Fred Grau
Joseph Greshbach
M. Hecht
Ernest Henning
S. B. Hicok

Peter Higgins
E. J. Huber
Ray Lambert
Paul Maihak
H. McCarl
Tom O'Day
F. Patton
Robert Poe
Mike Quinn
M. Sapper
Carl Schell
S. Shurin
Leo Stark
J. Walberg
George Wenger

APPENDIX III

LIST OF I.W.W.'S CONVICTED IN THE CHICAGO CASE

NAMES	One	Two	Three	Four	Fines
			YEARS		
Carl Ahlteen	6	10	2	20	$30,000
Olin B. Anderson	5	5	2	5	30,000
George Andreychine	6	10	2	20	20,000
Charles Ashleigh	6	10	2	10	30,000
John Avila	5	5	2	5	20,000
Aurelion Vincente Azuara	6	10	2	20	20,000
John Baldazzi	6	10	2	10	30,000
J. R. Baskett	1	1	1	1	30,000
Charles Bennett	6	10	2	10	30,000
J. H. Beyer	5	10	2	10	30,000
R. J. Bobbs	1	1	1	1	30,000
Arthur Boose	5	5	2	5	30,000
G. J. Bourg	6	10	2	10	30,000
Richard Brazier	6	10	2	20	20,000
Roy A. Brown	1	1	1	1	30,000
Dan Buckley	6	10	2	10	30,000
Ralph H. Chaplin	6	10	2	20	30,000
Stanley J. Clark	6	10	2	10	30,000
Ray Corder	1	1	1	1	30,000
Alexander Cournos	6	10	2	10	30,000
C. W. Davis	6	10	2	10	30,000
J. T. Doran	5	5	2	5	30,000
E. F. Doree	6	10	2	10	30,000
Forrest Edwards	6	10	2	20	20,000
James Elliott.	5	5	2	5	30,000
Ray S. Fanning	5	5	2	5	30,000
Ben Fletcher	6	10	2	10	30,000
Ted Fraser	5	5	2	5	30,000
Harrison George	5	5	2	5	30,000
Joseph J. Gordon	6	10	2	10	30,000
Joe Graber	5	5	2	5	30,000
Peter Green	6	10	2	10	30,000
C. R. Griffin	5	5	2	5	30,000
Ed Hamilton	6	10	2	10	30,000
George Hardy	1	1	1	1	30,000
William D. Haywood	6	10	2	20	30,000
Clyde Hough	5	5	2	5	30,000
Dave Ingar	5	5	2	5	20,000
Fred Jaakkola	6	10	2	10	30,000
Charles R. Jacobs	1	1	1	1	30,000
Charles Jacobson	1	1	1	1	30,000
Ragner Johannsen	6	10	2	10	30,000
H. F. Kane	5	5	2	5	20,000
Charles L. Lambert	6	10	2	20	20,000
Leo Laukki	6	10	2	20	20,000
Jack Law	6	10	2	10	30,000
Morris Levine	5	5	2	5	30,000
W. H. Lewis	5	5	2	5	30,000
Harry Lloyd	5	5	2	5	30,000

NAMES	One	Two	Three	Four	Fines
			YEARS		
Burt Lorton	6	10	2	10	30,000
Vladimir Lossieff	6	10	2	20	20,000
Herbert Mahler	5	5	2	5	30,000
James H. Manning	5	5	2	5	30,000
John Martin	6	10	2	10	30,000
Francis Miller	6	10	2	10	30,000
William Moran	5	5	2	5	20,000
J. A. MacDonald	6	10	2	10	30,000
Charles H. MacKinnon	5	5	2	5	30,000
Jo McCarthy	5	5	2	5	30,000
Herbert McCutcheon	5	5	2	5	30,000
Pete McEvoy	5	5	2	5	30,000
Charles McWhirt	1	1	1	1	30,000
Fred Nelson	1	1	1	1	30,000
Walter T. Nef	6	10	2	20	20,000
Pietro Nigri	18 months on each count				
Joseph A. Oates	5	5	2	5	20,000
V. V. O'Hair	5	5	2	5	30,000
John Pancner	6	10	2	10	30,000
Louis Parenti	5	5	2	5	30,000
Grover H. Perry	6	10	2	10	30,000
James Philips	5	5	2	5	30,000
Charles Plahn	5	5	2	5	30,000
Albert Prashner	6	10	2	10	30,000
Manuel Rey	6	10	2	20	20,000
C. H. Rice	6	10	2	10	30,000
Charles Rothfisher	6	10	2	20	20,000
James Rowan	6	10	2	20	20,000
Sam Scarlett	6	10	2	20	20,000
Archie Sinclair	6	10	2	10	30,000
Don Sheridan	6	10	2	10	30,000
James M. Slovick	6	10	2	10	30,000
Walter Smith	1	1	1	1	30,000
Alton E. Soper	1	1	1	1	30,000
George Speed	1	1	1	1	30,000
Vincent St. John	6	10	2	10	30,000
Siegfried Stenberg	6	10	2	10	30,000
William Tanner	5	5	2	5	30,000
James P. Thompson	6	10	2	10	30,000
John I. Turner	6	10	2	10	30,000
John Walsh	6	10	2	10	30,000
Frank Westerlund	5	5	2	5	30,000
Pierce C. Wetter	5	5	2	5	20,000
William Weyh	5	5	2	5	20,000